NAVIGATING THE INTERNET WITH COMPUSERVE

Wes Tatters

201 West 103rd Street
Indianapolis, Indiana 46290

This book is dedicated to my parents, who willingly put up with my strange working hours, and to my girlfriend, Cait, who knew nothing about the Internet before agreeing to proofread this book.

Copyright © 1995 by Sams.net Publishing

FIRST EDITION

International Standard Book Number: 0-672-30761-8

Library of Congress Catalog Card Number:95-67653

98 97 96 95   4 3 2 1

Interpretation of the printing code: the rightmost double-digit number is the year of the book's printing; the rightmost single-digit, the number of the book's printing. For example, a printing code of 95-1 shows that the first printing of the book occurred in 1995.

Composed in AGaramond and MCPdigital by Macmillan Computer Publishing

Printed in the United States of America

Trademarks

President, Sams Publishing	*Richard K. Swadley*
Publisher, Sams.net Publishing	*George Bond*
Publishing Manager	*Mark Taber*
Managing Editor	*Cindy Morrow*
Development Editor	*Fran Hatton*
Production Editor	*Sean Medlock*
Copy Editors	*Bart Reed, Johnna VanHoose*
Editorial Assistant	*Carol Ackerman*
Technical Reviewer	*Scott Loftesness*

Marketing Manager
John Pierce

Cover Designer
Tim Amrhein

Book Designer
Alyssa Yesh

Vice President of Manufacturing and Production
Jeff Valler

Manufacturing Coordinator
Paul Gilchrist

Imprint Manager
Kelly Dobbs

Team Supervisor
Brad Chinn

Support Services Manager
Juli Cook

Support Services Supervisor
Mary Beth Wakefield

Production Analysts
Angela Bannan, Dennis Clay Hager, Bobbi Satterfield

Graphics Image Specialists
Becky Beheler, Steve Carlin, Brad Dixon, Jason Hand, Clint Lahnen, Cheri Laughner, Mike Reynolds, Laura Robbins, Dennis Sheehan, Craig Small, Jeff Yesh

Production
Carol Bowers, Don Brown, Mona Brown, Charlotte Clapp, Terrie Deemer, Michael Henry, Kevin Laseau, Paula Lowell, Steph Mineart, Casey Price, Brian-Kent Proffitt, SA Springer, Tina Trettin, Mark Walchle, Dennis Wesner, Michelle Worthington

Indexer
Cheryl Dietsch

OVERVIEW

CONTENTS

Part III   WinCIM Internet Tools   75

6   E-Mail and CIS Mail   77

7   Mailing Lists   93

ACKNOWLEDGMENTS

Where I have directly quoted from additional sources throughout this book, you will find that I have attributed the quote to the appropriate person. However, because much of the information in this book comes from personal knowledge gained over a period of years, it has been impossible to directly attribute all sources of information.

To this end I would like to express personally my appreciation to all of the people I have corresponded with in the past few years, many of whom have provided me with valuable insights into the workings of the Internet and CompuServe as well. Special thanks also go to Andre Lackman and the staff at CompuServe Pacific Customer Support.

For his assistance with the "History of the Internet" section by producing the H'obbes' Internet Timeline, thanks goes to Robert H'obbes' Zakon. Thanks also to author Bruce Sterling for his "Short History of the Internet," and to Bernard Aboba for his interview with Vinton Cert, "How the Internet Came to Be." In addition, thanks to the Internet Society for the graphics and data they make so readily available.

And to Henry Hardy, whose Master's thesis "The History of the Net" prompted me to begin my own exploration of the Internet's history and whose writings are a valuable contribution to the historical understanding of the Internet today.

I would also like to acknowledge the work of the many hundreds of people responsible for the creation and collation of the thousands of Request for Comment, For Your Information, and Standards documents maintained by InterNIC, the historical and informational articles compiled by the Internet Society, and the Frequently Asked Questions documents produced so regularly and tirelessly by people whose sole interest is in promoting and developing the Internet.

And finally, thank you, to all the people who helped make this book a reality:

- ◆ My girlfriend, Cait Spreadborough, for reading and editing the original manuscript.
- ◆ Scott Loftesness, the Sysop of the Internet Forums on CompuServe, for his work checking the many sites, services, and technical aspects of this book.
- ◆ The staff at Sams.net who helped guide this project to its completion, and especially Mark Taber, Fran Hatton, and Sean Medlock.

ABOUT THE AUTHOR

Wes Tatters has worked in the computer industry since 1984 as a computer program and systems designer. During this time he worked on a number of computer platforms, using a variety of computer languages and communications tools. Currently, he operates a video production company while writing regular articles for a number of Australian computer magazines, dealing with the Internet and CompuServe, Amiga Computers, and database technology. He can be reached on the Internet at wtatters@world.net or taketwo@webcom.com, and on CompuServe at 100036,174.

INTRODUCTION

It seems that hardly a day goes by without some mention of the information superhighway or the Internet in the papers and on television. Over the past few years the Internet has begun to permeate many aspects of day-to-day life, moving what was once a system fixed staunchly in the world of scientists and academics to the forefront of public interest and accessibility.

In response to this growth in public interest, a number of previously closed communications services have begun to open their doorways to the Internet and the multitude of new capabilities it provides. Among these services, CompuServe has for some time been an industry leader in the development of Internet gateways that provide its members with easy access to Internet-based services.

But with the increased growth in popularity of the Internet, CompuServe realized that the level of access it was offering was still not sufficient to meet the growing demands of its members. As a result, in April of 1995 CompuServe decided to firmly position itself as an Internet service provider by acquiring Spry Inc., one of the leading developers of Internet-based software. At the same time, it also announced the global upgrading of all of its points of presence and dial-up connections to 14,400bps connection speeds, with the promise of 28,800bps connections by the end of the year. Then, still not satisfied, CompuServe also announced the availability of access to the World Wide Web and dial-up Internet connectivity via PPP through its own Internet dialer, called NetLauncher.

For CompuServe members, this now means that accessing the Internet is no more difficult than using the CompuServe Information Manger, which over the years has gained so many compliments. Today you can take advantage of FTP, Telnet, Usenet newsgroups, and with NetLauncher, even the World Wide Web, without any of the difficulties so often associated with doing so in the past.

What This Book Is All About

This book has been designed to guide you step by step through the various new Internet services CompuServe now provides. To do this, I have divided the book into five separate parts that deal with various aspects of the Internet and CompuServe's Internet Service:

♦ Part I—CompuServe and the Internet

This section takes a look at the history of the Internet and examines the path taken by CompuServe as it has moved from a dedicated communications service to a full Internet service provider.

- ◆ Part II—Getting Started on the Internet

  To give you a better understanding of the new capabilities the Internet brings to CompuServe, this section first looks at the range of services available on the Internet. Then, in the last two chapters, you will find information dealing with the Internet connection options CompuServe now offers and an exploration of the features offered by the CompuServe Information Manager—WinCIM.

- ◆ Part III—WinCIM Internet Tools

  Once you have an understanding of the concepts behind the Internet, this section expands on this knowledge by examining in detail many of the popular Internet services that can now be accessed using WinCIM. These include e-mail, mailing lists, FTP, Telnet, and Usenet newsgroups.

- ◆ Part IV—Internet Navigators

  Like WinCIM itself, which allows you to navigate around CompuServe with ease, the World Wide Web and its predecessor, Gopher, provide you with the best method of navigating the Internet. In this section, you learn about the World Wide Web and Gopher services provided by CompuServe.

- ◆ Part V—Where to Now?

  The Internet is not composed simply of software tools and communications services. Instead, it is best considered as an electronic world. To expand on this concept, in the closing section of the book you find examples of many of the different places you can visit on the Internet and a discussion of some of the ways that you can locate new information.

- ◆ Appendixes

  Appendix A—Information about the availability of alternate Internet service providers.

  Appendix B—Logging onto CompuServe via the Internet using Telnet.

  Appendix C—A short discussion of many of the popular Winsock client applications available for downloading from CompuServe and the Internet.

  Appendix D—A discussion of software-based compression and encryption tools, such as Wincode and PGP.

Conventions and Common Representations

Throughout this book I have adopted a few standard conventions to assist you in recognizing important pieces of information. These include special highlighting methods for information displayed by your computer and for information you need to type in yourself.

Typographical conventions used in this book

Typeface	Meaning
Bold	Text printed in bold represents information you need to type at your keyboard or fields and menu options that you need to choose while working with the various programs discussed in this book.
Computer Type	There are a number of Internet addresses, directory paths, and World Wide Web URLs defined throughout this book that are printed in computer type to make them easier to recognize.
Italic	When you encounter a word printed in italics, this indicates that you are about to examine a new concept and should pay close attention to what is being discussed.
Shortcut Key	Many menus and buttons associated with programs running under Windows support the use of shortcut keys, which allow you to bypass the mouse and instead select them by using a keyboard combination. Where a button or menu mentioned in this book supports the use of a shortcut key, the letter that corresponds to the key is printed in **B**old. To use this shortcut, hold down the Alt key on your keyboard and type the letter specified.

Information printed in Note boxes provides you with additional points of interest relating to the topic currently being discussed.

Tips offer additional suggestions about the use of programs and services.

Warning messages are designed to make you aware of important issues that may affect your use of CompuServe and the Internet in general.

PART *I*

COMPUSERVE AND THE INTERNET

CHAPTER 1

THE HISTORY OF THE INTERNET

Before looking at the powerful new services CompuServe now brings to its members, you first need to learn exactly what the Internet is.

This chapter looks at how the Internet began and how it evolved, and looks at some of the structures that keep the Internet running.

How the Internet Began

Not long after the first computer was invented, people began to look for ways to share the power these valuable machines offered. As the switch panels of early computer giants were replaced by paper tapes and punched cards, the first age of computer communications dawned.

Note

> Before the advent of keyboards or computer monitors or their early predecessor the teletype, the only way to communicate with a computer was by toggling banks of switches. Later, these switches were replaced by punched cards—small cards with holes punched in them to represent the sequence of instructions a computer was to perform. For long instruction sequences, rolls of paper tape were also used. Like the punched cards, paper tapes also had holes punched in them to represent information.

All of a sudden, people could share information and exchange computer programs, and for a short time everything was good. Progress nevertheless marches on, and before long, mailing punched cards and paper tapes around the country was deemed unacceptable. As teletypes began to replace punched cards and computers grew in power, a better alternative was needed—one that could physically connect computers separated by great distances.

Modems and Telephone Lines

After much experimentation, it was decided that telephone lines offered the most viable solution. However, this still left computer developers with a problem. Computers communicate using electronic signals that represent bits of information. Telephones, on the other hand, use sounds as the basis of their communication.

To resolve this problem, the *modem* was invented. This device, an early predecessor of the equipment you probably use now to connect to CompuServe, converts the electronic signals sent from a computer into a series of audible tones. These tones can be easily transmitted through a telephone line to a second modem, which converts them back to a form that computers can understand.

The U.S. Government and the RAND Corporation

While this development was taking place, the U.S. government was busying itself with its own research concerns. With the world locked in the grip of the Cold War, the government was concerned that in the event of a nuclear holocaust, America would need a command and control network that could still function despite the loss of any number of cities, states, or bases.

As author Bruce Sterling outlined in his paper titled a "Short History of the Internet," Paul Baran, an employee at the RAND Corporation, America's foremost Cold War think tank, was given the problem and, in 1964, made public the RAND proposal. In the quote that follows, Bruce Sterling explains the basics of the RAND proposal:

> The principles were simple. The network itself would be assumed to be unreliable at all times. It would be designed from the get-go to transcend its own unreliability. All the nodes in the network would be equal in status to all other nodes, each node with its own authority to originate, pass and receive messages. The messages themselves would be divided into packets, each packet separately addressed. Each packet would begin at some specified source node, and end at some other specified destination node. Each packet would wind its way through the network on an individual basis.
>
> *Bruce Sterling*
> *The Magazine of Fantasy & Science Fiction, Feb 1993*

By using a system such as the one described, the computer that sends the message does not need to concern itself with the path the message needs to take to reach its destination. In fact, the same message could quite possibly take entirely different routes depending on when it was sent and the condition of the network at the time it was sent.

What made this design so attractive was that regardless of the extent to which the network was damaged by a nuclear war, while any part of the network was still operating, messages would eventually reach all surviving nodes.

A copy of Bruce Sterling's "Short History of the Internet" is available online at the Internet Society. It is well worth the read because it puts into perspective much of the hype currently surrounding the Internet. To read this paper and one by Vinton Cerf, the current Internet Society president, use the following URL with your WWW browser: `gopher://gopher.isoc.org/11/internet/history`.

The Birth of the ARPANET

In 1969, as a result of numerous presentations and discussions regarding the potential of the modem and RAND's proposed network technology, the U.S. Department of Defense's Advanced Research Projects Agency (ARPA) launched an ambitious research project to further explore the possibilities of packet-based networking and the RAND proposal.

One of the main features of this proposed network was the use of *packet switching* as the means of inter-computer communications. Packet switching is the term used to describe the communications process, developed to implement the messages packeting concept, proposed by the RAND Corporation.

To test the viability of packet switching, ARPA decided to connect four high-speed computers—the supercomputers of their time—using a packet switched network. This would allow scientists to better explore and develop the emerging communications technology and, at the same time, better share the limited computer resources available to universities and other research bodies.

Three sites on the west coast, the University of California at Los Angles, the Stanford Research Institute at Stanford, and the University of California at Santa Barbara, were chosen for the project, with the University of Utah completing the network, which was given the name ARPANET after the Advanced Research Projects Agency that sponsored it.

Over the course of 1969, the computer hardware and software required to make the network a reality was gradually put into place, with all the effort finally culminating around September 1, 1969. On this day the first of the four packet switching nodes, or *interface message processors* as they were then known, was delivered from Bolt Beranek and Newman, the firm contracted to design them. During the weeks that followed, as the remaining sites took delivery of their interface message processors, the ARPANET was officially born.

The Dawn of E-Mail

Following this somewhat inauspicious start, interest in ARPANET grew slowly. Nevertheless, once the network became stable and the network communication protocol (NCP) software was officially adopted, other computing facilities began to take advantage of the technology offered by ARPANET. By 1971 there were 15 operational nodes on the network, connecting 23 independent host computer systems.

Ironically, as is so often the case, the force that seemed to drive the growth of ARPANET was not the opportunity to share computing resources or the availability of remote computing tools that the system's developers had predicted. Instead, the ARPANET had been turned into the world's first electronic postal service. People were using ARPANET to discuss research projects, exchange notes and documents, and eventually just to shoot the breeze. It is fair to say that e-mail took ARPANET by storm. In fact, by the end of 1972, it was accountable for more network traffic than all the other services.

Coming Out of the Closet

While network usage was booming, ARPA was still concerned that the number of network connections was still growing too slowly. To encourage even more involvement in ARPANET, it was decided that a public demonstration of the network should be arranged to coincide with the 1972 International Conference on Computer Communications. To stage this event, a packet switch and a terminal were installed in the basement of the Washington Hilton Hotel.

If ever there was a coming-out party for the Internet, this demonstration was it. Over a period of almost a year, plans were made and connections organized to ensure that the demonstration would be a success. Those in attendance were treated to an entirely new communications experience as they watched the Hilton terminal connect to an impressive 40 nodes—the largest number of ARPANET connections ever.

To put it mildly, the demonstration was an outstanding success. It impressed even its most persistent skeptics, and as of that day the ARPANET was officially here to stay. Indirectly, this demonstration also opened the way for the launch in 1973 of the first international ARPANET connections with England and Norway.

NCP and the Move to TCP/IP

As the expanding network grew in popularity, the Advanced Research Projects Agency became increasingly interested in the possibility of connecting other networks, including the new satellite and radio packet networks, to the existing ARPANET network. Unfortunately, the Network Control Protocol software (NCP), which until 1982 managed all network communications for ARPANET, was heavily reliant on the nature of the existing network, and as such was not capable of supporting the new internetworking requirements now being demanded of ARPANET.

To resolve these problems, a new network protocol was needed, one that could encompass all types of computer networks and the growing array of computer hardware that was beginning to appear.

The TCP/IP Protocol

Development of this new protocol, which was to become known as TCP/IP, started in 1973 in the lab of Vinton Cerf, then an assistant professor at Stanford.

Vinton Cerf, the current president of the Internet Society, is regarded by many as one of the founding fathers of the Internet. If you are interested in exploring the early life of the Internet, his account, "How the Internet Came to Be," as told to Bernard Aboba, makes for fascinating reading.

A copy of this paper, along with other information about the early years of the Internet, is available via FTP from `ftp.isoc.org` in the `/internet/history` directory. Alternatively, there is also a copy in the "Internet Society" library section of CompuServe's Internet New Users Forum (GO INETFORUM).

Unlike NCP, development of TCP/IP was to become a joint effort. Following the publication of "A Protocol for Packet Network Internetworking," by Vinton Cerf and Robert Kahn, three sites began to work on the project. The first site, naturally, was located at Cerf's lab, with the second site at Bolt Beranek and Newman, where Kahn had been instrumental in the development of the ARPANET's interface message processors. What made the effort truly international, though, was the third site at University College London, which also began working on the problem.

As the project progressed, it became obvious to developers that to ensure the success of TCP/IP as the globally adopted standard for internetwork computing, it had to be freely available. To achieve this ideal, the TCP/IP protocol was released into the public domain, giving any computer developer or operating system designer the right to include TCP/IP communications as a part of their product.

Interestingly, in many eyes, it was this decision that heralded the birth of the Internet and signaled its future potential.

Note

> A considerable amount of information dealing with the development of TCP/IP, and indeed many other aspects of the Internet, has been made available online in a collection of documents known as Request for Comments or RFCs. Copies of all the RFCs can be downloaded from `ftp.internic.net`. In addition, many of the more important RFCs can also be found in the "Standards/RFCs" library section of CompuServe's Internet Resource forum (GO INETRESOURCE).

The Birth of the Internet

While many dates, including September 1, 1969, have been put forward as the birthdate of the Internet, it is in fact very difficult to define how or when the Internet, as we now know it, actually came into being.

In many ways the Internet was never born, but more truly evolved from the collection of networks that many today consider its parents.

Network of Networks

As TCP/IP grew in popularity and availability, an ever-increasing number of sites began to form links with ARPANET. In fact, all of a sudden it seemed like anyone who owned a computer system wanted to be a part of ARPANET.

Ironically, while all the new sites were embracing TCP/IP in its entirety, many of the early ARPANET sites were reluctant to make the move themselves. It seemed the only option was to force these sites to change. As a result, in what was seen by some as an underhanded ploy, NCP was simply turned off on January 1, 1983.

Finally, the network of networks had begun, and with it the first true signs of the Internet as we know it today.

Growth Beyond Imagination

With this move the role of ARPANET began to change. No longer was it just a network. Instead it had become the *backbone* of the new Internet, carrying data from machine to machine and network to network.

In the years following the 1983 NCP switch-off, the Internet began to grow far beyond the expectations of even its most broad-minded prophets. According to the Internet host growth data published by the Internet Society (Figure 1.1), the 560 host sites reported in 1983 had, by the end of 1994, grown to include more than 3 million connected hosts.

FIGURE 1.1.

Summary of Internet host connections from 1969 to 1994. Data courtesy of the Internet Society.

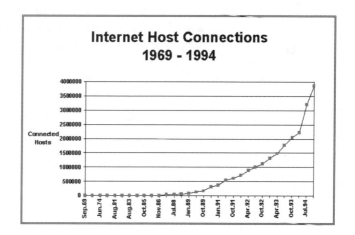

NSFNET

A large part of the Internet's growth can be attributed to the construction in 1986 of several publicly accessible supercomputing centers by the National Science Foundation (NSF).

To connect these centers and provide education and research institutions with direct computer access, the NSF initially planned to use ARPANET. However, ARPANET's minders, fearful of what this extra load would do to their network, decided not to allow ARPANET to be used. As a result, the NSF decided to construct their own backbone, which became known as NFSNET. However, in what was to become yet another irony of the Internet's development, ARPANET eventually opened network connections with NSFNET and thus the supercomputers it joined.

NSFNET brought with it a number of radical new developments that would again change the very nature of the emerging Internet. When the NSF was designing the network, it decided that instead of having individual computers connected to NSFNET, as was the practice with ARPANET, only regional networks would be permitted to have a direct connection. Computer sites in each region were to connect to the local network, which in turn would allow them access to NSFNET.

To support this plan, the concept of *service providers* was born. The NSF, not interested in managing the local networks, began to contract these regions to interested organizations—some of whom planned to make a profit by providing access to NSFNET and the Internet, and others who were looking simply to provide network services to their particular communities.

Out of this process grew the concept of Internet service providers, and thus, with the creation of NSFNET, the final foundation of the current Internet structure was laid.

The Internet Today

Not wanting to be left behind, many other government and non-government organizations also began forming their own networks.

Before long, networks such as BITNET, the LISTSERV network (see Chapter 7, "Mailing Lists"), and Usenet, the Newsgroups service (see Chapter 8, "Usenet—Newsgroups") were up and running. In addition, more specialized services, such as NASA's National Science Internet (NSI), the education and research network CSNET, and MILNET, the unclassified military network, which was separated from ARPANET in 1983, also began to service the needs of their communities.

Around the same time, networks were also beginning to appear in other countries, with services such as JANET in the United Kingdom, NORDUNET in Europe, and AARNET setting up an educational network in Australia.

Gateways

Before too long, however, users on many of these new networks began to encounter a problem. If two people wanted to communicate with each other, they had to make sure that they were both connected to the same network. This problem led to absurd situations in which computers in the same building could not communicate with each other because they were connected to different networks.

To alleviate this difficulty, special connections called *gateways* began to appear. These connections formed bridges between two unrelated networks. Once the individual networks were connected through one of these gateways, people on each of the networks were able to communicate as though they were connected to a single system. In fact, in many cases they did not even need to know that the computer they were communicating with was connected to another network.

The Internet Completed

As an ever-increasing number of networks began to open gateways with each other, the Internet as we know it today was finally formed.

For NSFNET, things were rapidly changing as well. By default, it had become the main backbone of the Internet for the mainland U.S., and in effect the global backbone as well. It had even surpassed and replaced ARPANET, which died a silent death in 1989. Unlike the upset caused by the 1983 switch-off of NCP, the closure of ARPANET occurred with hardly a murmur, as most of the early ARPANET sites had long since moved to NSFNET or one of the other networks.

Commercial Interest

As the Internet gained momentum, it did not take commercial interests too long to realize the potential power of this new resource. However, because ARPANET and NSFNET both grew out of educational and research projects, they were very dubious about letting commercial users onto their network backbones.

This resulted in a rather difficult situation. Even though many of the NSFNET service providers were quite willing to have the new commercial networks connected to their regional networks, NSFNET forbid any commercial information from being transmitted across the primary NSFNET backbone.

This resulted in a problem similar to the pre-gateway difficulties discussed earlier. This time, however, it was the commercial networks that were unable to communicate with each other. Obviously, this was not an acceptable alternative for the commercial users, who could only sit and watch the types of communications possible between NSFNET-approved services.

Out of this impasse between the NSFNET and the commercial networks, a new commercial backbone was formed. In March of 1991, Alternet, CERFnet, and PSInet, three of the largest commercial networks at that time, announced the formation of the Commercial Internet Exchange (CIX). With the introduction of CIX, the commercial community now had the same communications flexibility as its educational and research counterpart.

Managing the Internet

While no one actually owns the Internet, it was realized in the late 1980s that some structures needed to be put in place to ensure the ongoing reliability, integrity, and stability of the network.

Of primary importance was a method of issuing and tracking the IP addresses and domain names assigned to each host computer connected to the Internet. (See Chapter 6, "E-Mail and CISMAIL," for a full discussion of domain names.) In addition, the creation and maintenance of accurate address and user lists, not unlike the White and Yellow Pages provided by telephone companies, was also flagged for consideration.

To answer these suggestions, the NSF proposed the creation of an Internet Network Information Center (InterNIC). To manage this center, NSF issued tenders for three contracts. The first, awarded to Network Solutions, was for the creation of the Internet Registration service. The second contract, going to AT&T, was for the maintenance of Internet-related databases and directories. The third contract went to General Atomics, who provides and maintains the computer system that houses the Gopher, Web, and FTP sites that form the InterNIC service.

> Like most Internet services, information about InterNIC, including the AT&T databases, can be found on the World Wide Web at http://www.internic.org/.

The Internet Society

Due to the somewhat haphazard creation and growth of the Internet, many people over the years have likened it to living constantly in a state of total anarchy. What is amazing is that despite this tendency, the Internet has flourished and continues to do so.

One of the reasons for this success is the willingness, on the part of many people, to take part in working groups and other discussion forums. Over the years, many such meetings have taken place to plan, develop, and guide the Internet.

Despite all these good intentions, the Internet needed some direction. By the end of 1991, even NSFNET was being swamped by the astounding growth of popularity of the Internet. As a result, it was decided that an organization should be created to provide a forum for discussion about the operation and infrastructure of the Internet. This same body would also be responsible for facilitating evolution of the Internet as a global communications network and the promotion of new services and Internet-related developments.

In June of 1992, the Internet Society was officially chartered. At the same time, the Internet Architecture Board and its two major committees, the Internet Engineering Task Force and Internet Research Task Force, were also brought under the control of the new society.

Jointly, these bodies now plan and direct the development of the Internet by coordinating the input and efforts of the millions of people who continue to work for a better Internet.

Note

> The Internet Society offers membership to all members of the Internet community. More information about membership and the activities of the society, including online registration, is available from the Internet Society World Wide Web site at `http://www.isoc.org/`.

Toward the Future

With the Internet doubling in size on almost a yearly basis, its future is somewhat blurry. The one thing that is certain, however, is that in nearly every country in the world now connected to the network in one form or another (Figure 1.2), the Internet is here to stay.

FIGURE 1.2.

International connections as of November, 1994. Map courtesy of the Internet Society.

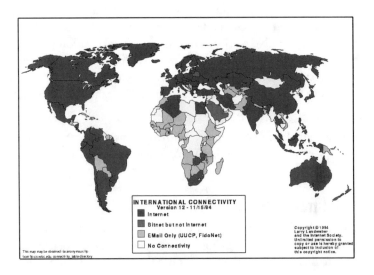

As the Internet expands its reach, it is rapidly changing the way people work, think, and even live. Banks and businesses now use it to conduct business transactions. Students are using it to share classes with children across the world. Even rock and roll bands like the Rolling Stones have fallen into its grip.

For many people, the Internet is now a part of their everyday life. As to exactly how it will affect your life—only time will tell.

Summary

What started out as a Cold War research tool is now the basis of the most complex global communications system known to man. Even the countries that were the focus of all the Cold War rhetoric are now encompassed by its global net.

For many people, however, its power lies not in the complex interplay of communications networks and computer systems that make it function. Instead, it lies in the ability to use the Internet without the need to understand how any of this technology works.

Whether by design or accident, the Internet now reaches into nearly every aspect of computer communications. While many commercial services such as CompuServe long resisted the move to connectivity with the Internet, they are now faced with a simple choice: Connect or be overrun!

The next chapter follows the process that brought about the linking of CompuServe with the Internet. At the same time, it explores some of the key differences between the two systems and introduces the range of new services the Internet offers to CompuServe members.

CHAPTER 2

THE HISTORY OF COMPUSERVE AND ITS CONNECTION TO THE INTERNET

Unlike the Internet, whose origin is grounded firmly in the hallowed halls of education and research institutions, CompuServe's history is deeply steeped in the commercial communications market. From its inception, CompuServe was designed to be a commercial commodity, a computer service available to anyone who wished to purchase the resources it provided.

As a result, CompuServe has become the world's largest private computer network. This chapter explores the development of this global network and follows the path that led to CompuServe's current links with the Internet.

CompuServe—The Early Years

In the late 1960s, educational institutions were not the only organizations with a growing need for computer resources. Commercial businesses had also begun to appreciate the capabilities of these powerful new machines.

For many companies, however, the cost of owning a computer was impossible to justify, even when the potential business benefits were weighed against the expense. The monetary cost of purchasing a computer was not the only factor that needed to be considered, either. These computers required special environments that provided filtered and cooled air, and in many cases they also required a highly trained staff just to keep the computers operating.

In the eyes of many businesses, these demands were simply not practical. What they wanted were computers that they could afford and that they did not have to maintain. Unfortunately, the desktop and portable computers that are so common today were still many years off, so businesses were forced to look for a more cost-effective solution.

Compu-Serve Network, Inc.

In 1969, at around the same time that ARPANET was being launched by the U.S. government, a man named Harry K. Gard formed a company call Compu-Serve Network, Inc. This company offered to take away the problems of high cost and maintenance by renting computer time on its computers to interested business organizations for computer data processing and data storage.

For many companies, this was the opportunity they had been seeking. Finally, they could obtain all the benefits of computerizing their business interests at only a fraction of the cost. From 1969 to 1972, Compu-Serve Network grew quickly through a coast-to-coast network of regional offices and data communications centers. By the end of 1972, the company was managing the computer interests of over 425 major business enterprises, including many Fortune 500 companies.

Batch Data Processing

Initially, Compu-Serve Network provided its clients with *batch data processing* capabilities. Companies would provide Compu-Serve Network with a list of data to be processed—

possibly a weekly payroll, an inventory update, or even a mailing list. This data would be fed into the Compu-Serve Network's computer and the results would be delivered back to the client.

While not exactly the type of computer access we are used to today, batch processing was a giant leap forward from the manual procedures companies had used since their inception. Batch processing meant that tedious jobs, such as the maintenance of accurate accounting ledgers, could be performed in a matter of hours instead of weeks, as had previously been the case.

Not satisfied with just offering batch processing services to its clients, the company soon began to explore the possibilities of *time-sharing* and computer access using telephone lines and modems.

Time-Sharing

Computer time-sharing uses a concept similar to that which made time-share holiday resorts so popular in the 1980s. Not everyone can afford to own their own private holiday resort, but by spreading the cost among a group of people, each person can use the resort for one or two weeks every year.

Similar principles were applied to time-share computer users. Instead of purchasing a computer, companies could purchase time on Compu-Serve Network's computers, paying only for the amount of time that they used.

In the early days, this type of time-sharing meant going to a computer center and using a terminal provided by the service provider. However, as modems became more readily available, computer centers were phased out in favor of dial-up access. Companies now had the best of both worlds—they had access to computer services from terminals in their own offices, and the cost of doing so was well within their budgetary constraints.

The Change to "CompuServe"

From 1972 until 1977, interest in the services Compu-Serve Network offered grew steadily. During this period, however, the cost of computers began to gradually drop, along with the level of maintenance needed to keep them operational.

By 1977, the first personal computers were beginning to appear, and minicomputers were now well within the reach of many company expense budgets. To survive in what would become a dwindling market, Compu-Serve Network began to explore new ways of utilizing its now extensive time-sharing computer network.

In order to keep the business relationships it had developed with its existing clients, Compu-Serve Network decided to add a wide range of value-added products to its time-sharing and batch-processing services. It was argued that even if companies installed their own computer systems, they would still want to connect to Compu-Serve Network to access these new services. As if to signal this new development, Compu-Serve Network changed its name to CompuServe.

Consumer Services

By the end of the 1970s, computers were no longer just the domain of educational institutions and corporate business ventures. Computer hobbyists and small businesses were joining the computerization explosion in ever-increasing numbers. To meet this demand, in 1979 CompuServe created MicroNET. This service, the forerunner of the CompuServe Information Service, gave members of the public night-time and weekend access to what was fast becoming the largest single general information service in the United States.

During the years that followed, CompuServe began to offer many new services to its customers. In 1980, an agreement was made with the Associated Press and ten of its member newspapers to provide continuous online delivery of news and information to CompuServe's customers. This was followed in 1983 by the development of the Electronic Mall, which for the first time allowed personal computer users to shop online.

By 1984, the newly named *CompuServe Information Service* (CIS) was providing over 100,000 users with 24-hour access to news, online shopping, and a wide array of business and general information services in what were to become known as *forums*. These forums provided the framework for CompuServe's information services. They often contained discussion areas, libraries of information, and even live conferences dealing with a specific topic or group of topics.

International Growth

Before long, other countries began to take an interest in the services CompuServe now offered. Japan was the first foreign country to offer personal computer users access to the CompuServe Information Service. As the result of a joint venture between the Japanese computer company NIF and CompuServe, Japanese users were offered access to a customized version of CIS in 1985.

This global growth did not stop at just connecting Japanese users to CompuServe. Soon people in Europe, the United Kingdom, and many other Asian countries were accessing CompuServe on a daily basis. Not all these services offered the same information to their customers, either. In many cases the service was individually tailored to suit the needs of the local community.

Probably the most significant single customization was for the French government's Minitel Network, which began to offer a limited version of CIS to its 6,000,000+ users in 1991. This was followed in August of the same year by the launch of CompuServe Pacific, a joint venture with the Fujitsu computer company, which offered CompuServe access to users in Australia and New Zealand.

CompuServe Today

CompuServe now provides more than 3 million users with worldwide access to over 2,000 forums covering a wide range of topics. It also offers access to Associated Press news services and thousands of forums and databases, with the Electronic Mall providing worldwide online shopping and CIS Mail allowing members to communicate using electronic mail.

What is amazing is that, while the Internet uses a network of millions of computers to achieve such a wide reach, CompuServe is still effectively a time-sharing computer service. Each information forum on CompuServe runs the same software, and every user who connects to CompuServe runs one of a small number of similar communications programs that display the same set of information.

For many people, this is CompuServe's main strength. A new user needs only to obtain a copy of WinCIM, CompuServe's navigation software, and they're up and running.

With CompuServe, there is no need to learn about the many complex systems that make services such as the Internet function. For the most part, getting connected is a simple process.

In this sense, CompuServe is a one-stop communications service, and it is in this definition that the difference between CompuServe and the Internet lies.

Online or Network

The Internet is in essence a network of separate computer systems, all sharing information and exchanging services. Although this process is what made the Internet so powerful, for the end user it has often been in the past (and probably will be well into the future) the source of many hours of heartache.

This difficulty comes from the greatly varying ways that each computer system handles the information it receives across the Internet. This has led to different programs being developed for each type of computer hardware, each with its own idiosyncrasies. Even a simple task such as e-mail can require the use of widely differing programs, depending on the computer system a user is connected to.

CompuServe, on the other hand, is still basically a single computer system with terminals connected to it, and this remains true even given the capabilities that programs such as WinCIM now offer to CompuServe users.

This is not to say the either system is better. Each offers users different communications options and, as is explored in the next section, when the two services are combined the users can obtain the best of both differing communications services.

The Internet Gateway

While CompuServe was building its global time-share computer service, the Internet was also rapidly developing its own global communications network of networks.

Eventually, it was inevitable that the paths of these two services would cross, and as had often been the case in the past, the driving force behind the initial meeting was electronic mail.

The E-Mail Gateway

By the end of the 1980s, both CompuServe and the Internet had well-established electronic mail systems operating on their respective networks. The problem was that users on one system couldn't send mail to users on the other. The reasons behind this problem were twofold. Firstly, there was no physical connection between the two services, and secondly, the methods of addressing mail were not compatible.

Although connecting separate networks through TCP/IP gateways was by this stage a popular Internet pastime, very little work had been done on linking non-TCP/IP-compatible systems to the Internet. As a result, for CompuServe and the Internet to be able to communicate, a new type of gateway was needed.

In addition, a number of new policies needed to be put into place by CompuServe to ensure that its users could both send and receive e-mail across the Internet. To make the whole system work, it was decided that each CompuServe user would be given an Internet address in addition to their existing CompuServe ID. This address was created by altering their existing CompuServe ID. For example, `100036,174` would become `100036.174@compuserve.com`. You don't need to be too concerned at this stage about exactly what this address means. It is discussed in greater detail in Chapter 6, "E-Mail and CIS Mail."

In 1989, once these policies were in place and the gateway constructed, CompuServe and Internet users were able to send electronic mail messages from the Internet to CompuServe and back.

Expanding the Gateway

As interest in the Internet began to grow, CompuServe users started to request expansion of the gateway to encompass other Internet services. In the early stages, the most requested service was connecting to CompuServe from the Internet using the remote computing capabilities for which the Internet was originally conceived.

To silence these requests and to further explore the possibilities of expanded Internet connectivity, CompuServe announced the availability of a Telnet connection to CompuServe in March of 1994. (See Appendix B, "Connecting to CompuServe from the Internet," for more information on this service.) With the opening of this service, Internet users could log onto CompuServe across the Internet in much the same way as modem users had done in the past.

This action was not a solitary one on the part of CompuServe, but instead signaled the start of the Internet connectivity that will be explored in the remainder of this book.

Usenet and FTP

Shortly after the Telnet gateway was opened, CompuServe began extensive testing of a Usenet gateway service. With the number of discussion areas on Usenet approaching the 8,000 mark, CompuServe decided that Usenet was the next logical Internet service to offer to its users. (See Chapter 8, "Usenet—Newsgroups," for full coverage of CompuServe's Usenet services.)

To correspond with the official opening of the Usenet gateway on August 15, 1994, CompuServe announced that it had joined the *Commercial Internet Exchange* (CIX). With this move CompuServe telegraphed its intentions to become a major player in the global Internet marketplace, and as such began the gradual introduction and education of its users in the ways of the Internet.

Following the opening of the Usenet gateway, which technically allows only discussions to be exchanged across the Internet, a number of users began asking for access to files stored on Internet host computers. CompuServe users familiar with CIS forums expected not only to be able to conduct discussions with other users, but also to be able to download files and computer programs in the same way that their familiar CIS forum software permitted. (See Figure 2.1.)

FIGURE 2.1.
WinCIM downloading a file from one of its forum libraries.

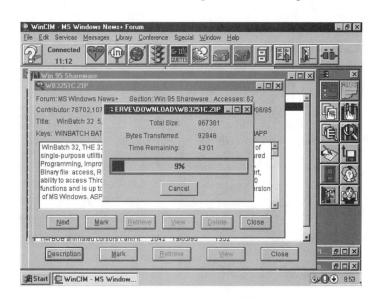

Unlike CompuServe, the Internet requires separate software to access libraries of files and computer programs. This software or *file transfer protocol* is commonly referred to as *FTP*. (See Chapter 10, "File Transfer Protocol (FTP)," for a full discussion of FTP.) To allow user's access to Internet file libraries, or anonymous FTP sites as they are known, a FTP gateway was opened by CompuServe at the end of 1994.

Telnet Comes Full Circle

Even though CompuServe opened its Telnet connection with the Internet in 1994, it was strictly a one-way affair. People on the Internet could use Telnet to log onto CompuServe, but CompuServe users could not use Telnet to log onto Internet systems.

In many people's eyes, this was considered the main indication that CompuServe and the Internet were still not yet fully linked together. To answer this concern, in March of 1995

CompuServe's Internet connection came full circle with the announcement that CompuServe users could now use Telnet to connect to systems outside of CompuServe. (See Chapter 9, "Telnet," for a full discussion of CompuServe's Telnet Services.)

CompuServe and the Internet Today

In March of 1995, a great number of changes began to take place at CompuServe. Not satisfied with its presence on the Internet, H&R Block—the company that now owns CompuServe—began discussions with Spry, one of the major Internet software companies.

These discussions resulted in the acquisition of Spry, Inc. and the formation of the CompuServe Internet Division. This new division, created out of existing services Spry offered, is to be responsible for the future development of all CompuServe Internet services. This will include a wide range of new Internet services that were also announced at the time of the takeover.

TCP/IP Connections

Probably the most stunning of these announcements, from a commercial perspective, was the announcement that as of April, 1995, all CompuServe network connections would automatically provide users with a direct TCP/IP link to the Internet.

For the 3 million plus CompuServe members, this meant that they were automatically given full access to the Internet, if they chose to use it. With the acquisition of Spry and the creation of CompuServe Internet Division, CompuServe now not only offered full access to the Internet, but also provided the software needed to make such a connection possible.

A full exploration of the use of TCP/IP connections with the Internet is outside the scope of this book, but Appendix C, "Internet Software," discusses some of the more popular TCP/IP software currently available.

There are also a number of very good books dealing specifically with TCP/IP connections to the Internet. *Teach Yourself TCP/IP* from Sams is a good book for people who are just beginning to explore the Internet, while *Using the Internet, Second Edition* from Que offers probably the best in-depth coverage of the Internet and the myriad of software programs that can be used in conjunction with it.

The World Wide Web

The other major announcement to surface in early 1995 was the release of full *World Wide Web* access for CompuServe users.

The World Wide Web is without a doubt the most talked about and hotly debated subject on the Internet today. In many ways the Web is not unlike a global version of the CompuServe WinCIM navigator. (See Chapter 11, "The World Wide Web," and Chapter 12, "World Wide Web Productivity," for an in-depth look at the World Wide Web.)

The World Wide Web is referred to by many terms these days. Often it is called the Web, or WWW, or even W3. For consistency, this book refers to it as WWW.

Note

With the release of an updated version of WinCIM that includes WWW capabilities, it can now truly be said that CompuServe has finally become a part of the network of networks we call the Internet.

The Future of WinCIM

Even with the introduction of TCP/IP connectivity, the future for dedicated CompuServe services looks very bright. Most important among all of these plans is the continued development of WinCIM. These include full support for access to the World Wide Web and secure data transactions.

Over the past few years, WinCIM has grown from strength to strength. As it now stands, it is one of the easiest to use all-in-one Internet navigators, and at the same time it still offers full CompuServe access to the many commercial services that will probably remain unavailable on the Internet for some years to come.

By offering users a consistent interface and simple one-click connectivity, WinCIM will be, for many new users, the tool that finally carries them onto the Internet and the global information superhighway.

Summary

As was so often the case with the development of the Internet, the creation of links between CompuServe and the Internet was driven, for the most part, by the needs of its users.

In opening up these links, CompuServe has brought its ability to provide highly user-friendly communications technology to the Internet. Using its existing network and familiar tools such as WinCIM, CompuServe users can now explore the Internet without needing to be concerned about the many problems and difficulties so often associated with Internet access.

At the same time it also brings TCP/IP and direct Internet access to millions of users who, in the past, never even considered the possibility of connecting to the Internet.

This brings us to an important point. With all the capabilities that CompuServe offers, why would anyone want to use the Internet?

To help answer this question, the next chapter explores some of the unique services that the Internet now offers to CompuServe users. In addition, it also looks more closely at the types of services that comprise the Internet today.

PART II

GETTING STARTED ON THE INTERNET

CHAPTER 3

USING THE INTERNET

For many CompuServe users, the foremost question in their minds is, "I'm happy with the services CompuServe offers me now, so why should I be concerned about using the Internet?"

On its own, this question is a hard one to answer. In much the same way that different people use CompuServe for different reasons, the Internet is different things to different people. As a result, the only person who can really answer this question is the person asking it.

This chapter will help you to answer this question by looking more closely at what the various Internet services, which were mentioned in Chapter 2, offer to CompuServe users. These services can be broken down into three main topic areas. To investigate the Internet further, this chapter deals with these topics in the following order:

- Communications Services
- Information Services
- Search Tools

Communications Services

At its heart, the Internet is primarily a communications tool. No matter how you look at it, using the Internet involves the exchange of information between two or more computers.

When the system was designed, it allowed computers to communicate and share resources. Before too long, people began to realize that if the system could allow two computers to communicate with each other, two people working on those computers should be able to communicate as well.

Electronic Mail

This realization led to the development of the service known today as *e-mail*. In essence, e-mail allows people to exchange messages using their computers. With e-mail, two people can correspond electronically in much the same way two people can write letters to each other using the postal service. (But it's much faster, of course.)

For CompuServe users, e-mail is probably one of the most important reasons for becoming aware of the Internet. As the use of e-mail becomes commonplace, more and more people are obtaining electronic mailboxes on one or more of the computer networks that now span the globe. However, not all of these people have accounts on CompuServe.

To send e-mail messages to these people, you will need to know at least a little bit about how the Internet works. You will also need to understand the procedures you need to follow to send e-mail using CompuServe. To ease the way, Chapter 6, "E-Mail and CIS Mail," explores these steps in detail.

Mailing Lists

One of the capabilities that eventuated when the first e-mail software began to appear on ARPANET was the ability to send the same e-mail message to more than one person. This was the electronic equivalent of photocopying a letter a number of times and mailing it to many different people.

Not long after this feature appeared, a few enterprising individuals realized that they could use this capability to conduct conference-like discussions. By setting themselves up as *moderators*, they could receive messages sent by people participating in a discussion. Then, using what was to become known as a *mailing list*, the moderators could forward each message to all *subscribers* of the discussion. Using this technique, there was no need for each person to have a copy of the mailing list. Instead, all they needed to do was send messages to the moderator, who would look after the distribution for them.

Although this system was suitable for small mailing lists, it soon became apparent that to manage some of the more popular mailing lists, a dedicated computer program would be a better proposition. Over time, two main computer programs have emerged to manage this task. Between them, LISTSERV and Majordomo handle a large percentage of the 10,000+ mailing lists now available on the Internet. Chapter 7, "Mailing Lists," discusses how you can participate in mailing lists using CompuServe.

> Mailing lists eventually became so popular that a dedicated network was created to look after the distribution process. This network became known as BITNET, the Because It's Time NETwork.

Newsgroups

Another service that grew out of the use of e-mail was the popular network known as Usenet. Usenet, like mailing lists, allows users to take part in online discussions.

However, where mailing lists use e-mail to automatically distribute a copy of each message to all participants, Usenet messages are stored on a network of computers in separate discussion areas known as *newsgroups*. Instead of receiving these messages by using e-mail, people use a special program called a *newsgroup reader* (Figure 3.1) to look through all the messages that have been sent to computers on the Usenet network. Newsgroup readers also allow users to post messages to Usenet newsgroups.

FIGURE 3.1.

By using a program like the Trumpet News Reader, you can read messages stored on Usenet.

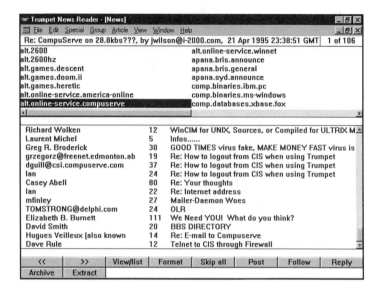

When someone posts a message to a newsgroup, it is stored on the Usenet computer that the person's newsgroup reader is connected to. A copy of the message is also sent to every other computer on the Usenet network, using a process known as *store and forward.* This name reflects the way that the newsgroup messages are distributed from computer to computer.

Like mailing lists, there are literally thousands of newsgroups available on Usenet. To assist you in getting the most out of newsgroups, Chapter 8, "Usenet—Newsgroups" explores the topic in depth.

Remote Computing

Even though the preceding discussion might seem to indicate that the only method of communicating on the Internet is by e-mail, this could not be further from the truth.

When ARPANET was first proposed, the big problem facing computer researchers was getting access to the limited number of high-powered computers that existed at the time. Naturally, people wanted to be able to use the most powerful machines available to reduce the amount of time their projects took. What the ARPANET team suggested was a way of sharing these computers that would allow researchers to log onto these machines from distant locations. In addition, unlike dial-up terminals, which require the use of dedicated phone lines, these remote connections would take advantage of the ARPANET network.

To achieve this goal, a remote logon service was developed that eventually become known as Telnet. Today, Telnet allows people to log onto computer systems all over the world. Some of these computers are very similar to the bulletin board systems (BBSs) that many of you have probably used in the past. Other systems offer access to databases, while some provide access to a wide variety of online computer gaming environments, such as MUDs and, more recently, MOOs.

Although Telnet is probably not going to be of use to everyone, it is a powerful tool that offers users a surprisingly wide range of capabilities. Chapter 9, "Telnet," looks at the Telnet capabilities offered by CompuServe and explores some of the sites you can connect to.

Real-Time Communications

As modem speeds and the speed of the Internet backbone increase, a new form of computer communications is becoming popular. Although all the standard e-mail communications tools are extremely fast when compared to services such as couriers and mail delivery, they lack the ability to compete with real-time services such as the telephone. To redress this failing, Internet relay chat (IRC) was developed.

IRC uses a party-line system that allows any number of people, anywhere on the Internet, to gather in virtual rooms or *channels,* where they can communicate in real time using their computers. (See Figure 3.2.) When a person types a comment on IRC, it is immediately displayed on the screen of every other person connected to the same channel. Using IRC, people can stage conferences, hold meetings, and simply spend time chatting with other people from all around the world.

FIGURE 3.2.

Using IRC, people all over the world can take part in real-time conversations.

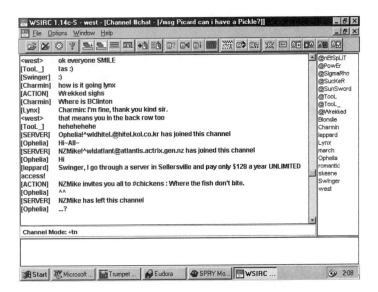

At this stage, CompuServe does not directly support the use of IRC using WinCIM. However, by using NetLauncher, it is possible to take advantage of the WinSock-compatible IRC program discussed in Appendix C.

Information Services

Apart from being a communications tool, the Internet is rapidly becoming a valuable source of information. Thousands of computers connected to the Internet now contain material stored in computer files, databases, and information systems, which for the most part are publicly available to people on the Internet.

To cope with this ever-increasing amount of information, a number of services have been created to assist people in retrieving data located on the Internet.

File Transfer Protocol

One of the first services developed on the Internet was the File Transfer Protocol (FTP). Using this tool, a person can exchange files with a remote computer system. In many ways, FTP is similar to Telnet. Both services allow you to log onto a remote computer and use it as though you were connected locally. In the case of FTP, however, instead of connecting to the remote system as a terminal, a special technique called a *client-server connection* is used.

Computer systems containing files that people can retrieve use a computer program called an *FTP server*. To obtain a file from one of these FTP servers, you need to run a program called an *FTP client* on your local computer. This program is responsible for all communications with the remote FTP server. These two programs communicate with each other and allow you to browse the directories and files located on the remote machine. When you locate a file you wish to retrieve, you tell your FTP client which one it is. Your FTP client communicates this to the FTP server, which in turn sends the file back to your FTP client to be stored on your local hard drive.

Note

> Not all computer systems that run FTP servers allow just anyone to access their files. To protect these sites, you must log on with a user ID and password when you connect to any FTP server. To get around this built-in FTP limitation, sites that allow anyone to access their files use a special user ID called anonymous. This user ID accepts anything you enter at the password prompt as a valid entry. As a result, these FTP sites have become known as *anonymous FTP servers.*

For CompuServe users, FTP is the ideal complement to the thousands of files already available in its forums. Chapter 10, "File Transfer Protocol (FTP)," looks at how CompuServe users can connect to FTP sites using WinCIM's built-in FTP client software. It also investigates some of the major FTP libraries located on the Internet.

Gopher

FTP offers users a good method of exchanging computer files, but it is often a very difficult job to actually locate the information you want to download. To reduce this difficulty, a number of menu-based tools began to appear in the early 1990s that allowed users to move around the Internet more easily.

Of these services, the most popular is a system known as *Gopher*. Like FTP, Gopher relies on the use of client-server communications. Computer systems that allow people to access their information using Gopher menus need to operate a Gopher server. This server, like an FTP server, communicates with a Gopher client running on your local computer.

The Gopher client displays the directories and files available on the Gopher server as a list of menu items. By selecting from these menu items, you can explore the information stored on the *host computer* and download items you are interested in.

Gopher also provides its users with a feature that FTP cannot provide. As well as providing easy access to files on a Gopher system, Gopher menu items can also contain *links* to other Gopher servers. When you select one of these links, you are automatically transferred to the new Gopher server and its menu items are displayed on your Gopher client's screen. To find out more about using Gopher with CompuServe, see Chapter 13, "Gopher."

World Wide Web

Unless you've just returned from the dark side of the moon, you've probably seen the name World Wide Web (WWW) mentioned somewhere in the past few months. To put it mildly, this client-server offering has taken the Internet by storm.

Developed by CERN, the European Laboratory for Particle Physics, in the late 1980s, the World Wide Web was designed to provide scientists and researchers with easy access to the thousands of documents and publications stored on computers throughout the Internet. At the time, many of the new users who were being introduced to the Internet quickly became confused and frustrated by the number of different tools they needed to achieve what were seemingly simple goals. The bold plan for the World Wide Web was to create a client-server tool that allowed people to move around on the Internet without needing to learn anything other than how to use a WWW client program.

> The acronym CERN comes from the French title for the project, "Conseil European pour la Recherche Nucleaire."

Note

In many ways, a WWW client is like a WinCIM navigator for the Internet. Using a simple point-and-click interface (Figure 3.3), a WWW client allows you to roam the Internet almost at will.

FIGURE 3.3.

Using the CompuServe WWW server, clicking on any underlined text transports you to the information it describes.

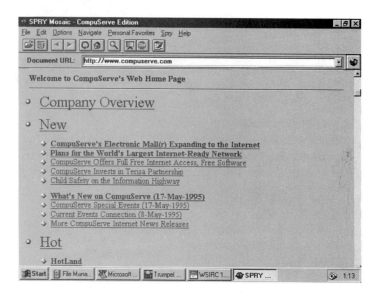

Instead of displaying menus as Gopher does, WWW clients display *documents* containing pages of information. These documents contain special links called *hypertext* links. By clicking on one of these links, a user can:

◆ Load a new WWW document

◆ Download files from an FTP site

◆ Browse the menus on a Gopher site

◆ Read newsgroup messages

◆ Open Telnet connections

◆ Listen to audio clips

◆ View pictures and digitized video clips

Note

WWW documents are written using a special format called the *hypertext markup language (HTML)*. This has led to WWW documents being more commonly referred to as HTML pages. Chapter 12, "World Wide Web Productivity," looks at how you can use HTML to create your own WWW documents and publish them on the Internet.

Given all the capabilities the World Wide Web offers, it should come as no surprise that its popularity has extended beyond the walls of the research institutions that developed it. Today, organizations of all shapes and sizes are setting up World Wide Web sites, and millions of people are using the World Wide Web to explore the Internet on a daily basis.

Many of the world's major computer companies now have WWW sites, as do a large number of software houses. What is more interesting, however, is the large number of non-computer-related pages being created each day. These pages cover everything from movies and television to home shopping to teddy bear ownership. To find out more about using the World Wide Web with CompuServe, turn to Chapter 11, "The World Wide Web."

Search Tools

With all the information now available on the Internet, finding the item you are looking for brings to mind the story of the needle in the haystack. To help lighten the load, a number of services now exist whose job it is to help you find the material you are looking for.

The InterNIC Database

As discussed in Chapter 1, when the NSF set up InterNIC, it appointed AT&T to look after the maintenance of a collection of Internet-related databases and search tools.

Using a World Wide Web client, InterNIC can be reached at `http://www.internic.net`. There is also a Gopher server at `internic.net port 70`. Failing this, you can also access InterNIC by Telneting to `ds.internic.net`.

Internet White Pages

With more than an estimated 30 million people now in possession of an e-mail address, one of the more popular tools provided by the InterNIC is the *Internet White Pages*. (See Figure 3.4.)

FIGURE 3.4.

Like a telephone directory, the Internet White Pages helps you locate people on the Internet.

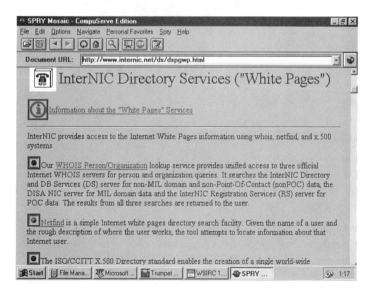

This service brings together many of the most popular Internet e-mail directories and listings. Using tools like Netfind and WHOIS or the experimental X.500 directory project, it is possible to look up a person's e-mail address and, in some cases, non-Internet related details such as phone numbers and postal addresses.

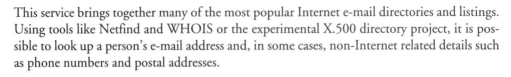

> Unfortunately, the White Pages project is still very much in its infancy, and as a result not all people with e-mail address are currently listed in the database. Over the coming months this should begin to change as the X.500 project expands, with the aim of eventually listing all e-mail users who wish their address to be known.

Directory of Directories

When you are trying to find a specific site, there is probably no better place to start than the InterNIC Directory of Directories.

This directory contains lists of nearly every machine known to be connected to the Internet. To assist you further, they are categorized into services such as those shown in Figure 3.5.

FIGURE 3.5.

The Internet Directory of Directories.

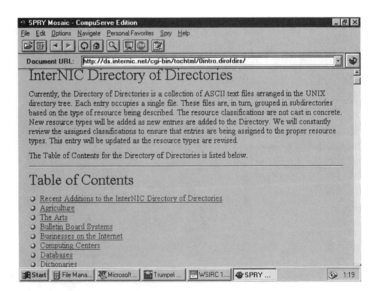

RFCs and FYIs

As mentioned in previous chapters, the InterNIC also maintains a full listing of all Request for Comment, For Your Information, and many other documents published by the Internet Engineering Task Force (IETF).

These documents contain a wide variety of valuable information dealing with all aspects of the Internet, including its operation, policies, and practices.

Archie

The InterNIC Directory of Directories may be of great assistance when you need to find a specific FTP site, but in many cases you may not actually know the location of a file you are trying to find. When this happens, you need to turn your attention to a different type of information database.

Archie was developed for the specific purpose of collecting the names of files and directories on every FTP site on the Internet and storing them in a publicly accessible database. When given a filename or the name of a related directory, Archie conducts a search of all FTP sites. When finished, it provides you with a list of every site that contains files or directories with names similar to the one you are looking for.

In Figure 3.6, an Archie client was asked to provide a list of all FTP sites that contain WinSock files. On the left side of the screen it has listed all the FTP sites that contain WinSock files. In the middle section it lists the directories where each site can be found. For more information on Archie, be sure you read "Archie" in Chapter 10.

FIGURE 3.6.

Using Archie, you can easily locate files stored at FTP sites.

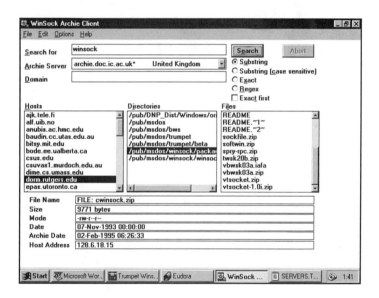

WAIS

Of all the search tools developed for the Internet, the Wide Area Information Service (WAIS) is the most amazing. Whereas most other Internet tools contain databases of files or Internet addresses, WAIS contains databases that index the documents themselves.

When the Thinking Machines Corporation decided to test the capabilities of its Connection Machine computer system, they developed an environment that was capable of bringing the library to the user's desktop.

When the Connection Machine was developed, it was a radically new type of computer system that worked on the principle that the best way to get a job done fast was to share the task between many computers. But instead of wiring these computers together using a network, the Connection Machine was designed in such a way that it consisted of many computer processors in a single box. As a result, this machine was capable of performing many tasks at the same time, or in parallel, which led to the Connection Machine being called a massively paralleled supercomputer.

To test this system, they combined the power of this machine with an extensive global library of documents, papers, and, in some cases, entire electronic books. The result was WAIS, a document indexing system capable of searching through the contents of hundreds of thousands of documents in a matter of seconds.

Using WAIS, it is possible to locate any mention of a specific word or phrase in documents as diverse as *Australian Aboriginal Studies, Tantric News*, the phone and fax numbers of members of the U.S. Congress, papers on mathematical studies at MIT, and *The CIA World Fact Book*. Not satisfied with doing just this, they added a technique called *relevance feedback*. Using relevance feedback, WAIS can take a document you have retrieved and use it as the basis for additional searches of the WAIS databases. In other words, the search says, "Now find anything that looks like anything in this document."

Like most Internet tools, you can access WAIS using Telnet, Gopher, WWW, or a dedicated WAIS client. The two most popular methods use either a WAIS client such as WINWAIS, discussed in Appendix C, or WAISgate, a WWW page operated by WAIS Inc., which is discussed in Chapter 12.

WWW Search Tools

With the number of pages on the World Wide Web now past the 2.5 million mark, finding your way around by pointing and clicking could take quite some time. To cope with this astonishing growth, a number of dedicated WWW search tools are appearing.

Using tools such as Lycos, Infoseek and Spry's own WWW Wizard, it is possible to quickly and efficiently search the World Wide Web and locate pages of information you are interested in. For many people, this is the best way to move around the World Wide Web, but others prefer to surf the Net using lists such as Yahoo. (See Figure 3.7.) Unlike WWW search tools, these lists provide a categorized index of hot pages and cool Web sites.

Chapter 12 looks at both types of World Wide Web tools, and also looks at how you can publish your own WWW pages.

FIGURE 3.7.

Yahoo helps people surf the Net in comfort.

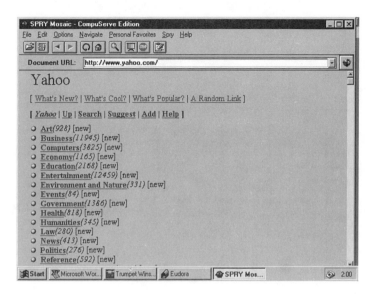

Summary

Since its inception, the Internet has been a service whose development is driven by its users. As a result, it can truly be said that the Internet contains something for everyone.

Like most areas of the computer world, the Internet is no longer the domain of scientists and researchers. Instead, it now offers everyone the ability to communicate, explore, shop, play, and even be entertained. Services like CompuServe have been providing these sort of capabilities for some time, but as the World Wide Web grows in size and popularity, many people are finding the incentive they need to make their first tentative steps onto the Internet.

To meet this demand, CompuServe now offers full access to all Internet services through the gateways and tools outlined in Chapter 2 and expanded upon in this chapter. The next chapter looks at how you can gain access to these new services and explore the capabilities offered by NetLauncher—the new PPP TCP/IP service—announced by CompuServe in April of 1995.

CHAPTER
4

GETTING CONNECTED TO THE INTERNET

Unlike many other Internet service providers (ISPs), CompuServe does not expect its members to come to grips with new software or strange utilities to access the Internet services it provides.

Instead, CompuServe has built onto the well-known interface provided by the CompuServe Information Manager (CIM) and, for Windows users, by WinCIM. You can access many of the current Internet services by using WinCIM, without ever needing to add a new program or service. By doing this, CompuServe has greatly reduced the enormous learning curve faced by most people when they embark on a first-time exploration of the Internet.

However, CompuServe has not been blinded to the fact that there are many useful software items available on the Internet that have something to offer to the Internet user in their own right. As a result, CompuServe has also developed a mechanism that allows all members to take advantage of these programs if they choose, or else they can stay with WinCIM's more comfortable environment.

This chapter explores CompuServe's various connection options by dealing with the following topics:

- The CompuServe Internet gateway
- WinCIM
- The CompuServe network and PPP
- NetLauncher
- Spry Mosaic
- Winsock
- The Internet Club

The CompuServe Internet Gateway

Before looking at the newer connection options, here is a recap of the services offered using the Internet gateway.

Ever since CompuServe began implementing Internet access, it has kept as its primary goal the seamless integration of these new services into those already offered to its members through the CompuServe Information Manager. To date, it has successfully achieved this, offering e-mail, FTP, USENET, and Telnet access through the menus and forums available on CompuServe. This has allowed many people to access Internet-based services with none of the difficulties usually associated with setting up an Internet connection or obtaining an Internet service provider account.

Note

Later this year, World Wide Web access will also be added to the capabilities supported directly by WinCIM.

WinCIM

The Internet gateway services' success largely springs from the capabilities inherent in the design of the CompuServe Information Manager (WinCIM). (See Figure 4.1.)

FIGURE 4.1.

CompuServe Information Manager for Windows offers users a simple point-and-click approach to online communications.

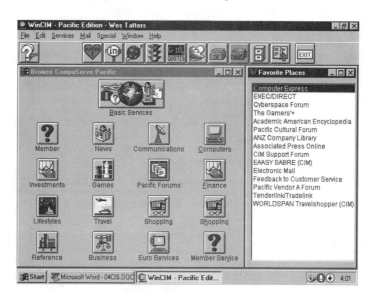

By adopting a point-and-click approach to online communications, WinCIM replaces the familiar text-based online terminal environment with an easy-to-use graphical interface.

The enhancements offered by WinCIM don't stop at fancy menus and windows. As you will learn in subsequent chapters, CompuServe has taken this environment's capabilities and used them to create graphic interfaces for such services as Usenet newsgroups (Figure 4.2) and anonymous FTP (Figure 4.3).

In Chapter 8, "Usenet Newsgroups," you will learn to use WinCIM to get the most out of Usenet and explore some of its many newsgroups. Then, in Chapter 9, "Telnet," you'll explore some of the ways that WinCIM allows you to log onto computers connected to CompuServe via the Internet.

As mentioned previously, WinCIM also gives you access to FTP (File Transfer Protocol), which allows people to exchange files using the Internet. To find out more about using this feature, Chapter 10, "FTP," covers the features that CompuServe offers and explores a few of the popular FTP sites to find out the types of files available.

In addition, CompuServe also provides you with a means of exchanging electronic mail and participating in Internet- and BITNET-based mailing lists. Chapter 6, "E-Mail and CIS Mail," covers what is involved in using this capability through WinCIM, and Chapter 7, "Mailing Lists," further explores the use of e-mail for mailing lists.

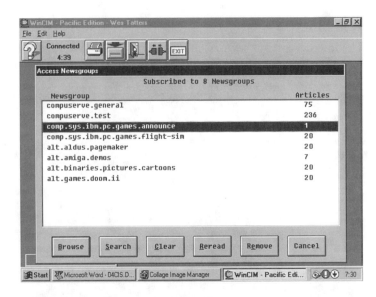

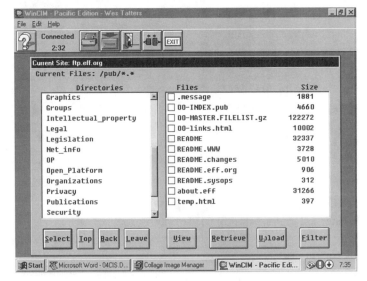

The CompuServe Network and PPP

Although the gateway services offered by CompuServe give its members access to the Internet, the services don't allow members to take advantage of some of the more popular Internet applications, such as dedicated Archie clients, IRC clients, or many of the popular World Wide Web navigators such as Netscape and Mosaic.

To use these programs, you need to create a more direct connection to the Internet, one that bypasses gateways and user interfaces and talks directly with the Internet as a physical part of the network. With the increased demand for this type of Internet access, CompuServe has decided to completely upgrade its dial-up network worldwide so that it now allows you to choose this sort of connection as an option when logging onto CompuServe.

For CompuServe members who have no need for this type of connection, the existing CompuServe Information Manager services still function as they did before. If you want to connect directly to the Internet, it only takes a few simple steps. In addition, CompuServe has also developed a special program that looks after the connection process for you and gives you direct access to the World Wide Web.

PPP Dial-Up Connections

For those of you who like to know about the technical details, CompuServe now supports the Internet Point-to-Point (PPP) serial protocol as an integral part of its dial-up services.

This is the same protocol used by many Internet service providers to give users dial-up access to the Internet. By adopting this protocol, CompuServe gives its members the ability to directly connect their computers to the Internet and become a physical part of the network. Once connected to the Internet in this way, you can run any of the popular Internet client programs currently available. (See Appendix C.)

NetLauncher

Connecting to the Internet in this way requires the use of a special dialer program and access to a collection of communication routines known collectively as the Winsock library.

To help its members out, CompuServe has developed its own dialer program called NetLauncher. This dialer is fully compatible with WinCIM and uses many of the same features, including the same session information. In addition, it also contains a copy of the Winsock library and a full working version of the Spry Mosaic World Wide Web browser.

You can download a free copy of NetLauncher by clicking on the Go icon in the WinCIM toolbar. This opens a dialog box similar to the one shown in Figure 4.4. In this dialog box, type the word **netlauncher** and click on the OK button.

FIGURE 4.4.
*Open the Go dialog box and type **netlauncher**.*

When you do this, WinCIM opens the NetLauncher forum shown in Figure 4.5. From here you can read about the contents of NetLauncher and download a copy. In addition, there is also a support forum (GO NLSUPPORT) that you can enter by clicking on the button provided.

FIGURE 4.5.

The CompuServe NetLauncher for Windows area.

Installing NetLauncher

Once you have obtained a copy of the NetLauncher file from CompuServe, installing it is a very simple process. If you accepted all the default options when you downloaded NetLauncher, a file called CNL.EXE should now be stored in your C:\CSERVE\DOWNLOAD directory.

> Before you can install NetLauncher, you need to have installed a copy of WinCIM version 1.4 or later. NetLauncher uses the session information created by WinCIM to determine the phone number and service it needs to connect to.

To start the installation process, run CNL.EXE by selecting the **R**un option from the **F**ile menu in the Windows main menu, or by using Windows Explorer if you are using Windows 95. This launches the CompuServe NetLauncher Installation program shown in Figure 4.6. This program takes you through the steps required to complete the installation.

FIGURE 4.6.

The CompuServe NetLauncher Installation program.

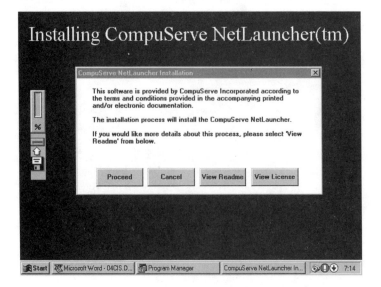

If you already have an Internet dialer installed, remove it before attempting to install NetLauncher. The NetLauncher Installation program renames any Winsock Library files that it finds.

Warning

Connecting to CompuServe

Installation adds three new programs to your CompuServe drawer or folder. (See Figure 4.7.) These are the CompuServe Internet dialer, Spry Mosaic, and ImageView. For the moment, let's leave Mosaic and ImageView aside and look at getting online using the Internet dialer.

FIGURE 4.7.

The CompuServe folder after installing NetLauncher.

To log onto CompuServe via PPP using the CompuServe Internet dialer, follow these steps:

1. Double-click on the CompuServe Internet dialer icon to start the program.
2. Once it starts, open the **S**ettings menu and select the **S**essions... option. This opens the Setup Session Settings dialog box shown in Figure 4.8. This dialog box should be familiar to you, because it is the same one used by WinCIM.

   You shouldn't need to change any of the items listed here if you aren't encountering any difficulties using WinCIM. However, if you haven't already done so, set your baud rate to the highest speed supported by your modem.

> If you are using an older modem that only supports speeds slower than 9,600bps, you seriously need to consider upgrading it to a 14,400 or 28,800bps modem. Working with services like the World Wide Web starts to become an impractical exercise, due to the time it takes to display each page of information. In addition, because CompuServe now charges the same rate for all connection speeds, the cost of connecting using a slower modem can rapidly add up to more than the cost of a new modem.

FIGURE 4.8.

NetLauncher and WinCIM share session connection settings.

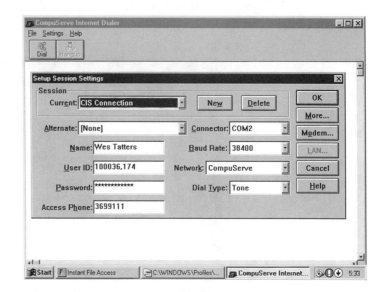

3. Click on the OK button when you are satisfied with your Session information.

4. Open the **S**ettings menu again and select the **T**imers… option. This opens another dialog box that allows you to define a number of timers. (See Figure 4.9.) These timers control whether the Internet dialer automatically closes your connection and hangs up the modem if there are no active Internet clients running on your system.

   For the time being, either accept the defaults provided or deactivate all the timers by selecting the Never Disconnect option.

5. When you're satisfied with the timer setting, click on the OK button to return to the Internet dialer menu window.

6. You are now ready to log onto the Internet. Click on the Dial icon in the toolbar to begin the connection process. Everything is automated from this point on. NetLauncher will look after dialing CompuServe, logging on, negotiating the PPP connection, and activating the appropriate Winsock drivers.

   With a successful connection, NetLauncher first displays the message shown in Figure 4.10 and then minimizes itself so that only a connection timer is showing.

FIGURE 4.9.

The Connection Timer Settings dialog box lets you define disconnection options for NetLauncher.

FIGURE 4.10.

A successful connection using NetLauncher.

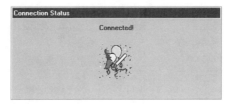

7. You can now launch any Winsock-compatible client currently installed on your computer and use it via the direct PPP connection NetLauncher has created.

8. When you decide to close your Internet connection, click on the minimized icon and reactivate it. Then click on the Hangup icon to log off the Internet and CompuServe.

Spry Mosaic

Once NetLauncher has logged on to the Internet, you can then start Spry Mosaic and begin your exploration of the World Wide Web. (See Figure 4.11.)

FIGURE 4.11.

Spry Mosaic connected to the CompuServe WWW home page.

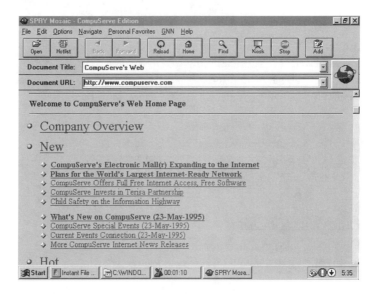

To find out more about using Spry Mosaic, take a look at Chapter 11, "The World Wide Web." Chapter 12, "World Wide Web Productivity," takes a closer look at some of the services the World Wide Web offers. In the closing chapters there are also a number of references to the World Wide Web, or more correctly, some of the *home pages*.

ImageView

As an added bonus, NetLauncher also includes a copy of the ImageView graphics program. (See Figure 4.12.) This program is used by Spry Mosaic when it needs to display images contained on WWW pages. It is capable of displaying files stored in many popular graphic formats including JPEG, GIF, TARGA, BMP, and DIB.

FIGURE 4.12.

ImageView can display and manipulate images stored in a wide variety of graphics formats.

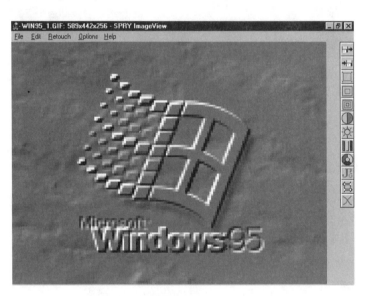

In addition to acting as an image viewer for Spry Mosaic, ImageView can operate as a standalone image viewer. It can also be configured to run as a slide show when you need to display picture sequences. This feature often comes in very handy at trade shows and other demonstrations when a full-blown presentation system is not warranted.

> ImageView can also perform a number of image manipulation functions that can assist you when you need to enhance or improve the quality of less-than-perfect images. The features can all be found in the **R**etouch menu and on the floating toolbar.

Other Winsock Clients

Obviously, Spry Mosaic is not the only Winsock client you can use, although for the purposes of this book it is the only one covered in any detail.

For more information about the types of programs currently available, Appendix C includes a short summary of the most popular programs, including some suggestions about where you can obtain copies of each.

> The Internet New Users Forum (GO INETFORUM) is a good place to go for information about the various programs available, as is the Internet Resource Forum (GO INETRESOURCE).

Note

Trumpet Winsock Dialer

NetLauncher is not the only Internet dialer currently available, and is certainly not the only one you can use with CompuServe's dial-up PPP connections. Of all these dialers, the most popular one is TCPMAN (the dialer that comes bundled with the Trumpet Winsock). This Winsock package has become the de facto standard for Winsock compatibility.

If you prefer to use this dialer instead of NetLauncher, you can obtain a copy from the Internet Resource Forum (GO INETRESOURCE). After you install it, you need to configure the dialer so that it can talk with CompuServe. To do this, run TCPMAN and select the **S**etup option from the **F**ile menu. Doing this opens the Network Configuration dialog box shown in Figure 4.13.

FIGURE 4.13.

The Trumpet Winsock Network Configuration dialog box.

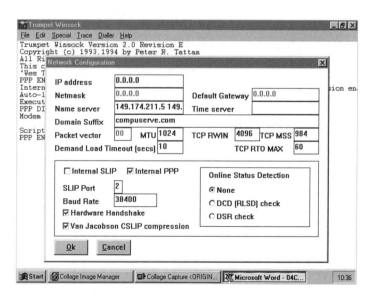

To configure TCPMAN for CompuServe, follow these steps:

1. In the Name Server field, enter the IP addresses for CompuServe's primary and secondary domain name server, separating them with a space:

   `149.174.211.5 149.174.213.5`

2. The CompuServe's domain name is entered in the Domain Suffix field:
   `compuserve.com`

3. Select the Internal PPP option.

4. Set the SLIP Port to the number corresponding to the Com Port your modem is connected to.

5. Set the baud rate to the highest speed supported by your modem.

6. Select Hardware Handshake.

7. Select Van Jacobson CSLIP Compression.

8. Leave all other fields at their default settings.

9. Click on the OK button to accept your new settings. You now need to exit TCPMAN by selecting the **Q**uit option from the **F**ile menu and then restarting TCPMAN so that it registers the new configuration information.

At this stage, you can either manually log onto CompuServe by selecting the **M**anual Login option from the dialer menu, or create a login script to automate the process. Naturally, most people will want to create a login script. To get you started, here is a sample script that you can alter to suit your needs.

Save this script as `LOGIN.CMD` and place it in the same directory as TCPMAN. The lines with "#" symbols in front of them are only there to help you understand what the script is doing. There is no need to include them in your script.

```
# initialize modem
output AT&F\n
input 10 OK\n
# now set up some modem defaults
output at&c1&k3\13
input 10 OK\n
# You need to enter the phone number for your local CompuServe
# connection on the next line instead of the ? characters
output atdt??? ????\13
input 30 CONNECT
# Once the modem connects wake up the Terminal Server
output \13
# Wait for the Host Prompt
input 30 Name:
output CIS\13
# and wait for the ID: prompt
input 30 ID:
# Place your own CompuServe ID number on the next line
output 100036,174/GO:PPPCONNECT\13
input 30 Password:
# replace PASS-WORD with your own password
output PASS-WORD\13
# Logon connection complete now negotiate PPP
```

After saving the script, select the **L**ogin option on the Dialer menu to start the connection process. TCPMAN then uses the commands stored in your script to connect to CompuServe and open a PPP connection. When the connection is complete, it displays the dynamic IP address negotiated by CompuServe for this session.

You can now run Spry Mosaic or any other client program in the same way you did using NetLauncher.

Using Other Computers and Dialers

Windows is not the only platform that allows you to take advantage of CompuServe's new dial-up PPP capabilities. Macintosh and OS/2 Warp users can also configure their machines by following the instructions outlined in the Dialup PPP information menu (GO PPP).

This menu also contains some additional documentation useful to people attempting to configure their dialers for CompuServe. This information is in a Frequently Asked Questions (FAQ) document.

If you are still encountering difficulties at this stage, take a look at the CompuServe Dial PPP message area and its corresponding library. This message area can be found in the Internet New Users Forum (GO INETFORUM). It has been set aside specifically for discussions dealing with using CompuServe's Dialup PPP facilities. Also, in the corresponding library area, there are a number of documents that discuss in detail the steps involved in using a number of different Internet dialers and operating systems.

The Internet Club

To accompany the release of the dial-up PPP service, CompuServe has also announced the creation of a new pricing plan. Called the Internet Club, this pricing plan offers CompuServe members considerable savings when using PPP or services included under the newly formed Internet Services umbrella. These services include:

◆ File Transfer Protocol (FTP)

◆ Remote Login (Telnet)

◆ Usenet Newsreader ASCII

◆ Usenet Newsreader CIM

> When you enter any of the services included under the Internet Service banner, an (I) appears next to the name of the service to remind you that this service is being charged at special rates.

People who plan to use PPP or any of CompuServe's Internet Services for more than 9 hours a month should consider taking advantage of this plan. When using the standard pricing plan, you automatically receive three hours of Internet access each month as a part of the monthly service charge. If you then spend more than three hours a month connected to Internet Services, you will be charged an additional $2.50 per hour.

If, on the other hand, you become a member of the Internet Club, which costs $15.00 dollars a month, you receive 20 hours of connection time up front, and are then charged only $1.95

for each additional hour over the first 20. Based on these figures, by taking advantage of the Internet Club you can access the Internet for around $1.25 an hour, which is one of the best commercial rates you will find anywhere, considering the level of support provided. Additionally, this rate does not even take into account the fact that the first $9.95 also provides you with access to all of CompuServe's standard services, including the Mall, News, and CIS Mail.

Warning

> In countries like Australia where an hourly network surcharge applies, you are billed for your connection time at the rates set down by your local provider, even if you choose to become a member of the Internet Club.

To find out more information about the Internet Club and also become a member, open the Go dialog box and type in **INETCLUB.** This opens the information area shown in Figure 4.14, where you can sign up as a club member.

FIGURE 4.14.

The Dialup PPP information area provides information about connecting to CompuServe from a variety of platforms.

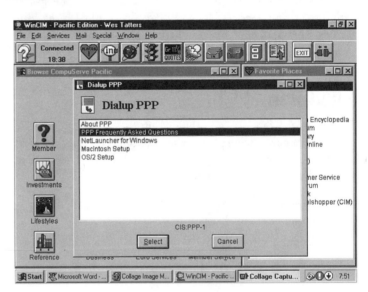

Summary

As seen in this chapter, the new dial-up PPP services now offer CompuServe members direct access to the Internet as a logical extension of the gateway services provided through WinCIM.

For many users, however, access to dial-up PPP connections is a step they have yet to take, being quite content with the services already provided via WinCIM. For these people, and those of you new to WinCIM, the next chapter looks at the way WinCIM operates and discusses in general terms some of the concepts that are expanded on in later chapters.

CHAPTER 5

WINCIM AND THE INTERNET

Many of the Internet services discussed in the remainder of this book take advantage of capabilities built into the CompuServe Information Manager (WinCIM). This chapter takes a brief look at how WinCIM operates by exploring the following topics:

- ◆ Downloading WinCIM
- ◆ Installing WinCIM
- ◆ Logging On
- ◆ Working with WinCIM
- ◆ The Toolbar
- ◆ WinCIM Menus
- ◆ The Internet Forum

Introducing WinCIM

Like many online computer services, there are number of ways you can connect to CompuServe. Of these, the most basic method takes advantage of any of the communications programs currently available.

Using a program like HyperTerminal, you can log onto CompuServe and navigate your way around the services provided by selecting items from the text-based menus presented through the ASCII version of WinCIM. (See Figure 5.1.) There are, however, a number of weaknesses appearing in the ASCII version. These include the lack of multitasking capabilities, such as reading messages while downloading a file, and the inability to use some of the newer services, such as the Internet File Transfer Program (FTP).

FIGURE 5.1.

HyperTerminal lets you log onto CompuServe using the ASCII version of WinCIM.

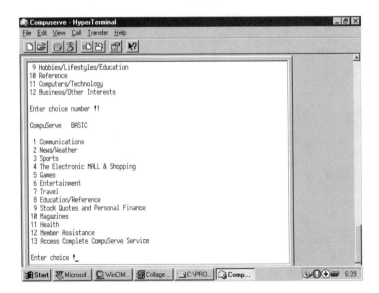

As a result, you need to use the graphic version of the CompuServe Information Manager to take full advantage of all the services offered by CompuServe. On Windows-based computers this program is known as WinCIM, and on Apple Computers it's MacCIM. WinCIM replaces the text-based menus provided by the ASCII version of the CompuServe Information Manager with pop-up windows, pushbuttons, and toolbars, which make navigating CompuServe a simple matter of clicking on the item you're interested in.

FIGURE 5.2.

WinCIM replaces text-based menus with pop-up windows, pushbuttons, and toolbars.

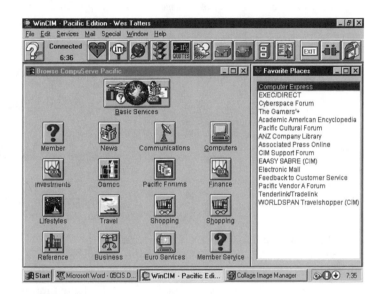

Downloading the Latest Version

Since WinCIM's release it has gone through a number of substantial changes, resulting in the release of four major upgrades in the past few years.

With each of these upgrades, many new features and capabilities have been added, making it vitally important that you always use the latest version of WinCIM. Although the older versions of WinCIM still operate correctly in some circumstances, this is not the case for some of the newer tools discussed later in this book.

To take advantage of these new tools, you need to have version 1.4 of WinCIM installed. Otherwise you may find that some strange things will happen when you try to follow some of the examples mentioned in later chapters. There are a number of ways that you can obtain a copy of the latest version of WinCIM, but the easiest is to download a copy from CompuServe itself.

Note   You can order a copy of WinCIM that includes a user's manual and some other helpful information by visiting the CompuServe shop while online (GO ORDER, or GO CPORDER if you live in the Pacific region).

Note   Throughout this book, the locations of CompuServe forums and services are described using the format GO WINCIM, where WINCIM is replaced by the forum address of the service currently being discussed.

You can download a copy of WinCIM by following these steps:

1. Using WinCIM, open the Go... dialog box by clicking on the traffic light icon in the toolbar or by selecting the **G**o option from the **S**ervices menu. (See Figure 5.3.)

FIGURE 5.3.

The Go... dialog box lets you move quickly to any CompuServe area.

2. Type **wincim** in this dialog box and click on the OK button. If WinCIM is not currently logged onto CompuServe, it uses your modem to dial up the network and negotiate a connection. (Throughout the remainder of this book it is assumed that you are already connected to CompuServe. If at any time you are not connected, WinCIM automatically negotiates a connection for you whenever you press the OK button in the Go... dialog box.)

3. Once WinCIM negotiates a connection between your computer and CompuServe, it displays a window similar to the one shown in Figure 5.4.

FIGURE 5.4.

Select the Download WinCIM option to retrieve a copy of the latest version of WinCIM.

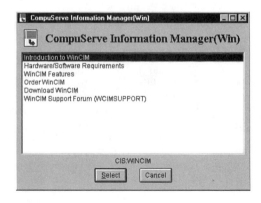

4. In this window you can select the Order WinCIM option to open the CompuServe Shop, or the Download WinCIM option to retrieve a copy and install it on your computer. For now, highlight the Download WinCIM option by clicking on it. Then click on the **S**elect button, or, alternatively, double-click on the Download WinCIM option.

5. When the Download WinCIM window opens, highlight the Download Version 1.4 option and again click on the **S**elect button.

6. You should now be presented with one of two options. CompuServe allows you to either download a full copy of WinCIM or download the individual components separately. Unless you have a thorough understanding of WinCIM, you should highlight the Download Complete WinCIM Program option and click on the Select button.

If you choose to download the components separately, you should first read the Download Instructions item listed at the top of the current window.

7. Once you select a download option, WinCIM opens a terminal window similar to the one shown in Figure 5.5. A message is displayed on the screen advising you of the estimated time the download will take, which depends on the version of WinCIM you are downloading. If you want to proceed with the download, type **Y** at the prompt and press the Enter key. To abort the download, type **N**.

FIGURE 5.5.

*Type **Y** and press the Enter key to begin the download.*

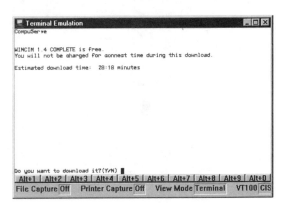

8. If you select **Y**, WinCIM opens a save requester like the one shown in Figure 5.6. Unless you want to store the update file in a different directory, click on the OK button to commence the transfer. By default, WinCIM saves the file in the C:\CSERVE\DOWNLOAD\ directory under the name WCINST.EXE.

FIGURE 5.6.

Use the save requester to nominate the directory where WinCIM stores the new file.

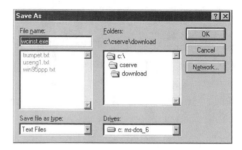

Installing WinCIM

Once you have obtained a copy of WCINST.EXE, either by downloading it or by purchasing a copy from the CompuServe Shop, you need to install it.

To do this, start WCINST.EXE by selecting the **R**un option on the **F**ile menu of the Windows desktop, or via the **R**un option on the **S**tart menu if you are running Windows 95. Once the program starts, the CompuServe Installer, shown in Figure 5.7, appears on your screen. From here, all you need to do to complete the installation process is click on the OK button. When you do this, the installer takes over and performs all the necessary steps required to install WinCIM and prepare it for use.

FIGURE 5.7.

CompuServe's install program automates the installation process.

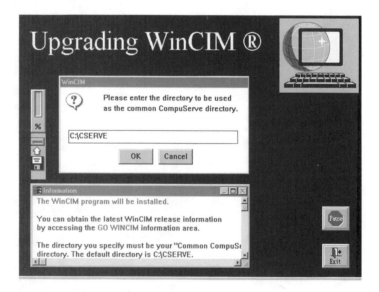

By default, WinCIM installs itself in the C:\CSERVE directory on your hard drive. As a rule, you should accept this directory even though the installer allows you to alter it.

Starting WinCIM

During installation, a new folder called CompuServe is created on your desktop, and the installer places the WinCIM program in it along with some additional support files. (See Figure 5.8.) These files include a copy of the CompuServe Almanac (a listing of all available forums and services) and a Windows Help file that contains detailed information about the use of WinCIM.

Open this folder now and click on the CompuServe Information Manager icon to start the newly installed version of WinCIM.

FIGURE 5.8.

Click on the CompuServe Information Manager icon to start WinCIM.

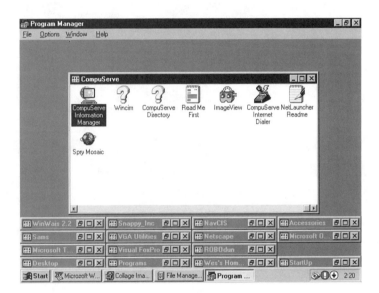

Setting Up the Dialer

Before WinCIM can connect to CompuServe, you need to adjust the settings for its dialer program so that they are correct for your particular location. If you are upgrading WinCIM, you can ignore this step because WinCIM copied your old settings during the upgrade process.

If not, open the **S**pecial menu and select the **S**ession Settings… option, as shown in Figure 5.9. Doing this opens the Setup Session Settings dialog box, shown in Figure 5.10. This dialog box allows you to adjust all of the settings that control the way WinCIM connects to CompuServe.

FIGURE 5.9.

Select the Session Settings option from the Special menu to configure WinCIM's dialer.

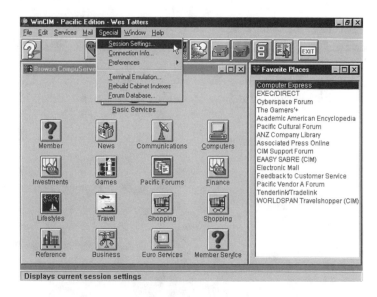

FIGURE 5.10.

Adjust the settings to configure WinCIM for your local connection point to CompuServe.

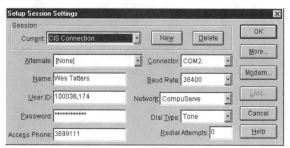

To set up WinCIM for your local dial-up point, follow these steps:

1. Leave the Session setting as it is for now. If you have a number of different connection options, such as Internet access, you can add these later.

2. Leave the Alternate: setting as None. If you later configure additional session options, you can nominate an alternate connection if your primary connection method fails.

3. Enter your name in the Name: field as you want it to appear on CompuServe.

In recent months it has become common practice in many forums to include your place of employment as a part of your name. If you were an employee at Microsoft, for example, you could add "[MSFT]" to the end of your name. There is no actual rule that says you should do this, but it does tell others your background and potential expertise.

4. Type your CompuServe ID in the User ID: field.

5. Enter your CompuServe password in the Password: field. WinCIM displays an asterisk to represent each character you enter. This protects your password from being seen by others.

6. In the Access Phone: field, enter the most suitable phone number for CompuServe in your local area.

GO PHONES to obtain a list of all the CompuServe access phone numbers worldwide.

Tip

7. Using the Connector: field at the top of the next column of information, select the COM port that your modem is connected to. In most cases this is either COM1 or COM2.

8. Select the fastest speed supported by your modem using the Baud Rate: field. Because CompuServe now charges the same rate for all connection speeds, selecting a slower baud rate will result in increased online charges.

9. The next field is the Network: field. If you are connected directly to a CompuServe network node, select CompuServe as the network. Otherwise, select the entry describing the network you plan to connect to.

10. If your modem uses tone dialing, select the Tone option in the Dial Type: field. You can also select Pulse for older pulse dialing modems, or Direct if you have direct access to CompuServe via a network.

11. If you occasionally get a busy signal when trying to connect to CompuServe, type a number in the Redial Attempts: field to allow WinCIM to automatically redial the connection point. If you leave this field set to zero but have nominated an alternate connection, WinCIM attempts to connect using the alternate settings if the primary connection fails.

12. Clicking on the **M**ore button opens a small dialog box that allows you to configure some special settings. For the moment, don't worry about the contents of this dialog box.

13. Finally, click on the M**o**dem button to tell WinCIM what type of modem you have. When you select this button, WinCIM displays the Modem Control Strings dialog box, shown in Figure 5.11. If your modem is listed as an option in the drop-down window that you can access by clicking on the Modem field, select it. Otherwise, you can select either the Hayes Default option or manually set up the correct information using your modem manual.

14. When you are satisfied that all of the modem and connection settings are correct, click on the OK button to save them.

FIGURE 5.11.

Adjust the settings to configure WinCIM for your local connection point to CompuServe.

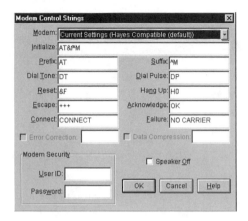

Working with WinCIM

With all the configuration details out of the way, you are now ready to connect to CompuServe.

Unlike a terminal-based program that requires you to first log onto CompuServe before you can do anything, WinCIM takes a more interactive approach. There is never a need to physically select a logon button or Connect option when using WinCIM. Instead, when you select any of the various services CompuServe makes available, WinCIM automatically connects to CompuServe.

The Toolbar

The most direct way to access many of the features provided by WinCIM is through the toolbar across the top of the main window. (See Figure 5.12.) Clicking on any of the icons displayed in this toolbar instantly transports you to the activity it represents. Although a full discussion of the capabilities offered by WinCIM is best left to books dedicated to this purpose, the following list discusses each of the icons available on the toolbar, in order from left to right.

Help icon—This icon opens the online help system.

Connect Counter—While you are connected to CompuServe, a counter keeps track of the amount of time you are online.

Favorite Places icon—Clicking on this icon opens the Favorite Places window, where you can store the locations of forums and services you use on a regular basis.

Find icon—This icon opens a dialog box where you can nominate the name of a topic you are interested in. When you then click on the OK button, WinCIM searches all of the forums and services available on CompuServe and displays a list of those containing information that may be relevant to the topic you nominated. You can then click on any of the forums listed to automatically open it, or you can store forums in your Favorite Places window.

FIGURE 5.12.

To access CompuServe's main functions, click on the appropriate icon in the toolbar.

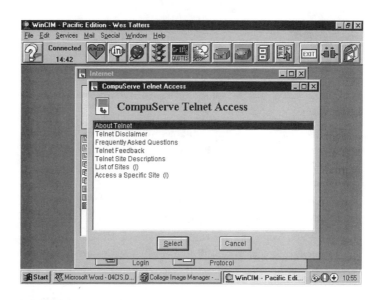

World icon—When you select this icon, WinCIM opens a window showing all the main services. (See Figure 5.13.) You can then click on any of the icons in this window to open windows containing the services they represent.

FIGURE 5.13.

The Browse window displays all of the major services offered by CompuServe.

Go icon—This icon opens a dialog box where you can enter the access name of any CompuServe forum or service. When you click on the OK button, WinCIM transports you straight to the forum without making you navigate through layers of menu windows.

Quotes icon—For those interested in the stock market, this icon opens the Stock Quotes dialog box, where you can obtain up-to-the-minute stock prices and rates.

Weather icon—Want to know what the weather's like? Then click on this icon to obtain weather forecasts from all around the world, including satellite weather maps for many countries.

In-Basket icon—When you receive new mail, WinCIM stores it in your in-basket by default. To read any of the messages stored in your in-basket, click on this icon.

Out-Basket icon—WinCIM allows you to create new e-mail and CIS Mail messages without actually being connected to CompuServe. When you do this, the messages are stored in your out-basket until you decide to log onto CompuServe and actually send them to the intended recipients. If there are currently any messages stored in your out-basket, clicking on this icon opens a window where you can make changes to them or even delete ones you no longer want to send.

Filing Cabinet icon—After reading a message stored in your in-basket, you may want to keep a copy of it for future reference. WinCIM allows you to do this by providing you with an electronic filing cabinet. (See Figure 5.14.) To open this filing cabinet, all you need to do is click on this icon.

FIGURE 5.14.

The WinCIM Filing Cabinet.

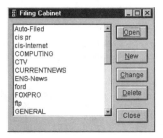

Address Book icon—When you select this icon, WinCIM opens your personal address book. In this address book you can store the names and CompuServe IDs of those with whom you correspond on a regular basis.

Exit icon—When you click on this icon, WinCIM disconnects you from CompuServe and closes WinCIM.

Disconnect icon—To disconnect from CompuServe without exiting WinCIM, click on this icon.

New Mail icon—If WinCIM detects that you have new messages in your CompuServe mailbox, it adds this icon to the toolbar. To retrieve any new mail, simply click on this icon.

The Menus

Most of the functions the toolbar provides are duplicated on the drop-down menus at the top of the WinCIM window. Of these menus, the three you will use most often are:

- ◆ Services
- ◆ Mail
- ◆ Special

The Services Menu

The options available on the Services menu (Figure 5.15) are nearly identical to those offered by the toolbar. To help you better understand the options this menu offers, Table 5.1 lists each of the menu options and gives brief descriptions of their functions.

FIGURE 5.15.

The Services menu.

Table 5.1. Functions available on the Services menu.

Menu Item	Hotkey	Description
Favorite Places		Like the Favorite Places icon, the menu item opens your favorite places.
Find...		Opens the Find dialog box.
Browse...		Displays the Browse window, listing the top-level services available on CompuServe.
Go...	Ctrl+G	Opens the Go... dialog Box.
What's New...		Requests a list of the latest entries on the CompuServe What's New window.
Pacific Forums...		If you live in the Pacific region, this option takes you directly to the Pacific forums. If you live in Europe, this is replaced with a local option for your area.
Executive News	Ctrl+E	Opens the Executive News Service dialog box. This allows you to define search profiles for the newsfeeds offered by CompuServe.
Quotes...		Opens the Stock Quotes dialog box.
Weather...		Opens the Weather Forecasts and Satellite images dialog box.
CB Simulator		Join the CB Simulator and participate in real-time conversations with other members.

In addition, some menu items can be accessed by using *hotkey combinations*. For example, the Go... dialog box can also be opened by holding down the Control key and the letter "G" at the same time. For any of the menu items that support hotkeys, the appropriate combination is listed.

The Mail Menu

As the name implies, all the functions you ever need when sending and receiving electronic mail are available from the Mail menu (Figure 5.16), along with access to your filing cabinet, in-basket and out-basket, and address book.

FIGURE 5.16.

The Mail menu.

In Table 5.2 is a list of all the available options, followed by a brief description of each. (To find out more about sending electronic mail, take a look at Chapter 6, "E-Mail and CIS Mail.")

Table 5.2. Functions available on the Mail menu.

Menu Item	Hotkey	Description
Get New Mail		Retrieves a list of all the new mail currently stored in your CompuServe mailbox.
Search **N**ew Mail...		Selectively retrieves a list of new mail based on the address of the sender, the subject, importance, sensitivity, or the date it was mailed to you.
Create Mail...		Opens the Create Message dialog box.
Send/**R**eceive All Mail...		Sends all the mail held in your out-basket and retrieves copies of all new messages and stores them in your in-basket.
Send File...		Opens the Send File dialog box, which allows you to send a file to anyone using CIS Mail.
In-Basket...		Opens your in-basket.
Out-Basket...		Opens your out-basket.

Menu Item	Hot Key	Description
Filing Cabinet...	Ctrl+F	Opens your filing cabinet.
Address Book...	Ctrl+A	Opens your address book.
Create Forum **M**essage...		Creates a new message and sends it to a CompuServe forum instead of using CIS Mail.
Member **D**irectory...		Opens a dialog box that allows you to search the CompuServe Membership Directory. You can nominate the first name, last name, city, state, and country to help narrow down the search.

The Special Menu

Whereas the other two menus give you access to tools and services provided by CompuServe, the Special menu (Figure 5.17) lets you configure WinCIM itself. Table 5.3 lists the functions provided by each of the Special menu's options.

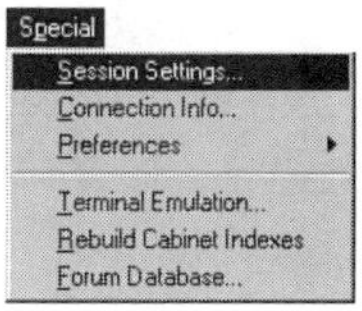

FIGURE 5.17.

The Special menu.

Table 5.3. Functions available on the Special menu.

Menu Item	Description
Session Settings...	Opens the Session Setting dialog box discussed earlier in this chapter and defines your connection options.
Connection Info...	Opens an information dialog box that gives you information about either the last or current connection to CompuServe. It also includes a counter that keeps track of the total amount of time you have been connected to CompuServe.
Preferences	Selecting this option opens a submenu from which you can select any of the configuration dialog boxes provided by WinCIM. These include general, mail, forum, and news configuration areas where you can tailor many of WinCIM's features to suit your needs.

continues

Table 5.3. continued

Menu Item	Description
	To find out more information about any of these features, open the dialog box you are interested in and click on the **H**elp button. This opens the Online Help system, which contains a detailed description of all the available features.
Terminal Emulation...	There are certain occasions when you may need to log onto CompuServe using the ASCII version of CIM instead of the graphical version. By selecting this option, WinCIM provides access to its own built-in terminal emulation program if necessary.
Rebuild Cabinet Indexes	Under certain circumstances, the indexes created by WinCIM to maintain your filing cabinet may become corrupted. If this happens, select this option to reconstruct them.
Forum Database...	Whenever you enter a CompuServe forum, information about it is stored in a special database maintained by WinCIM. This way WinCIM can open the forum faster the next time you choose it. However, on rare occasions this database may become corrupted. If this occurs, you can delete the information stored in the database by selecting this option.

The Internet Services Window

All the Internet-based gateways and services provided by CompuServe are now managed by its Internet division, which operates its own area as the main access point to all Internet services.

To access this area, open the Go... dialog box and type the word **internet** in the space provided. After doing this, click on the OK button to tell WinCIM that you want to open the Internet Services main window. (See Figure 5.18.)

FIGURE 5.18.

The Internet Services window gives you access to all the Internet-related services offered by CompuServe.

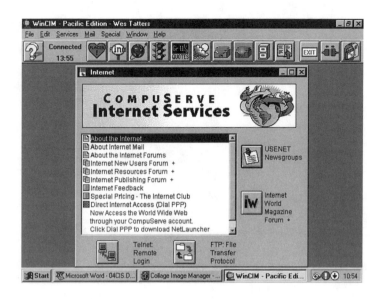

Internet Support Forums

There are a number of Internet-related forums and information services that you can access from the Internet Services window, including:

◆ The Internet New Users forum

◆ The Internet Resource forum

◆ The Internet Publishing forum

◆ The Internet World Magazine forum

To access any of these forums, click on the appropriate menu item or icon.

> In Chapter 14, "Internet Resources on CompuServe," you'll find a detailed discussion of the features provided by each of these forums, along with a general discussion of forum usage.

Usenet

To access each of the major Internet services provided by CompuServe, click on the icon associated with each one in the Internet Services window.

When you click on the Usenet icon, WinCIM opens the main Usenet Newsgroups window, shown in Figure 5.19. This window provides you with information about Usenet and the CompuServe newsreaders, along with two options that allow you to use either the text-based newsreader or the more popular graphical newsreader.

FIGURE 5.19.

Click on the Usenet icon to open the Usenet Newsgroups window.

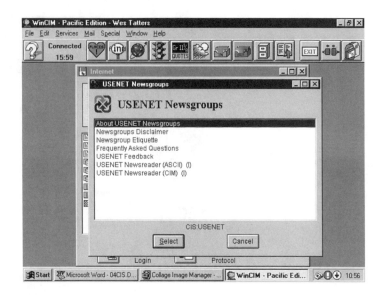

In Chapter 8, "Usenet—Newsgroups," you'll find a detailed discussion of newsgroups and WinCIM, along with a list of some of the more popular discussion areas.

Telnet

Since April of 1995, CompuServe has provided a means of logging onto other computers through the Internet. To take advantage of this capability, click on the Telnet icon in the Internet Services window. This opens the CompuServe Telnet Access window, shown in Figure 5.20.

FIGURE 5.20.

Click on the Telnet icon to open the CompuServe Telnet Access window.

This window lists a number of information files that contain details of the CompuServe Telnet gateway. You can also see descriptions of some of the more popular sites you can Telnet to by choosing either the List of Sites or Access a Specific Site options.

> To find out more about Telnet and some of the sites you can log onto using CompuServe, you should take a look at Chapter 9, "Telnet."

FTP

If you are unable to locate a file in any of the thousands of forum libraries contained on CompuServe, maybe you need to take a look at the many file archives available via the Internet. To do this, click on the FTP icon in the Internet Services window.

When you click on this icon, WinCIM displays the File Transfer Protocol window, shown in Figure 5.21. Along with a list of information files and a Frequently Asked Questions document, this window provides you with four icons that give you access to the various FTP services offered by CompuServe.

FIGURE 5.21.

Click on the FTP icon to access the File Transfer Protocol window.

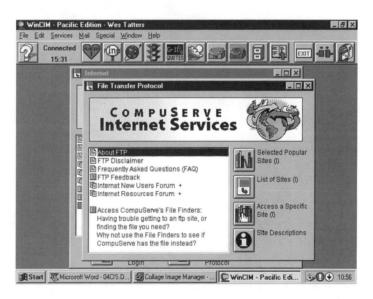

> Chapter 10, "File Transfer Protocol (FTP)," explains in detail the FTP client software provided by CompuServe, and looks at the types of files you are likely to find on some of the more popular FTP servers that CompuServe recommends.

Summary

Now that you have some understanding of the features offered by CompuServe and WinCIM, it is time to begin in earnest your exploration of the Internet.

In Part III of this book, "WinCIM Internet Tools," each of the main Internet services offered by CompuServe is explained one chapter at a time, beginning with a discussion in the next chapter that covers techniques you need to learn to exchange e-mail with others on the Internet.

Then in Part IV, "WinCIM—The Internet Navigator," you will examine the ways in which you can access the World Wide Web, and other Internet navigation tools like Gopher, through the services offered by CompuServe.

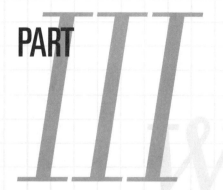

WINCIM INTERNET TOOLS

CHAPTER 6

E-MAIL AND CIS MAIL

Electronic mail, or e-mail, as discussed in previous chapters, has long been the driving force behind the widespread growth of the Internet.

Even though the original developers of ARPANET may not have foreseen the popularity of e-mail or even imagined its potential, for many people it is the main reason that they have an Internet connection. So, why is it so popular?

Firstly, e-mail is fast! Unlike traditional communication methods, such as courier and postal services, e-mail can be sent and received almost instantly. There is no need to make trips to a mailbox or to wait for a postal worker to deliver an important letter. In addition, the same e-mail message can be sent around the corner, across the country, or to the other side of the world, all in a matter of minutes.

Secondly, e-mail can be sent and received at any time of day and from just about any location—provided that you have access to a computer and a phone line. For people who travel regularly, e-mail has become an invaluable tool. Using e-mail, they can keep in almost constant contact with company offices, their families, and their friends while on the road.

This chapter looks at how CompuServe members can exchange messages with people on the Internet. It explores the following topics:

◆ IP addresses and Internet domain names

◆ Internet e-mail addresses

◆ Your CompuServe Internet address

◆ Sending e-mail to the Internet

◆ Sending files using e-mail

◆ Receiving e-mail from the Internet

Understanding Internet Addresses

Before looking at the steps required to send an e-mail message through the Internet from CompuServe, you need to understand the addressing system used by the Internet.

When you send e-mail to a person on the Internet, you need to consider the fact that she could actually be connected to any one of the thousands of separate networks that make up the Internet. In addition, most of these networks are entirely independent. As a result, in many cases the same user ID is assigned to different people on different networks. Simply addressing a message with a user ID, as is the case on CompuServe, could result in the message never reaching its desired destination.

To resolve this problem, the Internet uses an addressing system. This system gives each computer a unique address, not unlike the street or city address you use when sending someone a message through the mail.

Addressing the Internet

When TCP/IP was developed, it was realized that there needed to be a method of uniquely representing every computer connected to the network. To do this, a special numbering system was developed that assigned each machine a unique value known as an *IP address.*

This value consists of four separate parts, each containing a number between 1 and 255. When combined, these four values form what is known as a *dotted quad* or IP address. The reason for the term "dotted quad" relates to the way the address is written. The four numbers are written one at a time with a dot separating them. For example, the Internet site that maintains my e-mail mailbox is represented as 190.192.215.5.

The actual process of assigning IP addresses to new computer systems is not a simple matter of picking the next number in the queue. However, since a full discussion of the procedures involved in determining an IP address is outside the scope of this book, you should take a look at the InterNIC WWW site or the Internet Society WWW site for additional information.

Internet Domain Names

Even though IP addresses give each machine a unique identifier, it was not long before people began to dislike them. As the number of computers connected to the Internet continued to grow, remembering all these somewhat confusing numbers became an increasingly difficult task.

After much discussion, a new addressing system was proposed. Instead of representing each site as a number, it was suggested that each site could be represented by a unique name. From a user's standpoint, this seemed like a wonderful idea. On the technical front, however, changing the way the entire Internet operated was deemed to be impractical.

A compromise was needed. Internally, TCP/IP needed to use the IP addressing system, while externally, users wanted to use a simpler naming method. To achieve this compromise, a system similar to that used by phone companies was developed. A phonebook-like database was put in place that allowed people to use system names while TCP/IP retained the use of IP addresses.

When a system name (or *domain name,* as they have become known) is used where an IP address was expected, the computer in question contacts a special machine called a *domain name server.* The domain name server contains a list of IP addresses and domain names that it can cross-reference. After conducting a search of its records, the domain name server tells the calling computer the IP address that corresponds to the domain name it was given. This allows the computer to continue its use of IP addressing, while at the same time freeing end-users from the need to remember complex numbering systems.

This process is helped even further by the way domain names are formed. Much of the reasoning behind the term "domain name" comes from the fact that the name is used to describe not only the computer, but also the type of network it is connected to. In some cases it describes the geographical location of the network as well.

As Figure 6.1 shows, the domain name is broken into four parts. Not all parts are needed to create a valid domain name. However, regardless of which parts are used, the end result must be a name that is unique throughout the entire Internet.

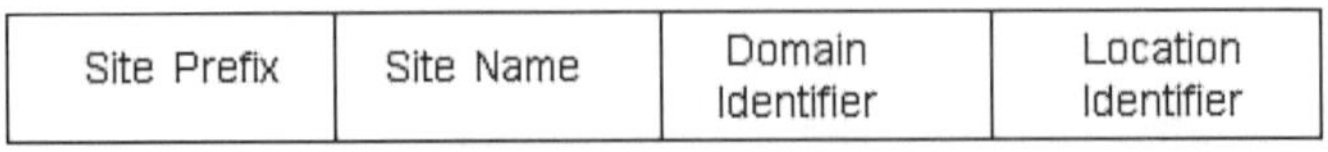

FIGURE 6.1.
Internet domain name structure.

Site Prefix	Site Name	Domain Identifier	Location Identifier

The two most common parts of a domain name are the *site name* and the *domain identifier*. Of these two, the domain identifier defines the type of network or type of organization that owns the site, and the site name usually represents the actual name of the organization.

While the site name can be just about anything an organization wishes to use, the domain identifier is expected to be one of a group of common names listed in Table 6.1. These identifiers are assigned by InterNIC, which, along with its other responsibilities, looks after the approval and administration of domain names.

Table 6.1. Common domain identifiers.

Identifier	Description
.com	Commercial companies
.edu	Educational institutions
.gov	Government bodies
.mil	Military networks
.net	Internet-related network hosts
.org	Any organization that fails to fit into any of the other categories

Like the domain identifier, the *location identifier* is used to describe a site in greater detail, and in some cases actually replaces the domain identifier. While the domain identifier describes the type of organization, the location identifier defines the geographical location of the system. For example, a company such as Acme Dingdongs could use the domain name dingdongs.com, which tells people that is it a commercial operation. If it was based in the United Kingdom, it could also use dingdongs.com.uk, which would better describe both its activities and location.

In a perfect world, such a system should result in unique names for every host. Unfortunately, there are sometimes clashes that prevent organizations from being granted the domain names they desire. In addition, with InterNIC already overloaded, there is little time to consider copyright and trademark issues when authorizing domain names. As a result, if the National Biscuit Company registers the name `nbc.com` before the popular broadcaster with the same initials, the domain name will be owned by the Biscuit company and there is very little that NBC—the broadcaster—can do about it.

Note

With organizations increasing the number of machines connected to the Internet, the use of *site prefixes* has also become a common occurrence. When an organization decides to connect a new computer to the Internet, they usually want to give it a domain name similar to the one they are currently using. To do this, they add site prefixes to the front of their existing domain name. For example, if Acme Dingdongs decided to link the computer in its northern office to the Internet, they would probably give it a domain name such as `north.dingdongs.com`.

The other reason for using site prefixes is to indicate the type of activities a computer can handle. For example, when Microsoft decided to open up a World Wide Web site, it set up a new machine with the address `www.microsoft.com`. In this case, the site prefix WWW is being used to describe the type of service that the machine provides to the Internet. Table 6.2 provides a list of some of the more common site prefixes.

Table 6.2. Common site prefixes.

Prefix	Description
ftp	File Transfer Protocol servers
gopher	Gopher servers
news	Usenet News servers
wais	Wide Area Information servers
www	World Wide Web servers

Internet E-Mail Addresses

The basic e-mail building blocks are computer programs known as *e-mail servers*. These programs, which are a lot like electronic post offices, handle the distribution of e-mail messages between all the different computers and interconnected networks on the Internet. In addition, they also collect and hold messages for users who have *accounts* with the e-mail server. These messages are stored in the electronic equivalent of a mailbox.

Each person who has an e-mail account on one of these servers is given a user ID similar to a CompuServe ID. They use this ID to access their mailbox. In addition, this user ID, when combined with the e-mail server's domain name, represents the user's e-mail address.

For example, the domain name of my e-mail server or mailbox is world.net, and my user ID is wtatters. To form my Internet e-mail address, take these two pieces of information and join them together with the @ symbol. My resulting e-mail address is wtatters@world.net.

It is interesting to note that you can also use a site's IP address instead of its domain name when forming an e-mail address. In that case, my e-mail address could also be written as wtatters@192.190.215.5

CompuServe IDs and the Internet

As discussed in Chapter 2, "The History of CompuServe and Its Connection to the Internet," it was inevitable that CompuServe users and Internet users would eventually want to be able to exchange electronic mail messages with each other.

Apart from the technical difficulties involved in opening the gateway, the biggest problem facing CompuServe was determining how its members could be contacted from the Internet, and in turn how they could properly address e-mail messages to go back onto the Internet.

The CompuServe Domain Name

The first part of the problem was relatively easy to fix. As is the case for every computer that opens a link with Internet, when CompuServe opened its Internet gateway, it needed to obtain a domain name and an IP address.

The domain name CompuServe selected was compuserve.com. People who wish to send e-mail to CompuServe members or who want to connect to CompuServe via a Telnet connection must use this name. In addition, CompuServe now operates a World Wide Web server located at www.compuserve.com.

The CompuServe ID

The second part of the problem was not as easily rectified. Unlike Internet user IDs, which for the most part consist of alphabetic names or codes, a CompuServe user ID consists of two numbers separated by a comma. Although the numbers themselves did not pose any problems, the comma in the ID was not permitted by the Internet.

To make CompuServe IDs compatible with the Internet, it was decided that the comma would be replaced with a period.

I now have the two pieces of information needed to form my Internet e-mail address: a valid user ID and a domain name. As a result, my CompuServe ID, `100036,174`, can easily be converted into its corresponding Internet e-mail address, resulting in `100036.174@compuserve.com`.

Using E-Mail

Now that you understand the principles behind the Internet's e-mail addressing system, you are ready to look at how messages are exchanged between CompuServe and the Internet.

As is the case with the majority of this book, this discussion concentrates on using WinCIM with the Internet. That said, the same basic procedures outlined in the following pages can easily be adapted for those people using terminal-based programs, and also for many of the popular CompuServe offline readers.

Sending Mail through the Internet

The procedure for sending e-mail messages to the Internet is a relatively simple one. If you have ever used WinCIM to send someone on CompuServe a message, you are well on the way to sending your first Internet e-mail message.

For the sake of this example, let's look at the steps involved in sending a message to my Internet mailbox at `wtatters@world.net`:

1. From the WinCIM main screen, open the **M**ail menu and choose the **C**reate Mail option, as shown in Figure 6.2.

FIGURE 6.2.

Creating a new e-mail message with WinCIM.

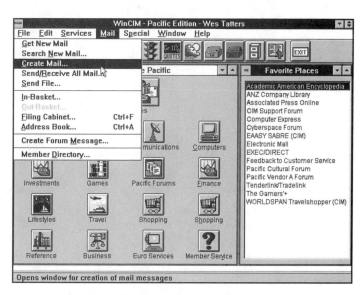

2. Once selected, the Recipient List dialog box (Figure 6.3) is displayed on the screen. Into the Name field of this dialog, type the name of the person that the mail is addressed to. In this case I have entered **Wes Tatters.**

3. Now touch the Tab key or use the mouse to move to the Address: field. Into this field, you need to type the person's Internet address. You also need to tell CompuServe that the address is an Internet address. To do this, first type the word **INTERNET:** and then the e-mail address.

FIGURE 6.3.

*Placing **INTERNET:** before an e-mail address informs CompuServe the message is to be sent to the Internet.*

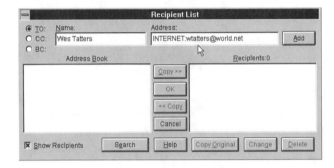

4. Once you are satisfied that the address information is correct, hit the Enter key or click on the OK button.

5. The Create Mail window, shown in Figure 6.4, should now be displayed on the screen. Before proceeding any further, type a brief description outlining the contents of the message in the Subject field.

FIGURE 6.4.

*Hitting the **Send Now** button mails the message to the Internet.*

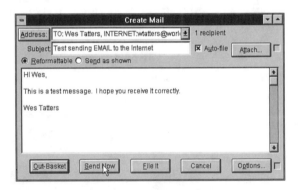

It is considered bad form to send someone an e-mail message without a subject line. To ensure that that messages you send are read by their recipients, make sure you include something in the subject line. If you don't include a subject, it is highly unlikely that your message will ever be read.

6. With all the paperwork out of the way, type your message in the body of the Create Mail window. There is no need to worry greatly about the length of each message, but you should keep in mind the fact that any single message can contain up to 2 million characters.

7. To mail the message, click on the **S**end Now button located at the bottom of the Create Message window, as shown in Figure 6.4.

If you've been following along through all these steps, congratulations! You have just sent your first e-mail message to someone on the Internet.

Sending Files through the Internet

Sometimes sending a typed message to a person is just not good enough. Maybe you want to send someone a copy of a spreadsheet, a picture, or a word processing document. To answer this need, as of version 1.4, a new button was added to the WinCIM Create Mail window.

Clicking on the **A**ttach button opens a File Attachment dialog box. (See Figure 6.5.) This dialog allows you to attach almost any file that's stored on your computer to a message. When you mail the message, a copy of the file is sent along with it.

FIGURE 6.5.

With WinCIM, you can now attach a file to a CompuServe mail message.

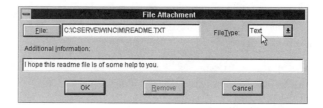

Unfortunately, due to the way Internet mail works, this facility is only partially available when you're sending a message to someone on the Internet. Internet messages can contain only *ASCII text*, unlike CompuServe messages, which can contain what are known as *binary files*.

> Computers store information as numbers. This is great for doing mathematical calculations, but it is of little use if you need to use a computer to store written information. To get around this problem, a table was developed called the ASCII table, which assigned each letter of the alphabet to a number. Using this table, a computer stores text as a long list of numbers.

As a result of this incompatibility, you can use the **A**ttach button to send a text file to an Internet address, but you cannot use it to send someone a copy of a spreadsheet or a word processing document. Luckily, this problem is not unique to CompuServe. The same problem has existed throughout the Internet since the use of e-mail first began.

To get around this weakness, a number of programs have been developed that can convert a binary file into a special type of ASCII text file.

UUENCODE and UUDECODE

The most popular method of doing this involves the use of a program made popular by the UNIX operating system. This program, called UUENCODE, when given the name of a binary file, converts the file into a ASCII text file. This text file is created in such a way that it uses only the letters listed in what is called the 7-bit ASCII table.

Once created, this file can be easily transmitted as a part of an e-mail message. When the message arrives at its destination, all the receiver needs to do is run UUDECODE—UUENCODE's sister program—to convert the ASCII text file back into a binary file.

However, as the effects of the 1990s multimedia explosion have begun to work their way into the Internet, a number of UUENCODE's weaknesses have started to become apparent. Specifically, some types of binary files are not encoded properly, resulting in garbage files when the file is decoded.

MIME

Because people obviously want to be able to send all types of files using e-mail, a new encoding standard was developed. Although specially targeted at the multimedia market, it also provides a number of benefits for all encoding purposes.

The Multipurpose Internet Mail Extension format, or MIME, can properly encode and decode numerous types of binary files, including:

> Images and pictures
>
> MPEG and full-motion video
>
> Sampled and computer-generated sound files
>
> Executable computer programs
>
> Compressed files created by PKZIP and other utilities

In addition, the process that MIME uses to build its special ASCII text files creates files that are noticeably smaller than those created using UUENCODE.

Note

Files created by UUENCODE and MIME are often much larger than the original files that they are generated from. This is due to the way they are created. This should be taken into consideration when you send files using e-mail, as not all e-mail systems can handle large files.

Wincode for Windows

Even though UUENCODE is a UNIX program, users of other operation systems have also been well provided for. On computers running Windows, the most popular program available is called Wincode. Copies of this program can be downloaded from a number of CompuServe forums, including Library (5) of the Windows Shareware Forum—GO WINSHARE.

> Appendix D provides an in-depth look at all the options and functions offered by Wincode.

Note

This program can encode and decode both UUENCODE and MIME format files. In addition, it can also look after the process of splitting large files into small segments suitable for use on e-mail systems that can't handle large files.

As a result, by using Wincode in combination with WinCIM, you can very easily attach binary files to a message destined for an Internet e-mail address:

1. Assuming you have installed a copy of Wincode, start Wincode and select the File Encode menu option. You can also start the Encode module by clicking on the Encode icon on the Wincode toolbar, as shown in Figure 6.6.

FIGURE 6.6.

Clicking on the Encode button starts Wincode's encode module.

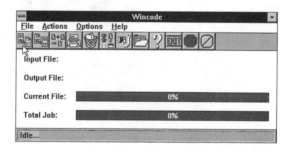

2. Using the File to Encode dialog box, shown in Figure 6.7, select the file you wish to encode and then hit the Enter key or click on the OK button.

FIGURE 6.7.

The File to Encode dialog allows you to select the file you want to encode.

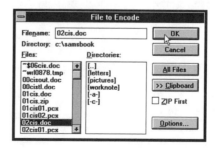

3. If you have not altered any of Wincode's default settings, a UUENCODE version of the file you selected will be saved in the `c:\wincode\ncode` directory with a `.UUE` file extension. For example, the `02CIS.DOC` file in Figure 6.7 was saved as `02CIS.UUE`.

4. Now open WinCIM and follow the steps discussed earlier for sending an e-mail message to an Internet address. This time, however, click on the Attach button once the Create Message window opens. This will allow you to select the file that you want to attach.

> You can also send a file using the **S**end File option located in the **M**ail menu. However, to emphasize the attachment process, this list follows the steps required when using the Create Mail option.

5. With the File Attachment dialog open, either type the name of the file you want to attach in the File: field or click on the **F**ile button. This will bring up a File Requester dialog that allows you to select the file you want.

6. Finally, make sure that you set the File **T**ype to Text, as shown in Figure 6.8, and then click the OK button to attach the selected file.

FIGURE 6.8.

If the File Type is not set to Text, the file will not be sent to the Internet address.

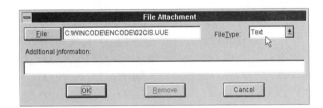

7. Back in the Create Mail window, click on the **S**end Now button to mail the attached file to the Internet.

> Due to a peculiarity of WinCIM, the Send Now button does not activate until you type something in the Message area. If, after you attach your file, the Send Now button is not operational, simply type a short message describing the contents of the file in the message area, and the Send Now button will activate.

Receiving Mail from the Internet

All mail messages sent to a person on CompuServe are stored in a private mailbox. Each time WinCIM connects to CompuServe, it checks to see if there are any unread messages in this mailbox. If there are any new messages, WinCIM puts a letterbox icon on the WinCIM toolbar (Figure 6.9) and also displays a message at the bottom of the screen telling you how many messages have arrived.

Reading New Messages

To read the new messages, follow these steps:

1. Select **G**et New Mail from the WinCIM **M**ail menu, as shown in Figure 6.9, or click on the letterbox icon. WinCIM will open your CompuServe mailbox and retrieve a list of all the messages currently stored in it.

FIGURE 6.9.

When WinCIM displays the New Mail letterbox, selecting Get New Mail will open your CompuServe mailbox.

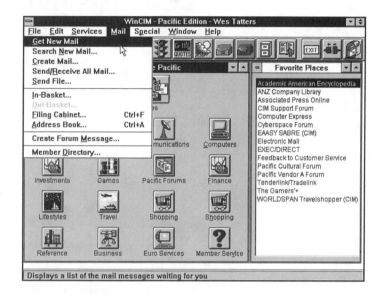

2. The Get New Message window will then display a list of all the new messages, showing the subject, sender and message length. (See Figure 6.10.)

FIGURE 6.10.

The Get New Mail message window displays all messages stored in a person's CompuServe mailbox.

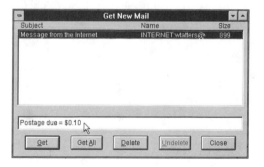

3. To read a message, double-click on it using the mouse or select it and then click on the **G**et button. WinCIM will retrieve the message and display it in a message window. Alternatively, you can click on the Get **A**ll button to have WinCIM automatically retrieve all the new messages and store them in the WinCIM In-Basket. You can then read these messages at some later time.

4. In the message window (Figure 6.11), in addition to reading the message, you can select any of the options provided by the buttons below the body of the message. These allow you to store the message in your **In**-basket, **F**ile it in a filing cabinet, mail a **R**eply back to the sender, For**w**ard a copy of the message to someone else, or **D**elete it from your mailbox.

FIGURE 6.11.

The WinCIM message window allows you to read new messages.

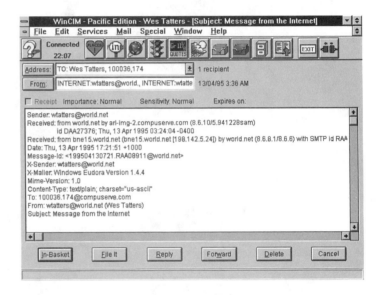

Unlike messages you receive from CompuServe members, messages you receive from people on the Internet attract a handling surcharge. This fee is not charged until you actually retrieve the message, however. For this reason, it is a good idea not to use the Get **A**ll button, as you will be billed automatically for any Internet messages waiting in your mailbox.

To find out more information about the CompuServe Internet e-mail surcharges, open the Go… dialog box, type **RATES**, and click on the OK button.

Receiving Files from the Internet

Obviously, if it is possible for you to attach a file to a message you send, it should also be possible for someone on the Internet to send attached files back to you.

When you receive a message from the Internet that includes an attached file, the message will look something like Figure 6.12.

FIGURE 6.12.

An e-mail message containing an attached file.

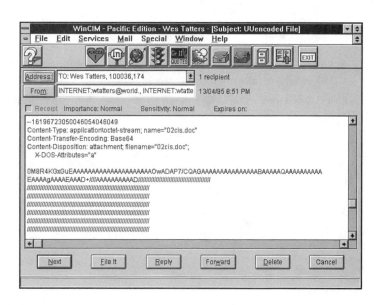

On the Internet, the attachment process physically includes the file as ASCII text in the body of the message. The jumble of letters near the bottom of the message area in Figure 6.12 is, in fact, the start of the encoded file.

Unlike attached files received from CompuServe members, which WinCIM automatically decodes, it is unable to decode files attached to Internet messages. As a result, you need to use a program like Wincode to decode the file and convert it back into binary format. This is achieved by doing the following:

1. Retrieve the message as discussed in the previous section using the Get New Mail window.

2. Once the e-mail message is displayed in a message window, select the Save **As** option from the WinCIM **F**ile menu. This will open a Save As dialog box similar to the one shown in Figure 6.13.

FIGURE 6.13.

The Save As dialog allows you to store a copy of the message in a format suitable to Wincode.

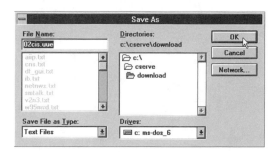

3. You need to give the message a filename. In this case I used **02CIS.UUE**. The UUE file extension is the default expected by Wincode. You also need to set the directory to **C:\CSERVE\DOWNLOAD** or some other appropriate location on your hard drive. When all the information is correct, click on the OK button to save the message.

4. The message can now be handed to Wincode for conversion back into a binary format. For a full explanation of the various decoding options available using Wincode, see Appendix D.

Tip

> If you are having trouble decoding a message, it may be due to the fact that it has been encoded using a format other than UUENCODE or MIME. In this case, you will need to talk to the person that sent you the message to find out how the message was encoded.

Summary

Over the course of the last 25 years, e-mail has opened communications doors that, in the past, people would never have thought possible. The ability to conduct written exchanges using e-mail is changing the way people communicate. It is expanding their horizons, changing the way they do business, and making global communications as commonplace as a chat over the back fence with your neighbor.

For CompuServe users, access to Internet e-mail opens up a wide range of new possibilities, not least of which is the ability to join any of the thousands of mailing lists currently running on the Internet.

Chapter 7, "Mailing Lists," takes a look at how you go about joining one of these lists, and also explores the benefits of doing so.

CHAPTER 7

MAILING LISTS

With the advent of e-mail, all of a sudden people were able to communicate more freely and effectively than they had ever thought possible.

As they became more familiar with the capabilities e-mail offered, the idea of using e-mail to conduct discussions and share ideas with groups of people dawned. This realization eventually led to the development of mailing lists.

Today mailing lists are used for a wide variety of reasons. Some allow people to discuss topics of mutual interest, while others are more like magazines or periodicals, delivering the equivalent of electronic newspapers to their subscribers.

This chapter looks at how CompuServe users can participate in mailing lists by discussing the following topics:

◆ What Are Mailing Lists?

◆ Communicating with Mailing Lists Using CompuServe

◆ The Different Types of Mailing Lists

◆ Using LISTSERVE

◆ Using Majordomo

What Are Mailing Lists?

Essentially, a mailing list is a register of people who have requested or *subscribed* to a special e-mail service. This e-mail service is used to forward copies of each message it receives to every person on the mailing list. In this way, electronic messages can easily be shared by many people.

In practical terms, this capability provides a mechanism that allows general discussions, conferences, and even electronic debates to be conducted using e-mail. It does this by ensuring that every participant is mailed a copy of each e-mail message sent to the mailing list.

Today there are mailing lists covering thousands of topics, hosted by computer systems all over the Internet. Many of these mailing lists discuss educational topics, while others deal with practical issues such as food and nutrition. Some, on the other hand, deal with less conventional subjects, such as David Letterman's nightly Top Ten List. To give you an idea of the wide variety of topics available, Table 7.1 lists the 10 most popular mailing lists on LISTSERV— one of the major mailing list services.

Table 7.1. The LISTSERV Top 10.

List Name	Subscribers	Description
TOPTEN	66,184	David Letterman's Top 10
MINI-AIR	23,173	The Mini-Annals of Improbable Research
TIDBITS	19,253	A newsletter for Mac users
ROADMAP	17,180	Roadmap workshop subscription list

List Name	Subscribers	Description
NEW-LIST	14,760	New list announcements
OMRI-L	10,630	Open Media Research Institute Daily Digest (SUNY)
INDIA-D	10,373	The India News & Discussion Network at BGSU
CCMAN-L	9,794	Chinese Magazine Network
LOOKING	9,327	The Personals India Network at BGSU
CHINA-ND	8,773	China News Digest (US News)

Although some of the smaller mailing lists are managed by hand, this is not a practical option when you begin to deal with lists that have tens of thousands of subscribers. To cope with these large lists, a special type of computer program known as a *list processor* was developed. Using such a program, it is possible to manage both the registration of names on a mailing list and the distribution of messages to each member of the list.

BITNET

For the researchers and scientists who began to use mailing lists in the early 1970s, they were like a dream come true. They made possible a whole new level of interaction and flexibility of discussion. Previously, the only way to communicate findings and engage in scientific discussions with your peers around the world was to attend conferences and meetings. Unfortunately, for many people these were held far too infrequently to be of much practical day-to-day use. Mailing lists replaced all this with daily correspondence and rapid feedback.

During the 1970s, however, only research and government institutions were permitted to connect to ARPANET. This left a large number of people in the education community out in the cold, so to speak. Many of them were beginning to hear about e-mail and mailing lists from their acquaintances, but because they did not have access to ARPANET, they were unable to participate. Eventually, some of these people decided to create their own network, and as a result, in 1981 BITNET was born.

By connecting to BITNET, any education or research body could offer e-mail and mailing list communications to all members of its campus community. Due to this more open connection policy, BITNET soon became a popular network, with nodes rapidly springing up across the country and eventually around the world.

Unlike ARPANET, which was built for the purpose of remote computing, BITNET was designed from the ground up as an e-mail and mailing list service. Instead of using packet network connections such as those operated by ARPANET, BITNET was built around a *store and forward* communications system based on a popular IBM protocol. Using this system, it was possible for even small organizations to use BITNET without the costs associated with the connections required of ARPANET. Today BITNET is managed by the Corporation for Research and Education Network (CREN), which represents over 1,000 academic and research centers in 50 countries worldwide.

In addition, as the ARPANET was gradually replaced by NSFNET and connectivity limitations decreased, gateways were opened to the emerging Internet. This permitted BITNET and the Internet to exchange e-mail. As an added bonus, these gateways also gave Internet users the ability to participate in any of the 4,000+ public BITNET mailing lists.

LISTSERV

LISTSERV—a computer program written for VAX/VMS computers—is the list processor responsible for the distribution of all mailing lists operated by computers connected to BITNET.

In addition to managing the distribution process, LISTSERV also looks after subscription requests and other user-related activities. You communicate with LISTSERV by sending it e-mail messages containing a set of simple commands or instructions. Using these commands, you can:

◆ Subscribe to a mailing list

◆ Cancel a current subscription

◆ Request catalogs of available mailing lists

◆ Retrieve files stored on BITNET computers

The section titled "Using LISTSERV" later in this chapter looks at the commands used to perform these actions and discusses how you use WinCIM to deliver them to LISTSERV.

LISTPROC

In recent years, CREN has begun to promote the use of a replacement for LISTSERV called LISTPROC. This software, unlike LISTSERV, runs on computer systems based on UNIX— the popular system of choice for Internet servers.

From a user's standpoint, LISTPROC operates in much the same way as LISTSERV and supports the same basic set of commands. At this stage, there are only a relatively small number of mailing lists using LISTPROC, but over the coming years, it is likely that more and more lists based on this program will appear.

Note

> A full discussion of the capabilities offered by LISTPROC is available from the CREN WWW server at `www.cren.net`. This site also contains information about BITNET and many of the new services CREN currently has under development.

Majordomo

Although LISTSERV is a very popular tool for mailing list management, it is suitable only for use on computers connected to BITNET. Computers connected to the Internet that want to operate mailing lists need to use a program that can take advantage of Internet-based e-mail services. To meet this need a number of different programs have been developed, but by far the most popular is the list processor known as Majordomo.

Majordomo is not a computer program in the true sense of the word. Instead, it is a collection of script files written in a computer scripting language called PERL. By using PERL, it is possible for Majordomo to operate correctly on a wide variety of computer platforms and operating systems. Because of this portability, Majordomo has become the most popular mailing list processor available on the Internet.

Like LISTSERV, Majordomo uses e-mail messages to control its operations. However, some of the commands and capabilities offered by Majordomo differ from those supported by LISTSERV. The section titled "Using Majordomo" later in this chapter discusses the differences between LISTSERV and Majordomo and looks at how you communicate with Majordomo using WinCIM.

Note

> The developers of Majordomo operate a WWW server at www.greatcircle.com. This site also contains a number of discussion papers, dealing with mailing lists in general, that some of you may find of interest.

Communicating with Mailing Lists Using CompuServe

As mentioned in the previous section, list processors use e-mail messages to control their operations. For this to occur, each list processor needs an e-mail mailbox and a corresponding e-mail address. (See "Where to Find Mailing Lists" later in this chapter for tips on locating these addresses.)

In most cases there are actually a number of e-mail addresses that the list processor uses for different tasks. These e-mail addresses can be categorized into two types—list processor addresses and mailing list addresses.

List Processor Addresses

The first e-mail address you need when communicating with mailing lists is the e-mail address of the list processor. This is the address you use when you want to communicate with the list processor itself.

For a LISTSERV list processor, this will be an address such as `listserv@bitnic.cren.net`. This address is in fact the e-mail address of the list processor operated by CREN. Messages you send to this address tell the list processor what actions you require it to perform. (See "Using LISTSERV" and "Using Majordomo" later in this chapter for a full discussion of the commands available using these two services.)

As was the case when sending regular e-mail, all you need to do to send messages to a list processor address from CompuServe is add the word `INTERNET:` to the beginning of the address. Therefore, to send a message to the CREN list processor, you would use the address `INTERNET:listserv@bitnic.cren.net`.

List Addresses

Each mailing list operated by a list processor will also have its own e-mail mailbox and corresponding address. This is where you send messages that you want the list processor to distribute to the mailing list's subscribers.

It is important to understand that you should not send command messages to this e-mail address. Instead, they need to be sent to the list processor's e-mail address.

Receiving Messages from a Mailing List

As discussed in Chapter 6, any e-mail messages you receive from the Internet are stored in your CompuServe mailbox until you retrieve them. Because messages distributed by mailing lists are essentially e-mail messages, CompuServe does not differentiate between them in any way.

When you get new mail using WinCIM, any mailing list-based messages will appear in the New Mail window, along with any other messages you receive from CompuServe or the Internet.

Warning

> Every message received by CompuServe from the Internet attracts a handling fee. This includes messages from all mailing lists. If you plan to become an avid mailing list user, this fee can rapidly add up to a considerable monthly expense. If this is the case, you should probably consider obtaining an account with an Internet service provider (ISP) that does not charge you a per-message fee.

Types of Mailing Lists

Regardless of which list processor a mailing list is managed by, each list falls into one of the following categories:

- Unmoderated
- Moderated

◆ Publications

◆ Digests

Unmoderated Lists

Most mailing lists tend to allow a fairly free range of discussion. However, you are expected to keep the conversation in line with the mailing list's subject. These mailing lists are called *unmoderated* lists.

Basically, there are no traffic cops watching these lists to ensure that the subject is maintained. However, most people who subscribe to a list have done so for a good reason, so moving off the topic is a surefire way of getting your mailbox stuffed with messages from people telling you to get in line.

Although these lists may sound like a free-for-all, you are still expected to play by the rules, and failing to do so can result in your removal from the list.

Moderated Lists

Moderated lists, on the other hand, have an *administrator* who views and approves each message before it is distributed. As opposed to unmoderated lists, these mailing lists tend to deal with more intellectual discussions and operate in a orderly fashion.

Unfortunately, there is one downside to participating in moderated lists. Whereas messages sent to unmoderated lists are usually distributed within minutes of being sent, messages sent to moderated lists can sometimes take days to be distributed. How long it actually takes often depends on the amount of time the administrator can give to the list, and also on the number of messages that need to be approved.

Publications

Not all mailing lists are used for discussion purposes. There is a special type of list that can best be thought of as an electronic newsletter or magazine.

A number of organizations now use this type of list to keep people up to date or to communicate information. In recent months, Microsoft has started one such mailing list, which has received considerable publicity, to keep people informed regarding the latest Windows 95 developments. Every 14 days, each WinNews subscriber receives an electronic newsletter from Microsoft in the form of an e-mail message. This e-mail message contains various tips and hints and other useful information dealing with Windows 95.

Unlike a normal mailing list, you do not send messages to these mailing lists for automatic distribution. As such, they are strictly a one-way affair from the list's administrator to its subscribers.

Digests

For many people, one of the big problems with mailing lists is the large number of messages that flood into their mailbox at all hours of the day and night.

To get around this problem, *digests* were developed. Instead of each message being distributed immediately, they are collected by the list processor or by the list's administrator and compiled into one large message or digest. At a predetermined time—usually once a day, once a week, or once a month—a copy of this compiled digest is mailed to all subscribers.

Instead of receiving hundreds and maybe thousands of individual messages, subscribers receive a single message that contains all the discussions since the last digest was distributed. There is one disadvantage with digests, however. Because all the messages arrive together, it is more difficult to make replies to individual participants and to follow individual conversations.

Many moderated and unmoderated lists now offer you the choice of receiving a digest or continuous messages. Also, some of the newer systems allow you to tailor the type of digest you receive to your own needs.

Where to Find Mailing Lists

With all this discussion about the thousands of mailing lists that are available, you are no doubt saying, "Great—but how do I find out which ones are best for me?"

It will probably come as no surprise to discover that you are not the first person to ask this question. As a result, over the years a number of lists have been compiled that attempt to catalog all of the mailing lists currently available. To help you locate these catalogs, this section looks at some of the popular mailing list catalogs.

The List of Lists

The first place to start is with the mailing list systems themselves. All the major list processors offer a facility that permits them to e-mail you a catalog of the mailing lists they maintain.

For example, if you send an e-mail message containing the word "LIST" or "LISTS" to a LISTSERV processor, you receive an e-mail message in return that details the name and description of each mailing list it manages. (See "Using LISTSERV" and "Using Majordomo" later in this chapter for a full description of commands and options offered by these services.)

LISTSERV can also provide you with a list of all the mailing lists operated by every LISTSERV processor.

FTP Sites

An extensive list of publicly accessible mailing lists is also posted on a regular basis in a number of locations, including the `news.answers` Usenet newsgroup. A copy of this list is stored in an *archive* on the public FTP site at `rtfm.mit.edu`.

Using FTP, you can retrieve a copy of this 14-part listing from the `/pub/usenet/news.answers/mail/mailing-lists/` directory. Each part is stored in the directory as a separate file given the name `part01` through `part14`.

WWW Sites

If you prefer not to wade though pages of mailing list names looking for the one you are interested in, maybe one of the WWW pages devoted to mailing lists will be more to your liking.

InterNIC

One of the first places you should consider investigating is the InterNIC Directory of Directories mentioned in previous chapters.

Not all mailing lists are currently listed in the directory, but there are a sufficient number there to get most people started. At the very least, this list can provide you with the e-mail addresses of a good number of list processors. The other advantage of this list is that it is available using the World Wide Web or a Telnet connection.

TILE.NET

One of the latest arrivals on the WWW scene, and at the same time one of the most useful, is the catalog service developed by the Walter Shelby Group Ltd. Called TILE.NET, this WWW server contains a list of all known LISTSERV mailing lists.

Using the sorting and search capabilities offered by TILE.NET, it is possible to locate mailing lists by name, type, popularity, and special categories such as membership policy.

> Located at `http://tile.net/`, TILE.NET also contains an extensive list of newsgroups, anonymous FTP sites, and computer vendors with a presence on the Internet.

Note

Indiana University Support Center

There are also a number of other WWW servers that contain mailing list compilations. To find out how to locate these servers on the World Wide Web, read the "Search Tools" section in Chapter 12, "World Wide Web Productivity."

Of special note among these is the database maintained by the Indiana University Support Center for the UCS Knowledge Base. As of April, 1995, this list contained the names and locations of 11,254 mailing lists located at over 300 sites, including not only LISTSERV but also Major-domo and LISTPROC list processors.

To allow people to search this database, the university has set up a special WWW page at http://www.ucssc.indiana.edu/mlarchive/.

Using LISTSERV

To participate in a mailing list, the first thing you need to do is *subscribe* to it. This registers you as a member and places your name in the distribution list.

Two pieces of information are needed before you can subscribe to a list. Firstly, you need to know the *list name* assigned to the mailing list by LISTSERV. In most cases, this name will be a single word like TOPTEN or a hyphenated name such as NEW-LIST. You also need to know the e-mail address of the LISTSERV processor that operates the mailing list. In the case of TOPTEN, the LISTSERV address is listserv@listserv.clark.net, and for NEW-LIST it is listserv@vm1.nodak.edu

Subscribing to a LISTSERV List

With this information in hand, you are ready to subscribe to your first list. To subscribe to TOPTEN, you need to follow these steps:

1. Using WinCIM, select **C**reate Mail from the **M**ail Menu.
2. Enter **TOPTEN** into the Name field of the Recipient List dialog, as shown in Figure 7.1.

FIGURE 7.1.

*When sending mail to the Internet, remember to add **INTERNET:** to the address.*

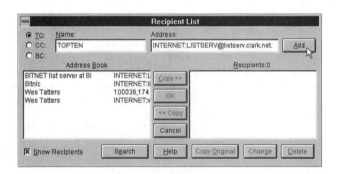

3. In the Address field, enter the list processor's e-mail address—remembering to add **INTERNET:** so that CompuServe will send the message via the Internet gateway. For TOPTEN, enter:

    INTERNET:listserv@listserv.clark.net.

> Due to the fact that all LISTSERV processors are connected using BITNET, you can actually use the address of any LISTSERV when subscribing to a mailing list. If the list name is not found by the LISTSERV processor you specify, a global register of all known LISTSERV mailing lists will be searched. If the list name is located, the message will be forwarded to the correct LISTSERV address.

4. Click on the **A**dd button or hit Enter to accept the e-mail address and then click on OK to open the Create Mail window.

5. Although LISTSERV ignores anything placed in the Subject field, you need to enter something in it before WinCIM will allow you to send the message. I entered the message **TESTING LISTSERV** in Figure 7.2, but any entry would have sufficed.

FIGURE 7.2.

WinCIM won't let you send a message without a subject.

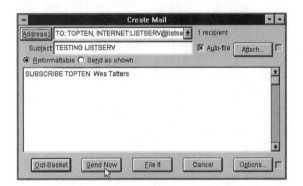

6. The last step you need to take to complete the subscription procedure is to tell the LISTSERV processor which mailing list you want to subscribe to and who it is that wants to subscribe. To do this, in the message area type **SUBSCRIBE TOPTEN**, followed by your full name. In this case I entered:

SUBSCRIBE TOPTEN Wes Tatters

7. Finally, click the **S**end Now button to mail the message.

If everything goes according to plan, the next time you log onto CompuServe, you will have received at least two messages from the LISTSERV processor.

The first message is a housekeeping message from the LISTSERV processor. It should look something like the message in Figure 7.3, which contains a list of the instructions you sent to the LISTSERV processor and a report outlining their completion. As a rule, this message can be safely ignored if the actions you requested appear to have been carried out correctly.

In most cases the second message you receive will be a Welcome message. This message contains some important information and should always be read. Probably the most important piece of information contained in the Welcome message is the name of the e-mail address known as the list address.

FIGURE 7.3.

Housekeeping messages can safely be ignored unless you seem to be encountering problems.

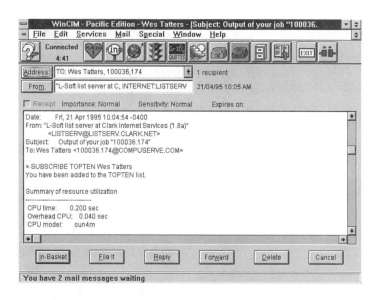

> Using the File It button on the Message Window, save a copy of all Welcome messages in a WinCIM folder devoted to mailing lists. This way, whenever you need to refer to one, they will all be stored in the same place.

The Welcome message from TOPTEN, shown in Figure 7.4, indicates that the TOPTEN list address is topten@listserv.clark.net. This is the e-mail address you use to participate in the conversations and discussions distributed by the mailing list. Usually the Welcome message will also provide you with instructions on how you cancel your subscription using the list processor's e-mail address.

Unsubscribing from a LISTSERV List

If you decide that you no longer wish to subscribe to a particular mailing list, you need to send an e-mail message to the mailing list's LISTSERV processor.

To unsubscribe to TOPTEN, follow the steps used when you subscribed to the mailing list, making sure that you send the message to the list processor e-mail address listserv@listserv.clark.net and not to the list address. This time, however, instead of entering **SUBSCRIBE TOPTEN Wes Tatters** in the body of the message, enter **SIGNOFF TOPTEN**.

This tells LISTSERV to remove your name from the TOPTEN distribution list and cancel your subscription.

You can also direct a LISTSERV processor to cancel your subscription to every mailing list it manages by sending the message **SIGNOFF ***.

FIGURE 7.4.

The Welcome message contains a list of all the e-mail addresses needed by the mailing list.

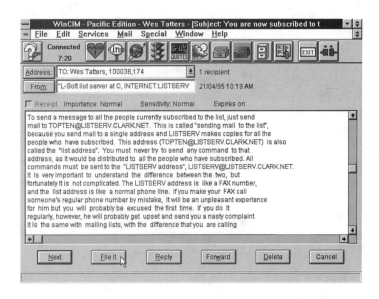

Taking this one step further, because all LISTSERV processors are connected using BITNET, you can instruct any single LISTSERV processor to cancel your subscription to every LISTSERV mailing list on all LISTSERV processors by sending it the following command: **SIGNOFF * (NETWIDE**.

> This is a handy command to use if your e-mail or CompuServe ID ever changes. The last time you use your old address, e-mail the message **SIGNOFF * (NETWIDE** to `listserv@bitnic.cren.net` to ensure that you are not leaving any old mailing lists registered to an invalid address.

Finding LISTSERV Mailing Lists

As I mentioned in the section titled "Where to Find Mailing Lists," each LISTSERV processor holds a list of all the mailing lists it manages.

If you send an e-mail message to a LISTSERV processor containing the word **LISTS**, an e-mail message similar to the one shown in Figure 7.5 will be sent back to you. This message shows the list name of each mailing list managed by the LISTSERV processor, followed by a short description.

> Some earlier versions of LISTSERV may not recognize the **LISTS** command. In versions before 1.8a, you may need to use **LIST** instead of **LISTS**.

FIGURE 7.5.

A list of all the mailing lists managed by the LISTSERV processor at `listserv.clark.net`.

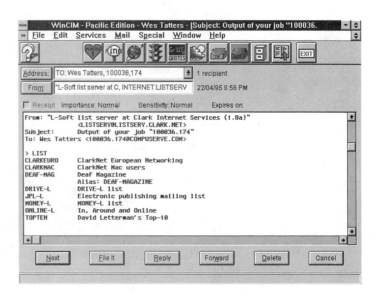

It is also possible to obtain a list of every mailing list located anywhere on BITNET. You can request a copy of this List of Lists by sending the command **LISTS GLOBAL** to any LISTSERV processor.

> Because this list is very large—over 600KB—it can be somewhat expensive to receive using CompuServe. Retrieving a copy of the list stored on the FTP server at MIT or browsing one of the WWW pages listed in the "Where to Find Mailing Lists" section probably offers you a better means of locating mailing lists.

LISTSERV also allows you to perform rudimentary searches of the List of Lists by adding a list of keywords to the LISTS GLOBAL command. For example, to obtain a list of mailing lists that deal with sporting activities, you could try sending an e-mail message containing the command **LISTS GLOBAL SPORT.**

Other LISTSERV Commands

In addition to the standard commands already discussed, each LISTSERV processor also provides subscribers with a number of other commands. Although the exact commands available at each site may differ slightly depending on which version of LISTSERV the system is running, there are a few commands that remain constant.

The HELP Command

Sending a message to a LISTSERV processor containing the word **HELP** results in an e-mail message outlining the most commonly used commands available on that LISTSERV. This message will contain information similar to that listed in Figure 7.6.

FIGURE 7.6.

Common LISTSERV commands.

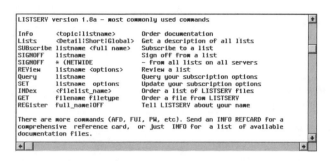

This figure also raises an interesting point. Up until now, you have been using the full name for all mailing list commands. It is possible to abbreviate many of the commands, using just the letters shown as capitals in the Command column.

As a result, **SUBSCRIBE TOPTEN Wes Tatters** could also be written as **SUB TOPTEN Wes Tatters**.

Getting Additional INFO

You can also obtain more detailed instructions covering all the commands supported by LISTSERV by using the INFO command.

This command can be used in two ways. If you send the word **INFO** to LISTSERV on its own, LISTSERV will send you back an e-mail message containing information similar to that shown in Figure 7.7. This list outlines all the information files that the LISTSERV processor can provide you with.

FIGURE 7.7.

Information files available from LISTSERV.

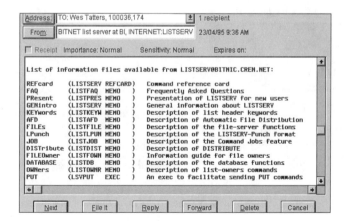

Once you have a copy of this list, you can send LISTSERV the INFO command followed by the name of the document you are interested in. For example, to request a copy of the LISTSERV Reference Card document, you would send the following command: **INFO REFCARD**.

New LISTSERV users should also consider requesting a copy of the "Presentation of LISTSERV for new users" document, called **PRESENT**, and **GENINTRO**, the "General information about LISTSERV" document.

The REGISTER Command

Regular LISTSERV users often choose to register their full names with LISTSERV. By doing this, they do not need to include their names when subscribing to new LISTSERV mailing lists.

To register your name, send the command **REGISTER**, followed by your full name, to any LISTSERV processor. To register myself, I sent **REGISTER Wes Tatters** to the LISTSERV processor at `listserv@bitnic.cren.net`.

Now, instead of typing **SUB TOPTEN Wes Tatters**, all I need to type is **SUB TOPTEN** and LISTSERV will fill in my full name for me.

Grouping Commands

Until now, all the LISTSERV messages you've seen have been restricted to a single line. However, LISTSERV can handle any number of instructions in a single message. Provided that each command is placed on a line of its own, LISTSERV will treat each one as a separate action.

Many people use this capability, when subscribing to a new mailing list, to obtain updated information about LISTSERV and alter default settings for the mailing list. For example, when I wanted to subscribe to a blues mailing list, I sent the following messages to `listserv@brownvm.brown.edu`:

> **SUB BLUES-L**
> **SET BLUES-L DIG**
> **INFO REFCARD**

The first line you should recognize as a subscription command that assumes that I have registered my name with LISTSERV.

The second line, on the other hand, you probably won't recognize. The **SET** command allows you to alter distribution options that relate to the **BLUES-L** mailing list. This mailing list can deliver messages in either message-by-message or digest form. By issuing the command **SET BLUES-L DIG**, I am instructing the LISTSERV processor to send the digest version of the mailing list.

Finally, the last line simply requests a copy of the reference card for this LISTSERV processor.

Sending Messages to the Mailing List

Although you can have hours of fun exchanging messages with the LISTSERV processor itself, the real reason for subscribing to a mailing list is to communicate with other people by sending messages that they, not the list processor, will receive.

To send e-mail to the mailing list itself, you need to know its list address. In most cases, this address will consist of the list name and the domain name of the list processor that manages it. For the blues mailing list discussed in the preceding section, this means that its list address is `blues-l@brownvm.brown.edu`.

Occasionally, there are situations where this may not apply, in which case the best approach is to look up the list address in the Welcome message you received when you first subscribed to the mailing list.

With the list address in hand, you are now ready to send a message to the mailing list by following these steps:

1. Create a new message using WinCIM and address it to **INTERNET:blues-l@brownvm.brown.edu**. Remember to type something into the Name field so that WinCIM accepts the address. Now click on the Add button and then the OK button to open the Create Mail window.

2. Unlike messages you send to LISTSERV, messages sent to the mailing list are expected to have a subject. This allows people to follow the flow of conversations in the mailing list. Because this is my first message to the BLUES-L list, I used the subject line to introduce myself. (See Figure 7.8.)

FIGURE 7.8.

When you join a mailing list, don't forget to introduce yourself.

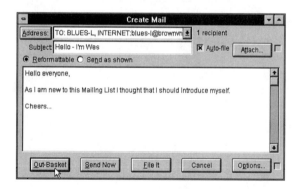

3. Finally, type your message in the body of the Create Mail window and click the **S**end Now button to mail your message.

If you are planning to send a number of messages to different mailing lists or simply to a number of people, click on the **O**ut-Basket button instead of the **S**end Now button. This will hold all the messages you enter so that you can send them all to CompuServe the next time you log on.

Tip

Using Majordomo

Like LISTSERV, Majordomo handles the maintenance and distribution of messages for mailing lists. In many ways, the two services are alike, using most of the same commands and supporting many of the same features. There are, however, a number of differences that merit a separate discussion.

These differences fall into two major categories. Firstly, there are some common actions that require different commands on each system. In a real sense, coming to grips with these differences merely involves the learning of some additional commands.

The other major difference is not as easily dealt with, and is viewed by many as a major weakness. This difference revolves around the fact that there are no interconnections between Majordomo list processors. As a result, there are no LISTS GLOBAL-like commands available on Majordomo. You must also know the correct e-mail address of a Majordomo processor before you can subscribe to any of the lists it maintains.

Subscribing to a Majordomo List

Because of the lack of LISTS GLOBAL, you will need to rely on the various catalogs and archives containing addresses of mailing lists to locate lists managed by Majordomo.

One of the first things you will notice about Majordomo mailing lists is that the list name can be almost any length, unlike LISTSERV list names, which tend to be kept quite short. By using longer names, it is a lot easier to work out what a mailing list does. For example: **biz-marketing-consulting**. This list, which is operated by the Majordomo processor at majordomo@world.std.com, obviously discusses subjects relating to marketing and consulting in the business world.

Once you find a Majordomo list that you want to subscribe to, the steps you take to subscribe are basically the same as those for a LISTSERV mailing list:

1. Create a new message by selecting **C**reate Mail from the WinCIM **M**ail Menu.

2. In the Name field of the Recipient List dialog box, enter the list name for the mailing list. Although this is not required by the list processor itself, WinCIM will not allow you to proceed if the name field is empty.

3. Now type **INTERNET:majordomo@world.std.com** into the Address field, as shown in Figure 7.9.

Note

> Unlike LISTSERV, this *must* be the address of the list processor that manages the mailing list you are subscribing to.

4. Click on the **A**dd button or hit Enter to accept the e-mail address, and then click OK to open the Create Mail window.

FIGURE 7.9.

You must use the address of the list processor that manages the mailing list.

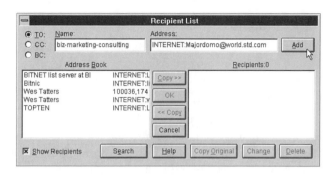

5. Majordomo, like LISTSERV, ignores anything placed in the Subject field. However, you still need to enter something in it before WinCIM will allow you to send the message.

6. Now enter **SUBSCRIBE biz-marketing-consulting** in the body of the message, as shown in Figure 7.10. You should also note that there is no need to enter your name when using a Majordomo List.

FIGURE 7.10.

Subscribe to biz-marketing-consulting.

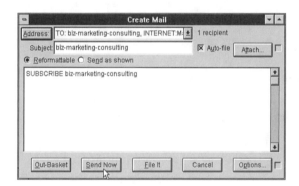

7. Finally, click the **S**end Now button to mail the message.

Like LISTSERV, the next time you log onto CompuServe, you will begin to receive messages from the mailing list.

Unsubscribing from a Majordomo List

To cancel a list, instead of using **SIGNOFF** you need to use **UNSUBSCRIBE**. Apart from this change, the process remains the same. To cancel your subscription to biz-marketing-consulting, send this message to majordomo@world.std.com:

UNSUBSCRIBE biz-marketing-consulting

Unfortunately, there are no global unsubscribe capabilities available with Majordomo. For this reason, make sure you keep a record of all the Majordomo mailing lists you subscribe to and remember to unsubscribe from them all if your CompuServe ID or e-mail address ever changes.

Other Commands

There are a few other commands available when using Majordomo that either function differently or are not supported by LISTSERV.

Getting Mailing List Information

Of these, the INFO command is probably the most relevant. With Majordomo, you use the INFO command to request information about the different mailing lists a Majordomo processor maintains. If you send a message containing the words **INFO biz-marketing-consulting** to `majordomo@world.std.com`, you will receive a message similar to the one shown in Figure 7.11.

FIGURE 7.11.

The INFO command requests information about mailing lists, not the list processor itself.

```
>>>> info  biz-marketing-consulting

Welcome to biz-marketing-consulting mailing-list!
This mailing list is dedicated to discussing ideas, plans, contacts and
experiences with all aspects in performing Marketing in a consulting
role. This includes, but is not limited to, Advertising, Public
Relations, Product Positioning, Corporate Identity, Product Strategy and
Marketing Communications in general.  In addition, we         d all like to
hear the ups and downs of marketing consulting, your best clients and
your clients from hell.  This mailing-list is _not_ moderated, so feel
free to be open and honest in your mailings.

To post messages send to:
biz-marketing-consulting@world.std.com
```

Using the LIST Command

As mentioned at the beginning of this section, the LIST command cannot perform all of the functions offered by LISTSERV.

That said, you can still use the command to obtain a catalog of all the mailing lists operated by any given Majordomo list processor, provided that you know its e-mail address in advance.

The WHICH Command

The one command that you may find useful that LISTSERV does not support is the WHICH command. This command requests a list of all mailing lists you subscribe to on the Majordomo list processor the e-mail message is addressed to.

Unfortunately, the WHICH command cannot tell you about mailing lists you subscribe to on other Majordomo list processors, but nevertheless it can come in handy when you're trying to track down a stray mailing list.

Communicating with the Mailing List

Like LISTSERV, each mailing list has a separate list address that you need to use when sending messages to the mailing list itself.

To find the name of the list address, use the INFO command discussed previously or look at the Welcome message you received when you first subscribed to the mailing list.

> Make sure you do not send Majordomo commands to the list address. As was the case with LISTSERV, they should be sent only to the list processor address. Sending them to the list address is a surefire way to get the other people who have subscribed to the list upset.

Summary

The big advantage of using mailing lists for electronic discussions is that you do not need to use anything other than simple e-mail messages to make them work.

For many Internet users, this offers a number of advantages in terms of flexibility and ease of use. For CompuServe users, however, mailing lists may not be the best choice, due to the surcharges incurred when receiving Internet e-mail messages. Luckily, there is an alternative discussion and conferencing system that in many cases duplicates the messages distributed by mailing lists.

Chapter 8, "Usenet—Newsgroups," looks at how this service, known as Usenet, operates, and explores some of the discussions or *newsgroups* it offers. It also looks at how WinCIM can be used to gain access to Usenet and discusses the concepts this involves.

CHAPTER

8

USENET—
NEWSGROUPS

Until the recent arrival of the World Wide Web, Usenet and its newsgroups were the only reason many people even wanted access to the Internet.

Newsgroups are discussion areas, not unlike CompuServe forums, where people can exchange ideas and discuss just about any topic imaginable. In this sense, they are also a lot like the mailing lists discussed in the previous chapter. To be more precise, unlike mailing lists, newsgroups do not rely on e-mail for the delivery of their messages or articles.

Instead, when you send an *article* to a newsgroup, Usenet distributes a copy to all the computers (Usenet servers) joined to the Usenet network via the Internet. This article is then made available by the server to everyone who wants to read that particular newsgroup.

At last count there were over 11,000 Usenet newsgroups discussing topics as diverse as gardening and human relationships, making Usenet one of the largest forums for free discussion in the world. There is a newsgroup for just about every topic imaginable, and for those subjects without a dedicated newsgroup, chances are there is a general discussion group of some description that will be only too happy to discuss the topic you are interested in.

To cover all the issues relating to Usenet and also look at how you can read newsgroups using WinCIM, this chapter covers the following topics:

- A short history lesson
- How newsgroups differ from CIS forums
- Newsgroup categories
- Netiquette
- Using WinCIM to access newsgroups
- Attached files and UUENCODE

Introduction to Newsgroups

The UNIX User Network, or Usenet, is an example of one of the more common distributed processing systems used by the Internet. Usenet consists of two separate components. The first component, called a *server*, monitors the day-to-day management of Usenet, the distribution of messages, and maintenance of all the newsgroups. There are thousands of Usenet servers all over the world devoted to ensuring that a copy of every article posted to a newsgroup on any server is automatically distributed to every other server.

The second component, called a *client*, is a program used to read any of the articles stored on a server. This type of client program is more commonly known as a *newsgroup reader,* which in some ways is a misnomer because the reader can be used to post new articles as well. By using a client/server approach to newsgroup management, there is no need for you to operate your own server. Instead, all you need is access to a client program and permission to use one of the many Usenet servers or hosts.

What Is Usenet?

Like so many of the services currently available on the Internet, the early history of Usenet can be traced back to a simple experiment developed by someone for their own needs. In the case of Usenet, it was a University of North Carolina graduate named Steve Bellovin who, in 1979, decided to write some simple shell scripts on his UNIX system to simplify the exchange of news and information between his campus and Duke University.

A Short History Lesson

For some time prior to the creation of these scripts, students at both Duke and North Carolina had been experimenting with a program called UUCP (UNIX to UNIX copy) as a means of exchanging messages between two UNIX servers. The idea for using UUCP in this way was first proposed by Jim Ellis and Tom Truscott, two graduate students at Duke. Steve Bellovin took the process one step further by automating it.

Once people began to hear about what Steve Bellovin had done, copies of the scripts, known collectively as "News," began to appear on a number of other UNIX computers. These computers then started to exchange messages with the North Carolina and Duke News servers using the News scripts. Over a short period of time, the Usenet was born.

As News grew in popularity, Steve Bellovin and Tom Truscott eventually rewrote the scripts using the C programming language. This allowed them to include new capabilities and improve the service's performance. With the release of this News version, the idea of newsgroups came into being, as did an early version of the hierarchical structure now used by Usenet. In this version there were two main Usenet hierarchies, called mod and net. In the mod hierarchy, newsgroups could be created that were moderated by a single user, while the net hierarchy handled unmoderated newsgroups.

Hot on the heels of this release, known as version A, another version of News was released by Matt Glickman and Mark Horton in 1981 as version B. This new version removed the limitation of version A that forced moderated newsgroups to be stored only in the mod hierarchy. This event signaled the first restructuring of Usenet and pointed the way for its future development.

In the years following, Usenet went through many changes, the most noticeable of which was the eventual replacement of UUCP. As ARPANET grew in popularity, many Usenet sites began to take advantage of its backbone for newsgroup discussion distribution. To do this, a new protocol called NNTP (Net News Transfer Protocol) was developed that allowed Usenet sites to exchange articles using TCP/IP.

TCP/IP and the Great Renaming

With the move to TCP/IP, which added many new sites to the growing list of Usenet servers, the structure of Usenet was forced once again to adapt so that it could cater to this increased popularity.

Until 1986, there were still only three top-level hierarchies on Usenet: `mod`, `net`, and `fa`. Because there were relatively few newsgroups on Usenet, having just three hierarchies did not pose any real problems, but as the number of newsgroups began to increase rapidly, many people started to suggest the need for a new structure.

This led to what has become known as the "Great Renaming" and spurred the biggest *flame war* in the history of Usenet. Although it was very easy to say, "Let's restructure Usenet," it seemed that everyone had different ideas about how it should be done. Following thousands of sometimes heated exchanges, it was decided that seven new top-level hierarchies should be created to replace the three original ones.

Newsgroup Hierarchies

These seven new top-level hierarchies were designed to represent equally the wide cross-section of discussion topics that Usenet was handling at the time. These seven hierarchies are listed in Table 8.1 with a brief description of the newsgroups they contain.

Table 8.1. Newsgroup top-level hierarchies.

Identifier	Category
comp	Computer-related discussions
misc	Unclassified newsgroups
news	Internet/Usenet news and information
rec	Recreation, sports, and hobbies
sci	Scientific newsgroups
soc	Social newsgroups
talk	Debate-oriented newsgroups

The Great Renaming did not happen overnight, however, because the very nature of Usenet meant that each server needed to be reorganized. At the same time, all existing newsgroups needed to be sorted into the new hierarchies, often with lengthy debates ensuing over the exact location of some of the less generic newsgroups.

To categorize newsgroups even further, additional hierarchical levels have also been added to the Usenet specification. This allows newsgroups to be categorized by subtopics within each top-level hierarchy. For example, the `rec` hierarchy is devoted to newsgroups that discuss recreation, sports, and hobbies. Within this hierarchy, a number of subcategories have been created describing the primary areas of discussions. These include `rec.arts`, `rec.autos`, `rec.game`, and `rec.sport`, to name just a few. Below this primary subject area, you will also sometimes find additional subgroups and eventually the newsgroups themselves.

In the `rec.sport` area, for example, newsgroups are further categorized by type of sport, including `rec.sport.baseball`, `rec.sport.cricket`, and `rec.sport.football`. The end result of all this subclassification is a newsgroup name, such as `rec.sport.football.australian`, that clearly defines the newsgroup's contents.

> In most cases, newsgroups are classified by no more than three levels, but it isn't uncommon to find newsgroups with up to five classification levels as well. Naturally, there is always an exception to the rule, as one newsgroup proves:
> `alt.help.me.get.out.of.trouble.trouble.trouble-please`

Usenet Today

Since 1987, Usenet has grown from strength to strength, with thousands of newsgroups being added each year. To accompany this growth, other hierarchies have also been added to cater to both location-specific and topic-specific newsgroups.

Of all these new hierarchies, by far the most popular is the `alt` hierarchy, which caters to many alternative discussion areas. This hierarchy, while being very popular, is often the cause of considerable consternation as well, due to its acceptance of newsgroups whose subject matter is often "racy," to put it politely.

> Some of the `alt` newsgroups are so lewd that a number of Usenet sites have chosen not to distribute them, and this is why the `alt` hierarchy exists at all. When people were prevented from setting up groups like `rec.sex` and `rec.drug` in the more respectable hierarchies, they decided to create a hierarchy catering to this type of discussion. By doing this they also provide a mechanism allowing these groups to be excluded by servers as required.

Netiquette

Although Usenet does provide a free environment for the exchange of information and ideas, there are still a number of rules to which participants are expected to adhere. These rules, or guidelines, are designed not so much to restrict users' personal space, but instead to help keep the enormous community of people who spend time on Usenet happy.

Language

The first rule of Usenet is that any rude, insulting, or degrading comments are simply not welcome. If you feel you need to express yourself in this way, either send your comments as a private e-mail or visit some of the `alt` newsgroups that are somewhat more tolerant of such outbursts.

Racist comments and opinions will also not be tolerated on any newsgroup and can result in a user being barred from a Usenet server, as can the use of foul language or swearing.

Usenet Grammar

There are also a few grammatical precedents applying to newsgroups.

You should only use capital letters when you need to make a point. TYPING IN CAPITAL LETTERS IS REFERRED TO AS *SHOUTING* and should be avoided wherever possible. For one thing, it makes your articles very hard to read and is considered to be very rude. In most cases, people will simply ignore articles typed in capital letters, apart from possibly firing off a message to you telling you not to shout.

If you want to make a point, the placement of an *asterisk* or two around the words you want to highlight is considered to be far more effective. Some people also use the _underline_ symbol in the same way.

Apart from this, there is very little need for such punctuation in your articles, because people tend to be interested in the content and not the grammatical quality. However, you should keep your articles as short as possible and resist the desire to write pages of flowing prose when a simple Yes or No would suffice.

Flame Wars

A *flame* is a sarcastic or rude message sent to someone in response to a comment or article the reader did not appreciate. Although the sending of flames is not regarded as accepted behavior, such messages are usually tolerated and sometimes even admired, especially when the contents of the flame are particularly well thought out.

If you are in the habit of making stupid comments, you can expect to be flamed, although sometimes even the most well-written article can attract a flame if one of its readers disagrees with your particular point of view. When you receive a flame, there are two ways that you can treat it. You can ignore it and accept it as a simple fact of life, or you can respond to the sender. However, if you do choose to respond, be prepared for yet another response.

By responding to a flame, you can also ignite what is known as a *flame war*. Often other people in the newsgroup decide to make their own comments about the flame or one of its ensuing replies and counter-flames. It is not uncommon on such occasions for the conversation on a newsgroup to degenerate into a flame war, replacing for a short time all other conversations on the newsgroup.

Smileys, Emoticons, and Abbreviations

To help keep your articles to a readable length, a number of abbreviations and other symbols have become a common part of the Usenet language.

For example, you can replace the commonly used "by the way" with <BTW>. Some of the more common abbreviations are shown in Table 8.2.

Table 8.2. Commonly used abbreviations.

Abbreviation	Description
<IMHO>	In my humble opinion
<PMFJI>	Pardon me for jumping in
<ROTFL>	Rolling on the floor laughing
<GD&RFC>	Grinning, ducking, and running for cover
<G>	A grin
<BG>	A big grin
<VBG>	A very big grin
<OTOH>	On the other hand
<FWIW>	For what it's worth

Another popular form of abbreviation is known as a *smiley* or *emoticon*. This form of abbreviation is used not so much to replace words, but instead to express the writer's state of mind. These symbols are often used to express complex emotions and feelings not otherwise apparent in a normal message. The most well-known smiley is :-) or :), the happy face. You can also use a similar symbol to express sadness (:-() or surprise (:-o). The number of possible combinations is extensive, with some of the more unique combinations including a happy person wearing glasses (8-)) and a person winking (;-)).

Tip

Even though the use of abbreviations and emoticons can seem like a good idea at first, you should use them sparingly. They should be used to enhance what you are writing, not to overwhelm it.

Signature Lines

Another popular part of many Usenet articles is the *signature*. This usually consists of one or two lines of information that your newsgroup reader automatically appends to every article you send.

On these lines, people often include messages and quotes along with their names and e-mail addresses. Unlike in CompuServe, which tends to prefer simple signatures, a complex or clever signature is a sign of prestige in a newsgroup. These messages also serve as your calling card on the Usenet, and people often look to the signature line in an article to find out something about the author.

Although a clever signature line is appreciated by most people, you should make sure you keep the length down to no more than four or five lines. There is nothing worse than loading a 20- or 30-line article only to find that it contains a 2-line message and a 28-line signature.

Using WinCIM to Access Newsgroups

Since August, 1994, CompuServe has provided its members with access to Usenet through the Internet gateway it created. Using either the older ASCII terminal interface or the more recent graphical interface provided by WinCIM, you can subscribe to any of the thousands of newsgroups currently available and both send and receive articles.

To gain access to the Usenet forum area, open the Go... dialog box by selecting the **G**o option from the **S**ervices menu. Type **Internet** in the dialog box to open the Internet Services window, shown in Figure 8.1.

FIGURE 8.1.

The Internet Services window allows you to access Usenet.

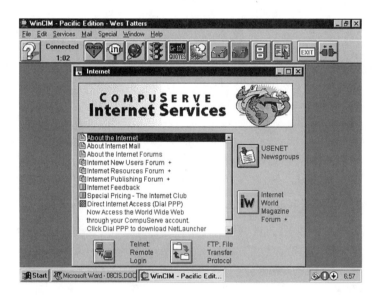

The Internet Services window is the base window for all the services covered by Internet Services. From here you can access any of the Internet Support forums and obtain information about CompuServe's Internet gateway and all the currently supported options.

In this case, you want to access the Usenet services. To do this, click on the Usenet newsgroups button to the right of the menu list. This instructs WinCIM to open the Usenet Newsgroups window, shown in Figure 8.2.

FIGURE 8.2.

The Usenet Newsgroups window.

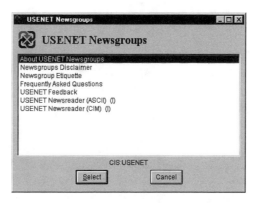

You can also jump directly to the Usenet Newsgroups window by typing **usenet** instead of **internet** in the Go… dialog box.

The Usenet Newsgroups Window

The first four items in the Usenet Newsgroups window provide you with information about using CompuServe's Usenet services. Before you begin to experiment with Usenet, take a few minutes to read through these entries to familiarize yourself with the latest information.

Of these items, pay particular attention to the Frequently Asked Questions entry. This item contains a document listing many of the common questions and problems encountered by Usenet users. For each question listed, the document contains an explanation of the problem and a suggested solution. If you are encountering any difficulties at all with Usenet, this is the best place to start.

There is also a Feedback option on the menu for sending queries and suggestions to CompuServe's support staff. Usually you'll receive an answer to any queries within 48 hours, depending on the query's complexity and the number of questions currently being handled.

The final two options in this window open either of the two Usenet newsreaders provided by CompuServe. The first opens the ASCII-based newsreader in a terminal window, while the second opens the graphical newsreader discussed in detail later in this chapter. (See Figure 8.3.) Both newsreaders provide you with the same level of functionality, but most people find the graphical interface considerably easier to use.

The main reason for using the text-based newsreader is because some of the offline navigators such as TAPCIS and OZCIS can be set up to retrieve newsgroup articles automatically.

FIGURE 8.3.

CompuServe's ASCII Usenet Newsreader.

The Graphical Newsreader

To open the graphical newsreader, highlight the Usenet Newsreader (CIM) (I) entry and click on the **S**elect button. This opens the newsreader and presents you with a window similar to the one shown in Figure 8.4. The options provided on this menu allow you to browse your currently selected newsgroups, subscribe to newsgroups, create articles, and configure various optional settings.

FIGURE 8.4.

The Newsreader main menu.

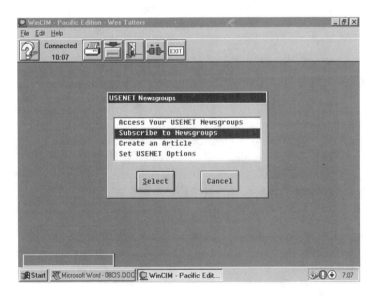

Subscribing to Newsgroups

Before you can read any newsgroup article, you need to tell CompuServe that you are interested in reading it. To do this, subscribe to the newsgroup by following these steps:

1. Highlight the Subscribe to Newsgroups entry as shown in Figure 8.4 and click on the **S**elect button. You can also achieve the same result by double-clicking on the Subscribe to Newsgroups entry. This opens the dialog box shown in Figure 8.5.

FIGURE 8.5.

The Subscribe to Newsgroups dialog box lets you choose the newsgroups you are interested in reading.

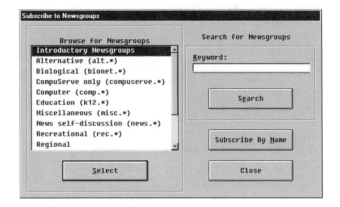

2. Down the left side of this dialog box there is a list of the top-level hierarchies carried by CompuServe on its Usenet server. To look at any of the newsgroups in these hierarchies, double-click on the one you are interested in or highlight it and click on the **S**elect button. For now, double-click on the CompuServe only hierarchy.

3. You should now see a dialog box like the one shown in Figure 8.6. This window lists all the newsgroups currently available in the hierarchy you selected. Down the left side of this dialog box are empty check boxes you select to nominate the newsgroups you want to subscribe to. To select a newsgroup, click on the check box. When you do this, an "X" appears in the box to indicate you have selected it.

FIGURE 8.6.

Newsgroup in the CompuServe only hierarchy.

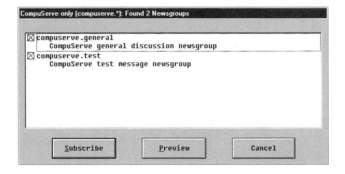

After selecting all the newsgroups you are interested in, click on the **S**ubscribe button. When you do this, CompuServe displays a message informing you that your subscription request was successful. Now click on the **C**ancel button to return to the main Subscribe to Newsgroups dialog box.

> You should not actually need to subscribe to the two newsgroups shown in the CompuServe only hierarchy, because CompuServe automatically subscribes to them for you the first time you enter Usenet.

4. If you are not sure where a newsgroup is located, you can search through the available newsgroups by typing a keyword in the space provided above the **S**earch button. To locate all the newsgroups relating to Microsoft Windows, type **windows** in the Keyword: field and click on the **S**earch button.

   After a few seconds, a dialog box similar to the one shown in Figure 8.7 opens, listing the newsgroups containing the keyword you nominated. Like the hierarchy list discussed previously, you select the newsgroups you are interested in by clicking on their check boxes. Once you have located all the newsgroups you want, click on the **S**ubscribe button and then the **C**ancel button to return to the previous screen.

FIGURE 8.7.

Select the Windows newsgroups you are interested in and click on the Subscribe button.

5. There is one final option available when you already know the name of the newsgroup you are interested in. Click on the Subscribe by Name button. This opens a small window where you can enter a newsgroup name. (See Figure 8.8.)

> Because some of the newsgroups in the `alt` hierarchy contain material that is less than savory, CompuServe has decided not to display these newsgroups in the various newsgroup listings it provides. However, if you already know the name of one of these newsgroups, you can still subscribe to it using the Subscribe by Name option.

FIGURE 8.8.

To take advantage of the Subscribe by Name option, you must already know the full name of the newsgroup you are interested in.

Working with Newsgroups

The first option listed on the newsreader's main menu lets you perform a number of activities relating to the newsgroups you have subscribed to. To explore the options this menu item provides, double-click on the Access Your Usenet Newsgroups option. Doing this opens the Access Newsgroups dialog box, shown in Figure 8.9. This dialog box displays all the newsgroups you have subscribed to, along with a number indicating how many unread articles are stored in each newsgroup.

> The Articles Available number takes into account any articles you have already read and deducts them from the number of articles currently stored in the newsgroup.

FIGURE 8.9.

The Access Newsgroups dialog box lists all the newsgroups you have subscribed to.

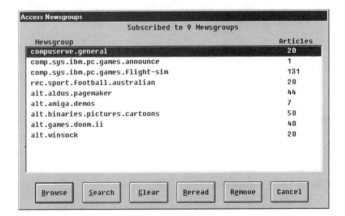

Across the bottom of the Access Newsgroups dialog box there are a number of buttons that let you browse articles and perform a number of newsgroup-related functions. Table 8.3 lists each of these buttons and explains what actions they perform.

Table 8.3. Options available using the Access Newsgroups dialog box.

Button	Action
Browse	Before you click on this button, highlight the newsgroup containing articles you want to read. Then, when you click on

continues

Table 8.3. continued

Button	Action
	the **B**rowse button, a new dialog box is opened displaying a list of all the articles currently available.
Search	If you don't want to scan all the articles in a newsgroup manually, you can use this button to search all the subject lines in a newsgroup and list only those that match the keyword you nominate.
Clear	This button marks all the articles in the currently highlighted newsgroup as read. When you do this, the article number associated with this newsgroup is set to zero.
Reread	This button performs the opposite function of the **C**lear button. If you click on this button, a dialog box opens asking you to nominate how many previously read articles should be marked as unread, starting with the last article you read and moving backward. When you do this, the article number associated with the newsgroup is also updated accordingly.
Remove	This unsubscribes the currently highlighted newsgroup and removes it from the list.
Cancel	This closes the Access Newsgroups dialog box and returns to the top Usenet newsreader menu.

Reading Articles

When you choose either the Browse option or the Search option, you are eventually presented with a Browse dialog box similar to the one shown in Figure 8.10. In the body of this dialog box, the subject line of each *thread* containing unread articles is listed, along with the number of articles included in the thread.

Note

> All articles in a newsgroup containing the same subject line are grouped together into *threads*. This makes it much easier to follow a conversation that may have taken place over a period of days.
>
> If the newsreader did not sort the articles into threads, you would need to scan the entire newsgroup, article by article, to follow a conversation.

In addition to the list of threads, there are buttons at the bottom of this dialog box that allow you to work with a selected thread. Table 8.4 is a list of the actions performed by these various buttons.

FIGURE 8.10.

The Browse dialog box displays all the unread articles in the currently selected newsgroups.

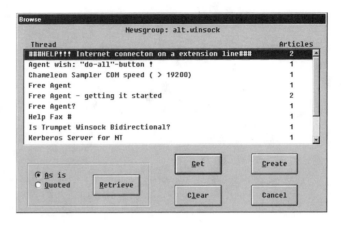

Table 8.4. Actions performed by the buttons on the Browse dialog box.

Button	Action
Get	Retrieves the first article in the currently selected thread and displays it in the Thread dialog box.
Clear	Marks all the articles in the selected thread as read and removes them from the browse list.
Create	Opens the Create Usenet Message dialog box with the current newsgroup selected as the destination.
Retrieve	Saves a copy of the selected thread to a file. If you select the As is option, the articles in the selected thread are saved in the same way they appear in the Message dialog box. On the other hand, if you select the Quoted option, the articles in the thread are formatted in a manner suitable for use as a quote in a reply.
Cancel	Closes the Browse dialog box and returns to the Access Newsgroups dialog box.

In most cases, when you open this dialog box you want to read the contents of the articles. To do this, highlight the thread you are interested in and select the **G**et button, or just double-click on the thread itself. When you do this, the newsreader retrieves a copy of the first article in the selected thread and displays it in an article dialog box, like the one shown in Figure 8.11.

Once you open the article dialog box, there are a number of additional functions to choose from, including viewing the current thread's other articles and moving to the next or previous thread in the current newsgroup. To take advantage of these functions, use the buttons displayed along the bottom of the article dialog box. To help you better understand all these features, Table 8.5 has a listing of the buttons and the actions they perform.

FIGURE 8.11.

When you select a thread, the newsreader always displays the first article.

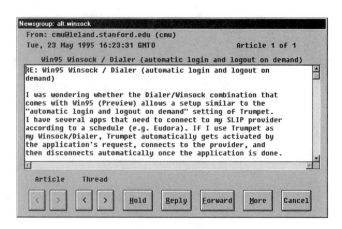

Table 8.5. Actions performed by the buttons on the Message dialog box.

Button	Action
Article < >	If there is more that one article in the currently selected thread, these two buttons let you move between them without returning to the Browser dialog box.
Thread < >	These two buttons allow you to move from thread to thread in the currently selected newsgroup.
Hold	Usually, once you have read an article the newsreader marks it as read and doesn't display it the next time you enter this newsgroup. If you click on this button, however, the article is displayed again next time.
Reply	This button opens a Reply to Usenet Message dialog box that allows you to send a new article to the current newsgroup as a reply to the current article.
Forward	This button opens a Forward Usenet Message dialog box that allows you to send a copy of the article via e-mail. By default, the address of the current article's author is used.
More	Selecting this button opens a dialog box that displays additional information about the current article and allows you to store a copy of the article on your local hard drive.
Cancel	This button closes the article dialog and returns to the Browser dialog box.

Creating an Article

There are a number of places in the WinCIM newsreader that enable you to create articles. Although each of these locations technically demands the creation of slightly different types of articles depending on whether you are replying to an existing article, forwarding a message to an article's author, or creating an entirely new thread, they all use the same message creation dialog box.

To use this dialog box, you should follow these steps:

1. For this example, select the Create an Article entry on the newsreader's main menu. This will open the Create Usenet Message dialog box, shown in Figure 8.12.

FIGURE 8.12.

The Create Usenet message dialog box, the Reply to Usenet message dialog box, and the Forward Usenet Message dialog box all use the same basic layout.

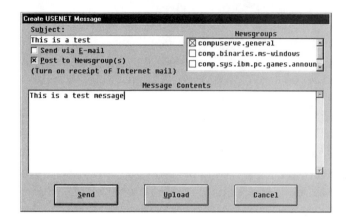

2. Whenever you create a new article, there must always be something in the Subject field. If you are creating a new thread, you should come up with a subject line that accurately describes the point of your posting. If you are replying to an existing thread, on the other hand, the subject line is automatically filled in for you by the newsreader.

3. To send a personal message using e-mail instead, select the Send via E-mail check box. Later, when you hit the **S**end button you will be asked to enter the e-mail address of the person you want to send the message to.

4. To post an article to a newsgroup, select the Post to Newsgroup(s) check box. When you select this option, you will need to select at least one of the newsgroups listed in the Scroll box located in the top-right corner of the dialog box.

You can select both the Send via E-mail option and the Post to Newsgroup(s) option at the same time. However, you should keep in mind that every time you send an e-mail message, CompuServe charges you a handling fee.

Note

If you are replying to an article, the newsreader automatically selects the correct newsgroup for you. On the other hand, if you are forwarding an article this option is disabled.

Warning

> Although the newsreader allows you to post an article to multiple newsgroups, this type of activity tends to be frowned upon under most circumstances. As a result, you should avoid multiple posting.

5. Once you have the "paperwork" out of the way, enter your message in the Message Contents area located in the middle of the dialog box.

6. By clicking on the **U**pload button, you can include the contents of any text file stored on your hard drive in the article you are writing. This feature comes in handy if you want to send UUENCODED files or quote from the original article, if you saved a copy of it using the **R**etrieve button mentioned earlier.

7. Click on the **S**end button to transmit your article to the nominated newsgroup or e-mail address.

Advanced Techniques

Now that you understand the basics of Usenet and the mechanisms required to send and receive articles stored in newsgroups, it's time to take a look at some of the more advanced options provided by CompuServe's Usenet newsreader.

Newsreader Options

To begin, let's look at some of the ways you can tailor the newsreader by selecting the Set Usenet Options entry on the main newsreader menu. When you do this, the newsreader displays the Options dialog box, shown in Figure 8.13. To explain the settings available in this dialog box, Table 8.6 contains a brief description of each and some comments on its use.

FIGURE 8.13.

The Options dialog box allows you to tailor the newsreader to your needs.

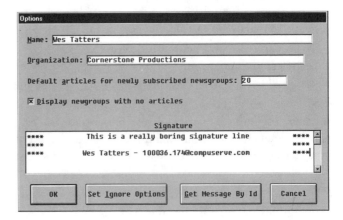

Table 8.6. Settings available in the Options dialog box.

Option	Description
Name	When Usenet creates an article, it includes your full name and e-mail address in the article's header.
Organization	You can also include the name of the organization you belong to in the header by nominating it in this field.
Default Articles	When you subscribe to a newsgroup, there may be hundreds or even thousands of old articles currently held on file. By setting this number, you tell the newsreader to mark all these articles as read, except for the newest 20 or so articles, depending on the number you nominate in this field.
Display Newsgroups	By default, if one of the newsgroups you subscribe to currently has no new articles in it, the newsreader does not list it in the Access Newsgroups dialog box. To override this option, select the check box next to Display newsgroups with no articles.
Signature	If you want the newsreader to automatically append a signature to every article you send, enter the message you want to append in the space provided. When you do this, each time you post an article or send an e-mail message, the newsreader will append the contents of this field to the end of the message.
Set Ignore Options	This button opens a dialog box that allows you to tell the newsreader to ignore articles from certain people or those that contain certain words in their subject.
Get Message by ID	Every article stored on CompuServe's Usenet server is assigned a unique ID that you can find by clicking on the More button in the article's dialog box. Once you know an article's ID, you can use this button to retrieve it by typing the ID in the space provided.
OK	Clicking on this button accepts any changes you have made to the configuration options.
Cancel	Clicking on this button cancels any changes and reverts the reader to the original settings.

UUENCODED Files and Usenet

In many different newsgroups, you will occasionally come across an article that looks something like the one shown in Figure 8.14. This is an example of a binary file that has been encoded using UUENCODE.

FIGURE 8.14.

Binary files sent using Usenet are UUENCODEd.

As discussed in Chapter 6, before you can send a binary file across the Internet using e-mail, or in this case Usenet, it first needs to be converted to a special ASCII text format. When it is received at the other end, it needs to be reconverted to its original format.

If you discover such an article in a newsgroup, first save a copy of it on your hard drive by clicking on the **M**ore button at the bottom of the article dialog box. Then click on the **R**etrieve button with the As is option selected. Doing this opens a save requester. (See Figure 8.15.)

FIGURE 8.15.

Save the article with a .UUE extension so your decoder programs recognize it.

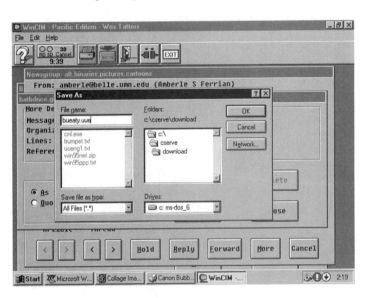

In the Save As dialog box, nominate a suitable name for the new file and give it a .UUE extension so your UUDECODE program recognizes it. Once you have saved the file, you can then use either of the programs mentioned in Appendix D that are capable of decoding UUENCODEd files—Wincode or WinPack.

You can also send your own files to Usenet newsgroups by first encoding them using Wincode. Then, when you open the Create Usenet message, click on the Upload button.

The Top 40 Newsgroups

With over 11,000 newsgroups now available, it isn't practical to even consider creating a long list of newsgroups you may or may not be interested in. Instead, to give you some idea of the diverse range of topics available, Table 8.7 lists the 40 most popular newsgroups, according to the information produced by the DEC Network Systems Laboratory in Palo Alto, California.

Table 8.7. The top 40 most popular newsgroups as of April, 1995.

Ranking	Newsgroup	Estimated number of readers
1	alt.binaries.pictures.erotica	280,000
2	alt.binaries.multimedia	94,000
3	alt.binaries.pictures.erotica.female	140,000
4	alt.binaries.sounds.tv	37,000
5	alt.binaries.pictures.erotica.male	50,000
6	alt.binaries.pictures.erotica.orientals	87,000
7	alt.binaries.sounds.music	54,000
8	alt.binaries.pictures.misc	160,000
9	alt.binaries.pictures.supermodels	200,000
10	alt.binaries.pictures.celebrities	90,000
11	alt.binaries.pictures.erotica.amateur.female	28,000
12	rec.games.trading-cards.marketplace	22,000
13	alt.binaries.sounds.movies	41,000
14	alt.binaries.multimedia.erotica	28,000
15	alt.binaries.sounds.mods	37,000
16	alt.sex.pictures	110,000
17	alt.test	47,000
18	alt.binaries.pictures.tasteless	120,000
19	bionet.molbio.genbank.updates	11,000
20	alt.binaries.pictures.erotica.blondes	120,000

continues

Table 8.7. continued

Ranking	Newsgroup	Estimated number of readers
21	alt.sex.pictures.female	76,000
22	alt.binaries.warez.ibm-pc	6,800
23	alt.binaries.sounds.misc	91,000
24	alt.binaries.pictures.utilities	140,000
25	alt.binaries.pictures.erotica.bondage	22,000
26	alt.binaries.pictures.erotica.teen	4,300
27	alt.binaries.pictures.erotica.bestiality	19,000
28	alt.binaries.sounds.erotica	43,000
29	alt.binaries.pictures.erotica.fetish	22,000
30	alt.sex.stories	270,000
31	misc.jobs.offered	330,000
32	alt.binaries.pictures.anime	32,000
33	alt.binaries.pictures.erotica.anime	21,000
34	alt.binaries.pictures.erotica.breasts	15,000
35	alt.binaries.misc	25,000
36	alt.binaries.doom	41,000
37	alt.binaries.pictures.girlfriends	160,00
38	alt.binaries.pictures.erotica.cartoons	400,00
39	alt.binaries.sounds.cartoons	12,000
40	alt.religion.scientology	26,000

Summary

As seen in this chapter, Usenet offers CompuServe members access to an entirely new world. With thousands of newsgroups covering every topic imaginable, there is bound to be at least one area of discussion that interests you.

But unlike mailing lists, you are not charged a fee for each article you send or receive. This makes using Usenet a far more financially viable option that, when used in conjunction with the pricing structure offered by the Internet Club, results in access rates similar to those offered by most commercial Internet service providers.

With all this discussion of e-mail, mailing lists, and now newsgroups, you are probably beginning to wonder if CompuServe offers any Internet services that don't involve discussions or the sending of messages. Well, you will be pleased to know that the answer is yes, it does offer other Internet services.

The next chapter takes a look at the first of these services, Telnet, and looks at how you can use CompuServe to open remote connections to the computers on the Internet.

CHAPTER 9

TELNET

When the ARPANET was first proposed back in 1969, one of the main goals set down for the project was to develop the capability for remote computing using the ARPANET network, as opposed to dedicated telephone lines.

The motivation behind this goal was the desire to share the capabilities and resources of the most powerful computers available at the time with as many scientists and researchers as possible. In addition, by using ARPANET to make the physical connections, the cost of maintaining separate dedicated lines for each user who wanted a connection was removed completely.

In the early developmental stages, all the work required to maintain these remote links was handled by the host computer system. This put a very heavy load on the computer, and was often the cause of system failures and other downtime events. As the need for remote computing began to increase, an alternate system was sought that could reduce these loads by sharing the work between the host computer system and a remote computer.

The answer to this problem was Telnet. Using Telnet, the remote system looks after the physical screen display and keyboard processing, leaving the host computer free to get on with the job it was designed for.

This chapter looks at the Telnet capabilities available to CompuServe users by dealing with the following topics:

◆ What Is Telnet?

◆ How Does Telnet Work?

◆ Using Telnet with WinCIM

◆ Popular Telnet Sites

What Is Telnet?

Like many of the services previously discussed, Telnet is a tool that enables you to use the Internet for some form of communication.

In Telnet's case, you use the Internet to log onto computer systems located anywhere on the network and use them as though they were sitting in the room next to you. From a user's standpoint, running Telnet is a lot like using a communications program to connect to CompuServe or a local *bulletin board system* (BBS).

However, whereas communications programs create a physical connection between your computer and the host system, Telnet uses a client/server approach that physically separates the actions of the host and remote systems.

How Does Telnet Work?

This client/server mechanism, or more correctly the *Telnet protocol*, allows two computer systems to share the workload required to perform a remote logon.

For this to happen, two separate computer programs are required. On the host computer—the one you want to connect to—there is a computer program called a Telnet server. It is the job of this program to wait for Telnet *remote logon* requests to arrive from computers connected to it using the Internet.

When such a request arrives, the Telnet server opens a communications channel with the computer making the request. To make a remote logon request, the person on the remote computer needs to run a Telnet client program. (See Figure 9.1.) This program looks and feels very much like a standard VT100 terminal. Internally, however, it is actually conducting a conversation with the Telnet server instead of connecting directly to the remote computer system.

FIGURE 9.1.

WinCIM running in VT100 terminal emulation mode.

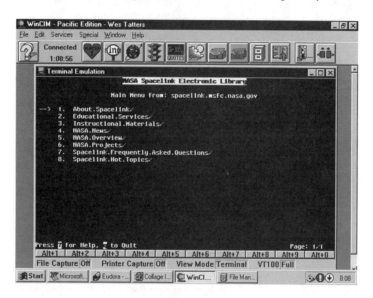

The VT100 terminal—developed by DEC—is the de facto standard terminal used by computer systems worldwide. Nearly every computer system available supports the use of VT100 terminals for both remote login and local connections. For this reason, it was also adopted as the default when using Telnet.

Using Telnet with WinCIM

Although CompuServe opened an inbound Telnet connection in 1994 to give Internet users remote Telnet connections to CompuServe, it was not until April of 1995 that a reciprocal service was opened. This service allows CompuServe users to make Telnet connections to sites on the Internet.

To use Telnet with CompuServe, all you need is WinCIM and the domain name of a computer you want to connect with. To actually log onto the remote site, in most cases you will also need a user ID and password.

> You can also use the IP address of a remote computer you want to Telnet to. Like e-mail addresses, the domain name and IP address are interchangeable.

If you don't know of any sites that permit Telnet connections, CompuServe can assist you there as well. The "Popular Telnet Sites" section later in this chapter looks at the sites suggested by CompuServe to help get you started.

> Using NetLauncher, you can also open Telnet connections from dedicated, Winsock-compatible Telnet clients. Appendix C looks at two of such programs and discusses places where you can obtain a copy of each.

The Internet Services Window

Like many of the Internet services offered by CompuServe, you can gain access to the CompuServe Telnet client via the Internet Services window.

To call up Internet Services, open the Go… dialog box by selecting the **G**o option from the **S**ervices menu, as shown in Figure 9.2. The Go… dialog box can also be opened by clicking on the traffic light icon in the Toolbar, which is visible just to the right of the Services menu in Figure 9.2.

FIGURE 9.2.

*Select Go to open the Go…
dialog box.*

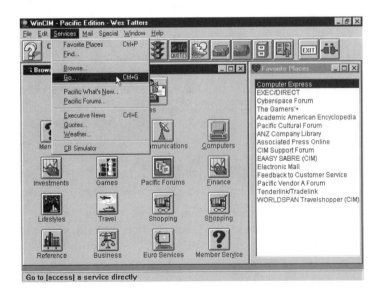

In the Go… dialog box (Figure 9.3), type the word **INTERNET** and then click on the OK button. This tells WinCIM to request a copy of the Internet Services window from CompuServe.

FIGURE 9.3.
The Go… dialog box helps you to navigate around CompuServe.

> Forum names and services can be typed in either upper- or lowercase. For example, you could also have typed **internet** in the Go… dialog box.

After some communications with CompuServe, WinCIM will display a window similar to the one shown in Figure 9.4. This is the Internet Services main window. To access Telnet from this window, click on the Telnet: Remote Login icon as indicated by the arrow cursor in Figure 9.4.

FIGURE 9.4.
The Internet Services main menu provides access to Telnet.

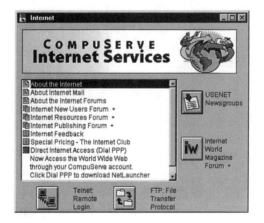

The Telnet Menu

Clicking on the Telnet: Remote Login icon directs WinCIM to open the main CompuServe Telnet Access window. This window, shown in Figure 9.5, provides direct access to all of the Telnet functions available to CompuServe users.

> You can also bypass the Internet window completely and jump straight to the Telnet Access window by entering **TELNET** in the Go… dialog box instead of **INTERNET**.

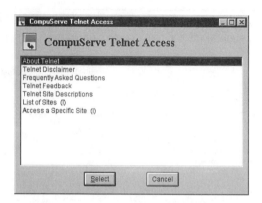

FIGURE 9.5.

The CompuServe Telnet Access window on WinCIM.

Information About Telnet

The first three options listed in the Telnet Access window offer you some general and specific information about using Telnet with CompuServe. When you begin to use Telnet, it is a good idea to spend a short time reading through these items to familiarize yourself with the latest information available relating to Telnet.

You should pay special attention to the Frequently Asked Questions option, the third item in the list in Figure 9.5. This menu item opens a message window that displays a list of questions asked by people encountering difficulties with Telnet. If you have a question about Telnet, it is highly likely that you are not the first. By browsing through the answers offered to these frequently asked questions, it is likely that the answer to your difficulties can be found.

If you are still encountering problems after reviewing these answers, the fourth menu item— Telnet Feedback—allows you to send a message to CompuServe to request assistance with the difficulties you are encountering.

The List of Popular Sites

To help you get started with Telnet, CompuServe has compiled a short list containing some of the more popular Telnet sites available. (See Figure 9.6.) By selecting the Telnet Site Descriptions option, you can request a list of sites recommended by CompuServe and a short description of each. The "Popular Telnet Sites" section later in this chapter looks briefly at what these sites offer to CompuServe users.

Your First Telnet Connection

CompuServe offers you two methods of connecting to Telnet sites. The first method uses the list of sites offered by CompuServe, and the second allows you to enter the address of any Telnet site manually.

This section first looks at how to connect automatically to one of the CompuServe recommended sites and then at how to connect to a site using its domain name.

FIGURE 9.6.

Popular Telnet sites available from CompuServe.

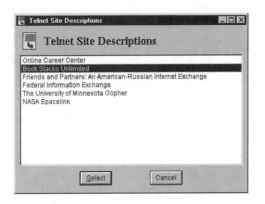

Connecting to the Online Career Center

Using WinCIM to connect to one of the sites listed in the Telnet list of sites is a relatively straightforward process:

1. If you have not done so already, open the CompuServe Telnet Access window by clicking on the traffic light icon and entering **telnet** at the GO… dialog.

2. Highlight the List of Sites option, as shown in Figure 9.7, and click on the Select button. You can also select the list of sites by double-clicking on it.

FIGURE 9.7.

Select List of Sites to open the Telnet window.

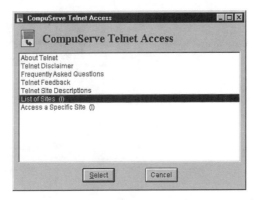

3. With the Telnet window open, double-click on the Online Career Center option (Figure 9.8) to start the Telnet connection. Using this window, you can Telnet to any of the sites listed without needing to know its domain name. CompuServe looks after the connection process for you, and in most cases handles the initial logon process as well. (See "Sites Recommended by CompuServe" later in this chapter for a discussion of the services these sites provide.)

FIGURE 9.8.

The Telnet window lets you connect to selected Internet sites.

4. After a few seconds, WinCIM displays an Alert message similar to the one in Figure 9.9. This message informs you that a Telnet connection is about to be opened and that you are leaving CompuServe. To start the Telnet connection, click on the **P**roceed button. Although this message is in many ways a formality, there is one piece of information it offers that you should pay attention to. Once the Telnet session begins, the only way to exit from a site—other than by the menus and options the site offers—is to use what is known in the Telnet world as the *escape sequence.* To use this option, press Ctrl+]. This will force WinCIM to break the Telnet connection with the remote computer and return you to WinCIM's Telnet Access window.

FIGURE 9.9.

Click Proceed to open the Telnet connection.

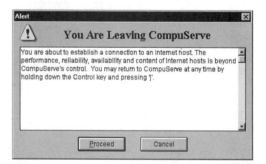

5. WinCIM automatically starts its internal VT100 Terminal Emulation program when the Telnet connection process commences. Once the Terminal Emulation window opens, the steps WinCIM takes to complete the Telnet connection are displayed on the screen. (See Figure 9.10.)

On some occasions WinCIM may not be able to complete the Telnet connection. This often depends on how many people are currently trying to open a Telnet connection with the remote system. If the Terminal Emulation window just sits on a message like "Trying 192.207.21.25" for a long time with no other activity, this is probably a good indication that the host is heavily overloaded. In that case, press Ctrl+] to cancel the connection attempt.

FIGURE 9.10.

A Telnet connection to the Online Career Center.

6. Once WinCIM has completed the Telnet connection and possibly the logon process, control of the Telnet connection is given to the operator. In this case, I was prompted with the message "Press RETURN to continue," but the actual message may vary depending on the site selected. On some systems, you may also be prompted for a user ID or some other information.

7. Hit the Return key, as prompted in Figure 9.10.

Most UNIX computers refer to the Enter key as the Return key. On most terminals, and when using WinCIM, these two terms are interchangeable.

Tip

8. You should now be presented with the menu of options similar to those shown in Figure 9.11. At this stage, you are on your own—but by reading the information displayed on the screen, it is usually not too hard to find your way around.

The Telnet connection that CompuServe makes to the Online Career Center automatically runs a Telnet-compatible version of Gopher. (See Chapter 13, "Gopher," for more information.) This allows you to navigate around the services offered by the Career Center by selecting from the numbers listed on menu items.

FIGURE 9.11.

The Online Career Center main menu.

At this stage, take some time to explore the options listed on the Gopher menus. If you do manage to get stuck, hitting the ? key should bring up a help menu. Failing that, hitting the escape sequence (Ctrl+]) will allow you to terminate the Telnet connection.

Manual Connections to Telnet

To demonstrate a manual connection to Telnet, let's look at the steps needed to connect to the InterNIC site discussed in previous chapters. When making a manual connection, you need to know the site's Telnet address and also have a valid user ID. For InterNIC, these are:

> Telnet address: `ds.internic.net`
>
> Log-in name: `guest`

As mentioned earlier, when you log onto most sites that support Telnet, you will need a user ID and password. Some sites, however, get around this requirement by offering a number of special guest user IDs, which allow people to log on without an individual user ID.

The InterNIC system is one of these services. Instead of logging on using a normal user ID, you use the special ID—guest. This automatically starts the InterNIC services program and completes your Telnet connection.

Note

There are also a number of other guest accounts available at the InterNIC site. These include Archie and Gopher, which launch specialized programs using Telnet. (See the "Archie Host Sites" topic in Chapter 10, "File Transfer Protocol (FTP)," for a full discussion of the Archie guest account.)

With the address information in hand, you can now connect to InterNIC by following these steps:

1. From the CompuServe Telnet Access window, highlight the "Access a specific site" option and click on the Select button.

2. WinCIM opens the dialog box shown in Figure 9.12. Type the Telnet address of the site you want to connect to in the Site Name field, and then hit the Enter key or click on the OK button to start the Telnet connection. To connect to InterNIC, type **ds.internic.net**.

FIGURE 9.12.

The Site Name dialog box.

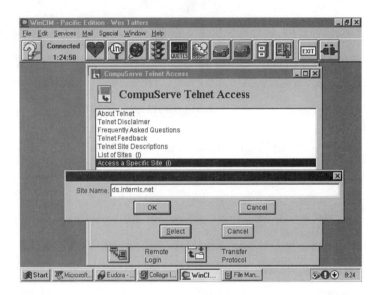

3. Like the automatic connections discussed previously, WinCIM will again display the You Are Leaving CompuServe alert box. Hit **P**roceed to acknowledge this message and open the Telnet connection.

4. Once the Terminal Emulation window opens, the connection process is displayed on the screen. After a short wait, the InterNIC Telnet server should respond and request a user ID. (See Figure 9.13.)

5. Enter guest as the user ID at the Login: prompt and hit the Enter Key.

Due to slight differences in the way some Telnet servers operate, on rare occasions hitting the Enter key results in "^m" being displayed on the screen. If this occurs, you need to use Ctrl+j to force Telnet to recognize a Return key.

FIGURE 9.13.

The InterNIC Telnet site waiting for a user ID.

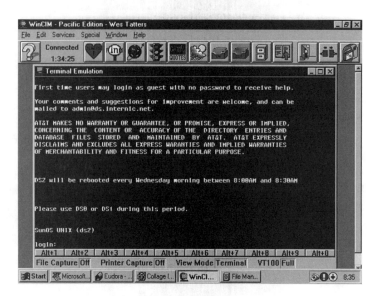

6. You are now presented with a number of housekeeping screens that tell you some information about the InterNIC. Once you've read each screen, hit the Enter key to proceed.

7. The last housekeeping screen asks you a question about the number of lines on your terminal. When using the WinCIM Terminal Emulation, simply hit the Enter key to accept the 24-line default.

If you have followed all the steps, you should now be logged onto the InterNIC Directory and Database Services Telnet connection. Like the Online Career Center, this system offers you a menu of options to choose from. (See Figure 9.14.)

FIGURE 9.14.

The main menu of the InterNIC Directory and Database Services.

Feel free to explore these options and maybe take a moment or two to look up some of the facilities that were discussed in previous chapters. A good place to start is the directory of RFCs and FYI documents or the Internet Directory of Directories.

When you have finished exploring the site, find your way back to the main menu and select the End Application option or hit the q key. This will close the Telnet connection and return you to WinCIM's CompuServe Telnet Access menu.

Port Numbers

During your travels, you may occasionally come across the address of a Telnet site that mentions something called a *port number*.

Port numbers are actually an internal addressing system used by Internet computers. Just as an IP address uniquely represents a computer connected to the Internet, a port number uniquely represents the different types of connections that can be made to a computer. For example, when you open a Telnet connection, you actually need to contact port 23 on the host system. A WWW client, on the other hand, needs to contact port 80, and a Gopher client port 70.

There is usually no need to worry about these port numbers, however, because each client automatically appends the correct default port number to any address she enters. Where you encounter problems, though, is when for some reason you need to connect to a port number other than the default for a particular service. You may encounter this situation when using Telnet to connect to MUDs or MOOs or some other multi-user games. Although these games are accessed using a Telnet client, they are usually not assigned to the default Telnet port.

For example, the MUD server located at `alexmud.stacken.kth.se` (mentioned in the CompuServe Telnet FAQ) is described as using port 4000 instead of port 23. To inform Telnet that this is the case, you need to append the port number to the Telnet address by separating them with a colon. Therefore, to connect to Alex's MUD site, you would enter the Telnet address as **lexmud.stacken.kth.se:4000**.

Security Issues

There are a number of security issues that arise when you begin to discuss remote login capabilities. Unfortunately, we don't live in a perfect world, and as a result sometimes people choose to abuse the services they are offered.

To protect yourself from such people and the effect they can have on computer systems, you need to consider the following issues when using services such as Telnet.

Passwords

The most important of these relates to the use of user IDs and passwords. Like your CompuServe ID, it is most important that you keep your passwords a secret to prevent other people from illegally using and abusing your connection privileges.

Unlike CompuServe, however, you will rarely be assigned a password on Internet systems. Instead, you will usually be asked to make up your own password. You should take great care when making up passwords to ensure you use a combination of letters that only you know. Also, never use any of the following:

◆ Your name

◆ Your birthday

◆ Your initials

◆ The word "password"

Although this may sound crazy, many people use one or a combination of these items in their password, and doing so only serves to tempt disaster.

To complicate matters further, due to the nature of the Internet, you should change your passwords on a regular basis to ensure that no prying eyes have managed to obtain a copy of your password information.

Credit Cards

From the time that online computer services began, the concept of electronic shopping has become a popular part of the Internet.

To enable these services to operate in a society that expects payment before delivery, credit cards have become a popular method of payment for electronic purchases. Although using such services is certainly convenient, you should make sure that you know exactly who you are dealing with before you ever consider giving someone your credit card details.

This also raises an important point about the security of information you send across the Internet. From the time a message leaves your computer to the time it arrives at its destination, it may have passed through any number of machines that may be able to both intercept and copy the message.

Although such practices are illegal, this does not mean that they don't sometimes occur. For this reason, as a rule you should avoid sending any confidential or private information across the Internet.

Public Key Encryption

Although these warnings may sound like a lot of doom and gloom, you do need to take them into consideration when using any of the Internet's communication services.

In fact, they have become so critical that some people have begun to experiment with ways to encode information distributed on the Internet, to prevent it from being read by the wrong people. Based on these experiments, a popular system known as *public key encryption* is now available to help protect your private information.

Appendix D examines one of these public key encryption systems and explains how to use it on the Internet.

Popular Telnet Sites

With over a million computers connected to the Internet, I could spend the rest of this book discussing the thousands of Internet sites that offer Telnet connections. Doing so, however, would only serve to duplicate the efforts of many others who have already spent considerable time and effort researching and exploring many of these sites.

Instead, this section looks briefly at each of the sites recommended by CompuServe in its Telnet Sites list, and then looks at some ways to locate other Telnet sites using the services offered by the Internet.

Sites Recommended by CompuServe

Although far from being an extensive list of Telnet sites, the short list offered by CompuServe provides a very good cross-section of the types of services available using Telnet.

Online Career Center

The Online Career Center is one of the most comprehensive online electronic job placement and career advice systems available anywhere in the world.

Using the Online Career Center, you can obtain up-to-date information about employment-related activities, obtain career assistance, and review college and university resume books. In addition, there is also an extensive database of current employment opportunities. Using keyword searches and other browse tools, you can review the thousands of job opportunities offered online and obtain application details and other relevant information. (See Figure 9.15.)

FIGURE 9.15.

The Online Career Center Jobs Search menu.

There is also a resume placement service that allows you to enter your resume or CV into a database that prospective employers can search when looking for new employees. As is the case with the job opportunities database, employers can search the resume database using keywords and location-specific queries.

Book Stacks Unlimited

This site is operated primarily as a commercial online bookstore. At last count, there were over 240,000 books listed in the Book Stacks Unlimited catalog, all indexed by author, title, keyword, ISBN, and even Dewey Decimal number.

Using the tools provided, you can search the catalog and request lists of relevant books. (See Figure 9.16.) When you find a book you are interested in, you can then place an order for it online and have the book delivered to your home or office. To assist you in choosing the right book, many books in the catalog are also accompanied by reviews that you can browse before placing your order.

FIGURE 9.16.

Books about the Internet at Book Stacks Unlimited.

Book Stacks Unlimited's online system also provides a number of customer services. These include public conference areas and a book review section where anyone can submit reviews of books they have read.

Note

> The first time you connect to this site, you will be asked to enter your full name and then select a password. This information will be stored on the Book Stacks Unlimited system, along with some other information you are required to enter once you log on. You should make a note of this password so you won't need to go through the registration process the next time you log onto the system.

Friends and Partners

The Friends and Partners initiative is a joint venture between the people of the United States and the people of the former Soviet Union.

Based around the capabilities offered by the World Wide Web, this Telnet connection example uses Lynx—a text-based World Wide Web client—to provide terminal-based access to the World Wide Web, and more specifically the Friends and Partners project. (See Figure 9.17.)

FIGURE 9.17.

Lynx—the Telnet-compatible World Wide Web client.

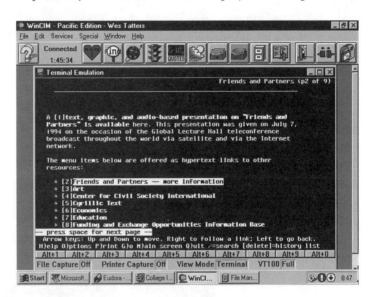

The purpose behind this project is simple. For the better part of the 20th Century, the peoples and cultures of the former Soviet Union and those of the United States have been completely isolated. Now, by providing a common meeting place, the Friends and Partners project is seeking to close the gaps created by this isolation.

In creating this project, its designers have set themselves no small task. To quote from the information CompuServe provided about the project, they seek to "Create and link together information on our nation's histories; our art, music, literature, and religion; our educational and scientific resources; our business and economic opportunities; our geography and natural resources, our languages; and our opportunities for communicating, traveling, and working together."

Moving around the Lynx environment is somewhat different than using the Gopher-styled menus seen previously in this chapter. This is due to the fact that Lynx is based on the World Wide Web navigation system.

Using Lynx, the menu items are often buried within the text displayed on the screen. These are what the World Wide Web calls *hypertext links.* To select one of these links, use your arrow keys to move the highlighted box over the item you want to select, and then hit the Enter key to choose the item.

Although this site offers a good example of how Telnet can be used to gain access to the World Wide Web, to get the most out of it you really need to use a dedicated World Wide Web client such as Spry Mosaic, as discussed in Chapter 11, "The World Wide Web."

Federal Information Exchange

This Telnet site is operated by a private company called the Federal Information Exchange, Inc. Its job is to provide information to the public about business opportunities within the U.S. Federal Government. This includes public grants, tenders, draft proposals, and a wide variety of other potential business partnerships.

In addition, this site also houses the Minority On-Line Information Service, which contains numerous publications, journals, and discussion papers dealing with minority issues.

Like the Friends and Partners project, this Telnet service also uses Lynx to provide World Wide Web hypertext access to the information it provides. Of special note here, however, is the Lynx Tutorial, available from the main logon page. (See Figure 9.18.) If you are interested in learning more about using Lynx, this tutorial is a very good place to start.

FIGURE 9.18.

The Federal Information Exchange offers a very good Lynx Tutorial.

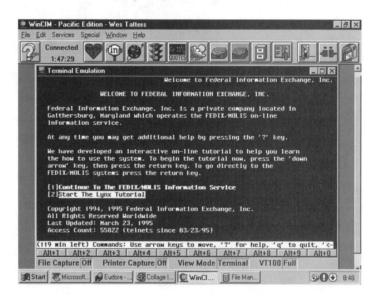

The University of Minnesota Gopher

The main reason for this Telnet example is to demonstrate the capabilities that Gopher systems offer to Telnet users. Based at the University of Minnesota, this Gopher server is regarded by many to be the home of Gopher itself. (See Figure 9.19.)

Although Telnet will certainly give you access to Gopher services, for serious *Gopherspace* exploration, a dedicated navigator such as a Gopher or WWW client offers a far better alternative. (See Chapter 13, "Gopher," for a full discussion of Gopher and Gopherspace.)

FIGURE 9.19.

The Home Gopher server at the University of Minnesota.

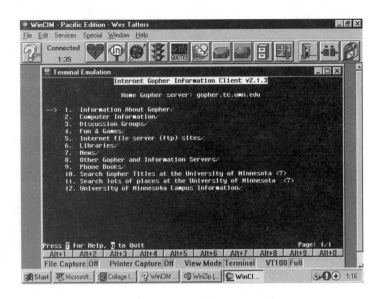

When you Telnet to some systems, such as the Minnesota Gopher server, you will be asked to enter the type of terminal you are using. If you are ever asked for this information, enter **vt100**.

Note

NASA Spacelink

To cater to the persistent fascination many people have for all things interplanetary, NASA has set up a Gopher server to provide up-to-the-minute information about the many projects it conducts.

The service also caters to the wide variety of educational institutions that frequent the system, offering materials and resources for all grades from kindergarten though post-graduate studies. To complement this material, the NASA News Service contains a regularly updated directory of all news releases, shuttle and space probe status reports, and even the complete shuttle launch schedule.

If up-to-the-minute isn't good enough for you, NASA also offers a Hot Topics menu, which covers late-breaking stories and details of current and upcoming shuttle missions. (See Figure 9.20.)

Other Places of Interest

The best source of information about the addresses of Telnet sites is the Internet itself. Over the years, a number of comprehensive lists have been developed that offer users a good guide to the types of Telnet sites available.

FIGURE 9.20.

Hot Topics on the NASA Spacelink Gopher server.

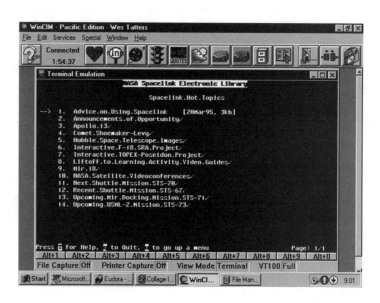

The Big Dummies Guide to the Internet

One of the most popular sources of information, not only about Telnet but also about the Internet in general, is a publicly available document known as the *Big Dummies Guide to the Internet*. Recently renamed the *Electronic Frontier Foundation's (Extended) Guide to the Internet*, this document is available from many locations.

An up-to-date copy can always be found in Section 2 of the Internet New Users forum (GO INETFORUM). The filename to look for is NTGD31.ZIP, although this may change in the future.

Tip

> Files ending with the extension .ZIP use a special compression technique to reduce the size of the file. Before you can use a file compressed in this fashion, you need to run it through a special program to decompress the file, expanding it back to normal size. Appendix D looks at two programs that perform this decompression for you—WinZip and WinPack.

An online version of the guide is also available for use with WWW clients. The Electronic Frontier Foundation operates such a version on its WWW server at www.eff.org. If you want to jump straight to the home page for the EFF guide, you can do this by calling up this http address: http://www.eff.org/papers/eegtti/eegtitop.html. (See Figure 9.21.)

HYTELNET

Without a doubt, the most comprehensive listing of Telnet sites is maintained by a program known as HYTELNET. This service contains the addresses of hundreds of Telnet sites located on computers in all parts of the world. Until recently, the University of Saskatchewan offered a public Telnet site running HYTELNET, but its popularity grew to such an extent that the service had to be closed.

FIGURE 9.21.

The EFF Guide to the Internet provides an ideal introduction to many Internet services.

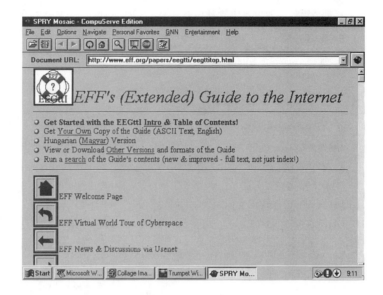

In its place, a WWW page was created that offers the same capabilities without the problems associated with the direct Telnet connection version. (See Figure 9.22.) You can reach this page at `http://www.usask.ca/cgi-bin/hytelnet`.

FIGURE 9.22.

HYTELNET lists hundreds of Telnet sites.

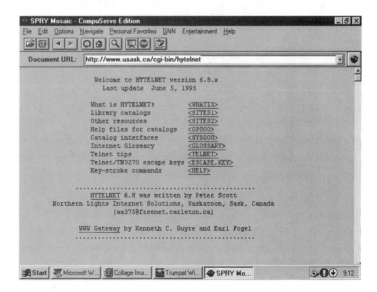

Other Favorites

If you're still hungry for more Telnet sites, here is a list of some additional sites that you might like to explore, in no particular order. For each site, I have listed the domain name and, where necessary, the port number. When you Telnet to most of these sites you will be logged on automatically, but for those where you aren't, I have also listed the appropriate user ID you will need to use to log in.

Table 9.1. Popular Telnet sites.

Address	Login	Description
news.janet.ac.uk	news	JANET news desk
locis.loc.gov	N/A	The U.S. Library of Congress information database
madlab.sprl.umich.edu:3000	N/A	Weather, crop, and ski reports
consultant.micro.umn.edu	gopher	The Online Electronic Books initiative
quake.think.com	wais	Wide Area Information server at Thinking Machines
enews.com	enews	The Electronic Newsstand
info.umd.edu	N/A	The University of Maryland Information Service
leo.nmc.edu	visitor	Traverse City Free-Net
cdnow.com	N/A	CDnow!: The Internet Music Store
martini.eecs.umich.edu:3000	N/A	The Geographic Name server
baymoo.sfsu.edu:8888	guest	BayMOO—Palo Alto, California

Summary

For the avid Internet explorer, Telnet offers access to many unique and varied services. Using the global connectivity offered by the Internet, it is possible to connect to computer systems all over the world from the comfort of your own home.

Yet despite these capabilities, during the past two years the popularity of Telnet has begun to wane. As most existing Telnet sites move their services onto Gopher and World Wide Web servers, the need to use Telnet has been greatly reduced for many people. Regardless of this decline, you can rest assured that Telnet will be around for many years to come.

As you have seen in this chapter, Telnet still has a lot to offer the Internet user. What's more, when combined with services such as Gopher and WWW, it opens up a whole new range of connection possibilities.

More importantly, Telnet is not the only service that allows you to log onto remote computer systems. Using FTP—Telnet's sister service—you can connect to remote computers and retrieve copies of files, documents, and computer programs.

The next chapter, "File Transfer Protocol (FTP)," looks at how this service works and examines a number of computer archives and mirror sites containing Internet computer software.

CHAPTER 10

FILE TRANSFER PROTOCOL (FTP)

The reason many people first purchase a modem is not to explore the World Wide Web or reap the benefits of electronic mail. Instead, it is to log onto local bulletin boards (BBSs) and download copies of games and other computer files.

While they are connected to these BBS systems, most people inevitably discover e-mail and discussion forums, but for many the main attraction remains the downloading of files. This love affair with inexpensive access to copies of computer software and games has not been lost on the Internet world, either. Using the tools discussed in this chapter, it has been estimated that Internet users have access to more than 300 gigabytes, or the equivalent of over 400 CD-ROMs worth of computer files.

To obtain access to these files, the Internet uses a program known as the *file transfer program* and its corresponding communications protocol, the *file transfer protocol*. It is common practice to refer to both by the common acronym FTP. Through FTP (the program and protocol), it is possible to log onto thousands of remote computer systems and transfer copies of the files they contain onto your own computer.

This chapter explores the use of FTP and some of the tools that assist you in locating files available via FTP by discussing these topics:

◆ What Is FTP?

◆ FTP Archives and CompuServe

◆ Using WinCIM with FTP

◆ Archie

What Is FTP?

The file transfer program is in many ways a special version of Telnet. As was the case with Telnet, you use FTP to log onto remote computer systems. Whereas Telnet lets you use the remote computer as though it were directly connected to your local computer, FTP uses similar techniques to exchange files between your computer and the remote system.

The File Transfer Protocol

To achieve this, FTP uses a client-server environment that allows your computer and the remote computer to communicate using a *file transfer protocol.*

This is yet another example of a remote computer running special server software and your computer running a local client program. In this case, the remote computer needs to be running an FTP server while your computer runs an FTP client. Using this set of programs, you can open a connection with a remote host computer, access and retrieve copies of the files stored on its disk drives, and in some cases transfer files to the remote system as well.

In the early days of the Internet, the similarities between FTP and Telnet did not stop at just the logon process. Visually, running FTP was very much like running a Telnet terminal. To browse the directories on the remote computer, the user entered commands such as **ls** or **dir** using a terminal-like interface, and to change directories he issued commands like **cd /pub**.

For people who were comfortable with the vagaries of DOS or UNIX, these commands were quite familiar. But as more and more people with little understanding of the workings of command line-based interfaces began to use FTP, more elegant interfaces were designed that allowed these commands to be hidden from the user. Modern FTP clients—like the one in WinCIM—now use point-and-click menus and action buttons to navigate through remote directories and send or receive files.

FTP Sites on the Internet

Obviously, if FTP allows you to log onto remote computers, there must be computers on the Internet that allow you to log onto them.

These computer sites fall into two basic categories: private FTP sites, which require you to have an account with the site before you can FTP to it, and public sites, which allow anyone to log on. This chapter deals mainly with public sites. However, for those of you who have access to private FTP sites, the steps involved are identical.

Like the guest accounts provided by some Telnet servers, FTP also uses a special account to permit users to log onto public FTP sites. The account name used by FTP for this purpose is *anonymous*. To reflect the use of this account name, publicly accessible FTP sites are commonly known as *anonymous FTP servers*.

Domain Names

Like all computers connected to the Internet, FTP sites are referred to by domain names.

For the most part, these domain names are easily recognizable as belonging to an FTP server, due to the fact that they are usually prefixed with ftp. For example, the FTP site operated by my Internet service provider at world.net uses the domain name ftp.world.net. Although this is not a hard-and-fast rule, it is a handy way to work out the most probable domain name for an FTP site.

If you were trying to find the domain name for Spry's FTP server, it would be reasonable to assume it to be ftp.spry.com. The first part, ftp, describes it as an FTP server, followed by .spry to represent the name of the organization and .com to indicate that it is a commercial operation.

> When using WinCIM, you can substitute a site's IP address wherever a domain name is requested.

Note

Internet Archives

Many of these sites have also become known by another name due to the nature of the files they contain. In recent years, the terms *FTP archive* and *Internet archive* have become popular when referring to a special group of FTP sites that contain entire collections of files covering many types of computer systems. (See "CompuServe's List of Sites" later in this chapter for a discussion of some of these archives.)

These archive sites contain copies of literally thousands of public domain and shareware computer programs. In addition, there are copies of transcripts from popular newsgroups and mailing lists, graphics, photographs, sound files, and a wide variety of text files and documents covering just about every topic known to man. Basically, if a file has ever been publicly distributed by computer, chances are that a copy of it will be available from one of the Internet FTP archives.

Hosts and Mirrors

As a result of the sheer number of files located in these FTP archives, the number of people who want to access them at any one time can become quite large. Like any computer system, there comes a point when the system cannot handle any more connection requests. When this happens, any additional users who attempt to open an FTP connection are effectively locked out.

To cope with this overload problem, some of the major FTP archives are now duplicated on other computer systems in different parts of the world. These sites are said to *mirror* the main FTP archive because they contain exact copies of all the files stored on the main site. As a result, if you are locked out of an FTP archive because it is overloaded, it is possible that the file you are looking for may be available from one of the archive's mirror sites.

Note

> Although not all FTP sites have mirrors, in many cases copies of files can be found at completely unrelated sites as well. To assist you with the task of finding these files, a program called Archie was developed to create a global index of all FTP sites. (See the "Archie" section later in this chapter for more information.)

CompuServe File Libraries

When CompuServe announced the availability of FTP access using WinCIM, few of CompuServe's users realized the powerful resource they had been given. For the most part, this is due to the extensive library of files already available to CompuServe users in its forums and on ZIFFNET. Yet in reality, FTP is the ideal complement to CompuServe's file libraries.

There are files available at FTP sites that will never be available in CompuServe's own libraries, and likewise some of the files stored on CompuServe are not available on the Internet. In this sense, by combining the two resources, CompuServe brings the best of both worlds to its users.

CompuServe and FTP

Like Telnet and Usenet, CompuServe lets you use FTP in much the same manner as you'd use any of CompuServe's standard services. In this way, you don't need to learn a new program for each service. Instead, all you need to do is learn how to use one or two new windows displayed by WinCIM itself.

Internet Services

FTP is one of the services offered by CompuServe Internet Services in the Internet Services window. To open this window, click on the traffic light icon located on the WinCIM Toolbar. (See Figure 10.1.)

FIGURE 10.1.
The Go icon is represented by a set of traffic lights.

This opens the Go... dialog box shown in Figure 10.2. Using this dialog box, you can tell WinCIM to open any of the forums and services CompuServe offers. In this case you want to call up Internet Services. To do this, type **internet** into the Go... dialog box and hit Enter.

FIGURE 10.2.
The Go... dialog box lets you move around inside CompuServe.

Opening the Internet Services window gives you access to all the tools and forums provided under the CompuServe Internet Services banner. From here you can move easily to any Internet Service by clicking on the appropriate menu item or icon.

FTP is represented here by the icon indicated in Figure 10.3 by the arrow cursor. Click on this icon to open up the FTP Services window.

FIGURE 10.3.
The Internet Services window gives you access to all Internet tools and forums.

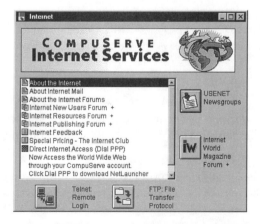

The File Transfer Protocol Window

The File Transfer Protocol window (Figure 10.4) provides you with the means of accessing all of the FTP-related services currently provided by CompuServe. From this window you can access information about FTP, choose any of the FTP services, and even open CompuServe's own file finder.

FIGURE 10.4.

The File Transfer Protocol window.

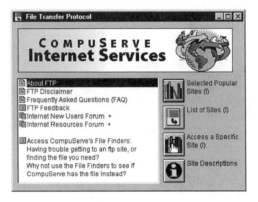

The following pages examine all of the options available through this window and look at the steps involved in retrieving a file using FTP.

> To call up the File Transfer Protocol window without first opening the Internet window, open the Go... dialog box and type **ftp** instead of **internet.**

Information Updates

Before you proceed any further, now would be a good time to take a look at the information offered in the first four items listed in the File Transfer Protocol window.

These items contain information about late-breaking FTP news and offer valuable assistance if you encounter any difficulties while using FTP. You should pay special attention to the Frequently Asked Questions (FAQ) item, which contains a list of answers to problems and operational queries regularly asked by CompuServe members.

Internet Support Forums

The File Transfer Protocol menu also allows you to open the two Internet Support forums provided by CompuServe. If you are encountering difficulties using FTP, or maybe just want to know the domain name of a good FTP site, the Internet New Users forums are a good place to start.

Like the File Transfer Protocol FAQ, these forums are a good place to turn for help. Because people like yourself ask questions and receive answers to their problems on these forums every day, it is highly likely that the answers to your questions have already been discussed. In this sense, the New Users forums are like a 24-hour help line. To find out more about what these forums have to offer, see Chapter 14, "Internet Resources on CompuServe."

CompuServe's File Finders

In many cases, copies of files you plan to retrieve using FTP are probably also stored in one of CompuServe's forum libraries.

For this reason, you should first search CompuServe's libraries using one of its file finders (Figure 10.5) before trying to retrieve them though FTP. In the long run this can save you both time and money, especially if the FTP site you want to connect to is busy and no mirror sites are available.

FIGURE 10.5.

The CompuServe File Finders main menu.

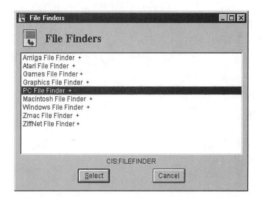

To access the CompuServe file finders, click on the last item shown in the File Transfer Protocol window. This calls up the File Finders window.

From this window, you can easily search any of the file libraries located on CompuServe by following these steps:

1. Firstly, you need to decide what type of file you want to find. In this case, let's look for any recent files that contain lists of anonymous FTP sites.

2. Select the file finder that most closely relates to this criterion. It is likely that such lists can be located in either the PC or Mac file finders, so highlight the PC File Finder option and click on the **S**elect button. (Double-clicking on the PC File Finder item will also achieve the same purpose.)

3. You should now see a window with the title PC File Finder, similar to that shown in Figure 10.6. In addition to providing access to the PC File Finder search options, the items listed in this menu also offer some good advice and various tips about how to use CompuServe's file finders. The first time you use a file finder, it is a good idea to spend some time familiarizing yourself with the information these items provide.

FIGURE 10.6.

The PC File Finder main menu.

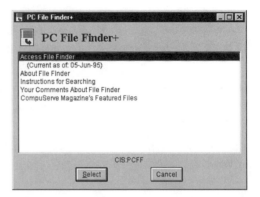

4. To open the PC file finder itself, highlight the Access File Finder option and click on the **S**elect button. This opens the Select Search Criteria window, shown in Figure 10.7. Using the items displayed in this menu, you can define a list of *keywords* that describe the files you are looking for. You can also narrow down the search by including:

◆ Submission dates

◆ Forum names

◆ File types

◆ File extensions

◆ Filenames

◆ File submitters

FIGURE 10.7.

Select Search Criteria lets you define the types of files you are looking for.

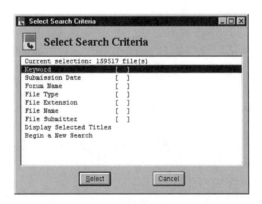

5. To look for files containing lists of FTP sites, highlight the Keyword item and click the **S**elect button. This action opens the Keywords dialog box (Figure 10.8), which allows you to enter up to three keywords relating to the files you are looking for. Where possible, try to use all three keywords to limit the number of files located. In Figure 10.8 I entered **internet**, **ftp,** and **sites** as the keywords.

FIGURE 10.8.

You can enter up to three keywords for every search.

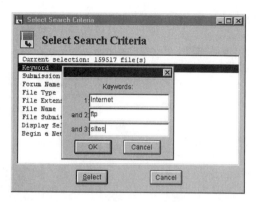

A similar result would also be obtained by just entering **ftp** and **sites** as keywords. However, you should try to narrow down the search as much as possible. Even though it is highly unlikely that the **ftp** and **sites** keywords would be used in conjunction with files not related to the Internet, adding **internet** as a keyword ensures that only Internet-specific files are found.

6. When you click on the OK button, WinCIM performs a search based on the keywords you enter. When it completes the search, it reports the number of files found on the Current Selection line located at the top of the Select Search Criteria window. (See Figure 10.9.)

FIGURE 10.9.

WinCIM located seven files that possibly contain a list of Internet FTP sites.

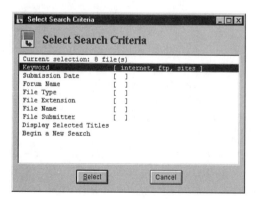

7. Although not totally necessary due to the small number of files the keyword search returns, you can refine the search further by adding additional criteria. For example, select the Submission Date item. This opens a dialog box that lets you define the oldest file you are interested in looking at. Because I was only interested in the most recent list of FTP sites, entering **02/24/95** into the Start Date dialog box limited the search to files that were no more than 2 months old. (See Figure 10.10.)

FIGURE 10.10.

The Start Date dialog box lets you indicate the oldest file you want to look at.

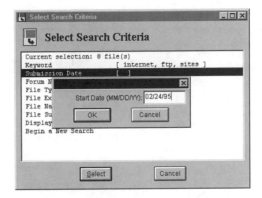

8. Once you are satisfied that all your search criteria have been met, click on the Display Selected Titles option, highlighted in Figure 10.11, to request a listing of all the files located by the search.

FIGURE 10.11.

With two criteria selected, WinCIM reports that only five files meet your requirements.

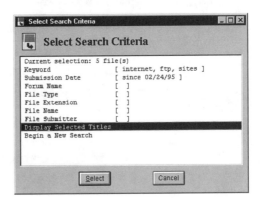

9. Judging from the list shown in Figure 10.12, it would appear that CompuServe does indeed have a file that meets your needs precisely. To make certain, double-click on the file's description line to request a more detailed description of the file's contents. (See Figure 10.13.)

10. From this dialog box, you can download a copy of the file by clicking on the **R**etrieve button. In addition, if the file is an ASCII text file, clicking on the **V**iew button will allow you to examine the file's contents.

FIGURE 10.12.

The Display Selected Titles option opens a window that lists the search results.

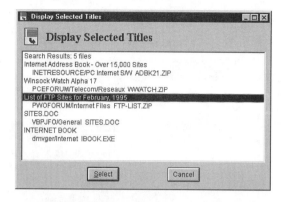

FIGURE 10.13.

The Description dialog box lets you download a copy of the selected file.

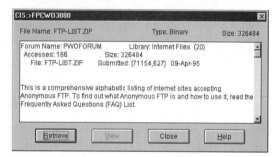

Using WinCIM for FTP Connections

Now that you are familiar with the support that CompuServe provides for FTP, it is time to look at how to use WinCIM to connect to an FTP site.

There are four buttons down the right side of the File Transfer Protocol window. (See Figure 10.14.) The first three provide you with different methods of connecting to FTP sites, and the fourth button gives you a description of all the sites recommended by CompuServe.

FIGURE 10.14.

You access the FTP connection options using the buttons down the right side of the File Transfer Protocol window.

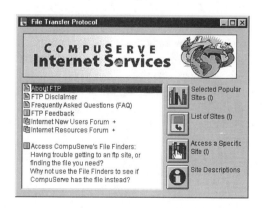

Connecting to a Popular Site

Clicking on the Selected Popular Sites button opens the window shown in Figure 10.15. Listed in this window are eight of the most popular FTP sites that are currently available on the Internet. Between them, these sites provide access to files covering nearly every resource you could possibly need.

FIGURE 10.15.

Selected popular FTP sites recommended by CompuServe.

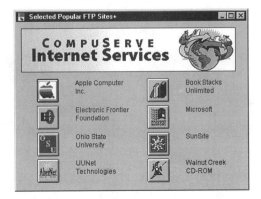

CompuServe has chosen these sites because they represent a good cross section of the sites available on the Internet, and also because they tend to provide access to files that may not be available on CompuServe. Two of these sites are of special importance as well, because they represent the primary locations for access to support files dealing with Apple Computers and Microsoft computer software.

Logging On

To open an FTP connection with one of these sites, all you need to do is the following:

1. Click on the button that represents the site you want to connect to. Let's say you're interested in obtaining a new Internet add-on for Microsoft Windows. Click on the Microsoft button.

2. After a few seconds, WinCIM displays the Access a Specific Site window, shown in Figure 10.16. Because you selected a recommended site, CompuServe has already filled in all the information needed to open the FTP connection. Before you go on, let's look briefly at what WinCIM has done. In the Site Name field, CompuServe has entered Microsoft's domain name, `ftp.microsoft.com`, and has placed anonymous in the User Name field to indicate that you need to use the anonymous FTP facility to connect to Microsoft. You should also note that WinCIM has entered your Internet address in the Password field. This is a requirement for most anonymous FTP connections that allows the FTP site to keep a record of every user who connects to that site. In most cases, if you do not type your Internet address in the Password field, the FTP site will prevent the FTP connection from occurring. That leaves you with one field unaccounted for. By default, WinCIM leaves the Directory field empty so

that when the FTP connection opens, you start off in the remote site's *root* directory. If you happen to know the exact location of the file that you are looking for, you can enter the directory path to the file in this field.

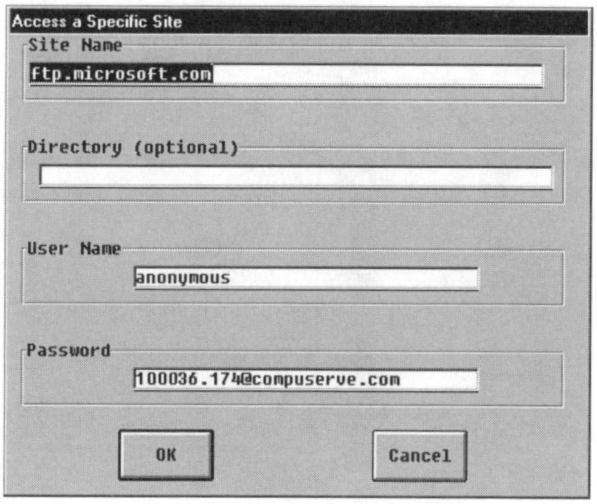

FIGURE 10.16.

The Access a Specific Site window shows the information needed to open an FTP connection.

Access a Specific Site

Site Name
`Ftp.microsoft.com`

Directory (optional)

User Name
`anonymous`

Password
`100036.174@compuserve.com`

OK   Cancel

3. Click on the OK button to open the FTP connection with `ftp.microsoft.com`.

4. Once the connection between CompuServe and the remote FTP site is complete, a welcome message will appear on the screen, similar to the one displayed in Figure 10.17. You should also note that the standard WinCIM toolbar has been replaced by a smaller toolbar. Working from left to right, the buttons on this toolbar allow you to open the WinCIM online help system; print the contents of the current Information Manager text box (when you view the contents of a file located at an FTP site, you can print a copy by clicking on this icon); save a copy of the contents on the current Information Manager text box; leave FTP without disconnecting from CompuServe; disconnect from CompuServe without closing WinCIM; and disconnect from CompuServe and then close WinCIM.

If WinCIM is unable to complete the FTP connection for some reason, it will display a message advising you of the problems it is encountering. (See "Troubleshooting" later in this chapter for a discussion of what these messages mean.)

5. After reading the message, click on the OK Button to open the WinCIM FTP Client window.

You should now be logged onto the Microsoft FTP site, looking at a screen showing the contents of the root directory. The next section looks at how to use this screen to explore an FTP site.

FIGURE 10.17.

The Microsoft FTP site Welcome message.

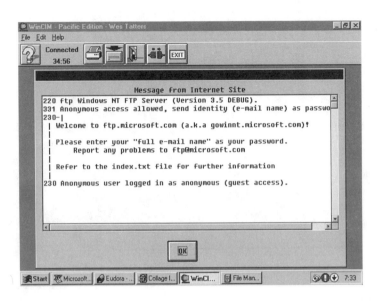

Working with WinCIM's FTP Client

When the connection process is completed, your screen should look like Figure 10.18. The main feature of this screen is the FTP Client Navigation dialog box. Using this dialog box, you can move through the directories located on remote FTP sites and send and receive files with the tools provided.

FIGURE 10.18.

The WinCIM FTP Client lets you navigate easily around remote sites.

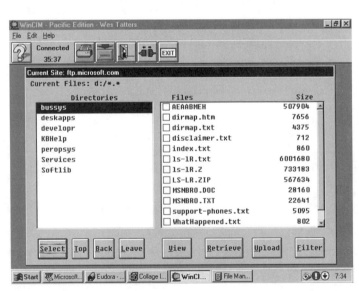

The dialog box is broken into three main areas that deal with the different tools you use to manage an FTP connection: the Directories window, the Files window, and navigation buttons.

The Directories Window

Files at FTP sites are organized using a hierarchical structure similar to that used by MS-DOS. All files are stored in directories and subdirectories, starting at a root directory. When you first connect to an FTP site, the window on the left side of the dialog box lists all the subdirectories accessible from this root directory.

By double-clicking on any of these subdirectories, you can move down the directory tree. As you move into successive directory layers, the Current Files: message in the top-left section of the dialog box will change to reflect the location of the current directory.

When you first connect to an FTP site, the Current Files: message will show something like `d:/*.*`, as shown in Figure 10.18. When you double-click on the `deskapps` directory, this message will change to `d:/deskapps/*.*` to reflect the fact that you have moved to a new directory. The information listed in the Directories area will also change to show the subdirectories accessible from the `deskapps` directory, which is now the current directory.

The Files Window

To correspond with the information listed in the Directories area, the window on the opposite side of the dialog box contains a list of all the files available in the current directory, as indicated by the Current Files: message.

Both the name and size of each file are listed in alphabetical order, with a small box drawn in front of each. This box is a *check box*, which you use to select the file or files you want to retrieve. When you click on a file to select it, an X is placed in the box, and if you click on it again the file is deselected and the X removed.

Navigation Buttons

To help you work with the information displayed in the Directories and Files windows, there are two groups of buttons across the bottom of the dialog box. The first group is used to navigate through the FTP site's directories:

Select	Open the currently highlighted subdirectory and make it the new current directory.
Top	Return to the root directory and update the Directories and Files windows to reflect this change.
Back	Move one level back to the next highest directory level and refresh the Directories and Files windows to reflect this change.
Leave	Close the FTP connection and return to CompuServe.

The second group serves a slightly different purpose. It lets you control all the actions possible when dealing with the files stored at an FTP site. Clicking on one of these buttons instructs the FTP client to perform the following actions:

View	If any of the currently selected files—ones with X in their check boxes—are ASCII text files, clicking on this button will display their contents in a Message window.

Retrieve   Clicking on this button will retrieve copies of any files that have their check boxes selected.

Upload   Using this button, it is possible to send copies of files located on your computer to a remote FTP site.

> Not all FTP sites will permit you to send them files, and in most cases those that do will let you upload files only to certain directories. On sites that do allow you to upload files, there is usually an /incoming directory set aside for that purpose.

Filter   This button allows you to define the types of files displayed in the Files window.

Important Files at FTP Sites

In the root directory of each FTP site, you will usually find a number of special files with information that can help you find your way around the site. The next section shows you how to view and retrieve copies of these files, but for the time being, all you really need to be aware of is what they contain.

index.txt

A good place to start when connecting to any FTP site is the index.txt file, sometimes also called just index or INDEX. This file will usually contain a description of every file in the root directory. Reading this file gives you a good idea about which files contain information about the site's contents.

The root directory is not the only place that you'll find index.txt files. In most cases there will be an index.txt file in each directory as well, containing a list of the files that it contains.

ls-lR.txt

The ls-lR.txt file always contains a full directory listing of all the files held at the site. As a result, this file can often be quite large. When this happens, you may also find a file with a name such as ls-lR.ZIP or ls-lR.Z. If this file exists, it contains a compressed version of the ls-lR file, which you will need to decompress once you retrieve a copy of it.

On some sites, you will find that the ls-lR.txt file is listed as just ls-lR. In fact, this is the original name given to these directory files, and actually represents the command used on UNIX computers to generate the list.

dirmap.txt

A number of sites also provide an abbreviated version of the ls-lR file that lists the directories without their contents. This file is often referred to as a directory map, hence the name dirmap.txt or dirmap.

readme.txt

You should also pay close attention to any `readme`, `read.me`, or `readme.txt` files stored in the root directory. These files often contain important information about the way the site is operated and special details regarding the files it contains.

.message

Some directories, including the root directory, contain special information that, when you're using some FTP clients, is displayed every time you change directories. The current version of WinCIM does not display this information automatically, but it does allow you to read these files once you enter the directory.

They are listed in the Files window using the name `.message`. If you find that some strange things are happening in a directory that contains a `.message` file, reading this file may help to explain what is going on.

links.txt

Some sites use a special process to create connections between their different directories. These connections, called *linked directories,* allow you to move quickly from one directory to a different directory, possibly on a different hard drive or in a completely different path.

For example, at `ftp.cdrom.com`, a number of its archives are stored in directories with names such as `/.1` or other cryptic descriptions. To get around this problem, they have a directory called `/pub/` that consists entirely of links to these cryptic locations. In `/pub/` these cryptic directories are described using names such as `/pub/doom` and `/pub/games`, which you must agree are much easier to understand.

However, not all FTP clients are able to handle these special links. To get around this problem, most sites that use these links will include a file called `links.txt` that shows you how these directories are linked together.

> The current version of WinCIM does support the use of directory links, but this situation may change in the future.

Retrieving a File

The Internet add-on for Microsoft Word that I mentioned in the "Logging On" section is stored in one of the subdirectories at `ftp.microsoft.com`.

You can describe the location of this file by writing down the path you need to follow to reach it, starting at the FTP site's root directory. The path to the file you are looking for is `/deskapps/word/winword-public/ia`.

This path indicates that the file is stored in the ia directory, which is a subdirectory of winword-public. In turn, winword-public is a subdirectory of word, and word of deskapps. Because deskapps is the first directory listed, this indicates that it is a subdirectory of the root directory.

To retrieve a copy of this file once you are connected to an FTP site, follow these steps:

1. To get to the ia directory using WinCIM, you use the Directories window to move from the root directory through each successively lower directory level. In the Directories window shown in Figure 10.19, you can see that the first subdirectory, deskapps, is listed as one of those available from the Microsoft FTP root directory. Click on this directory to highlight it, and then hit the **S**elect navigation button to make it the new current directory.

> By entering a file's full path into the directory field on the Access a Specific Site window, you can instruct WinCIM to open this subdirectory instead of opening the root directory when it first connects to an FTP site.

FIGURE 10.19.

Highlight the deskapps subdirectory and hit the Select button.

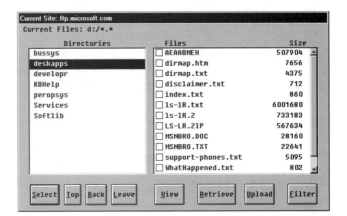

2. Once you hit the **S**elect button, WinCIM sends a message to the remote FTP site to request a change of directory. When WinCIM receives a response from the FTP site, the Current Files: message changes to d:/deskapps/*.*. At the same time, the information displayed in the Directories window will also be updated, as shown in Figure 10.20.

3. Listed in this updated Directory window should be word, the next directory listed in the file's path. Click on this subdirectory to highlight it and again hit the **S**elect button to move down another level. Alternatively, double-clicking in the subdirectory will perform the same action.

FIGURE 10.20.

Microsoft's deskapps *directory.*

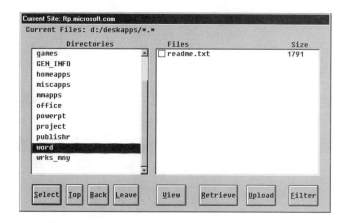

If there are more subdirectories than can fit in the Directories window, you may need to use the scroll bar to the right of the window to display the rest of the list.

4. Now repeat step three twice, once to move down into winword-public and then again to open the ia directory.

5. Now that you have reached the correct directory, it is time to turn your attention to the Files window. (See Figure 10.21.)

FIGURE 10.21.

The Files window lists all the files stored in the ia *directory.*

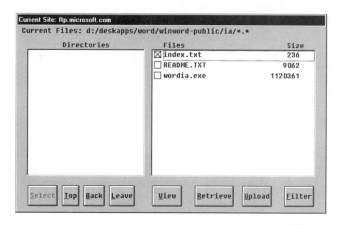

There are three files stored in this directory, each of which serves a different purpose:

index.txt   At most FTP sites, there is a special file stored in each directory that describes its contents. In this case the file is called index.txt, but at other sites it may simply be called index. To look at the contents of this file, click on it to toggle its check box, as shown in Figure 10.21, and then hit the **V**iew button located below the Files window. This tells WinCIM to request a copy of the `index.txt` file. When the file arrives, it will be displayed in an Information Manager message window similar to the one shown Figure 10.22.

FIGURE 10.22.

WinCIM displays the contents of `index.txt` in a message window.

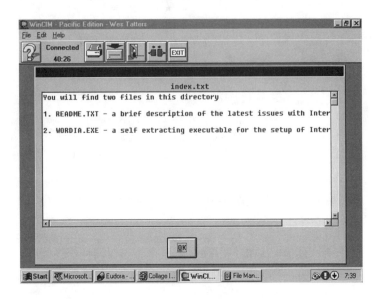

`readme.txt`   Depending on the FTP site, large files are often accompanied by a small description file. This file is designed to tell you about the contents of the larger file before you download it. The name of this file usually takes one of two forms: `readme.txt` if there is only one main file in the directory, or `filename.readme` if there is more than one main file. However, `filename` would be replaced by `wordia.exe` without its extension, resulting in `wordia.readme`. Like the `index.txt` file, these files can be looked at by hitting the **V**iew button.

> If more than one text file is selected when you hit the **V**iew button, each file will be retrieved and displayed in the message window, one after the other.

`wordia.exe`   By reading through the `index.txt` and `readme.txt` files, it would appear that this is the file you are looking for.

6. To retrieve a copy of this file, select it by toggling its check box and then hit the **R**etrieve button.

7. WinCIM opens a Save Requester similar to that shown in Figure 10.23. By default, all retrieved files are stored in your local `/cserve/download` directory using the same name as that used at the remote FTP site. However, by using this Requester you can change

the directory and even the filename before commencing the transfer. Once you are happy with the name of the file and the location where it will be stored, click on the OK button.

FIGURE 10.23.

Click OK to store
wordia.exe in the
/cserve/download
directory.

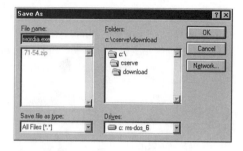

8. When you click on the OK button, the remote FTP site will then be asked to commence the transfer process. Once the transfer begins, WinCIM will display a progress dialog box indicating how much of the file has been received and the estimated time remaining. (See Figure 10.24.)

FIGURE 10.24.

The Cancel button allows
you to stop the transfer at
any time.

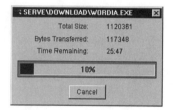

> Depending on the number of requests an FTP site is handling, the transfer speed may sometimes fall below an acceptable standard. In these situations, it is often better to abort the transfer by clicking on the Cancel button and to make another attempt at a later time.

Tip

9. When the transfer is complete, the progress dialog closes and you are returned to the FTP Client dialog. From here you can retrieve additional files or hit the **Leave** button to close the FTP connection.

Uploading a File

This option is one that most people will rarely—if ever—need to use, although the steps needed to upload files are fairly simple:

1. Connect to the site where you want to upload a file. I connected to the Electronic Frontier Foundation FTP site for this example. This site permits users to upload files that relate to the issues it deals with.

2. In the root directory of this site, there is a `readme.incoming` file that outlines the site's upload requirements. This file tells you that all files should be uploaded to the `incoming` directory and each must be accompanied by a separate `readme` file outlining the new file's contents.

Tip

> Before you upload files to any site, make sure that you have read all the relevant documentation. This includes any `readme`, `read.me`, `readme.txt`, and `readme.incoming` files located in a site's root directory, and sometimes in the `/pub` directory.

3. Using the Directories window, move to the location where you want to store the file; in this case, `/incoming`.

4. Click on the **U**pload button.

5. Before you can upload any file to CompuServe or any FTP sites it connects to, you must indicate that you have the legal rights to do so. To allow you to do this, WinCIM will display a dialog box like the one shown in Figure 10.15. If you do not own the rights to upload the file, hit the Cancel button now! On the other hand, if you do have the right to distribute copies of the file, click on the OK button.

FIGURE 10.25.

You must own the distribution rights for any file you want to upload.

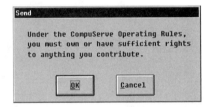

6. Once you get past the legal jargon, WinCIM opens a dialog box to allow you to select the file you want to upload. (See Figure 10.26.) To enter the filename, either type the name and location in the field provided or click on the **F**ile button to open a File Requester. You also need to tell WinCIM what type of file you are uploading by selecting the correct option from the File Type list.

7. When you are satisfied that all the information is correct, click on the OK button to start the transfer. As the transfer proceeds, WinCIM will display a progress dialog similar to the one you saw when retrieving files. Again, this dialog will show you how much of the file has been sent and how much time is left.

8. If the file transfer completes successfully, you will be returned to the FTP Client dialog, where you can hit the **L**eave button to close the FTP connection. (See "Troubleshooting" later in the chapter for a discussion of some of the problems you may encounter.)

FIGURE 10.26.

Enter the name of the file you want to upload and select its type.

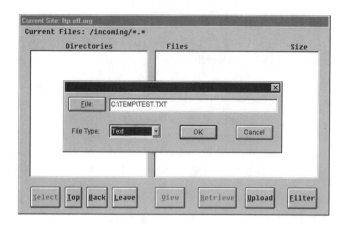

Basically, the only difficulty you will encounter when trying to send files to an FTP site is locating sites that permit you to do so. Unlike bulletin board systems, which thrive on files uploaded by users (often awarding special benefits for those who do so), most FTP sites tend to discourage the uploading of files.

That said, there are still some sites where you can upload files. These tend to fall into one of two categories: archive sites and private accounts.

Archive Sites

Most archive sites that hold large collections of files allow people to submit new files through a special directory, usually called /incoming. At these sites, this is the only directory that allows you to upload files.

There are also usually strict guidelines and rules that need to be followed when you're submitting a file to one of these sites. In most cases, the file must be compressed using a program like WinZip (see Appendix D) and must also be accompanied by a readme file describing the file's contents.

Private Accounts

Some Internet service providers offer their users access to a private directory on their host system, where they can store files using FTP.

For these people, this is a bit like having a filing cabinet stored in someone else's building. As a rule, only the owner of the directory has access to it, so these sites can often be used to store copies of private information with little concern about possible theft or copying.

Although it's not currently supported by CompuServe, in the future you may be able to access your own private storage area on CompuServe using FTP.

Setting File Filters

The one button on the FTP Client dialog box that has not been discussed to any degree is the **Filter** button. This button allows you to selectively control the types of files listed in the Files window.

By default, all files held on a remote FTP site are displayed in the **Files** window. However, when you begin dealing with very large directories—sometimes holding hundreds of files—it can often be difficult to locate the exact files you are looking for. This is where the **Filter** button can come in handy. When you click on it, WinCIM opens a dialog box like the one shown in Figure 10.27. In this dialog box, you can enter what CompuServe calls a File Mask using either DOS or UNIX *wildcards*.

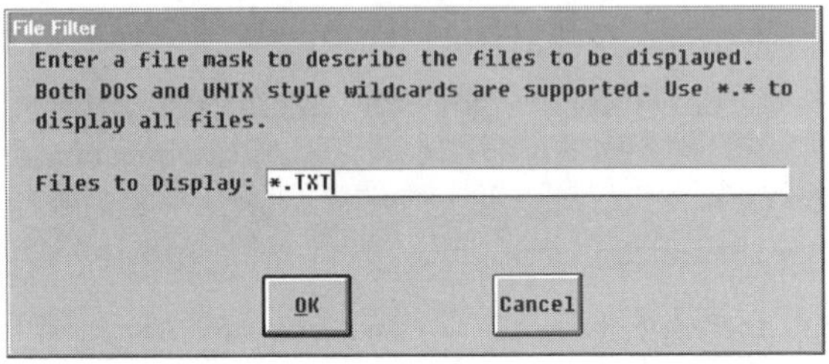

FIGURE 10.27.

The File Filter dialog box lets you define the type of files you want to be listed in the Files Window.

```
File Filter
   Enter a file mask to describe the files to be displayed.
   Both DOS and UNIX style wildcards are supported. Use *.* to
   display all files.

   Files to Display: *.TXT

              OK              Cancel
```

In fact, you have already seen this file mask in use, although there has not been any great mention of it. At the end of the Current Files: path, you probably recall seeing the symbol *.*. This is actually telling you that all the files in the current directory are being shown in the Files window.

This mask uses the * wildcard, which basically means that this symbol can be replaced with anything. As a result *.* indicates that any file with any extension will be displayed. If you change this mask to *.txt using the File Filter dialog, you are telling WinCIM that you only want to see a list of files that end in .txt.

This can also come in handy when you are trying to locate a specific file. For example, if you know that the name of the file begins with the letter M, you could set the File Mask to M*.* and receive a list of all files beginning with M.

Tip

> The Current Files: message will always reflect the File Mask. If you connect to a site and find that no files appear to be listed, check Current Files: to make sure that it ends in *.*.

Connecting to an Unlisted Site

The only real difference you encounter when connecting to an unlisted site is that you need to find the domain name on your own.

Using the list of sites provided by CompuServe, the domain name is added to the Access a Specific Site screen by WinCIM before you see it. However, if you hit the Access a Specific Site button in the File Transfer Protocol window, the Access a Specific Site window is displayed without any site name. Until you enter something into the Site Name field, you should also note that the OK button is disabled.

There are a number of ways to find the addresses of the different FTP sites located around the world. To start with, the file you located using the PC file finder offers an extensive list.

This process is somewhat hit and miss, however, so you would probably benefit more from the results obtained using Archie, the FTP indexing and search tool. (See the "Archie" section at the end of this chapter for more information on using Archie.)

CompuServe's List of Sites

Like the Selected Popular Sites window, the List of FTP Sites window (Figure 10.28) can be reached from the File Transfer Protocol window. Open this list by clicking on the icon titled "List of Sites," which is the second icon from the top on the right-hand side of the File Transfer Protocol window.

FIGURE 10.28.

FTP sites suggested by CompuServe.

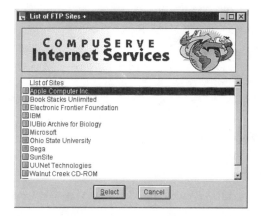

Note that all the sites shown on the Selected Popular Sites window are also listed in this window. As a result, most people tend to use the List of Sites as their regular starting point for FTP exploration. In addition, CompuServe may add new entries to this list over time.

CompuServe also maintains a description of each of these sites in the FTP Site Description window. To open this window, click on the Site Descriptions icon at the bottom-left corner of the File Transfer Protocol window. For those of you who would prefer to read about these in black and white, here is a short description of the sites currently offered by CompuServe.

Apple Computer Inc.

This site is operated by Apple Computers and is its primary FTP site for Apple Computer software updates, company and product information, and the Apple Assistance Center Q&A archive.

Book Stacks Unlimited

To complement the Book Stacks Unlimited Telnet site discussed in Chapter 7, this site contains a library of thousands of electronic books (or *Ebooks*), all of which are copyright-free or "used by permission."

To get started, retrieve a copy of the `dir.txt` file from the site's root directory to obtain a map showing the layout of various files stored here.

Electronic Frontier Foundation

Operated by the Electronic Frontier Foundation, this site is the repository of the Computers and Academic Freedom archives and the Computer Underground Digest online library.

Located in these archives are thousands of files dealing with networking, privacy, the information infrastructure, censorship, electronic activism, cryptography, and many of the computer legislation issues currently sweeping the world.

IBM

This site is the primary source of support and maintenance files for IBM software. These include software patches and bug fixes for IBM operating systems and applications.

There is also a large archive of text files covering many IBM company-, hardware-, and software-related issues.

IUBio Archive for Biology

Of all the sites offered by CompuServe, this one is the most unique. As the name suggests, this site is an archive for biological data and software.

Included in the list of files, dealing mainly with molecular biology, are computer programs suitable for use on MS-DOS, Macintosh, UNIX, and VAX/VMS operating systems. There are also a number of news and document archives stored at the site dealing with molecular biology.

Microsoft

This extensive site, operated by Microsoft, contains thousands of files dealing with business systems, desktop applications, developer tools and information, Microsoft education and certification, Microsoft shareholder information, instructions and index for the software library, personal operating systems and hardware, and information on TechNet.

To help you find your way around this large FTP site, download the `dirmap.txt` file from the root directory when you first connect.

Ohio State University

Although probably not suited to everyone, this site, operated by Ohio State University at Columbus, contains over 10,000 programs covering a wide variety of UNIX-related applications. This includes UNIX support files, applications, and anti-virus tools, as well as source code and Internet-related files.

Sega

Although not the repository of pirated computer games that some people might hope for, this site contains a valuable collection of hints and cheats and a list of much-sought-after game codes.

There is also a collection of screen shots, movie files, product descriptions, and some up-to-the-minute information about Sega business operations such as the Arcade division and the Sega Channel.

Sunsite

Sunsite is one of the main archive sites for a number of varied file collections. It is operated by the University of North Carolina Office for Information Technology, with assistance from Sun Microsystems and Cisco Systems.

Due to this relationship, the site contains an extensive collection of Sun Microsystems- and UNIX-related files and information archives. There is also a rapidly growing collection of *public domain* multimedia software tools and resources, including the Smithsonian photo archives, the Internet Underground Music archive, and the Collaborative Visual Arts archive.

For people interested in LINUX, the public domain version of UNIX, this site also contains one of the largest LINUX archives available.

UUNET Technologies

UUNET Technologies has been around almost as long as the Internet itself. Positioned as a global communications company through Alternet, its commercial TCP/IP network UUNET has accumulated the resources need to make this site one of the largest on the Internet.

In addition to its famous UNIX software archive, the site also contains a host of general-interest files unique to this site.

Walnut Creek CD-ROM

More commonly known as just CDROM.COM, this site is recognized as the home of a number of famous (or in some cases, infamous) Internet archives, including the Hobbes OS/2 collection, the Doom add-on repository, both FreeBSD and LINUX, the Games archive, the Online Book Project, Project Gutenberg, and the Handicapped Resource archive.

On top of all this, CDROM.COM also houses a large source code archive covering C, Ada, and Perl. Not wanting to leave anyone out in the cold, there are Macintosh, MS Windows, and MS-DOS archives as well.

Washington University

For many people looking for one-stop FTP access, this is the place to start. In addition to the large collection of files it maintains itself, it also contains mirrors of almost every other major archive site located around the world.

Although this is a great place to shop from a resource point of view, its popularity often means that it may take a number of hours to log onto the site once it becomes overloaded.

Wiretap

Wiretap is the electronic newshound of the Internet. Since 1992 it has been collecting and updating millions of press releases, legal documents, Usenet newsgroup discussions, historical records, and White House publications.

Troubleshooting

When you're using the WinCIM FTP client, you will probably encounter a number of messages indicating that WinCIM is having difficulties of some sort. To assist you with resolving these problems, Table 10.1 lists some of the more common messages and an explanation of why they occur.

Table 10.1. Common FTP error messages.

Error Message	Comments
Internet Site	Each FTP site can only handle a certain number of connections at any one time. If you try to connect to a site that is already overloaded, you will receive a message similar to this one. Under certain conditions, you will also receive this message if the FTP site needs to log you off for some reason.
Closed Connection	When you click on the OK button, the exact reason why your connection was closed will be displayed in a message window.
Specified Host is Unknown	This message indicates that WinCIM could not locate an FTP site with the domain name nominated on the Access a Specific Site window.

Error Message	Comments
Remote Site is Unresponsive	If the domain name for a site is valid but WinCIM cannot open a physical connection to the site, this message is displayed. Click the Retry button to tell WinCIM to try again, or click Cancel to abort the connection attempt.
No Files Selected	If you hit the **V**iew or **R**etrieve buttons and no files are selected, WinCIM displays this message.
Failed to Change Directory	When you attempt to select a directory that you don't have permission to enter, WinCIM reports a message similar to this one.
Connection Failed	Like the Remote Site is Unresponsive message, this indicates that WinCIM is encountering difficulties while trying to communicate with the remote FTP site.
Remote Site Denied Access to File	This message usually occurs when you attempt to retrieve a file that is actually a linked directory. To get around this problem, look for a `links.txt` file in the current directory. This file lists the actual path that this file is linked to.

Archie

With millions of files stored on FTP sites all around the world, locating the one you are after by wandering onto sites by chance is a fairly remote possibility. To help you locate the file you are after, a program called Archie was developed.

Archie is actually three separate computer programs, each of which performs a separate task. The job of the first program is to search the Internet and collect copies of the indexes stored at each FTP site. It does this on a regular basis to ensure that it has a copy of the latest file information possible. The second component of Archie is responsible for taking these files and compiling them into a global database. This database, in theory, contains an index that holds the location of every file stored at FTP sites.

Now, having such a database is wonderful, but at the same time it's fairly useless if no one can use it. This is where the third component of Archie comes to the fore. To search this database, you use an Archie client program. There are three main ways to gain access to an Archie client with CompuServe.

The first, which I will look at in this chapter, is to Telnet to one of the main Archie sites and make our queries using the Telnet Archie clients they provide. You can also use a tool called ArchiPlex on the World Wide Web. (See Chapter 12.) Finally, you can use a dedicated Archie client program such as WSARCHIE.

Archie Host Sites

The quickest way to start using Archie is to Telnet to one of the Archie Telnet clients listed in Table 10.2.

Table 10.2. Archie servers by location.

Location	Domain Name
North America	archie.internic.net
North America	archie.rutgers.edu
North America	archie.unl.edu
North America	archie.ans.net
North America	archie.sura.net
Canada	archie.mcgill.ca
Australia	archie.au
Europe	archie.funet.fi
United Kingdom	archie.doc.ac.uk
Middle East	cs.huji.ac.il

Usually, when I talk to people about which site they should use, I advise them to use the site located nearest to them. However, because of the CompuServe-Internet gateway, this is not a practical consideration. As a result, any of the North American sites are probably a good place to start, although archie.internic.net and archie.rutgers.edu are often fairly heavily loaded down, so they tend to take a long time to perform searches.

Using Archie Via Telnet

To Telnet to an Archie site, you can use either a dedicated Telnet client or the one built into WinCIM. If you want to use the Telnet client in WinCIM, you will need to follow these steps:

1. Open the CompuServe Telnet Access window and select Access a Specific Site, as shown in Figure 10.29. In the Site Name dialog box, enter the address of the Archie site you want to log onto. For this demonstration, I used the server operated by the University of Nebraska, Lincoln, located at archie.unl.edu.

2. When CompuServe establishes the Telnet connection, enter **archie** at the Login: prompt. Depending on the site, you may need to enter **archie** at the Password: prompt as well.

FIGURE 10.29.

Go Telnet to open the Telnet Access window and select Access a Specific Site.

3. Once you get past the logon procedure, the Archie server displays a screen similar to that shown in Figure 10.30, and a prompt similar to unl-archie> appears to indicate that your connection was successful. The unl-archie> prompt is also known as the command-line prompt, because this is where you will enter all your commands. Whenever a new command-line prompt appears on the screen, this indicates that Archie is waiting for additional instructions from you.

FIGURE 10.30.

A successful Telnet connection to the Nebraska Archie site.

4. At the command-line prompt, enter the instructions needed to tell Archie what actions you want to perform. To get started, type **help** and hit the Enter key. This displays the first page of Archie's online help system. By following the commands displayed on the help screen, you can learn about all the different options offered by Archie.

5. Before you make your first search, there are a couple of options that you need to take a look at. The first one is the set pager command. When you request a search using Archie, it can often generate a list of files that takes many pages to display. By default, when you run a search, Archie scrolls through all the entries without stopping at the end of each screen. To stop this from happening, type **set pager** on the command line and hit Enter. Now if you run a search, Archie stops after each page loads and waits for you to hit the spacebar before listing any additional entries. To turn this function off, simply type **set pager** again.

6. The second option is that you can limit the number of matches reported by Archie when you make a search request. To reduce the number of matches reported to ten, type **set matches 10** and hit Enter.

7. To look for any filename or directory containing the word "winsock," at the command line prompt enter **find winsock**. When you hit the Enter key, Archie begins the search for you. After a short wait—the length depending on the complexity of the query and the number of users on the system—Archie lists all the sites that contain files or directories that match your request. Figure 10.31 shows a small part of the result list for the "winsock" query.

FIGURE 10.31.

The results of an Archie search.

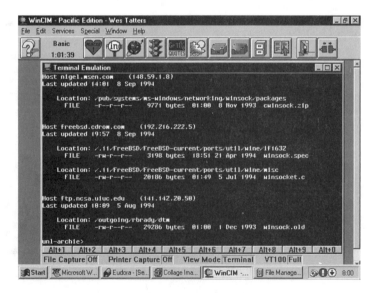

8. If you are happy with the results given by a search, you can tell Archie to send you a copy via e-mail. To do this, type **mail 100036.174@compuserve.com**. The next time you connect to CompuServe, a copy of the results of the last Archie search you ran before typing the mail request will be waiting in your CompuServe mailbox. Obviously, this would send the result to my CIS mailbox, so remember to replace "100036.174" with your own CompuServe ID.

9. You can also tailor the way Archie handles your request and even adjust the layout of the search results using the commands outlined in the Archie Online Help system. To give you an idea of what to look for, try typing **help set**. This lists all the configuration options available and explains their uses.

10. To close the Archie connection, press Ctrl+D. On some systems you can also type **quit** or **bye** to close the connection.

Although Archie does not allow you to perform the complex searches offered by WinCIM's file finders, when used with a bit of forethought, it still offers you a powerful tool for locating files stored at FTP sites.

Summary

For many people, the attraction of free computer software is reason enough to own an Internet connection. With FTP, you can obtain copies of just about any computer file ever made available to the public, either in the public domain or as shareware.

In this light, by bringing FTP to WinCIM, CompuServe now gives its members the best of both worlds. Not only do they have access to the extensive collection of files stored in CompuServe's forum libraries, but they now have access to the millions of files located at FTP sites all over the Internet.

CompuServe's connections to the Internet don't stop at Telnet and FTP, either. As of April, 1995, CompuServe has made a commitment to bring its skills with communications to the newest Internet arenas as well.

The next section of this book looks at how you can access the World Wide Web and Gopher via CompuServe.

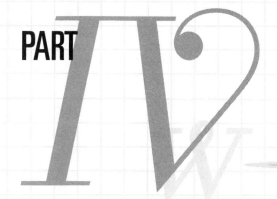

PART IV

WINCIM—THE INTERNET NAVIGATOR

CHAPTER 11

THE WORLD WIDE WEB

For many years the Internet was the domain of scientists and researchers who, for the most part, were willing to put up with its idiosyncrasies in return for the benefits it offered them. However, as more and more people began to understand the Internet's potential, these idiosyncrasies were deemed unacceptable and it was decided that a more efficient and user-friendly method of working with the Internet was needed.

The organization at the center of this debate was CERN—the European Particle Physics Laboratory. Since 1986, CERN has been one of the leading developers of Internet connectivity in Europe, allowing its researchers access to information and resources located on remote sites. However, its researchers were often forced to take extremely convoluted paths when trying to locate information using a combination of Telnet, FTP, and WAIS-based clients. Apart from being time-consuming, when new researchers were presented with such a task they were often left floundering and at a loss as to which way to proceed.

What was needed was a tool that could combine these different services into one easy-to-use program, a program that would give them easy access to the information they required and that could also display any figures or graphics associated with this information. In answer to this list of requests, the *World Wide Web (WWW)* was born.

In this chapter you will learn about the World Wide Web's early history and explore tools provided by CompuServe allowing you to access it. The following topics will be discussed:

- ◆ Early History
- ◆ Basics of the World Wide Web
- ◆ Spry Mosaic Browser
- ◆ WinCIM Browser
- ◆ Advanced Options

Early History

Unlike most other Internet tools, whose history can be traced back to the formative days of the Internet and ARPANET, the World Wide Web is the relative youngster of the group.

It was not until late in 1990 that the first World Wide Web browser, designed by Tim Berners-Lee, appeared at CERN. Over the next twelve months, this browser (and a less capable text-based version) was brought online at CERN and was gradually enhanced to include all the capabilities requested by the project staff. These features included the capability to read newsgroups, access anonymous FTP sites, and make use of both WAIS and Gopher servers with no need to access any other client program.

At the same time, they also adopted a new file format called HTML that has since become possibly the best-known file format in use on the Internet. HTML is basically an enhanced text file that contains embedded commands that let World Wide Web users easily create *hypertext* pages that can be displayed by a World Wide Web browser.

Although these browsers were still only available in-house at CERN, it was not long before people began to hear rumors about this exciting new tool and began to look for ways to make it available to the mainstream Internet world. To answer these rumors, in 1992 CERN began actively promoting the existence of the World Wide Web tool it had developed.

Following this announcement, a number of World Wide Web browsers began to appear on most computer platforms, including Windows, Apple Macintosh, UNIX, and even smaller platforms such as the Commodore Amiga. Since this time, the World Wide Web has erupted onto the Internet and single-handedly replaced many of the previously popular client applications, while giving people of different skill levels simple and efficient access to all aspects of the emerging information superhighway.

NCSA Mosaic

Without a doubt, the best-known of all World Wide Web browsers is the Mosaic browser, developed by the National Center for Supercomputing Applications at the University of Illinois at Urbana/Champaign. Since the first NCSA Mosaic browser appeared in early 1993, it has become the de facto standard for World Wide Web browsers. (See Figure 11.1.)

FIGURE 11.1.

NCSA Mosaic.

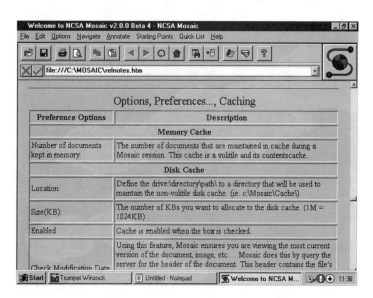

When the NCSA developed Mosaic, its aim was to create a World Wide Web browser that was freely available to all members of the Internet community. At the same time, the ongoing development of Mosaic, which will soon see the official release of version 2.0, will ensure that the World Wide Web continues to gain users and that it evolves to meet the new demands of an increasingly computer-literate community.

There are now versions of Mosaic available for Windows, Apple Macintosh, and a variety of Windows-based UNIX machines. In addition, the full source code is also available to those interested in exploring the internal works or in developing their own specialized version.

To this end, many of the other World Wide Web browsers now available demonstrate their obvious heritage, which, for so many, lies in the NCSA source code.

> NCSA Mosaic is available free of charge for nonprofit or private use. If you wish to use it for commercial reasons, on the other hand, the Mosaic license requires you to pay a licensing fee.

Netscape

If you are not using a copy of Mosaic or one of the browsers based on its code, chances are you are using Netscape. (See Figure 11.2.) For many people, Netscape is the *only* World Wide Web browser, but in most cases this is based purely on personal preferences and not on any performance or feature-for-feature comparisons between the two.

FIGURE 11.2.

The Netscape WWW browser.

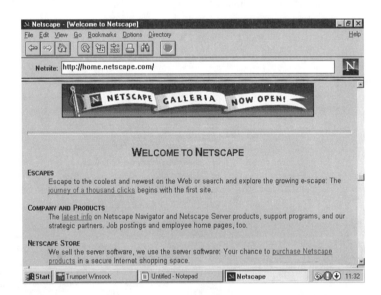

On the surface, these two programs' appearance is more than a little similar, possibly because many of the original NCSA staff who developed Mosaic now work for Netscape Communications, the company responsible for the Netscape browser. There are a number of features offered by Netscape that Mosaic does not support, however, not the least of which is that you can run Netscape on any Windows-based machine without the need for special 32-bit Microsoft libraries and support files.

Like Mosaic, Netscape is also available for private use free of charge, although users are encouraged to purchase a copy of the identical commercial version that includes a comprehensive users' guide.

> For more information about obtaining a copy of Mosaic or Netscape, take a look at Appendix C, "Internet Software."

W3 Consortium

Although CERN still maintains a presence on the Internet as the original developer of the World Wide Web, it is no longer directly responsible for the long-term coordination of the World Wide Web or the various standards such a global system now demands. To take over this responsibility, a group known as the W3 Consortium was formed by the Massachusetts Institute of Technology (MIT) and the French National Institute for Research in Computing and Automation (INRIA).

The purposes of the consortium are:

◆ To support the advancement of information technology in the field of networking, graphics, and user interfaces by developing the World Wide Web into a comprehensive information infrastructure.

◆ To encourage the industry to adopt a common set of World Wide Web protocols.

To achieve this, the consortium plans to design a common World Wide Web protocol suite, develop publicly available reference code, promote the common protocol suite throughout the world, and encourage industry to create products that comply with the common protocol suite.

If you are interested in finding out more about the consortium's activities and its members, a World Wide Web server has been set up to provide detailed information about many of the projects currently under development, along with a wide variety of resource documents dealing with all aspects of the World Wide Web. The home page for this server, shown in Figure 11.3, can be found at `http://www.w3.org/`.

FIGURE 11.3.

The W3 Consortium home page.

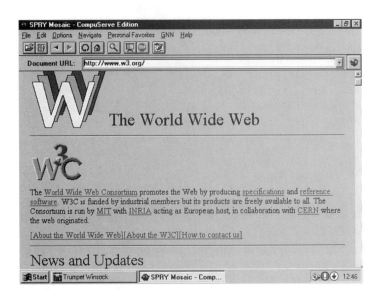

Basics of the World Wide Web

As mentioned previously, the tool used to access the World Wide Web, or more correctly, the Internet, is called a browser. This name stems from the way you can easily browse through many of the documents, files, and services provided by many different types of servers all over the Internet.

In this sense, a Web browser can best be thought of as an Internet client program for all occasions. Built into most browsers is the capability to communicate with FTP servers, Usenet newsgroup servers, and even WAIS or Gopher servers, and, more importantly, you access all these servers using the same familiar interface. If this were all that the World Wide Web was capable of, it would already be a valuable tool to many people. However, with the addition of its own special type of server as well, the World Wide Web truly is *the* Internet navigator.

Hypertext

To assist you as you explore the World Wide Web, its developers adopted the now popular hypertext system as the basis for its navigation environment.

Hypertext is a process that allows special connections or hotlinks to be embedded in the text displayed on the browser's screen. Clicking on one of these links tells the browser to automatically load the document the link points to. With these links, you can very easily move from document to document without ever needing to know the physical name of the document or even its location. You simply click on a word that says "CompuServe" or "bobsled" and your WWW browser knows where to go to locate this new information.

What's more, these links can also take you to files on FTP sites, newsgroups, and other services offered anywhere on the Internet.

URLs

To make such a system a reality, a new type of addressing system needed to be developed that could describe not only the location of a file or server, but its type as well. The World Wide Web uses an addressing system known as a Uniform Resource Locator (URL) to achieve this.

A URL consists of four separate parts that, when combined, completely define the location of any file or service located anywhere on the Internet. These parts are the protocol, domain name, path name, and filename. A completed URL will usually look something like this: `http://home.mcom.com/home/internet-search.html`.

The Protocol

The most important part of any URL is the protocol definition. This piece of information defines the type of server the selected link points to. Without this information, the WWW browser doesn't know which port and server it needs to talk to in order to obtain the information pointed to by the selected hotlink. The main protocols are listed in Table 11.1.

Table 11.1. URL protocols.

Protocol	Service
`file:`	In addition to referencing information located on the Internet, most WWW browsers can also access files stored on your local hard drive. If `file:` is followed by a `///C¦`, this indicates that the URL points to a file on your local C: drive. Otherwise it performs the same function as the `ftp:` protocol listed below.
`ftp:`	If the nominated link points to a file stored on an anonymous FTP server, the URL must begin with this definition.
`http:`	HTML documents are usually stored on a WWW server. *HTTP* (hypertext transfer protocol) refers to the protocol used by these servers.
`gopher:`	All WWW browsers can also navigate their way around a Gopher server by using this protocol definition.
`mailto:`	This is a special type of URL that lets you send an e-mail message.
`news:`	Links that point to Usenet newsgroups must be declared using this protocol.
`telnet:`	To indicate that a link needs to open a Telnet session, the URL begins with `telnet:`. Most WWW browsers can't open a Telnet session themselves. Instead, they will usually launch a separate Telnet client when such links are selected.
`wais:`	In theory, all WWW browsers can access WAIS servers, but most users prefer to use WAIS gateways such as WAISgate instead. (See Chapter 12, "World Wide Web Productivity.")

Domain Name

Following the protocol definition, the next item of information to be defined by a URL is the location of the server housing the file or information pointed to by the hotlink.

Like all other Internet services, this can be done by using either the domain name of the server or its corresponding IP address. However, the use of IP addresses is frowned upon by most of the WWW community because it does not describe the name of the site that the URL refers to in an easily understandable form.

When the protocol definition and the domain name are combined using the `//` symbol, the result is a URL definition that accurately indicates the location and type of server. In addition, due to the nature of the World Wide Web, in most cases you can access a server's home page or root directory by using just these two pieces of information.

For example, the following URL takes you straight to the home page of the CompuServe WWW server without the need for either a path name or filename: `http://www.compuserve.com/`.

> WWW browsers use the protocol definition to determine the port number they should use to access a specific server. On certain occasions, however, this port number may need to be altered from the default port of 80. Simply append the port number to the domain name, separated by a colon, such as in `http://www.compuserve.com:80/`.

Path and Filename

The last two components of a URL may or may not exist, depending on the location and type of information any given hotlink points to. In most cases, however, you will find that both a path and a filename are listed as a part of the URL.

When describing the path to a file, a URL uses the standard UNIX method for path definitions, separating each directory by a forward slash (/). Windows users should be careful not to fall into the trap of using the DOS backslash (\) because most WWW browsers will fail to understand what you have entered.

Relative Addressing

There is also a special type of URL that does not contain a domain name, but may still contain a path and filename.

This type of URL is referred to as a *relative* address. Instead of supplying a full domain name and path itself, this type of URL adopts the domain name and path of the last URL that the server accessed and looks for the specified file based on this information.

Many WWW servers use this type of addressing to move between pages because it makes for considerably easier site maintenance, especially if a group of pages needs to be relocated to a different server or directory.

> URLs containing a domain name are referred to as having an *absolute* address.

Note

WWW Servers

To manage all these hypertext documents, a new type of server and a corresponding communications protocol were developed.

The protocol, known as the Hypertext Transport Protocol (HTTP), lets WWW browsers communicate with special WWW servers that contain collections of hypertext documents called *HTML pages.* These pages contain the information and links displayed by the WWW browser. There are now thousands of WWW servers in operation all over the world, joined by the many hotlinks in the over four million HTML pages that provide information as diverse as the Internet itself.

Although HTTP began life as a relatively simple communications protocol, recent developments have seen the addition of new capabilities, including secure transaction layers, firewalls, and proxy servers. All of these enhance the capabilities provided by the World Wide Web. Luckily, there is little need for you to learn about any of the capabilities in order to take advantage of the World Wide Web. For those of you who would like to know more, the best place to start is the HTTP information pages compiled by the W3 Consortium at `http://www.w3.org/hypertext/WWW/Protocols/Overview.html`.

HTML

To easily define the contents of a WWW page, a simple method was needed that could encompass the large amounts of text many pages include and incorporate all the graphical elements and combinations of hypertext links that may be included on any given page. Also, a system was needed that could allow the same information to be displayed on a wide variety of both text and graphical WWW browsers.

As a result, it was decided that instead of defining WWW pages in a rigid typographical sense, a language would be developed to describe the information and the way its creator expected it to appear. The WWW browser could then take this information and display it in the best way possible, given its particular operating environment.

To do this, the *Hypertext Markup Language* (HTML) was developed. HTML uses text files that include a limited set of instructions to define special items such as hotlinks, images, and a limited number of typographical elements. (See Figure 11.4.) This allows WWW pages to be created by anyone with a simple text editor or word processor. (See Chapter 12 for a more in-depth discussion of HTML.)

FIGURE 11.4.

The Hypertext Markup Language lets anyone with a text editor create pages that can be displayed by a World Wide Web browser.

Once a page of HTML has been created and stored on a WWW server, anyone can add links to the new document from their own HTML pages. By doing this, the new page effectively becomes part of the World Wide Web and can then be called up by anyone with a WWW browser and Internet access. For example, the page of HTML shown in Figure 11.4 is actually a part of the home page for the CompuServe WWW Server shown in Figure 11.5. If you look closely, you can see how the various references made in the HTML document become pictures and hotlinks in a WWW browser.

FIGURE 11.5.

HTML becomes graphics and hypertext when displayed by a World Wide Web browser.

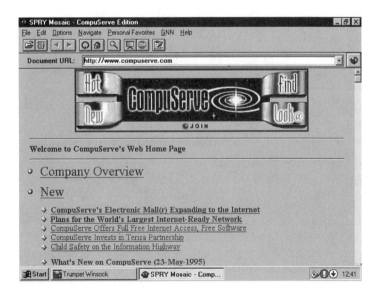

Home Pages

Because the World Wide Web effectively has no top or bottom, the concept of home pages was developed to give people some sort of reference points in what was otherwise a never-ending chain of links and interconnections.

There are many definitions of what actually constitutes a home page. Regardless of what the technical definitions are, most people consider a home page to be any location that acts as a front door to a collection of related WWW pages. For example, the WWW page shown in Figure 11.5 represents CompuServe's WWW server home page because it serves as an entrance point to all the other pages CompuServe provides.

Spry Mosaic

To allow you easy access to the World Wide Web, CompuServe has made available a special version of Spry Mosaic as a part of the NetLauncher package discussed in Chapter 4, "Getting Connected to the Internet." It is one of the WWW browsers based on NCSA Mosaic.

With NetLauncher installed, all you need to do to get Mosaic up and running is double-click on the Spry Mosaic icon in the CompuServe folder. (See Figure 11.6.)

FIGURE 11.6.

Double-click on the Spry Mosaic icon to start it running.

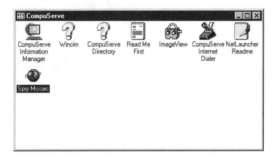

First Steps

Provided that you have set up NetLauncher correctly, when Spry Mosaic opens for the first time, it automatically starts the dialer utility and opens a CompuServe connection. To let you know what is happening, a series of message windows is displayed in the middle of the Spry Mosaic main window, as shown in Figure 11.7.

When NetLauncher completes the connection, the CompuServe home page is displayed. (See Figure 11.8.) By now this page should be reasonably familiar to you, although the layout may appear slightly different from some of the figures you have previously encountered. When Spry Mosaic is installed, a number of settings default differently than the configuration used. Later in the chapter you'll look at the different ways to alter Spry Mosaic to suit your own tastes, but for now, let's work with default configuration.

FIGURE 11.7.

NetLauncher keeps you up to date on its progress by displaying messages in the middle of the screen.

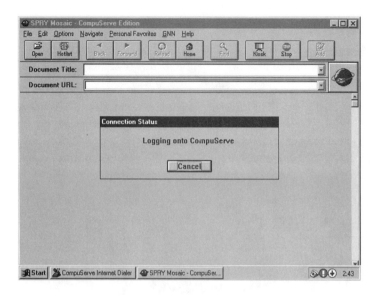

FIGURE 11.8.

Spry Mosaic is initially configured to automatically open the CompuServe home page.

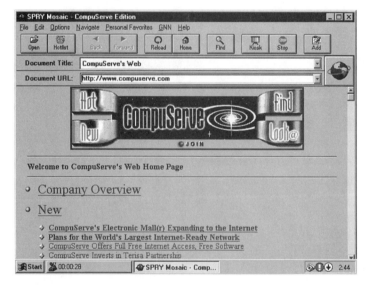

The Main Window

You are now on the World Wide Web. At this stage you can begin to explore it to your heart's content, but before you get too carried away, let's take a look at some of the features Spry Mosaic provides.

The Spry Mosaic window is broken into three main sections:

◆ The document area
◆ The control console
◆ The status bar

The Document Area

The most important part of any WWW browser is the *document area* where WWW pages are displayed. With Spry Mosaic, as with most WWW browsers, the middle section of the screen is devoted to displaying WWW pages as they are retrieved from the Internet.

In addition, you'll often find that a WWW page is larger than the space provided by the WWW browser. To read such a page, use the scrollbars at the top and sides of the document area.

Hotlinks

The first thing you need to know when working with any WWW browser is how to recognize a *hotlink*. In Spry Mosaic all hotlinks are defined as blue text and, optionally, are further enhanced by an underline. In addition, any graphics that have hotlinks associated with them are highlighted by a blue border.

When you click on any of these hotlinks, Spry Mosaic opens a copy of the document that the link points to and displays it on the screen in place of the current page.

The Control Console

The area at the top of the Spry Mosaic window, above the page display window, is referred to as the *control console*. You can easily navigate your way around the World Wide Web by using the various tools provided in this area.

The Menu Bar

Like all Windows-based programs, Spry Mosaic has a *menu bar* across the top of the main window. To access the options provided by this menu bar, click the various menu pad options listed. When you do this, a pulldown menu appears displaying the options available:

File	The File menu contains functions that allow you to open new documents located on either your hard drive or any of the WWW servers. In addition, you can also print copies of the page you are currently viewing or display the Hotlist window. For those of you interested in the workings of HTML, there is an option that allows you to display the current document's HTML source.
Edit	The Edit menu lets you copy URLs displayed on the document line or open the find requester.

Options
From this menu you can select any of the options that allow you to tailor the way Spry Mosaic looks and operates. (See "Configuring Spry Mosaic" later in this chapter.)

Navigate
Except for one, all the function lists on this menu are duplicated in the toolbar discussed below. The only one that is not, the **H**istory item, opens a window listing all the WWW pages you have visited during your current session.

Personal Favorites
The Add button on the toolbar allows you to add pages to your list of personal favorites. Once added, all these pages are listed on this menu so you can easily return to them whenever you want. When you select a page listed on this menu, Spry Mosaic opens it as though you had selected it by clicking on a hotlink in a WWW page.

GNN
Any of the hotlist sections installed by NetLauncher when Spry Mosaic was added to your hard drive can be placed on the menu bar to allow easy access to the sites they contain. GNN is one of these hotlists.

Help
This menu gives you access to the Spry Mosaic online help system and also allows you to send e-mail to the developers at Spry.

The Toolbar

The toolbar displayed below the menu bar gives you access to many of Spry Mosaic's features. (See Figure 11.9.) By default, the toolbar contains both a graphical and text description of its purpose. As you become more familiar with the use of Spry Mosaic, you will probably want to adjust the settings so that only the graphical elements are displayed. (See Figure 11.10.) By doing this, you increase the amount of space available in the Spry Mosaic window for displaying WWW pages.

FIGURE 11.9.
The Spry Mosaic toolbar.

FIGURE 11.10.
With the text turned off, the toolbar is considerably smaller.

Here are the toolbar items:

Open
This icon opens the file requester shown in Figure 11.11. It lets you load HTML pages stored on your hard drive into Spry Mosaic.

FIGURE 11.11.
The Open Local File requester lets you open WWW pages stored on your local hard drive.

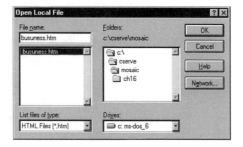

Although documents stored on a WWW server are all given an `.html` extension, due to the limitations imposed by MS-DOS, all HTML documents on your hard drive must have an `.htm` extension.

Hotlist
When you install Spry Mosaic, it comes preconfigured with a list of popular WWW sites. These sites are stored in the Spry Mosaic Hotlist. When you click on this icon, the Hotlists window is displayed so that you can select from the numerous sites provided. (See Figure 11.12.) The hotlist is broken down into a number of small lists relating to different types of services. To open any of these smaller lists, double-click on the category you are interested in. Doing this expands that section of the list. For example, the GNN section is currently expanded in Figure 11.12. By clicking on any of the WWW sites described in this area, you can tell Spry Mosaic to open the corresponding page, just as if you had selected it by clicking on a hotlink in a WWW page. You can also tell Spry Mosaic to add any of the sections displayed to the Menu bar. Sections that will be shown in the menu bar have a small "M" in their section icon. For example, the GNN section also appears in the menu bar. Finally, you can also add new sections and WWW pages, as well as maintain existing ones, by using the buttons provided on the right side of the Hotlists window.

FIGURE 11.12.

The Hotlists window displays all of the sites stored in Spry Mosaic hotlists.

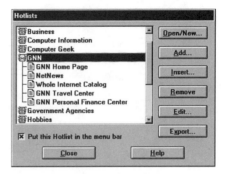

Back	As you begin to move around the World Wide Web, Spry Mosaic keeps track of where you have been. If you click on this icon, the previous page is recalled.
Forward	If you've used the Back icon, you can then use the Forward icon to move back up the list to the most current page.
Reload	Clicking on this icon forces Spry Mosaic to reload the current page. If you stopped the retrieval of a large page, for example, you can use this icon to retrieve the missing information.
Home	This icon always returns you to your own home page. When Spry Mosaic is installed, this icon opens the CompuServe home page, but you can adjust this to point to any page you choose.
Find	When you open a large WWW page, it is sometimes handy to be able to search quickly through the contents of the page. The Find icon allows you to do just that by opening a small dialog box where you can nominate a word or words you want to be located on the current page. (See Figure 11.13.)

FIGURE 11.13.

You can search rapidly through large WWW pages by using the Find dialog box.

| Kiosk | Selecting this icon places Spry Mosaic in Kiosk mode. (See Figure 11.14.) All the toolbars, menus, and other controls are removed from the screen to allow more room for displaying large WWW pages. |

FIGURE 11.14.
Spry Mosaic in Kiosk mode.

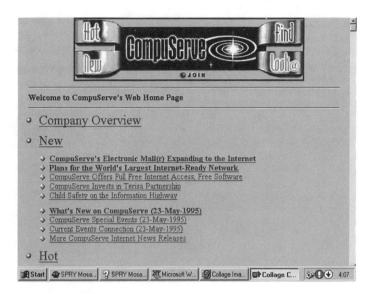

To exit Kiosk mode, hit the Esc key or Ctrl+K.

Tip

| Stop | If you need to halt the loading of a document, click on this icon. |
| Add | To add the current page to your list of personal favorites, click on this icon. |

Document Title

Immediately below the toolbar is a section displaying the name of the current WWW page. In most cases you will probably want to remove this section from the screen to free up more space for the document display area. (See "Configuring Spry Mosaic" later in this chapter for details.)

If you keep this area active, you can use it to return to any of the pages visited during the current session by clicking on it. Doing this displays a history list similar to the one shown in Figure 11.15. You can then select the page you want to recall, and Spry Mosaic locates the page for you.

Document URL

Like the Document Title field, this field displays information about the current WWW page. In this case, the information displayed relates to the URL of the current document. This field also allows you to type in the URL of a WWW page directly instead of selecting it from a menu or hotlist, or through a hotlink.

FIGURE 11.15.

The Document Title field lets you recall a page from a list of pages you have visited during the current session.

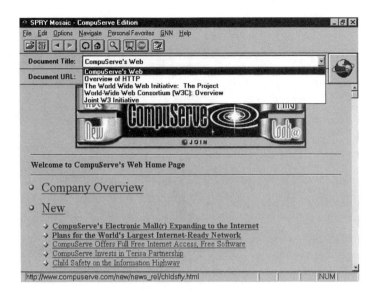

Doing this allows you to easily open any of the WWW pages listed in this book. For example, enter the following HTTP address into the document URL field: `http://www.webcom.com/~taketwo/sams.html`.

Did you receive the special message left for you?

> By clicking on the drop-down arrow to the right of this field, you can call up a history list similar to the one provided by the Document Title field. This time you received a list of URLs instead of document names.

Logo Animation

Apart from giving you something to look at, the animated logo to the right of the Document Title and Document URL fields is there to let you know when Spry Mosaic is retrieving a WWW page. If the animation is spinning, Spry Mosaic is busy. If it is static, no pages are currently being retrieved.

Status Bar

The last area of the Spry Mosaic window is the status bar. It is located below the main document display window. This area displays a variety of information depending on what the browser is doing. When you place your mouse pointer over a hotlink, the URL of the page or server that it points to is displayed in the status area on the left side of the status bar. Alternately, when a new page is being loaded, a counter is displayed in this area to indicate the page size and the number of characters already retrieved. The same thing also happens when inline graphics are being loaded.

On the right side of the status bar, there are five boxes. The first box displays a DISK message whenever the Load to Disk option is active. The next box displays a BUSY message whenever a page load is in progress. The last three indicate when the Caps Lock, Num Lock, or Scroll Lock keys are active.

> Like many of the elements already discussed, the status bar can be turned off to allow more room for displaying WWW pages.

Configuring Spry Mosaic

In the **O**ptions menu (Figure 11.16), there are a number of functions that allow you to tailor the appearance and operation of Spry Mosaic. This section examines each of these options and discusses their use.

FIGURE 11.16.

The Spry Mosaic Options menu.

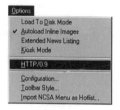

Load to Disk Mode

To choose this option, simply select it from the Options menu. A check mark is placed beside this option on the menu to indicate that it is active.

Once activated, whenever you attempt to open a new document, a save file requester is displayed so that you can specify a name for the file. Once you specify a name, the document is saved directly to your hard disk. The most popular use for this option is to save a page that you may want to study more closely once you disconnect from the Internet.

> When Load to Disk mode is active, none of the documents you select are displayed on the screen; they are only saved to your hard disk.

To save a page, activate the Load to **D**isk Mode option and click on the Reload icon. Enter a name for the new file in the save file requester and click on the OK button. Now deactivate the Load to **D**isk Mode option by again selecting it from the **O**ptions menu. After you disconnect from CompuServe, you can reload the document into Mosaic by clicking on the Load icon.

Tip

You can also selectively activate the Load to Disk option by holding down the Shift key
when you click on a hotlink. This will save the new WWW page to your hard disk
instead of displaying it on your screen.

Autoload Inline Images

When a WWW page is displayed, you will probably notice that the text of the document is
displayed first and then any images associated with the page are loaded.

When you turn off the **A**utoload Inline Images option, Spry Mosaic loads only the text of the
document and inserts placeholders where all the images are meant to go. (See Figure 11.17.)
The main advantage of doing this is that loading the same document with all the images included can take 3 to 4 minutes using a 14,400 bps modem (Figure 11.18), while loading it
with placeholders takes only a matter of seconds. When you consider that some pages may take
up to ten minutes to load with slower modems, deselecting this option makes a lot of sense.

FIGURE 11.17.

*The Spry HotLand page
takes about 15 seconds to
load with Autoload Inline
Images turned off.*

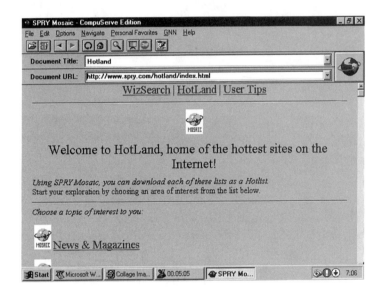

FIGURE 11.18.

With Autoload Inline Images turned on, the same page can take 3 to 4 minutes to load.

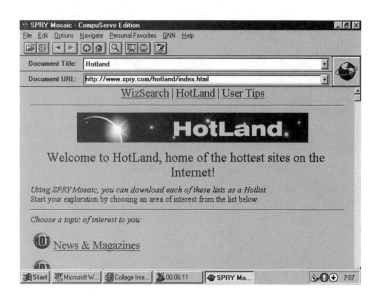

Extended News Listing

One of the more advanced features of Spry Mosaic allows you to read articles in Usenet newsgroups. When this option is turned on, both the name of the newsgroup and a short description of its contents are displayed. If this option is turned off, only the name of the newsgroup is displayed. For more information on reading newsgroups with Spry Mosaic, see "Advanced Capabilities" at the end of this chapter.

Kiosk Mode

This option performs the same action as the Kiosk icon discussed in the toolbar section. All the control panel information is removed from the screen to allow more of the current page to be displayed.

Once in Kiosk mode, you need to hit the Esc key or Ctrl+K to return the display to normal.

HTTP/0.9

This option is rarely needed these days because there are very few version 1.0 HTTP servers still in existence. For the most part, you should leave this option turned off.

Configuration

The most important function on the **O**ptions menu is the **C**onfiguration option. When you select this menu item, Spry Mosaic opens the Configuration dialog box, shown in Figure 11.19.

To help you understand the options available in this dialog box, Table 11.2 lists each function and gives a short description of its purpose.

Table 11.2. Spry Mosaic configuration options.

Option	Function
Show Toolbar	If this function is selected, the toolbar is displayed. Otherwise it is turned off.
Show Status Bar	The status bar is displayed when this option is turned on.
Show Document Title	Turn this option off to remove the Document Title field from the screen.
Show Document URL	This option displays or hides the Document URL field.
Save last window position	When this option is selected, Spry Mosaic records its location on the Windows desktop and restores itself to that position the next time you use it.
Autoload inline images	This option duplicates the item in the Options menu.
Show URL in Status Bar	If this function is turned off, the URLs of hotlinks under the mouse pointer are not displayed in the status bar.
Underline hyperlinks	With this option selected, all hotlinks are highlighted with an underline. Turn this option off if you don't want the underline to be displayed.
Animate logo	On some machines, the animated logo can decrease the performance of Spry Mosaic during file transfers. If your machine seems to be running slowly, try disabling this field.
Use 8-bit Sound	If you have a sound card, Spry Mosaic can take advantage of it when playing sounds. However, on some lesser-quality sound cards the sound may be tinny. If this occurs, select this option to force the use of 8-bit sound instead of 16-bit sound.
Redraw images	For most users this function doesn't affect Spry Mosaic's operation in any way. Leave it at between 1.5 and 5 seconds.
Home Page	When you click on the Home icon, the CompuServe home page is loaded by default. If you want to change this page to one of your own, enter the URL of the alternate page in this field. If you select the Load automatically at startup option, this page is automatically retrieved every time you start Mosaic.
Email Address	When NetLauncher installs Spry Mosaic, your CompuServe e-mail address is inserted into this field.
SMTP Server	To send e-mail messages using the `mailto:` protocol, you need to define an SMTP server. The address of the CompuServe SMTP server is the default.

Option	Function
News Server	To read articles stored in newsgroups, you must define a news server. The address of the CompuServe NNTP server is the default.
Cached Documents	Spry Mosaic keeps a record in a local cache of the last few pages you have loaded. This allows these pages to be reloaded without having to re-query the remote server where they are actually located. The number in this field defines how many old pages are cached. If you have a lot of memory you can set this as high as 15 or 20 documents, but as a rule you should leave it at around 10.
Documents in dropdown	This number determines the number of previous documents listed in the Document Title and Document URL history dropdowns.

FIGURE 11.19.

The Spry Mosaic Configuration dialog box.

There are also four buttons across the bottom of the Configuration dialog box that give you access to other, more technical options. In Table 11.3 each of these options is described. For a full discussion of the features provided by these buttons, you should refer to the online help information.

Table 11.3. Configuration buttons.

Button	Function
Viewers	If you want to configure any additional viewers for Spry Mosaic, click on this button. ImageView, the graphic display program delivered with NetLauncher, is an example of an external viewer.
Link Color	You can change the color of the hotlinks by opening the color selector provided by this button.
Fonts	This button opens a dialog box that allows you to change the font size and text style that Spry Mosaic uses when displaying WWW pages.
Proxy Servers	At this stage there is no need to configure any Proxy options when you're using NetLauncher and the CompuServe dial-up PPP.

Toolbar Style

The **T**oolbar Style entry on the **O**ptions menu opens the small dialog box shown in Figure 11.20. By using this dialog box, you can select a toolbar that displays both picture and text, picture only, or text only.

FIGURE 11.20.

Select the Picture Only option to display a more Windows-like toolbar.

Import NCSA Menu as Hotlist

This last option is of use only to those already using NCSA Mosaic. It allows you to import the contents of a NCSA Quick menu into a Spry Mosaic hotlist.

Advanced Capabilities

Now that you have an understanding of how the World Wide Web and, more specifically, Spry Mosaic works, let's take a look at some of the special features offered by World Wide Web browsers.

mailto

As you begin to explore the World Wide Web, you will occasionally come across a special type of hotlink that looks something like this: `mailto://wtatters@world.net`.

If you select a hotlink like this, Spry Mosaic opens a dialog box similar to the one in Figure 11.21. This dialog box allows you to send an e-mail message—usually to the creator of the WWW page or to some other e-mail address nominated by them.

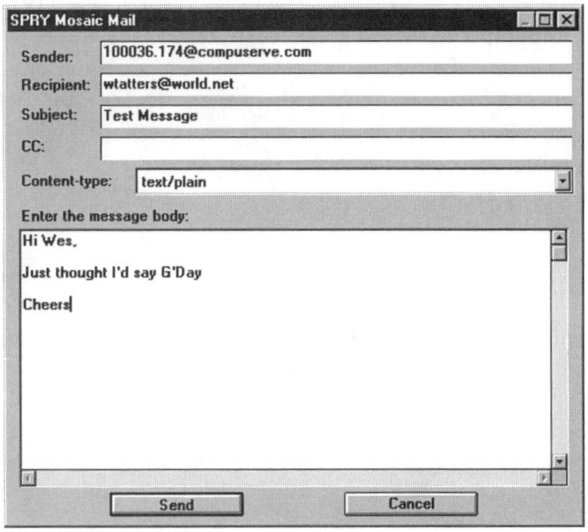

FIGURE 11.21.

The Mail dialog box allows you to send e-mail messages using Spry Mosaic.

SPRY Mosaic Mail	
Sender:	100036.174@compuserve.com
Recipient:	wtatters@world.net
Subject:	Test Message
CC:	
Content-type:	text/plain

Enter the message body:

Hi Wes,

Just thought I'd say G'Day

Cheers

[Send] [Cancel]

Your CompuServe e-mail address, or any other address that you nominated in the Email Address field of the Configuration dialog, is inserted in the first field of this dialog box. The next field contains the destination address of the e-mail message. The contents of the remaining fields are up to you. Obviously a subject line is important, as is a message in the dialog box's body. In the CC field, you can nominate people to whom you want to send a copy of the message.

When you are happy with the message you have entered, click on the Send button. Spry Mosaic then attempts to transmit the message via e-mail. If it is successful, a small Message Sent dialog box is displayed. Otherwise a message explaining the difficulties is shown.

> If you type `mailto:` on its own in the Document URL field, Spry Mosaic also opens the Mail dialog box. This allows you to use Spry Mosaic to send your own e-mail messages instead of using CIS Mail in WinCIM. Although you can use this method to send e-mail, at this stage it is not possible to receive e-mail this way.

FTP

It is also possible to use Spry Mosaic as an FTP client. Simply enter the domain name of the FTP site you want to visit in the Document URL field. To tell Spry Mosaic that you want to open an FTP session, first enter `ftp://` and then the domain name.

For example, if you want to visit the Microsoft FTP server discussed in Chapter 10, enter the following in the Document URL field and hit the Enter key: `ftp://ftp.microsoft.com/`.

After a few seconds you should see a page like the one shown in Figure 11.22. All the files and subdirectories in the root directory of the Microsoft server are displayed down the left side of the main document, each represented as a hotlink. All you need to do to enter any of these directories or retrieve any of the files is click on them.

FIGURE 11.22.

The root directory of the Microsoft FTP server.

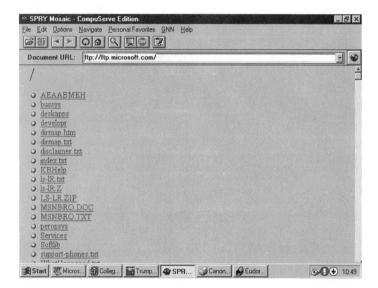

As an experiment, try to locate the subdirectory and file discussed in "Retrieving a File" in Chapter 10. To help you out, here is the full URL description for the directory you need to locate: `ftp://ftp.microsoft.com/deskapps/word/winword-public/ia`.

As you move down through the various directories, note that the top line of the document area is continually updated to reflect the path to your current location on the FTP server. When you get to the `ia` directory, your screen should look like Figure 11.23. The file discussed in Chapter 10 was `wordia.exe`. To download this file, click on it.

After a few seconds, Mosaic displays the dialog box shown in Figure 11.24. This dialog box tells you that Spry Mosaic is not familiar with the contents of that file and asks if you want to save it to your hard disk. Click on the Yes button if you want to proceed with the download.

A save requester is then displayed so that you can nominate the directory in which to save the new file. (See Figure 11.25.) You can also change the name of the file if it conflicts with one you already have. Click on the OK button to begin the transfer. Spry Mosaic transfers a copy of the file to your hard drive. While the transfer is in progress, Mosaic displays a counter on the status bar indicating how many bytes of data have been received.

FIGURE 11.23.

Click on the file
wordia.exe to download a
copy of it.

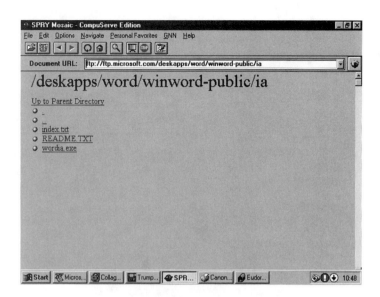

FIGURE 11.24.

When Spry Mosaic does not
recognize the contents of a
file, it always asks you what
you want to do with it.

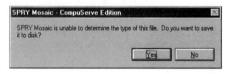

FIGURE 11.25.

Nominate the directory
where you want to save the
new file and click on the
OK button.

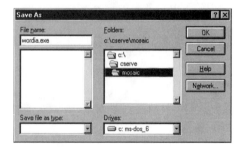

Newsgroups

The final major specification of the original WWW project was giving the user the ability to read articles stored in newsgroups by using a World Wide Web browser. As a result, this capability is built into Spry Mosaic, provided, of course, that you have access to a news server. To this end, CompuServe has made a Usenet server available to its members via the World Wide Web.

There are three ways that you can access a newsgroup using a WWW browser. The first is through a hotlink pointing to a newsgroup as part of a WWW page. Secondly, you can enter the full name of a newsgroup into the Document URL field, preceded by **news:**. For example, to open the newsgroup shown in Figure 11.26, you would enter the following URL: `news:comp.infosystems.www.browsers.ms-windows`.

> There is no need to include a // after the news: protocol.

FIGURE 11.26.

The Windows WWW browsers newsgroup in comp.infosystems.www.

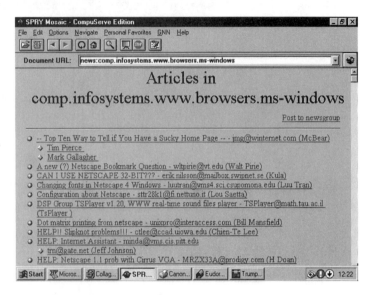

To post a new article to this newsgroup, click on the Post to newsgroup hotlink at the top of the document area, or click on any of the articles listed to read their contents. (See Figure 11.27.) Once you have read an article, you can post a follow-up message with the current message automatically quoted for you in the body of the new message, or you can send an e-mail message to the article's author. (See Figure 11.28.)

FIGURE 11.27.

When you select an article, Spry Mosaic displays it for you in the document area.

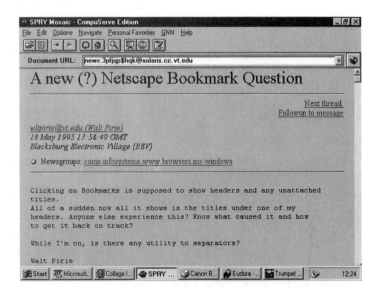

FIGURE 11.28.

The article you are replying to is automatically quoted at the beginning of the message you want to send.

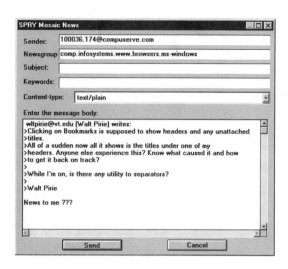

If you don't know the names of any newsgroups, you can use Spry Mosaic to display a list of all those available. Type **news:** in the Document URL file, followed either by a single asterisk or the name of one of the more popular hierarchies. For example, to retrieve a list of all the newsgroups in the comp hierarchy, type the following: **news:comp.***.

After a few seconds, a page similar to the one shown in Figure 11.29 appears, listing all the newsgroups in this hierarchy and a brief description, provided that the Extended Newsgroup Listings option is active in the Options menu.

FIGURE 11.29.

Spry Mosaic lists all the active newsgroups and a brief description of their contents.

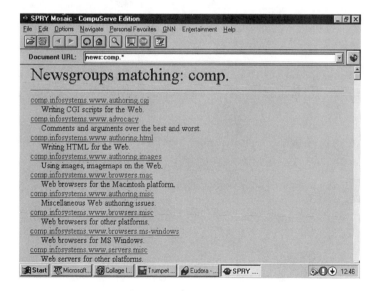

Data Entry Forms

One feature of the World Wide Web that sets it apart from other Internet services is its ability to interact with the users through *forms.*

On some WWW pages you will encounter fields like those in the form shown in Figure 11.30. These fields allow you to submit information to a WWW server by filling in the spaces provided. Depending on the WWW page, this information might relate to a membership application, a search form, delivery details for an online purchase, or even your responses to online messages on a service like WebChat.

FIGURE 11.30.

The GNN registration form allows you to become a registered GNN user.

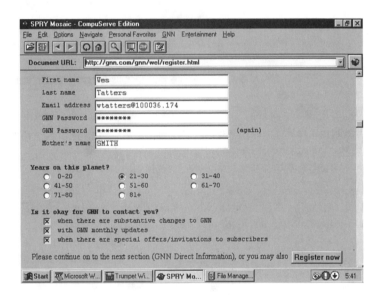

The form shown in Figure 11.30 is a part of the application form you are required to complete when subscribing to GNN—the Global Network Navigator. In addition to data entry fields, many forms also contain *radio buttons* like those under the "Years on this planet?" message. These buttons allow you to choose a single option from the list provided. Other forms include *check boxes* like those listed under the "Is it okay for GNN to contact you?" message. Check boxes allow you to select any or all of the corresponding options.

When you have completed the information requested by the form, you must then submit it to the WWW server. On most forms, you do this by clicking on a Submit button. In this example, however, you need to click on the Register button shown at the bottom on the screen.

If you mess up a form, you can often start fresh by clicking on the Reset Form button. Doing this removes all the information you have entered into the form. Not all forms include such a button, but those that do display it beside the Submit button in most cases.

Summary

Using the World Wide Web is both a simple process and one that offers you capabilities far beyond those provided by more conventional Internet clients. It allows you to explore the World Wide Web itself, retrieve files stored at FTP sites, and even read articles in Usenet newsgroups. So what else is it capable of doing?

The next chapter answers this question and takes a look at some of the more popular WWW directories and home pages. It also takes a brief look at what is involved in creating your own HTML pages, and offers some suggestions for places that may be able to assist you further in your understanding of the World Wide Web.

CHAPTER 12

WORLD WIDE WEB PRODUCTIVITY

Now that you have the world at your fingertips, so to speak, it's time to take a look at some of the ways that you can locate home pages and WWW sites by using the World Wide Web. Instead of creating a shopping list of popular World Wide Web sites, this chapter demonstrates ways that you can use the World Wide Web to locate interesting sites yourself.

To do this, this chapter first examines some of the major WWW directories and then looks at ways that you can search the World Wide Web and many other Internet services as well. Then, for those of you who really want http addresses and URLs, it briefly discusses a few of the more unique WWW pages.

Having said that, the World Wide Web is not just about pages of information provided by other people. It is also a place where you too can become a publisher. The final section of this chapter looks briefly at what you need to do to get your own home pages online and discusses, in general terms, the use of HTML.

WWW Directories

With the mind-numbing growth of the World Wide Web in the last two years, it is not surprising that more than a few people have become overwhelmed with it on their first few WWW outings. The fact that there is no front door or starting point is a concept that many people find difficult to grasp. This is to be expected, however, because our whole society is accustomed to the use of maps and step-by-step plans that always have a logical beginning and end.

For this reason, a number of WWW sites have been set up for the sole purpose of providing you with at least a logical starting point. The endpoint is still up to you, but at least these pages give you some idea about where to start.

Scott Yanoff's Special Internet Connections

The Special Internet Connections list (Figure 12.1) has been doing the rounds on the Internet in a variety of forms since 1991, when Scott Yanoff first published his personal list of Internet connections. The original list contained just six Internet sites, but since then the list has grown to contain links to thousands of World Wide Web sites, FTP servers, Telnet ports, Gophers, and mailing lists.

Since its inception, the list has been made available in a wide variety of formats, but with the growth of the World Wide Web, that version is now the most popular method of accessing the list. To explore the many links detailed in this list, use this http address: `http://www.uwm.edu/Mirror/inet.services.html`.

The list is collated by category, but not by service type. As a result, when you use this list you will often be transported to Gopher servers and FTP sites when you select a hotlink. To check the type of service that any link uses, examine the protocol section of the URL shown in the status bar when you place your cursor over its hotlink.

FIGURE 12.1.

Scott Yanoff's Special Internet Connections list includes not only WWW sites but FTP, Telnet, and Gopher servers.

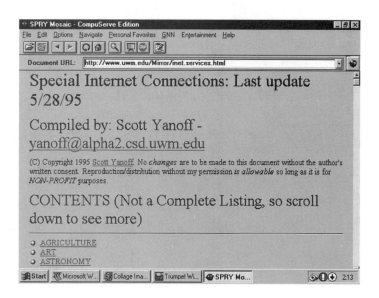

Yahoo

Yahoo was created by David Filo and Jerry Yang, who according to *Newsweek* are two of the 50 most influential people on the Internet. They prefer to describe themselves as "Yahoos," however, and will happily direct anyone who does not know what a Yahoo is to this http address: `http://c.gp.cs.cmu.edu:5103/prog/webster?yahoo`.

Yahoo contains a comprehensive listing of popular WWW pages categorized by type. (See Figure 12.2.) The site also contains a number of unique features, including:

◆ A What's New list, which is updated daily

◆ A What's Popular list, itemized by category

◆ David and Jerry's personal What's Cool listing

◆ An integrated search capability

◆ A random link page that takes you to a random WWW page

◆ The Yahoo rating system

Yahoo can be found by pointing your WWW browser to this http address: `http://www.yahoo.com/`.

`http://c.gp.cs.cmu.edu:5103/prog/webster?yahoo` is an automated version of Webster's dictionary, containing both definitions and full cross references. To look up the meaning of any word, replace `yahoo` with the word you are interested in.

FIGURE 12.2.

The Yahoo WWW sites listing.

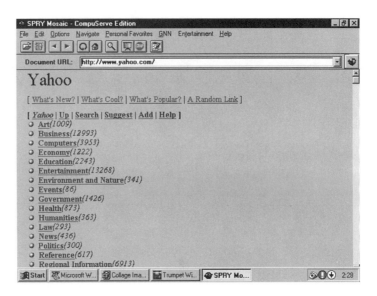

The Whole Internet Catalog

This site is based loosely on The Whole Internet User's Guide & Catalog and contains links to all of the sites this book mentions, along with many new updates and additional references. (See Figure 12.3.)

FIGURE 12.3.

The Whole Internet Catalog home page.

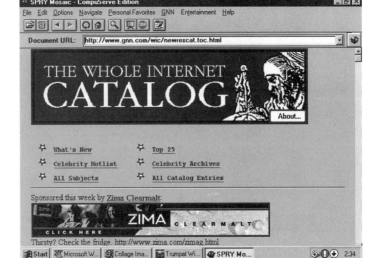

Like Yahoo, this site contains a hierarchical list, categorized by resource type. It is not a comprehensive list, however, containing only what its publishers consider to be the best WWW pages for each category listed. The advantage of this sort of list is the fact that it helps you wade through the many thousands of pages on the World Wide Web, each of which tends to cover a topic in many different, though not necessarily effective, ways. This catalog reduces the number of sites you need to explore in your effort to locate information.

In addition to the general resource list, there are also special pages that cover the following topics:

◆ The Celebrity Hotlist, a page where special Internet guest editors are invited to share their most popular WWW pages

◆ The What's New listing

◆ The Top 25 WWW sites

The Whole Internet Catalog is provided as a part of the Global Network Navigator (GNN). To explore the links this catalog provides, use the following http address: `http://www.gnn.com/wic/newrescat.toc.html`.

Global Network Navigator

The Global Network Navigator (GNN) itself, which is provided by O'Reilly and Associates, also contains links to many other popular sites and services. (See Figure 12.4.) To access this site, use the following http address: `http://www.gnn.com`.

FIGURE 12.4.

GNN—The Global Network Navigator.

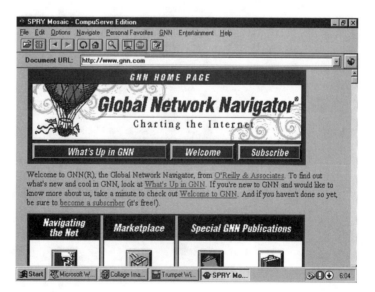

In addition to The Whole Internet catalog, GNN maintains a number of specialized WWW lists that include the following subjects:

◆ Best of the Net

◆ Personal finance

◆ Education

- ◆ Net news
- ◆ Sports
- ◆ Travel

The table of contents for GNN also provides a very good list of major WWW sites and popular home pages at `http://gnn.com/gnn/wic/internet.toc.html`.

> *Note*
>
> Before you can use many of the services offered by GNN, you will need to become a subscriber. There is no cost involved in doing this. All you need to do is complete the Online Information form that is available from the GNN home page by selecting the Subscribe option.

The WWW Virtual Library

By far the most comprehensive list of WWW pages currently available can be found at the WWW Virtual Library, whose http address is `http://www.w3.org/hypertext/DataSources/bySubject/Overview.html`. (See Figure 12.5.)

FIGURE 12.5.

The WWW Virtual Library contains links to most WWW pages.

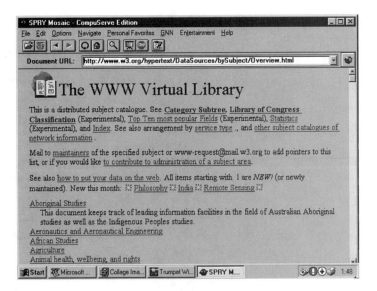

The WWW Virtual Library categorizes the pages it contains into over 150 major classifications, which themselves are often further broken down into more specific topic areas. As you may have already noticed, this service is provided by the W3 Consortium as the primary resource for WWW-related indexes. To this end, there are also a number of special pages that provide you with additional information, including:

- ◆ The Category Subtree
- ◆ The Library of Congress
- ◆ Top Ten most popular fields
- ◆ The Virtual Library Index
- ◆ The Virtual Library by service type
- ◆ A list of other Internet catalogs

This site also operates in a slightly different manner than most other major lists. If someone discovers a category that is not properly represented in the Virtual Library, instead of just letting the administrators know that they have been remiss, that person often takes over the maintenance of this new area and keeps the links it contains up-to-date. To make suggestions about new categories, select the "to contribute to administration of a subject area" hot link.

EINet Galaxy

EINet Galaxy (Figure 12.6) is organized in a slightly different manner than the other major WWW directories. At its core, Galaxy is driven by a complex database system that uses a *manufacturing automation and design engineering* (MADE) program. This program allows the categories, or information structures, Galaxy maintains to be indexed and cross-referenced in a manner not permitted by conventional hierarchical lists.

FIGURE 12.6.

EINet Galaxy lets you search a variety of databases for WWW pages.

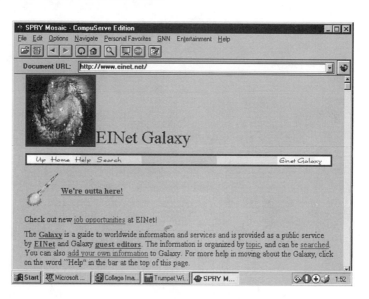

To access these indexes, Galaxy provides you with a navigation database that allows you to move easily around the Galaxy environment and quickly locate relevant information. Every information page on Galaxy contains a search field where you can enter words you want to locate. When you enter a word, a new information list is displayed that outlines all of the related information structures.

To complement the navigation database, there are also service-specific databases that allow you to search for Gopher, Telnet, and WWW links separately.

If you are interested in exploring Galaxy, you can reach it via the EINet home page at `http://www.einet.net/`.

Note

> This site also contains information about the variety of services and tools offered by EINet, which include the WinWeb WWW browser and a variety of other browser and server products.

Spry HotLand

Although far from being the most comprehensive list of WWW sites available, for Spry Mosaic users, HotLand (Figure 12.7) offers some unique capabilities.

FIGURE 12.7.

HotLand WWW categories can be downloaded to your computer in the form of Spry Hotlists.

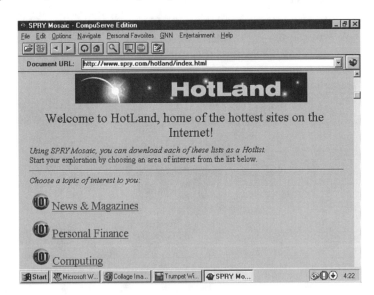

Spry bills this page the "home of the hottest sites on the Internet." To achieve this claim, they have spent a considerable amount of time combing the WWW looking for hot sites that offer both the best and most unique services. Although their choice of sites is still based very much on personal opinions, HotLand comes into its own because it allows you to download a copy of all of the links in each of the categories as a hotlist. Once downloaded, you can open the list as you would any other hotlist.

To obtain a copy of these hotlists or to simply browse the sites Spry nominates as the hottest on the Internet, use this http address: `http://www.spry.com/hotland/index.html`.

The Mother-of-all BBS

For a different approach to the categorization of WWW pages, you should take a look at the Mother-of-all BBS listing. (See Figure 12.8.) This site is very much a self-service directory that allows anyone to create new categories—called BBS's—and add new entries to existing ones. The http address for the Mother-of-all BBS is `http://www.cs.colorado.edu/homes/mcbryan/public_html/bb/summary.html`.

FIGURE 12.8.

The Mother-of-all BBS.

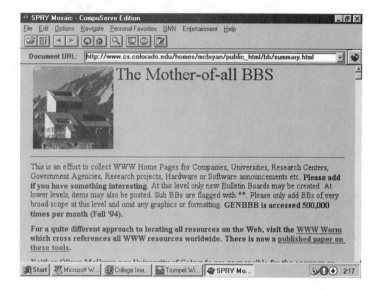

WWW Search Tools

If spending hours scanning endless lists of WWW pages is not your style, maybe a more direct approach will better suit your needs.

With more than four million pages of information now directly available via the World Wide Web, not to mention the countless FTP and Gopher sites, it did not take too long for a number of WWW search tools and utilities to appear. Many of these tools provide access to a variety of information sources, including WWW pages, FTP sites or files, and WAIS directories.

This section examines some of the more popular WWW search tools and provides you with details about the types of information indexed by each.

Lycos

By all accounts, the most comprehensive index of WWW sites is maintained by a search tool developed at Carnegie Mellon University. The name of this tool is Lycos. (See Figure 12.9.) As of the time of writing, Lycos had indexed 4.4 million WWW pages and was adding thousands of new pages each day.

FIGURE 12.9.

Lycos is the most comprehensive WWW index currently available.

Like many of the WWW search tools currently available, Lycos has created its impressive index by automatically exploring the World Wide Web, page by page and link by link, following all of the paths each page offers and recording each one as it visits it. In the last six months, Lycos has become one of the busiest places on the World Wide Web, with over 15 million requests for information being answered.

To access this index, Lycos provides you with a variety of search options that allow you to search either the full database or a smaller "recent pages" database. There is also a simple search page and a more complex form-based page that lets you configure details such as the number of matches reported and even the search benchmarks. On the home page shown in Figure 12.9, you can choose any of these search options and select from pages that contain information about the use of Lycos. You can reach this page at `http://lycos.cs.cmu.edu/`.

When you type a word or combination of words into one of the search fields provided, Lycos searches its index and displays a list of results that match your query on a page similar to the one shown in Figure 12.10. From here you can select any of the links that Lycos has returned to take you directly to the WWW page described. (See "The Web and Hubble" in Chapter 16, "Family Fun and Education," for more information on using Lycos.)

In spite of its popularity, Lycos is still only in beta release. In the future, its author plans to include extended Boolean features and possibly a search capability, known as relevance feedback, made popular by WAIS.

FIGURE 12.10.

You can select any of the links listed in the results of a Lycos search to move straight to the nominated page.

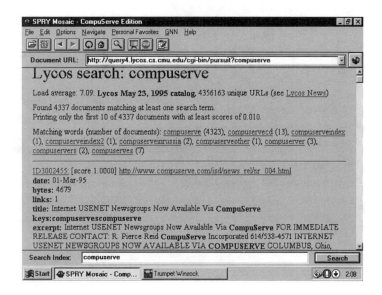

Spry's Wizard

For users of Spry Mosaic, there is a special search tool called the Spry Internet Wizard that allows you to create hotlists based on search results.

Like Lycos, the Internet Wizard lets you search an index consisting of WWW pages by entering a word or combination of words. Where it differs, however, is in the addition of the check box, shown in Figure 12.11, just below the search field. If you select this box, when the Internet Wizard completes its search, a hotlist is created that contains all of the links that were located. You can then download this hotlist to your local hard drive and install it on your menu in the same manner as any other hotlist you are currently using.

To access the Internet Wizard, select it on the CompuServe home page or use the following http address: `http://www.spry.com/wizard/index.html`.

ArchiPlex

The World Wide Web is not limited to providing WWW search tools. There are a number of other services currently available online that index many other popular Internet sources. Of these, one of the most popular is ArchiPlex.

ArchiPlex is a World Wide Web extension to the Archie server discussed in Chapter 10, "File Transfer Protocol (FTP)." Instead of using a Telnet connection or a dedicated Archie client, by taking advantage of ArchiPlex, you can use the World Wide Web to locate files stored at anonymous FTP sites. (See Figure 12.12.) In addition, once you have located the files you are interested in (Figure 12.13), you can also take advantage of the FTP capabilities built into each WWW browser to retrieve a copy of the files and store them on your local hard drive.

FIGURE 12.11.

Wizard creates downloadable hotlists based on the results of the searches it conducts.

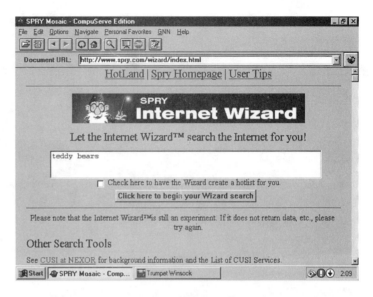

FIGURE 12.12.

ArchiPlex, the WWW gateway to files on FTP servers.

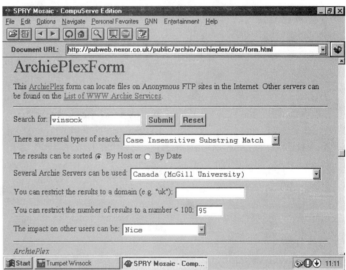

FIGURE 12.13.

When ArchiPlex returns the results of a search, you can simply select any of the files listed to download them.

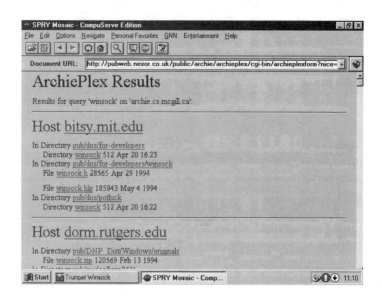

There are a number of ArchiPlex pages that you can choose from, operated by WWW sites all over the Internet. To view a list of all the ArchiPlex pages currently available, point your WWW browser to `http://pubweb.nexor.co.uk/public/archie/servers.html`.

> Depending on the time of day, Archie servers will respond to your queries with either promptness or downright tardiness. If you find that you have not received a response within a couple of minutes, you should cancel the request and try another server. You do not need to change ArchiPlex pages to do this. Simply adjust the Archie server field on the request form.

WAISgate

Although most WWW browsers are capable of directly communicating with WAIS servers, the results obtained when they do are often less than suitable. To get around this problem, WAIS Inc., one of the leading WAIS publishers and developers, provides a WWW gateway called WAISgate. (See Figure 12.14.)

FIGURE 12.14.

WAISgate gives you full access to the files and databases available via WAIS.

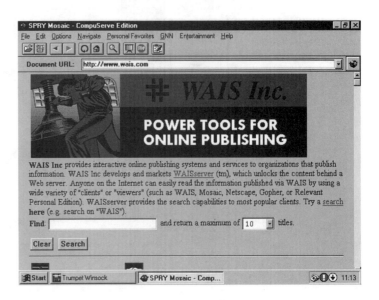

This gateway offers a form-based interface that greatly enhances the WWW/WAIS interface and provides a method of operation that seamlessly integrates the two services. (See "WAIS and Hubble" in Chapter 16 for a demonstration of WAISgate.)

To access WAISgate, use the following http address: `http://www.wais.com`.

> WAIS, Inc. is currently working on a new release of WAISgate, dubbed WAISgate 2.0. To try a sample of what they plan to offer, select the WAISgate 2.0 demo option on the WAIS Inc. home page.

Popular WWW Search Pages and Locations

Apart from the four services already mentioned, there are about 20 other major WWW or Internet indexes and search pages, each of which offers a slightly different user interface and index. Most are not as comprehensive as those already discussed, but at the same time they often contain information that may not be available on other pages.

There are a number of ways to locate these different pages, the simplest of which is to follow the links on one of the WWW search tool pages. Figure 12.15 shows the list provided by Netscape on its WWW search page at `http://home.netscape.com/escapes/internet_search.html`.

This page also features a direct link to the new commercial InfoSeek WWW index, which aims to provide the most comprehensive Internet index ever created.

FIGURE 12.15.

The Netscape list of search tools and utilities.

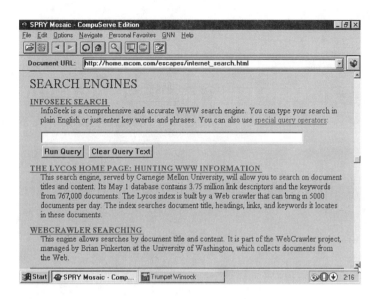

At the bottom of this page, there is also a link to a page known as the Configurable Unified Search Engine (CUSI). CUSI contains a list of all the known search engines that are accessible via the World Wide Web. These include:

Lycos, WebCrawler, InfoSeek, and Jumpstation

ALIWEB, Yahoo, Global On-Line Directory, and the CUI W3 Catalog

Veronica, WAIS, and the Whole Internet Catalog

ArchiPlex, CICA & SIMTEL Archives, HENSA Micro Archive

However, instead of just providing hotlinks to the appropriate pages, you can enter your search criterion in the space provided on the CUSI page (Figure 12.16) and click the related search button. The search page will look after the job of connecting to the search engine you selected and the submission of your query request.

To use the CUSI interface, take a look at `http://pubweb.nexor.co.uk/public/cusi/cusi.html`.

Access to CUSI is also available on the Spry Internet Wizard page at `http://www.spry.com/wizard/index.html`.

Note

For a slightly different service that provides many of the same features, try `http://cuiwww.unige.ch/meta-index.html`. (See Figure 12.17.)

FIGURE 12.16.

Select the search engine you want to use and enter your query parameters. The CUSI page will look after the rest of the job for you.

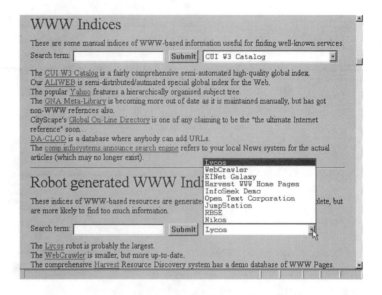

FIGURE 12.17.

Instead of dropdown boxes, this page lists each WWW search tool separately.

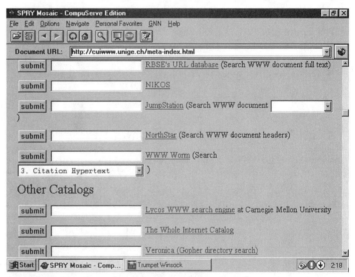

Cool and Unusual Places

Since it seems that just about everyone else on the Internet now publishes his own list of favorite places, why should I be any different? As a result, all of the WWW pages and links mentioned in this book are listed in chapter order at my home page: `http://www.webcom.com/~taketwo/sams/nav-int-cis.html`. This is also the site of my Take Two film and television directory, among other things. (Cheap plug.)

As for the other things, in the pages that follow I have compiled a list of cool and unusual places for you to explore. This list is an ideal place to start your own exploration of the Internet and maybe even your own personal list—but more about that later. First the list: `http://www.webcom/com/~taketwo/sams/cool.html`.

GNN's Best of the Net

GNN's Best of the Net (Figure 12.18) was first proposed in 1994 as a way of recognizing expertise in all areas of World Wide Web development. The nominees for this year's awards are currently being collated here, alongside the honorees for 1994. This list recognizes not just WWW pages, but also services such as Lycos and even programs like Netscape and NCSA Mosaic that have made an outstanding contribution to the development of the World Wide Web. It can be found at `http://gnn.com/gnn/wic/best.toc.html`.

FIGURE 12.18.

It may not be the Academy Awards, but for Netsurfers the Best of the Net is just as important.

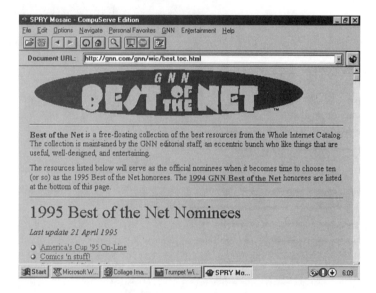

If you find a service that you think should be listed here, there are instructions for making a nomination at the bottom of the Best of the Net page.

ESPNET SportsZone

If you're into sports or just like to watch, ESPNET SportsZone is the place to be. (See Figure 12.19.) Each day, the latest news and information about many popular sports and sports personalities is brought to you live via the World Wide Web. The address is `http://web1.starwave.com:80/`.

FIGURE 12.19.

*The home of Internet
sportscasting.*

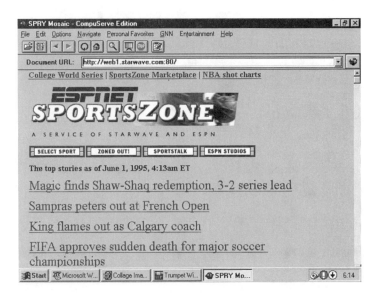

You can either select from the list of sports covered, find out who's zoned out, or catch up on all the latest sports talk. When you're done, drop by the ESPN studios for all the late-breaking excitement.

The Movie Database

Have you ever found yourself in one of those arguments that seem destined to occur over coffee? Frankly, who really cares what character Clint Eastwood played in the first movie he both directed and produced? Nevertheless, it's a debate that will often drag on into the small hours of the morning. To solve this dilemma, what you really need is your handy laptop computer, a cellular modem, and the Internet Movie Database (Figure 12.20). It can be found at either `http://www.cm.cf.ac.uk/Movies/` or `http://www.msstate.edu/Movies/`.

The Internet Movie Database is a classic example of what happens when a group of people with a good idea put their minds to making it happen. Since 1989, a small group of dedicated individuals has spent many thousands of hours creating what is one of the most comprehensive databases of movies and television programs available today. To search this database, select the search option displayed on the home pages shown in Figure 12.20. You will be presented with a list of search options that include:

◆ Actors and actresses

◆ Producers, directors, and writers

◆ Editors, cinematographers, and costume designers

◆ Movie titles, release dates, and running times

Based on these parameters and many others, you can search the database and examine movie plots, cast biographies, and even lists of goofs and crazy credits.

FIGURE 12.20.

A WWW interface to the Internet Movie Database.

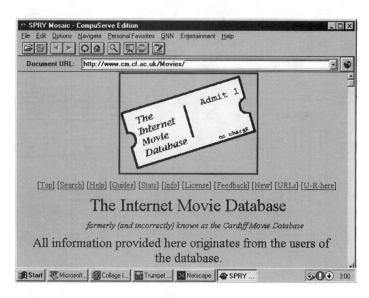

For those of you who are interested in these things, the movie was *Firefox*, made in 1982. Clint Eastwood played Mitchell Gant while both directing and producing the finished product.

The Electronic Zoo

For animal lovers, the Electronic Zoo (Figure 12.21) offers links to every related WWW page, along with a number of non-WWW sites. The Zoo was created by Dr. Ken Boschert, a veterinarian who spends many a late night surfing the Internet. It can be found at `http://netvet.wustl.edu/e-zoo.htm`.

At the Zoo, you will find sites categorized by both species and Internet service type. As a result, you can look for information by following a direct path to the animal of your choice or by a less direct, but often equally informative, path via a selection of Gopher, Telnet, mailing lists, electronic publications, and newsgroups.

To accompany this service, Dr. Ken also maintains the NetVet WWW and Gopher server, which contains information relevant to veterinary studies. The http address for NetVet is `http://netvet.wustl.edu/vet.htm`.

The White House

The White House site's biggest claim to fame is not the personal message recorded by the President or the Vice President. (See Figure 12.22.) It is not the guided tour of the White House by the First Family. Nor is it the list of publications and information about the executive branch of the United States government. Instead, it is the recording of Socks (the First Cat), which can be downloaded during the First Family tour. If you don't believe me, take a look for yourself. I won't tell you exactly where it is, but yes, it is in there.

The http address for the White House home page is `http://www.whitehouse.gov/`.

FIGURE 12.21.

If it's about animals and it's on the Internet, you can find it here.

FIGURE 12.22.

Ever wanted to hear a personal message from the President of the United States? Click the President's Welcome Message button.

Note

To hear any of the audio clips available on this site, your computer will need to be fitted with a suitable sound card. For those without a card, there is also a written transcript of each speech.

42—Deep Thought

If you are familiar with the five books in Douglas Adams' infamous *Hitchhiker's Guide to the Galaxy* trilogy, this page (Figure 12.23) might be of interest. Basically, it's all about the number 42. Far from being an example of a serious page, I have included it here to show that anything is possible on the World Wide Web. It's at `http://www.well.com/user/dljones/`.

For those of you who have not read any of the books in this series, in book 2, *The Restaurant at the End of the Universe*, Arthur Dent, the book's reluctant hero, discovers that the answer to the ultimate question of Life, the Universe and Everything is "42." The only problem is, no one knows what the question was.

FIGURE 12.23.

The Hitchhiker's Guide to what?

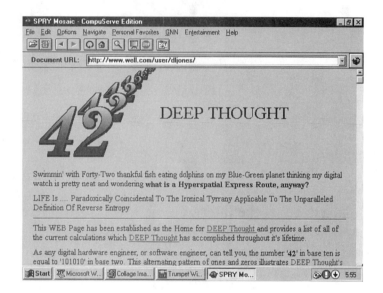

Useless Pages, or America's Funniest Home Hypermedia

It seems to be a fact of life that the moment you turn a video camera on even the most seemingly normal person, a strange metamorphosis takes place that often results in the most astounding actions. Now it seems this same affliction is starting to appear on the World Wide Web. Give a person the ability to publish her own WWW page, and you often get some strange results.

And like the popular *America's Funniest Home Videos* program, there is now America's Funniest Home Hypermedia page to catalog these pages. (See Figure 12.24.) If you really want to know the contents of Scott's sock drawer, this is the page for you. This is not to say that many of these otherwise useless pages are not worth paying a visit. Some, in fact, are extremely clever and in the past have resulted in their developers receiving considerable notoriety. This page is at `http://www.primus.com/staff/paulp/useless.html`.

FIGURE 12.24.

More pages that exist because someone felt like creating them.

> As a challenge, try to locate the HOTTUB page, which continually updates the temperature in Paul Haas's hot tub and refrigerator.

Understanding the Internet

To accompany their television special "Understanding the Internet," produced in conjunction with the Discovery Channel, Cochran Interactive Inc. has created this special WWW site that provides over 200 links to information that new Internet users will find invaluable. It's at `http://www.screen.com/start`. (See Figure 12.25.)

The Macmillan Web Site of the Week

The Macmillan Publishing WWW site at `www.mcp.com` is the home of the Web Site of the Week competition (`http://www.mcp.com/hypermail/website/`). Web publishers are invited to nominate themselves as contestants in this competition. At the end of each week, a new WWW site is selected based on its design, content, and overall originality. (See Figure 12.26.)

If you have created your own WWW site and would like it to be considered, all you need to do is follow the steps outlined on the competition page. To take a look at the winner for the 1st week of June, use this http address: `http://www.corelnet.com/`. (See Figure 12.27.)

FIGURE 12.25.

If you want to learn more about the Internet, check out this site.

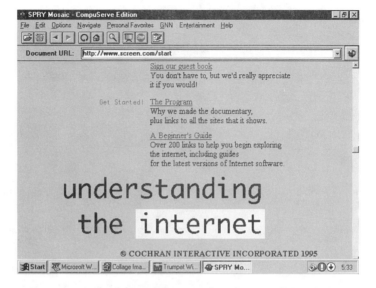

FIGURE 12.26.

Nominate your entrant for the Web Site of the Week competition.

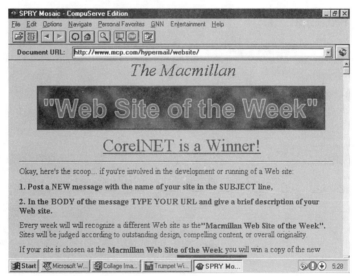

FIGURE 12.27.

CorelNET—site of the week as of June 1st.

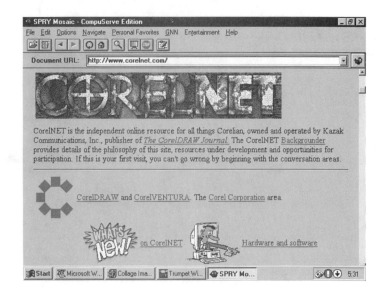

WebChat

In recent months, an innovation has appeared on the Internet that brings real-time communications like IRC to the World Wide Web. By taking advantage of the capabilities built into many new WWW browsers, it is now possible to use a site such as WebChat as an interactive alternative to IRC. (See Figure 12.28.) Although they are still very experimental, many of these chat environments are rapidly gaining popularity as more and more people become aware of their existence. WebChat can be found at `http://www.irsociety.com/webchat/webchat.html`.

FIGURE 12.28.

IRC meets the World Wide Web.

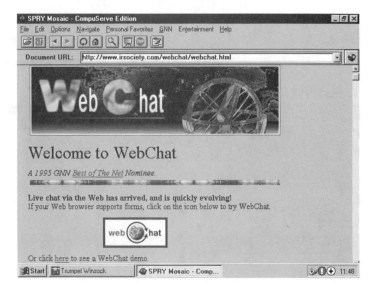

> To use WebChat, you need a modem that is capable of at least 9,600bps, with 14,400 or 28,800 offering better performance.

Publishing Your Own Home Page

If you're tired of looking at other people's WWW pages and thinking, "I could do better than this," maybe it's time you began to explore the possibility of setting up your own home page. Doing so is not as complicated as it may first appear, and the costs involved can be relatively small, depending on the type of WWW page you want to operate.

This section looks briefly at the steps involved in setting up your own WWW home page and points you towards a number of sources that can help make your personal WWW page a reality.

Finding a WWW Service Provider

There are basically two ways to go about setting up your own home page. You can either follow the expensive path of installing your own WWW server (see Chapter 17, "Business on the Net") or rent space from a WWW service provider.

For most people, the WWW server option is simply not practical unless they already have access to the Internet via a university or place of employment. The best alternative is to find a WWW server that will allow you to add your pages to its hard drive and provide you the appropriate access to manage the information your pages contain.

Depending on your location, there are a number of different approaches that different organizations provide to give you WWW access. Some Internet service providers will allow you to create your own WWW pages as a part of their standard service, while others provide a WWW server as an additional service.

> Although you cannot currently store WWW pages on CompuServe, there have been rumors that you may be able to do this in the future. Keep an eye on the What's New pages for future information on this and many other proposed developments.

On CompuServe, WWW server access is not available as a part of the services provided, but you can still obtain access to other WWW servers that have been set up specifically for the purpose of renting WWW space. Chapter 17 takes a closer look at one such service, WebCom, but there may be others more suited to your needs.

To locate the best WWW server for your needs, you should examine either of these two sites: `http://union.ncsa.uiuc.edu:80/HyperNews/get/www/leasing.html` or `ftp://ftp.einet.net/pub/INET-MARKETING/www-svc-providers`.

The main difference you will find between most of the services on these lists is one of support. If you don't mind doing the work yourself, you can usually get away with around $10 a month for a very capable service. On the other hand, if you own a business that just wants to get on the Internet, a fully maintained site will cost around $150 a month, and this price can go considerably higher.

For additional information on World Wide Web and Internet service providers in general, the documents maintained by the Internet Society are also a good place to start. The http address for the Internet Society is `http://www.isoc.org/`.

HTML

Once you have access to a WWW server, you're basically ready to create your home page and place yourself on the World Wide Web. Unless you have chosen a WWW service that will create these pages for you, your next step should be to do some research into HTML, the language used to write WWW pages.

There are a number of very good sources of information about HTML, including full tutorials and documents discussing all manner of design strategies, on the World Wide Web itself. Many of these documents have been collated by the W3 Consortium and placed on the page shown in Figure 12.29, whose http address is `http://www.w3.org/hypertext/WWW/MarkUp/MarkUp.html`.

FIGURE 12.29.
The W3 HTML page.

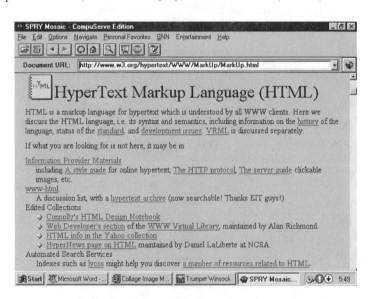

You should also take a look at the following pages as well, each of which provides additional information about using HTML to create functional and sophisticated WWW pages:

`http://www.ncsa.uiuc.edu/demoweb/html-primer.html`

`http://www.webcom.com/~webcom/html/`

```
http://www.netscape.com/assist/net_sites/index.html

http://union.ncsa.uiuc.edu:80/HyperNews/get/www/html/guides.html
```

Although creating WWW pages is not an overly complex task, it is a subject that is best left to the many online documents that do it the justice the subject deserves. One of the reasons for this is the fact that the entire HTML specification is currently in a state of flux.

The HTML design standard has been through two major releases in its relatively short life, and is at the moment about to undergo another revision for the release of HTML 3.0. To keep track of all the latest changes and updates, you should keep a close watch on the pages maintained by the W3 Consortium, which is administering the current development and design strategies that will be implemented in version 3.

Hello World by HTML

Having said that, let's take a brief look at the contents of an HTML file and look at how you go about the development of a simple "Hello World" home page.

An HTML document is basically a simple ASCII text file with a number of special instructions included that tell the WWW client how it should display the page. I created a simple WWW page, shown in Figure 12.30, by entering the HTML information into a text file using the Windows Notepad. When this page is displayed using Spry Mosaic, this information creates the page shown in Figure 12.31.

FIGURE 12.30.

You can create HTML pages using the Windows Notepad.

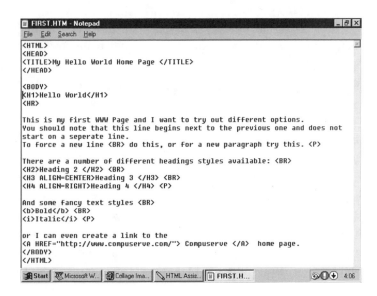

FIGURE 12.31.

You can use Spry Mosaic to display the page using the Load icon.

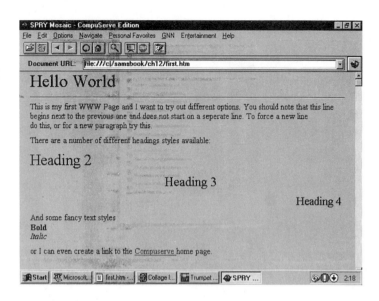

There are obviously many other commands available in HTML, but this example should at least take you some of the way toward the creation of your home page.

Building Blocks

To add an HTML command or *element* to an ASCII text file, enclose the element between a less-than sign (<) and a greater-than sign (>). When a WWW browser encounters a word contained within these symbols, it knows that it needs to interpret the command and perform some sort of action.

In Figure 12.30, you should be able to identify a number of such elements, including:

```
<HEAD>
```

```
<H2>
```

```
</BODY>
```

Each of these elements tells the browser how it should format the text contained in the file or provide the information required to create hotlinks and display inline graphics. The best way to think of elements is like a switch. An element like <H1> tells the browser to turn on the Heading 1 print style for any text that occurs after it in the document. Until the text style is changed or Heading 1 is turned off by issuing a </H1> command, the text will be printed in large bold letters. The slash (/) after the < symbol acts as an off switch for the element command that follows it.

Let's go through this line by line:

```
<HTML>
```

The `<HTML>` element tells the browser where the start of the HTML information is. Although many browsers automatically assume that the start of the document is the start of the HTML information, you should always include an `<HTML>` element.

> If you want to add descriptive notes to a WWW page, place them before the `<HTML>` element so they won't be displayed by WWW browsers.

`<HEAD>`

At the top of every HTML document, you should always create a Heading section so that the browser knows some basic information about the page.

`<TITLE>My Hello World Home Page </TITLE>`

The Title element is not actually displayed on the page itself, but instead in the Document URL field mentioned in the previous chapter. If you have this field turned on, the words "My Hello World Home Page" will be shown.

`</HEAD>`

Use this element to close the Heading section of your WWW page.

> Although it is possible to insert displayable text into the Heading section, it is not technically correct to do so. You should only include information in the Heading section that describes the contents of the page.

`<BODY>`

All of the text that will be displayed on your WWW page should be included in the Body section. This element indicates the start of the body of your page.

`<H1>Hello World</H1>`

This is the first piece of actual text that will be displayed on the WWW page. By placing it inside the `<H1> </H1>` element set, the WWW browser will display "Hello World" using the Heading 1 text format.

`<HR>`

The `<HR>` (Horizontal Rule) element is a graphical element that tells the WWW browser to place a line across the screen. (No `</HR>` is needed for this type of element.)

Any text that is typed into the document is displayed on the WWW page in normal text format unless any special formatting elements are active. You should also note that the WWW browser takes no notice of the layout of the text you have entered. It ignores any carriage returns, line feeds, or new lines you place in the text.

To force a new line to be inserted into the WWW page, place a `<BR>` element in the text. All the text that appears after this element is placed on a new line. Alternatively, you can use a `<P>` element to force a new paragraph, which is effectively a double new line element.

> In HTML 3.0, the paragraph option may support a `</P>` element. This will allow you to define each paragraph as a separate block of text.

```
<H2>Heading 2 </H2>
```

There are six different heading Type Styles, which represent different size text formats. As the heading number increases, the size of the text decreases, with `<H5>` being approximately the same size as normal text and `<H6>` slightly smaller again.

```
<H3 ALIGN=CENTER>Heading 3 </H3>
```

```
<H4 ALIGN=RIGHT>Heading 4 </H4>
```

By including the `ALIGN` command as a part of the Heading element, you can instruct the WWW browser to center or right justify the text contained within the element boundaries—that is, before the `</` element. For consistency's sake, there is also an `ALIGN=LEFT` command. However, this is rarely if ever used, since it is the default option.

> The `ALIGN` command is a part of the HTML 3.0 specification, and as such, not all browsers currently support it for all elements.

```
<b>Bold</b>
```

```
<i>Italic</i>
```

There are also a number of style elements that allow you to alter the way text is displayed. At this stage, though, this feature is very much WWW browser-specific, especially if you use some of the less well-documented styles. Where possible, stick to Bold and Italic for the moment, at least until the HTML 3.0 specification is adopted by all WWW browsers.

> There is also an Underline element, `<U>`, which has fallen into disuse due to the fact that so many people set their browsers to display all hotlinks with an underline. As a result, you should avoid using this element wherever possible.

```
<A HREF="http://www.compuserve.com/"> CompuServe </A>
```

This is by far the most complex element on the whole page. It is used to define a hotlink to the CompuServe home page at `www.compuserve.com`. The `<A ... >` element tells a WWW browser that the text between it and the `</A>` element should be marked as a hotlink. In this case, the word "CompuServe" becomes the hotlink.

The information contained inside the `<A ... >` element itself is used to indicate the action that will occur when this hotlink is selected. The `HREF="http://www.compuserve.com/"` following the `<A` is the physical declaration of the location of CompuServe's home page. `HREF` can point to either an absolute address like this one or a relative address such as `HREF="index.html"`. It can also be used to point to a location within the current page using `HREF="#someplace"`, where `someplace` was defined by using:

```
<A NAME="someplace"> </A>
```

To find out more about creating links, check out the excellent documentation at `http://www.webcom.com`.

```
</BODY>
```

At the end of the Body section, you need to remember to place a Close element. In most cases the browser will assume you have finished a page if you forget to include a `</BODY>` element at the very end of the document, but you should get used to including it, because in the future there may be other elements that require its existence.

```
</HTML>
```

Finally, close the HTML section by issuing an `</HTML>` command.

HTML Editors

As you become more familiar with the use of HTML, you will probably want to replace your text editor with a dedicated HTML editor. These programs provide you with a lot of special features that are designed specially for the creation of WWW pages.

There are currently about 15 different HTML editors available from various Internet sites, each of which offers slightly different capabilities. To give you some idea of the types of editors available, the following pages include short descriptions of the major contenders. For each site, you will find an FTP location where you can download a copy of the program and a home page address that contains additional information about it.

If you don't find an editor in this collection that suits your needs, there are a number of places on the World Wide Web that discuss the types of HTML editors available. By far, the most comprehensive list is maintained by Yahoo. To access this list, use the following http address: `http://www.yahoo.com/Computers/World_Wide_Web/HTML_Editors/MS_Windows/`.

Live Markup

FTP site: `ftp.mediatec.com/pub/mediatech/`

Home page: `http://www.digimark.net/mediatech/`

Live Markup (Figure 12.32) is the first of the new wave of HTML editors that bring true "what you see is what you get" (WYSIWYG) editing to the HTML world.

FIGURE 12.32.

Live Markup allows you to edit your page in HTML instead of text.

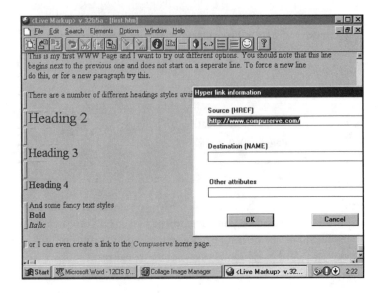

In Live Markup, you edit your HTML document in an environment that closely approximates the actual appearance of your finished document. By doing this, most of the HTML commands are hidden away, allowing you to get on with the job of designing WWW pages instead of worrying about whether you have used the correct element.

This approach also removes the need for switching back and forth between your editor and a WWW browser to check how your changes look. With Live Markup, you see the changes you make as they happen. On the downside, you will need at least a DX66 computer to cope with the amount of work the computer needs to do to maintain this environment, and 16MB of memory won't hurt either.

If you have the computer power and are serious about developing in HTML, this is one editor that you definitely need to check out. Included in the program is full support for inline graphics and all of the new HTML 3.0 features, plus many of the special Netscape 1.1 enhancements, all of which are displayed on-screen as you create them.

There are currently two versions of Live Markup available. The first is released as shareware, while the more powerful Pro version is available only as a commercial product. Depending on your needs, you can choose to use either version by visiting the Live Markup home page, which contains downloadable copies of the standard version and ordering information and comparison tables for the Pro edition.

> In the words of one HTML editor developer, "HTML 3.0 is currently a moving target." As a result, this editor is still in a constant state of development. For this reason, the developers of Live Markup are offering special rates to new purchasers of the Pro version, which includes free upgrades for the remainder of 1995.

Note

HoTMetaL

FTP site: `ftp://ftp.ncsa.uiuc.edu/Web/html/hotmetal/Windows`

Home page: `http://www.sq.com/hmpro.html`

HoTMetaL (Figure 12.33) is probably the most popular HTML editor currently available. It offers a powerful editing environment that represents each element as a tag. This allows for easy recognition of the element's purpose and correct placement. In addition, there is also a WYSIWYG viewing option, which approximates the appearance of your finished page, although it is not quite as accurate as Live Markup.

FIGURE 12.33.

HoTMetaL represents elements as easily recognizable tags.

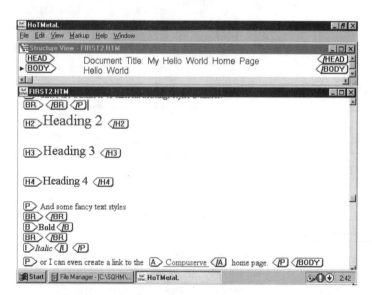

By far, the most popular feature of this program is its extensive error checking and document validation routines. Whenever you save a WWW page using HoTMetaL, it is first checked to ensure that the document complies with the HTML specification. If an element is out of place or has been incorrectly used, you will be given a message that tells you what needs to be fixed.

This program comes in a commercial version and a somewhat less-featured freeware version, but unfortunately the freeware version is incompatible with many of the new HTML 3.0 features. As a result, if you plan to do any serious work with HoTMetaL, you will need to purchase the commercial version. Ordering information and access to the downloadable version can all be found on the HoTMetaL home page.

HTML Assistant

FTP site: `ftp://ftp.cs.dal.ca/htmlasst`

Home page: `ftp://ftp.cs.dal.ca/htmlasst/lernhtml.htm`

HTML Assistant can best be thought of as a text editor that helps you create WWW pages; hence the name. For this reason, you will need to have a fairly good knowledge of HTML design methods to take full advantage of this program.

There are no fancy WYSIWYG displays or error checking. Instead, you get a solid text editor that allows you to insert HTML commands with a click of a button on the toolbar. Just about every possible HTML command has a button assigned to it or a corresponding menu option. (See Figure 12.34.) This allows you to quickly add HTML elements to your WWW page without having to remember how each one is written.

FIGURE 12.34.

The toolbar gives you access to all the major HTML commands.

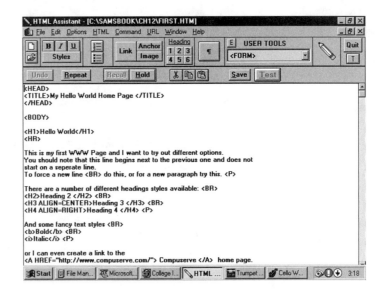

Although the WYSIWYG style of WWW page design is gaining popularity, many people find that the straightforward, click-and-go approach of HTML Assistant can get their pages up and running just as fast, if not faster. What's more, the freeware version is full-featured, with all of the major commands already supported. There is also a commercial version with a number of additional features, including wizards that automate much of the creation process and special filters that can strip HTML commands out of documents.

Note

The URL for the HTML Assistant home page is slightly different from those you have seen to date. Instead of starting with `http://`, it begins with `ftp://`. This home page is an example of a HTML document stored on an anonymous FTP server instead of a WWW server. Spry Mosaic will display the page correctly only if you use `ftp://`.

WebEdit

Home page: `http://wwwnt.thegroup.net/webedit/webedit.htm`

Like HTML Assistant, WebEdit (Figure 12.35) is a text-based HTML editor. Where it differs is in the way it helps you with the creation of your WWW page.

FIGURE 12.35.

The WebEdit URL builder guides you through the steps required to form a valid URL.

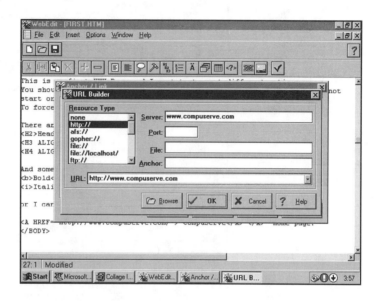

When you select many of the options on its toolbar, a dialog box opens to guide you through the steps needed to complete the information an element requires. This is especially valuable when you're designing complex forms and pages with many links. There is also a special feature that allows you to define your own commonly used tags so you can recall them for later use. For example, if you always place a `mailto:` link at the bottom of your pages so people can send you e-mail, you can easily add a copy to each page by placing this information in a tag.

Unlike all of the editors mentioned previously, there is no freeware version of this program. Instead, the authors have released it as shareware. If you choose to continue using WebEdit after the 30-day trial period, you will need to pay a registration fee to the program's developers.

Internet Assistant for Word 6.0

Home page: `http://www.microsoft.com/pages/deskapps/word/ia/default.htm`

If you cast your mind back to Chapter 10, you may recall that the file you downloaded as a demonstration was an add-on module for Microsoft Word called Internet Assistant. (See Figure 12.36.)

What Internet Assistant does is turn Word 6.0 into a WYSIWYG HTML editor. Once you install Internet Assistant on your computer, you can open an HTML document in much the same manner as a normal Word document, but instead of displaying the word processing editing tools, Word displays a special set of HTML editing tools. Using these tools, you can design WWW pages that include all the different heading and text styles and even URL links or inline graphics.

FIGURE 12.36.

Edit WWW pages and browse the Internet as well.

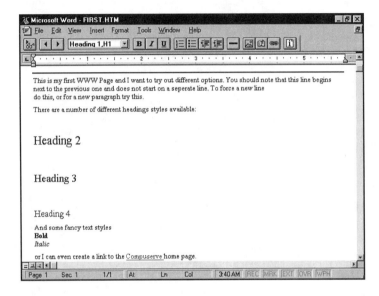

Then, when you have created your home page masterpiece, you can also use Internet Assistant as a fully featured WWW browser that even takes advantage of WinSock and NetLauncher, just like Spry Mosaic.

> You must already have Microsoft Word version 6.0a running on your computer before you can install Internet Assistant.

Summary

By now you should have come to the realization that with just a WWW browser you can take advantage of nearly everything the Internet has to offer. You can read newsgroups, download files, and even chat with other people in real time. By providing a single, easy-to use interface, the World Wide Web has done more to give people access to the Internet than any other tool.

But there is still one topic that we have not explored fully. The next chapter examines one final feature of the World Wide Web that allows you to access another type of Internet navigator, called a Gopher.

GOPHER

Before the World Wide Web came to popularity, there was another Internet navigator that provided many of the features offered by a WWW browser. This navigator was aptly named the Internet *Gopher*, due to its ability to dig through the layers of information contained on the Internet and in the world it created, called *Gopherspace.*

Although Gopher has been replaced by the World Wide Web as the navigator of choice, there are still many Gopher servers in operation. This chapter looks at how to access Gopherspace—using the World Wide Web, strangely enough—by dealing with these topics:

◆ What Is Gopher?
◆ The History of Gopher
◆ Veronica

What Is Gopher?

Gopher was developed by the University of Minnesota to assist the members of its campus community who had access to the university's computer facilities. Gopher gets its name from the university's mascot, and from the play on words that gives the word "Gopher" its alternate meaning. In many organizations a gopher is a person who fetches messages, runs errands, and picks up parcels—in other words, someone whose job it is to "gopher" things. Both definitions accurately describe the activities provided by this service. Like the World Wide Web, Gopher is a navigator that allows you to move around the Internet, without many of the inherent difficulties. Whereas a spider's web is the analogy used to describe the World Wide Web, for Gopher the concept of a system that fetches things for you by burrowing though the Internet was adopted.

The History of Gopher

By 1991, the computer staff at the University of Minnesota was constantly being inundated with what were, as a rule, relatively easy queries to answer. But the sheer number of queries was consuming a considerable amount of staff time and resources. The plan for Gopher was to place all of the answers to the more commonly asked questions into an electronic form. By doing this, the computer staff found that they could free up much of their time and also provide a service that, in most cases, would answer the questions of the past.

What was unique about Gopher was its design. Instead of developing a simple menu-based help system, the developers decided to create a client/server-based system to cope with the massive number of users on the university's computer systems. By doing this, each campus community could use its own computing resources to access the Gopher-based information without putting an enormous load on the main Gopher server.

Because of this design, people at other Internet sites soon began to realize that they could also take advantage of the Minnesota Gopher server and the extensive online help services it provided. All they needed to do was make a Gopher client available to their users, and they too could access information via Gopher. During the period between 1991 and 1993, the popularity of Gopher grew at an astounding pace. By the middle of 1994, it was estimated that there were over 5,500 Gopher servers in operation worldwide, providing users with access to over 10 million items of information in documents and on FTP servers.

How Gopher Works

Gopher is yet another example of a client/server system, something that by now you should have grown accustomed to. On each Gopher server, directories of information are maintained in the form of text-based menus.

The items on these menus can contain a variety of information, including:

◆ A pointer to another Gopher menu located on either the local server or any of the other Gopher servers that populate Gopherspace.

◆ A file stored on the local server in a text-based format. When you select a menu item of this type, Gopher displays the contents of the file on the screen of your Gopher client.

◆ A link to an FTP server or a direct link to a file contained on an FTP server.

◆ A Veronica server that allows you to search the contents of Gopherspace.

◆ A link to a Telnet site.

◆ A link to specialized services such as WAIS.

When you select any of the menu items listed on your local Gopher client, it either performs the action demanded by the menu item or queries a Gopher server for a new menu if the item selected requires this.

Gopher vs. WWW

Despite all of these capabilities, the popularity of Gopher has begun to decrease with the introduction of the World Wide Web. There are a number of reasons for this.

Firstly, the Gopher environment is too sterile for many people. In a world that now demands fancy computer graphics and images, the text-based format of a Gopher menu simply cannot compete. In addition, until the development of Gopher+, an extension to the Gopher environment, it was difficult to handle many of the now-popular multimedia file formats, which included image files and audio clips.

So which is better, Gopher or the World Wide Web? Basically, this is a question that you don't even need to answer. The reason for this is that the World Wide Web has been designed in such a way that it can access a Gopher server as though it were a Gopher client. In a more literal sense, the World Wide Web is capable of doing everything that a Gopher server can do, and considerably more as well.

In fact, if you have been exploring some of the sites mentioned in this book—the InterNIC server or the Internet Society server, for example—it is highly likely that you have already encountered a Gopher server without actually realizing it. If a URL on a WWW page points to a Gopher server, it will contain the word "Gopher:" in the protocol section.

Using Gopher

Although the World Wide Web provides you with an excellent means of accessing Gopherspace, there are also a number of dedicated Gopher clients that provide you with more direct access.

In Chapter 9, "Telnet," you encountered a number of terminal-based Gopher clients. These clients provide users with an elegant method of exploring a Telnet site without the need for complicated command-line instructions or a knowledge of the UNIX operating system. To access these public Gopher clients, you need to use either the built-in Telnet client available as a part of WinCIM or a Winsock-based client via NetLauncher. (See Figure 13.1.)

FIGURE 13.1.

Using the EWAN Telnet client, you can log onto any public Gopher client.

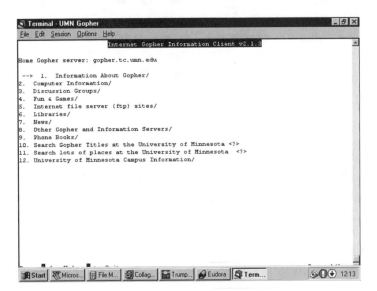

According to the Gopher FAQ, the sites listed in Table 13.1 represent the major public-access points for Telnet connections to Gopher. For each site there is a domain name, IP address, and user ID you must enter to start the Gopher client. Each site's physical location is listed as well.

Table 13.1. Public Gopher clients available via Telnet.

Domain Name	IP Address	Login	Area
consultant.micro.umn.edu	134.84.132.4	Gopher	North America
ux1.cso.uiuc.edu	128.174.5.59	Gopher	North America
sailor.lib.md.us	192.188.199.5	Gopher	North America

Domain Name	IP Address	Login	Area
panda.uiowa.edu	128.255.40.201	Panda	North America
gopher.msu.edu	35.8.2.61	Gopher	North America
gopher.ebone.net	192.36.125.2	Gopher	Europe
gopher.sunet.se	192.36.125.10	Gopher	Sweden
info.anu.edu.au	150.203.84.20	Info	Australia
tolten.puc.cl	146.155.1.16	Gopher	South America
ecnet.ec	157.100.45.2	Gopher	Ecuador
gan.ncc.go.jp	160.190.10.1	Gopher	Japan
gopher.th-darmstadt.de	130.83.55.75	Gopher	Germany
hugin.ub2.lu.se	130.235.162.12	Gopher	Sweden
gopher.uv.es	147.156.1.12	Gopher	Spain
info.brad.ac.uk	143.53.2.5	Gopher	United Kingdom

Telnet clients represent only one segment of the Gopher clients that are currently available. By using the Winsock capabilities built into NetLauncher, you can use a variety of Windows-based Gopher clients.

Winsock Clients

There are a number of locations on the Internet that contain copies of Gopher clients, including the sites listed in Appendix C, "Internet Software," but by far the most comprehensive list is maintained by the University of Minnesota on its Boombox FTP server. To access this FTP site using the World Wide Web, use the following URL: `ftp://boombox.micro.umn.edu/pub/gopher/Windows`.

You will find copies of all the major Gopher clients for Windows and other platforms at the site, along with instructions for locating some of the less well-known ones as well.

WSGopher

Archive Filename: `WSG-12.EXE`

WSGopher is a feature-packed Gopher client that uses the Windows environment to good advantage. All of the major functions are easily accessible through the toolbar across the top of the main window.

In addition, the latest version, 1.2, fully supports all of the current Gopher+ extensions, which include simple forms entry and extended file views. You can open any number of Gopher menus at the same time, and even perform file transfers using the built-in FTP features while you explore Gopherspace in another window.

Once installed on your system, WSGopher will automatically connect to its home gopher server whenever you start it. From there you can select any of the items displayed on the Gopher menu or alternatively open the comprehensive bookmark listing shown in Figure 13.2. Many of the major Gopher sites and services have been included in this list to give you easy access to many parts of Gopherspace. Bookmarks are very similar to the hotlists provided by Spry Mosaic, and like hotlists, you can also add any sites that you find to your list of personal bookmarks.

FIGURE 13.2.

WSGopher comes complete with a comprehensive list of bookmarks to help get you started.

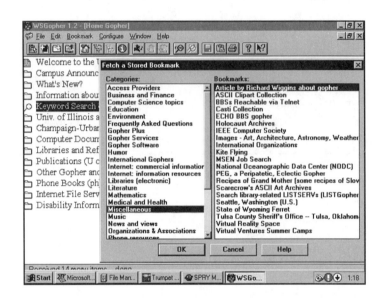

The authors have released WSGopher as freeware and place no limitations on its use. To obtain a copy of the latest version, visit the Boombox FTP directory.

HGopher

Archive Filename: `HGOPH24.ZIP`

Each Gopher client offers a slightly different approach to accessing the same basic information. Unlike WSGopher, HGopher does not provide you with a toolbar, but instead gives you a set of command buttons on the status bar at the bottom of the screen.

These buttons perform many of the same functions as those on the WSGopher toolbar, and also give you a means of controlling up to three simultaneous connections. (See Figure 13.3.) For example, this allows you to start a file transfer and then continue to explore Gopherspace while the file is retrieved in the background. The other major difference is in the way that HGopher uses bookmarks. Whereas most other Gopher clients open a menu on a home Gopher when they are started, HGopher opens your bookmarks list as though it were a Gopher menu.

FIGURE 13.3.

HGopher can maintain up to three simultaneous Gopher connections.

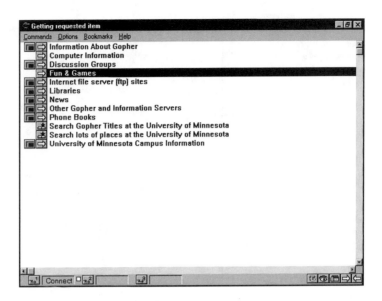

HGopher also provides a very comprehensive online help system that not only discusses the use of HGopher, but also contains some useful general information about both Gopher and Gopher+.

This program was released by the University of Illinois as freeware and is also available via FTP. But instead of using the Boombox site, you should first try the Consummate Winsock Applications list. This server always maintains a copy of the latest version of HGopher. The http address for this page is: `http://homepage.eznet.net/~rwilloug/stroud/cwsapps.html`.

BCGopher

Archive Filename: `BCG08B.EXE`

BCGopher offers yet another way of displaying Gopher menus. This time, the approach involves big icons that represent the various types of information each menu item contains. (See Figure 13.4.)

There is support for Gopher+, although this client is beginning to show its age because some of the newer features are not fully supported. It appears that this program is no longer supported, and since it was also released by Boston College as freeware, this makes getting any assistance unlikely.

Gopher for Windows

Archive Filename: `WGPH32.ZIP`

Gopher for Windows (Figure 13.5) is a fairly recent addition to the Gopher arena. It was released by the Chinese University of Hong Kong (CUHK) to provide students and faculty members with access to their Gopher server.

FIGURE 13.4.

BCGopher represents the different types of information available on each page by using icons.

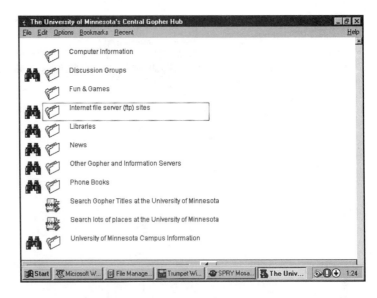

FIGURE 13.5.

Gopher for Windows displays each new menu in a separate window.

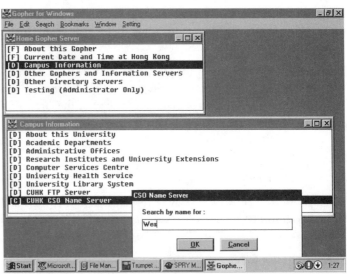

Many of its features are similar to those provided by WSGopher, but at this stage it still does not support all of the Gopher+ extensions. To obtain a copy of this Gopher client, you should use the CUHK FTP server located at `ftp://ftp.cuhk.hk/pub/gopher/PC/`.

A copy of Gopher for Windows can also be found in section 4 of the Internet Resource Forum (GO INETRESOURCE).

Spry Mosaic and Gopher

As mentioned at the start of this chapter, you can also use Spry Mosaic or any other WWW browser as a Gopher client. Doing this removes the need for a dedicated client or a Telnet connection.

To do this, you need to use a special type of URL that takes the following form: `gopher://<host>:<port>/11/<path>`.

In place of the `<host>` field, insert the domain name of the Gopher site you want to connect to. The `<port>` field usually contains a 70, which indicates the standard port for a Gopher server. Following the `/11/`, you then enter the path and name of the Gopher menu or action you want to use.

For example, to access the "Information About Gopher" menu on the University of Minnesota Gopher server (Figure 13.6), you would use this URL: `gopher://gopher.tc.umn.edu:70/11/Information%20About%20Gopher`. If you look closely at this URL, you will probably notice that the spaces between `Information`, `About`, and `Gopher` have been replaced with a strange combination of symbols—`%20`. You need to do this because any URL you enter cannot contain spaces. The `%20` symbol represents a space, which the WWW server will translate into the correct form at its end.

FIGURE 13.6.

Use `%20` *to replace any spaces in the Gopher menu path or name.*

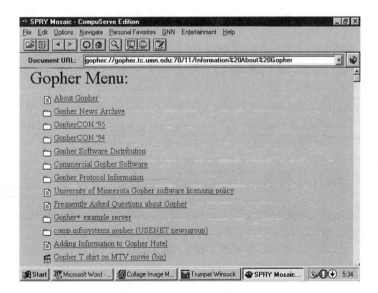

There is also a special form of the Gopher URL reserved for the top menu of each server. To open this menu, there is no need to include the `/11/`. To access the top menu of the Minnesota Gopher, use this URL: `gopher://gopher2.tc.umn.edu:70/1`. (See Figure 13.7.)

FIGURE 13.7.

There is no need to use /11/ when accessing the top menu of a Gopher server.

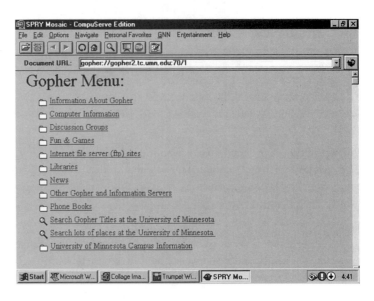

Once you open a Gopher server using Spry Mosaic, you can then navigate your way around it using the familiar hotlinks provided by the WWW browser. You can access all of the menus and features offered by Gopher from Mosaic and even request files via FTP.

> Although you can use the Gopher capabilities of Spry Mosaic to do file transfers, you will sometimes find that the filenames used by Gopher can cause strange things to happen when you try to start a download. If this happens, you may need to use the Save to Disk option to force Spry Mosaic to write the file to your hard disk, instead of trying to display it on the screen.

Gopher Search Tools

Although Gopher is a system that allows you to explore the Internet, in most cases you will want to locate information by a more than hit-and-miss approach. This section examines two of the search tools available via Gopher: Veronica and Archie.

Veronica

To allow you to wade through the millions of menu items stored on Gopher servers all around the world, an indexing and search tool known as Veronica was created for Gopher. Veronica provides you with a quick and efficient means of searching through menu items in Gopherspace. It does this by creating a Gopher menu with a list of just the items you are interested in.

Just about every Gopher server you visit will have a menu option that takes you to a Veronica search requester. On the top menu of the Minnesota Gopher, shown back in Figure 13.7, there are two such menu options. When you select either of these options, a page similar to the one shown in Figure 13.8 is displayed. In the field provided, type your search request and then click on the Search button.

FIGURE 13.8.

Enter the information you want to look for in the field provided and click on the Search button.

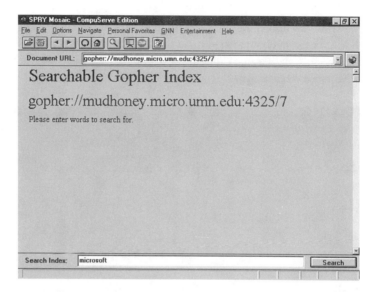

The Gopher server then searches all of the Gopher menu titles in the area of Gopherspace indexed by the particular search item you have selected. When the search is complete, a new Gopher menu is displayed that lists all of the menu items it located. (See Figure 13.9.) You can then select any of these menu items without needing to know which Gopher server it is on or how to access it.

FIGURE 13.9.

When you search Gopherspace, a new menu is created that contains the results of your search.

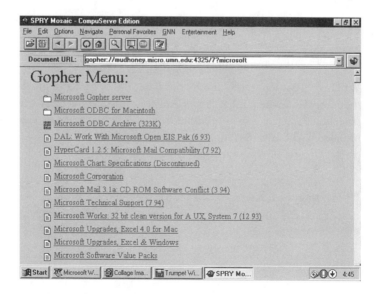

Whenever you encounter a Search/Index menu item, the title of the item will always indicate its scope. This is because not all Veronica-based indexes contain information about the same parts of Gopherspace. For this reason you will sometimes need to carefully choose the search index you plan to use to make sure that you don't miss information.

To assist you in making this decision, there are Gopher menus at a number of sites that provide links to many different search indexes. The menu shown in Figure 13.10 is an example of such a location. To open this menu using Spry Mosaic, use the following URL: `gopher://liberty.uc.wlu.edu:70/11/gophers/veronica`.

FIGURE 13.10.

Select the Gopherspace you want to search.

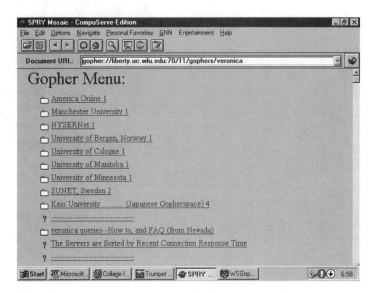

When you select any of these menu options, a Gopher menu that contains a list of all the possible search options available on the selected site is displayed. (See Figure 13.11.) Using this menu, you can select not only the type or category of information to be searched, but also the maximum number of results that each request will return.

With over 10 million titles in Gopherspace, it is not uncommon for a search request to match thousands of separate menu items. Therefore, unless you really need all of the possible links, you should choose a small number of results. This serves two purposes. Firstly, you are not inundated with useless results, but more importantly, you are not putting an unnecessary load on the Gopher servers that you access.

Note

For a slightly different list of sites, try `gopher://veronica.scs.unr.edu/11/veronica`.

FIGURE 13.11.

You can choose from a range of search parameters that include the maximum number of results your search will return.

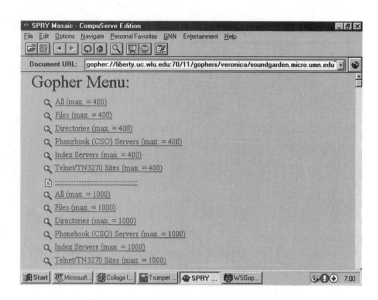

Archie

When Gopher was first developed, one of the main reasons for its existence was to provide an alternative way of accessing files stored on FTP servers. At the time, the only sort of FTP servers in popular use were terminal-based affairs that required you to enter UNIX-based commands.

With the advent of Gopher, all of a sudden it was possible to access files without having to worry about these commands. To accompany this capability, there also needed to be some easy way of locating files. As a result, an Archie gateway capability was added to Gopher. This provides capabilities not unlike the ArchiPlex form discussed in Chapter 12, "World Wide Web Productivity."

To access the Archie search menu on the Minnesota Gopher, select the Internet file server (ftp) sites option shown back in Figure 13.7. When you do this, a menu similar to the one shown in Figure 13.12 is displayed. There are a number of search options listed on this menu, along with a few options that take you directly to some of the major FTP servers.

If you choose any of the search options, a search requester similar to the one used by Veronica is opened. This time, you type the name of the file or directory you want to locate in the Search field. When you click on the Search button, a Gopher menu is created that lists all of the directories and files located by the Gopher search. From this menu you can choose the files you want to download and open the FTP directories listed, in much the same way as discussed for ArchiPlex.

FIGURE 13.12.

Gopher lets you search FTP sites using Archie.

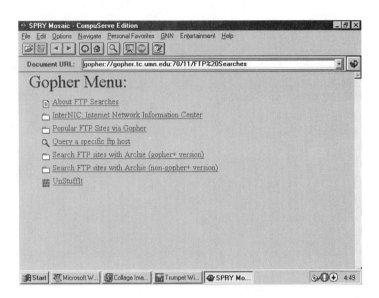

All of the dedicated Gopher clients provide you with identical file transfer capabilities. In addition, they don't suffer from the filename difficulties that sometimes cause problems with WWW browsers.

Searching Veronica via the World Wide Web

There is also a way to search the contents of Veronica via the World Wide Web itself. On the CUSI World Wide Web search page, mentioned in the previous chapter, you will find a Veronica Search option. (See Figure 13.13.) To open this page, use the following http address: `http://www.spry.com/wizard/index.html`.

If you use this option, a standard Gopher menu is created to display the results of the search. From here you can choose any of the Gopher menu items listed.

FIGURE 13.13.
The CUSI WWW Search page lets you query Veronica.

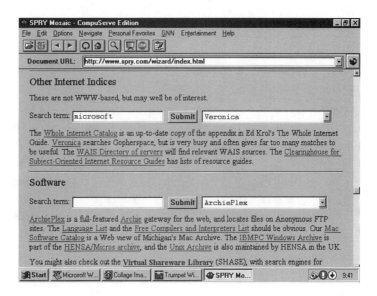

Popular Gopher Sites

Table 13.2 contains a list of URLs that provide a wide cross-section of Gopher servers or facilities, along with a brief description of what each one does.

Table 13.2 Popular Gopher sites.

URL	Description
gopher://gopher.enews.com:70/11/newsletter	Business publications and resources (electronic newsstand)
gopher://free-net.mpls-stpaul.mn.us:8001/1	Twin Cities Free-Net
gopher://nceet.snre.umich.edu:70/1	EE-Link, the Environmental Education Gopher
gopher://jei.umd.edu:70/1	Joint Education Initiative Gopher site
gopher://avril.amba-ottawa.fr:70/1	French Embassy / Ambassade de France (Ottawa, Canada)
gopher://jupiter.sun.csd.unb.ca:70/11/FAQ	Internet FAQs
gopher://gopher.nara.gov:70/1	U.S. National Archives
gopher://gopher.microsoft.com:70/1	Microsoft

continues

Table 13.2 continued

URL	Description
gopher://gopher.voa.gov:70/1	Voice of America and Worldnet Television
gopher://winftp.cica.indiana.edu:70/11/pc/win3	CICA Windows software archive (Indiana University)
gopher://info.csc.cuhk.hk:70/1	Chinese University of Hong Kong
gopher://cexpress.com:2600/1	Computer Express (online software and hardware)
gopher://mudhoney.micro.umn.edu:70/10/Gopher.FAQ	The Gopher FAQ
gopher://ice.ucdavis.edu:70/1	Information Center for the Environment
gopher://mudhoney.micro.umn.edu:70/11/gplustest	Gopher+ example server

Summary

With the completion of this chapter, you have now seen all of the Internet tools and services currently provided by CompuServe. At this stage you should now be able to work with all of the tools and begin your own exploration of the Internet.

To guide you through this new phase of your life on the Internet, the final section of this book, "Where to Now?" contains information that can act as both a starting point for your explorations and a resource tool.

PART

V

WHERE TO NOW?

CHAPTER

14

INTERNET RESOURCES ON COMPUSERVE

In addition to offering Internet gateway tools, CompuServe is an ideal source of Internet-related information, programs, and connectivity assistance.

For the Internet *newbie*, one of the most daunting tasks is coming to grips with the never-ending array of applications and the computer jargon associated with the Internet. CompuServe meets this challenge by offering one-stop Internet connectivity using WinCIM; but, more importantly, it also offers a level of support and user assistance many people regard as second to none.

Ironically, a large part of this support does not come from hundreds of operators who are waiting to take your call, but instead from other users like yourself who are more than willing to lend a hand or offer a helpful suggestion. To coordinate this growing resource, CompuServe offers a number of Internet forums that provide you with a place to meet and discuss the Internet and its complexities. They also act as a repository for the ever-increasing library of computer programs and information files that deal with using the Internet.

This chapter shows you how to work with CompuServe forums and how to explore the resources available in them that deal with Internet-related topics. It discusses the following topics:

◆ Using WinCIM with CompuServe forums

◆ CompuServe automation

◆ The Internet New Users forum

◆ The Internet Resource forum

◆ The Internet Publishing forum

◆ Other Software Support forums

Working with CompuServe Forums

The forum is the basic tool you use to access the thousands of discussions and topics managed by CompuServe. There are forums for computer-related topics, entertainment and recreation, employment and work, hobbies, sports, and many other general discussions.

A good place to find out about the different forums operated by CompuServe is the CompuServe directory (Figure 14.1), which comes with WinCIM. Using the standard Windows Help system, this directory allows you to browse through a list of all the forums, categorized by subject. Along with a description of the forum and a brief overview of its contents, each forum is assigned a *service name*. This is the name you need to type into the Go… dialog box to open the forum using WinCIM.

Another popular way of finding out about new forums—and old ones you may have missed— is to read the monthly *CompuServe* magazine. Each month this magazine features articles that discuss topics covered by CompuServe forums. Apart from being a good read, each article usually contains pointers to the various forums that deal with the topics mentioned. Like the CompuServe directory, these forums are usually referred to by their service names with the format GO INETFORUM. The word *GO* refers to the use of the Go… dialog box in WinCIM.

Once you know a forum's service name, you can access the forum using WinCIM or one of the other popular CompuServe navigators and offline readers discussed in the following pages.

FIGURE 14.1.

The CompuServe Directory.

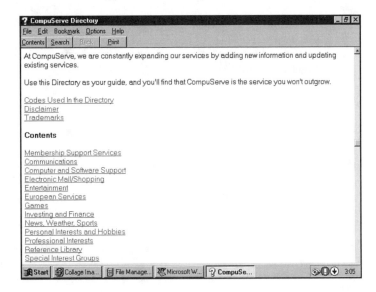

Using WinCIM with CompuServe Forums

Although most of this book has been related to the Internet-related functions offered by WinCIM, the main service provided by WinCIM revolves around the procedures for accessing and working with the thousands of forums available on CompuServe.

This section looks briefly at these capabilities. Because a full discussion of this topic is outside the scope of this book, you should refer to the WinCIM online help system or to books dedicated to CompuServe forum navigation for additional assistance.

The Practice Forum

For those of you who are unfamiliar with WinCIM and forum usage in general, the Practice Forum is a very good place to start. This forum is operated by CompuServe to allow you to experiment with WinCIM and practice using CompuServe's standard forum resources. As an added bonus, access to this forum is free, apart from any local network connection surcharges.

To use this forum, open the Go... dialog box by selecting the **G**o option from the **S**ervices menu or by clicking the Go icon (represented by a set of traffic lights). In the Go... dialog box, type the Practice Forum's service name: **practice**. (See Figure 14.2.) Now press the Enter key or click the OK button to enter the Practice Forum.

FIGURE 14.2.

*Using the Go... dialog box
to open the Practice Forum.*

If you are entering a forum for the first time, you will be presented with a dialog box similar to the one shown in Figure 14.3. This dialog box allows you to register yourself as a forum member. In doing so, you indicate that you are willing to abide by the rules and guidelines set down by the forum's operators. To register your acceptance of the terms and conditions, click on the **Join** Button.

If you are not sure whether you want to join a forum, you can look through the forum by clicking the **Visit** button. However, if you choose this option, not all of the forum's capabilities will be available to you.

FIGURE 14.3.

*Click the Join button to
become a member of a new
forum.*

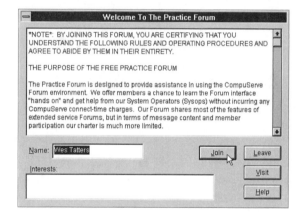

After you click the **Join** button, or when you return to a forum you have previously joined, the WinCIM screen changes to reflect the fact that you have entered a forum.

The most noticeable indication of this is the placement of the forum's name on the WinCIM backdrop. (See Figure 14.4.) In some forums, this name is accompanied by a customized picture that represents the forum's activities. Depending on how you have configured your preferences for WinCIM, the forum toolbox, shown on the right side of Figure 14.4, is opened.

The menu bar, located across the top of the screen, is also updated to reflect the fact that you have entered a forum. Three new menu options are added to give you access to the main forum features:

◆ Messages
◆ Library
◆ Conference

FIGURE 14.4.

The CompuServe Practice Forum, ready for use.

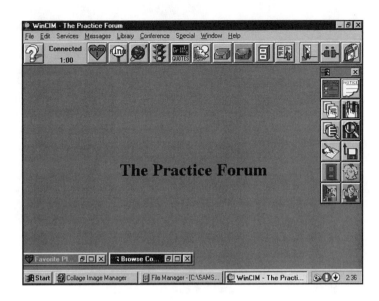

Message Sections

The main feature of many CompuServe forums is the *message area.* This is where you exchange messages dealing with topics related to the forum's area of interest with other CompuServe members. Forum message areas are a lot like Internet newsgroups, which also allow the public exchange of messages. See Chapter 15, "The Best of Both Worlds," for a full comparison of the two services.

To gain access to a forum's message area, you open the **M**essages menu (shown in Figure 14.5) and select the **B**rowse option. Doing this will open a window listing the different *message sections* offered by this forum. Each forum can support up to 24 separate message sections. These sections represent the major topics covered by a forum. In the Practice Forum (Figure 14.6), there are 18 sections. Each section contains messages dealing with the different aspects of CompuServe usage.

FIGURE 14.5.

The Messages menu.

FIGURE 14.6.

The 18 message sections in the Practice Forum.

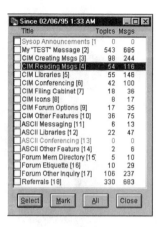

This window also lists the number of messages currently stored in each section and the number of separate discussion topics or *threads* to which these messages relate.

> WinCIM keeps track of the last time you visited a forum and displays the date you last read messages at the top of the message section's window. Because a forum can hold a large number of messages at one time, WinCIM uses this date to determine the earliest message it displays. You can change this date using the Set **D**ate option in the **M**essages menu.

Using the message section's window, you can open any section and browse or read the messages it contains. To do this, highlight a message section and then click the **S**elect button (or double-click the message section). This opens the CIM Reading Msgs window, which lists the discussion threads currently active in the section. (See Figure 14.7.)

FIGURE 14.7.

The CIM Reading Msgs window.

On CompuServe, messages with same subject line are kept together in threads in much the same way Usenet newsgroups relate messages together. In the CIM Reading Msgs window, each of the threads stored in a message section is accompanied by a number that indicates how many messages the thread contains.

To read the messages contained in one of these threads, you either double-click the message thread or highlight the thread and click the **S**elect button. This opens a message window, which displays the first message in the thread. (See Figure 14.8.) Using the buttons at the bottom of the message window, you can reply to the message, move to the previous message, follow the thread, or jump to the next thread topic.

FIGURE 14.8.

The WinCIM Forum Messages window.

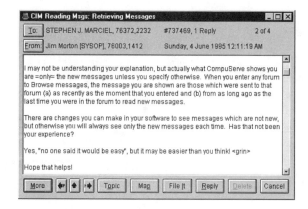

Library Sections

If the WinCIM Messages menu is similar to Usenet, the Library menu (Figure 14.9) can best be thought of as CompuServe's own version of FTP. (See Chapter 10, "File Transfer Protocol (FTP)," for a full comparison of WinCIM libraries and FTP.)

FIGURE 14.9.

The Library menu.

Over the years, CompuServe has accumulated a vast collection of files and software archives relating to the many forums it operates. By opening the **L**ibrary menu and selecting the **B**rowse option, you can explore the files available in each forum file library.

Like CompuServe's message areas, a forum's libraries are categorized into as many as 22 separate sections. (See Figure 14.10.) In the Practice Forum, there are three sections containing forum and CIS help files. Also, there is a special section to practice uploading files to CompuServe.

FIGURE 14.10.

*The Practice Forum's
library sections.*

To open any of these areas from the Library Sections window, highlight the section you are interested in and then click the **S**elect button, or just double-click the section. This will open a window similar to the one shown in Figure 14.11. From this window you can select the files you want to download.

FIGURE 14.11.

*The Forum Help & Info
file library.*

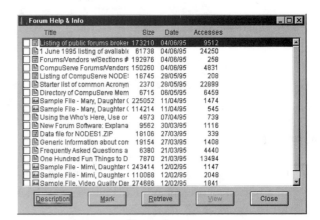

Online Conferences

Some forums also allow you to participate in online conferences and real-time discussions with other CompuServe members. To participate in a conference, select the **E**nter Room option from the **C**onference menu. (See Figure 14.12.) This opens a window that lists the conferences currently operated by the forum. Because the Practice Forum does not operate any conferences, here is a look at the conferences operated by the Internet New Users Forum. (See Figure 14.13.)

FIGURE 14.12.

The Conference Menu.

FIGURE 14.13.

The Internet New Users Forum conference rooms.

To participate in any of the listed conferences, highlight the one you want to join. Below the main window, a message will appear to let you know how many people are currently participating in the conference. Click the Enter button to participate in the conference, or click on the Listen button to simply watch what is being discussed.

The Internet Conference window (Figure 14.14) operates a bit like CB radio. All the comments entered by people participating in the discussion are displayed in the top section of the window. You enter your comments in the bottom section. Whenever you hit the Enter key, anything you have entered is sent to the other participants and is displayed in the top section of their Internet Conference windows.

FIGURE 14.14.

The Internet Conference window.

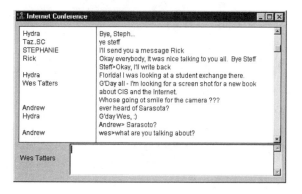

Tip

A number of forums stage special conferences attended by famous people from all walks of life. Keep an eye on the What's New area, GO NEW, for information on these special events.

The Forum Toolbox

Many of the services available from the forum menus can also be selected using the forum toolbox, shown on the right-hand side of Figure 14.15. If the toolbox does not open when you enter a forum, you can call it up by selecting the **T**oolbox item on the **S**pecial menu. Alternatively, you can select the Show Toolbox option in the Forum Preferences dialog box to force WinCIM to open it automatically.

FIGURE 14.15.

The Forum toolbox, which lets you easily work with forums.

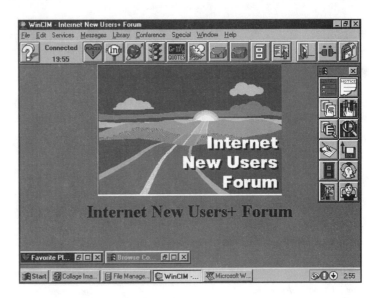

Internet New Users+ Forum

The top-left button only activates if there are messages in the forum addressed to you. If you click this button, WinCIM will retrieve these messages and display them for you in a message window. The top-right button, on the other hand, is always active. If you click this button, WinCIM will open the Notices menu to allow you to read the messages contained there.

The next three buttons on the left side are devoted to various forum message activities, while their counterparts on the right side perform corresponding functions for the forum's libraries. Selecting the first button on either side performs the same action as selecting the Browse option from the corresponding Messages and Library menus. The next button opens a dialog box that allows you to search for either specific messages or files. The last button on the left side of this group opens a Create Message dialog box, while the button on the right side opens the Contribute dialog box, which allows you to upload files to the current forum.

The last four buttons deal with the various online conference functions. Using the first button on the left side, you can enter an online conference. The button on the right side shows you who else is currently in the forum. The bottom two buttons allow you to invite other people to participate in a conference with you (the one on the left) and to decide whether you want to accept requests from other people (the button on the right).

CompuServe Automation

As you become more familiar with the forums available on CompuServe, you will eventually reach a point where you should consider the use of a CompuServe offline reader (OLR) to reduce the amount of time you spend connected to CompuServe.

Reading messages and browsing forum message areas while connected to CompuServe is time-consuming and an extremely inefficient use of connection time. To get around these problems, a number of programs have been developed that allow you to automate many of the activities you normally perform online. These activities include the sending and retrieval of CompuServe Mail, as well as many forum-related activities like the collection of threads or messages and the downloading of files. Using such programs, you can reduce your online time by a considerable amount. Some users have reported reductions of up to 75%.

WinCIM and CSNav

Although not the easiest program to use, CSNav is the most WinCIM-compatible OLR. (See Figure 14.16.) CSNav was designed by CompuServe to complement WinCIM. CSNav shares many of WinCIM's features, such as the Session and Connection utilities, the WinCIM filing cabinets, and the In/Out boxes.

FIGURE 14.16.

The CSNav offline reader.

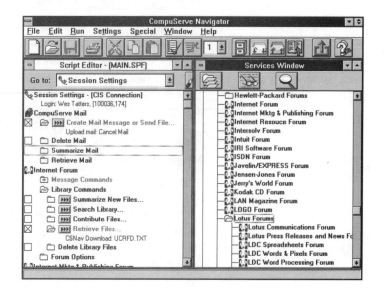

You can download a copy of CSNav from CompuServe by opening the CSNav Information Forum. To do this, type **CSNav** in the Go... dialog box. This will open a menu that allows you to purchase CSNav and download a copy to your PC. This menu also gives you access to the CSNav Support Forum, GO CSNAVSUPPORT, as well as other information about CSNav.

To use CSNav with CompuServe, you create scripts that tell CSNav what activities you want it to perform. These scripts can tell CSNav to collect mail from your CompuServe mailbox, open forums and retrieve message headers as well as the messages themselves, download files from forum libraries, and even manage your Executive News Service options.

Once you are satisfied that the script suits your needs, you tell CSNav to use it to log onto CompuServe. CSNav connects and follows the instructions stored in the script to retrieve the information requested and then hangs up when it is finished. You can now read your mail and examine the contents of the forums you selected without the costs associated with being connected to CompuServe.

Managing Threads and Messages with OzWIN

OzWIN, like CSNav, is an OLR for CompuServe. (See Figure 14.17.) The way it works, however, is considerably different. Instead of using scripts, OzWIN performs a set of predetermined actions for each forum.

FIGURE 14.17.

The OzWIN offline reader.

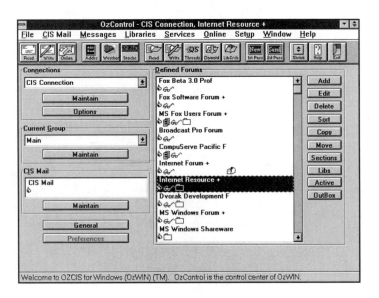

To use OzWIN, you nominate the forums you want to work with and select the actions you want to perform. As with CSNav, you tell OzWIN to log on, perform certain actions, and then hang up. From a usability perspective, many people prefer the nonscript-based process used by OzWIN.

However, this is not OzWIN's most popular feature. Where OzWIN really stands out is in the way it manages the messages and threads it retrieves from CompuServe. OzWIN allows you to collect threads and to sort messages by date or thread. It also enables you to watch for specific messages and to retrieve automatically any additional messages posted to the threads you are following.

You can always find a copy of the latest version of OzWIN in Section 10 of the OzWIN Support Forum—GO OZWIN. When you download OzWIN, you are free to use it for 30 days; if after this time you decide to continue using OzWIN, you must purchase a copy from Ozarks West Software, Inc., OzWIN's developer.

NavCIS by Dvorak

Although it is very hard to make a recommendation about which offline reader is best, NavCIS is considered by many to be the easiest to use. (See Figure 14.18.)

FIGURE 14.18.

The NavCIS offline reader.

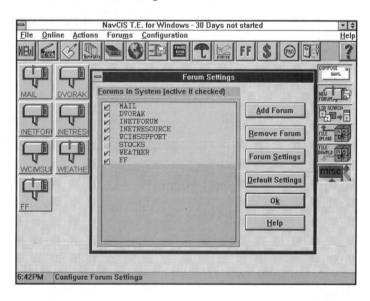

Like OzWIN, NavCIS does not use scripts to control its actions, but instead uses a predetermined set of functions. Where NavCIS differs from OzWIN is in its use of the Windows drag-and-drop functions and in its general layout. In addition, NavCIS offers a special feature that allows users to send messages to others who are using NavCIS that contain different fonts and text styles, such as bold and italic.

To obtain a demonstration copy of NavCIS, enter **DVORAK** in the Go... dialog box. This will take you to the NavCIS Support Forum. You can then download a copy of either the SE or TE version of NavCIS from the file library. The SE version of NavCIS is freeware but is limited in a number of ways; the TE version, on the other hand, is a full demonstration version of NavCIS Pro. However, the TE version can only be used for 30 days, after which time the program locks you out until you purchase a copy of the commercial version.

The Internet Forums

To assist you with your exploration of the Internet, CompuServe now offers a number of forums specifically dedicated to the Internet. These forums represent a major support component of CompuServe's Internet services.

To access them, you can either open the Internet Services area (Figure 14.19) and select from the menu options provided, or you can jump directly to them by using the service names outlined in the following pages, which show you how these forums can help you gain a better understanding of the Internet and provide answers to your queries.

FIGURE 14.19.

The Internet Services area, which lets you select any of the support forums.

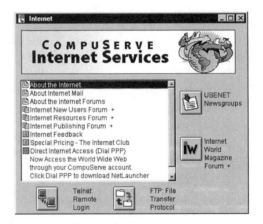

The Internet New Users Forum

The best place for new users to start is the Internet New Users Forum. To open this forum, type **INETFORUM** in the Go... dialog box and then press the Enter key. In this forum there are message areas and file libraries that provide basic assistance and support for all the major Internet services.

Message Areas

To help you get started, the first four sections are devoted to basic Internet queries for Internet beginners. These sections also cover accessing CompuServe from the Internet and accessing the Net in general. In these sections there are always people willing to offer you assistance and guidance, so don't be afraid to ask for help.

The next seven sections are devoted to discussions covering the use of the main Internet services, which include e-mail, FTP and Archie, Usenet, mailing lists, World Wide Web and Mosaic, Telnet, and Gopher and WAIS. These discussions include the use of tools provided by CompuServe and those used when working with Dialup Point-to-Point (PPP) and WinSock-based Internet connections.

There are also two sections devoted to locating people and resources on the Internet, and a section for discussion of business activities on the Internet. Messages relating to the Internet Society are given a separate section, as are general discussions dealing with CompuServe's PPP dial-up connections.

To round out the New Users Forum, there is a general conversation section called the Internet Coffee Shop. In this section you can chat about anything you want.

File Libraries

To correspond with the various message sections, there are file libraries that contain files dealing with the same topics. Unlike some libraries, which contain a large number of computer programs, most of the files in these sections contain information files.

Of particular interest to new users are the various files containing tutorials and guidelines relating to the Internet. There are also a number of files that contain directories of FTP sites, WWW pages, mailing lists, and Internet service providers.

The Internet Resource Forum

Whereas the New Users Forum deals with general discussions, the Internet Resource Forum deals more with the specifics of using particular programs and tools. It also deals with the various resources available on the Internet.

To open this forum, type the service name **INETRESOURCE** in the Go… dialog box.

Message Areas

The message areas in this forum deal with Internet-related resources, ranging from books and magazines to online games and Internet security. There are also sections that deal with PC software for the Internet, Mac software, WWW and hypertext tools, Internet servers, and online publishing.

In addition, a number of sections are allocated to the discussion of resources available on the Internet for academic, business, community, government, technical, and personal use. If you'd like to know about the detailed workings of the Internet, there is also a section dedicated to the discussion of standards and Request For Comment (RFC) documents. Finally, there is also a section dealing with online commerce and its implications for the Internet.

File Libraries

If you are looking for software to use with NetLauncher, this forum is the place to start. You can find copies of all the programs discussed in Appendix C, as well as a number of additional support files and tools, in the "PC Internet Software" section. To complement this collection, there is a library for Macintosh software as well.

Like the Internet New Users Forum, the library sections available in this section mirror the topics discussed in the forum's message areas. As a result, in addition to the collection of software files, there are a number of text files and other reference items that deal with the various resources discussed in the message areas.

The Internet Publishing Forum

As discussed previously, the World Wide Web is without a doubt the most rapidly developing segment of the Internet. In response to this growth, CompuServe has opened a forum dedicated to the World Wide Web and Internet publishing and marketing in particular.

To reach the Internet Publishing and Marketing Forum, type **INETPUB** in the Go… dialog box and then press the Enter key.

Message Areas

If you have a question that relates to publishing on the World Wide Web, chances are it has either already been answered in this forum or there is somebody lurking there who can answer the question for you.

As would be expected of any discussion dealing with WWW publishing, there are a number of message sections dealing with the use of HTML. These sections include the HTML language, HTML editors for the PC and Macintosh, CGI scripting, home page creation, and layout/design issues. There are two sections allocated to the discussion of PR and marketing issues and four sections for general publishing, as well as online commerce and news.

To cater to those interested in the business end of WWW publishing, the remaining sections are devoted to the use of WWW servers on PCs, Macintosh computers, and other platforms as well.

File Libraries

Although still a new forum in many respects, there are already a number of WWW-related files stored in this forum's libraries.

For people interested in creating their own home pages, these libraries contain a number of HTML and graphics editing tools, which simplify the task of developing HTML documents. To complement these editors, some of the more popular public domain WWW server tools and CGI scripts can also be found here.

The *Internet World* Forum

To access the Internet World Forum, type **IWORLD** in the Go… dialog box and then press the Enter key. Although not dealing with the Internet itself, this forum is the electronic arm of *Internet World* magazine.

Through this forum, you can communicate with the editors and staff of *Internet World* and discuss the various articles they have written. You can also obtain subscription information and download copies of files mentioned in the magazine, including those in the "Editor's Toolbox," a collection of files chosen by the *Internet World* magazine editor.

A special feature of this forum is the "Members Pick" section, which allows you to have your say and vote for the best items on the Internet—be they the WWW home pages or your favorite Internet tools.

Other Related Forums

Although not a part of the Internet services, there are a number of other forums that contain information dealing with the Internet.

Some of these forums deal specifically with the Internet, while others cover the Internet as a part of their particular area of interest. This section shows you some of these forums and discusses their relevance to the Internet.

The Electronic Frontier Foundation Forum

The Electronic Frontier Foundation (EFF) was formed in 1990 to ensure that there is freedom of expression in the digital media, with special attention given to the application of the principles embodied in the Constitution and Bill of Rights to computer-based communications. To promote these activities and extend them to CompuServe users, the EFF operates a forum on CompuServe.

You can join the forum by entering **EFFSIG** in the Go... dialog box. This forum offers Internet users a radically different perspective by dealing not with technical issues but instead with more esoteric topics, such as online activism, the virtual community, digital privacy, and the data superhighway. To encourage a better understanding of these important issues, the EFF invites all CompuServe members to participate in discussions and debates that deal with topics such as electronic civil liberties and online computer communications.

In the EFFSIG libraries, there are many files dealing with Internet culture, technical issues, and guide books and tools, including the *EFF Guide to the Internet*. In addition, a number of files discussing civil liberties and cyberlaw are also available for downloading.

The Telecommunications Issues Forum

For the technically minded, as well as for those interested in the many developments occurring in the telecommunications world, the Telecommunications Issues Forum is an ideal place to start. In this forum, you can discuss issues such as long distance communications, internetworking, ISDN, and satellite communications.

To join this forum, type the service name **TELECO** in the Go... dialog box.

The Working from Home Forum

With the development of remote computing capabilities, the Internet has fostered the growth of a new type of employee known as the teleworker or telecommuter.

In the Working from Home Forum, GO WORK, there are a number of message sections devoted to the use of the Internet and CompuServe by teleworkers. Of these message sections, the most interesting are the ones that deal with the tools used by information brokers— another Internet-fostered business opportunity. For CompuServe users, this includes IQUEST databases and WWW or WAIS resources.

The *Interactive Week* Forum

Like the Internet World Forum, the Interactive Week Forum is an electronic extension of a magazine. This time it is *Interactive Week* magazine. To access this forum, type **IAWEEK** in the Go… dialog box.

This forum is devoted to interaction between the various rapidly converging communications technologies, which include cable, broadcasting, online computing, and telephony. Although aimed at the professional end of the market, there are numerous discussions that point to the future of the Internet and the emerging information superhighway.

In the library section, along with numerous pictures, there are text transcripts of many of the articles published in past editions of the magazine. If you would like to subscribe to the printed version of the magazine, there is also information on how to do this online.

National Computer Security Association

The National Computer Security Association (NCSA) operates two forums on CompuServe that deal with a wide range of computer- and Internet-related security issues. The topics covered in these forums include computer ethics and privacy, data encryption, UNIX and Internet security, and disaster recovery. The service name for the main forum is **NCSA**. Enter this name into the Go… dialog box to participate in the forum.

To deal with the issue of computer viruses, the NCSA also operates a special forum for computer virus software vendors. You can join this forum by entering **NCSAVEND** into the Go… dialog box.

Software Support Forums

Apart from the forums already mentioned, there are a number of others that provide support and assistance for the various navigators and OLRs designed for use with CompuServe. In Table 14.1, I have compiled a list of many of the support forums operated by CompuServe.

Table 14.1. CompuServe software support forums.

Go...	*Description*
WINCIM	WinCIM information and download area
WCIMSUPPORT	Windows CIM support forum
WCIMGE	Windows CIM general support forum
WCIMTE	Windows CIM technical support forum
MACCIM	MacCIM information and download area
MCIMSUPPORT	MacCIM support forum
DCIMSUPPORT	DOSCIM support forum
OCIMSUPPORT	CIM for OS/2 support forum
CSNAV	CSNav information and download area
CSNAVSUPPORT	CSNav support forum
NAVSUPPORT	MACNAV support forum
NETLAUNCHER	NetLauncher information and download area
NLSUPPORT	NetLauncher support forum
OZWIN	OzWIN Windows support forum
OZCIS	OzCIS DOS support forum
DVORAK	NavCIS support forum
TAPCIS	TAPCIS DOS navigator support forum
CSAPPS	CompuServe applications forum

Summary

For all the capabilities and opportunities offered by the Internet, many people still consider it to be too hard to use and too hard to connect to.

By taking advantage of the support services offered through CompuServe and the one-stop connectivity provided by CompuServe's "Internet Made Easy" program, many of these complexities and difficulties can be completely removed. These factors, when combined with the willing and plentiful assistance offered by other CompuServe members in the Internet and CompuServe support forums, make using the Internet as simple as working with any of the standard CompuServe services.

In many ways, the forum services provided by CompuServe complement the new services offered though the expanded Internet gateway. The next chapter looks at the resources provided by CompuServe and the Internet so that you can compare and contrast these services.

CHAPTER 15

THE BEST OF BOTH WORLDS

With the integration of so many Internet services into CompuServe, its users now have the best of both worlds: the flexibility and simplicity of WinCIM and Internet Made Easy, and the expanded resources offered by the Internet. But how do these new services compare with those already available on CompuServe, and more importantly, why would anyone want to use them instead of CompuServe's existing services?

Because answering this question in any definitive way is an impossible task, this chapter looks at how the services offered by the Internet compare and contrast with the better-known CompuServe services. Once you have an understanding of the differences and similarities inherent in these services, you will be in a better position to answer this question for yourself.

This chapter looks at the Internet services that complement CompuServe's forums, and also at some of the more dedicated CompuServe tools, by discussing the following topics:

◆ Global support

◆ Forums and newsgroups

◆ FTP and CompuServe libraries

◆ Conferences and IRC

◆ The World Wide Web and WinCIM

◆ The Electronic Mall and Internet shopping

◆ IQUEST and WAIS

CompuServe's Internet Services

Before I dive in and look at specific CompuServe services, let's take a look at why people would choose to use CompuServe as their *Internet service provider* (ISP).

With the introduction of Internet Made Easy and dial-up PPP support, CompuServe is the first Internet service provider to offer people a truly global Internet service. While all ISPs allow people to connect to the world through the Internet, CompuServe is the first service that gives you the convenience of dial-up connections or *points of presence* (POP) in many parts of the world. At last count, CompuServe had over 450 points of presence providing more than 60,000 individual connections in countries throughout the British Isles, Europe, Asia, the Pacific Rim, and North America.

Global Dial-Up Connectivity

Talk of points of presence and dial-up PPP connections may sound impressive, but what does this mean for the user? To put it simply, if you are a CompuServe member, you can make a local phone call or, if you live in the U.S., dial a toll-free (800) number that will instantly connect you to both CompuServe and the Internet. At the same time, CompuServe is also upgrading all its dial-up connections to 28,800kbps and experimenting with the delivery of CompuServe services using high-speed ISDN connections.

To accompany this increased presence, CompuServe has also gone to great lengths to expand its service and support infrastructure in many of the countries where it offers services. On a global scale, it's now the largest single Internet support service, and for CompuServe members this means improved customer support wherever they are in the world.

While not wanting to denigrate the services offered by many Internet service providers, this kind of service was, prior to the launch of CompuServe's Internet services, unheard of in the Internet world.

Affordability

Although CompuServe may not offer the cheapest service around, it certainly does offer users an Internet service that gives them value for their money. This is especially the case when you consider the level of support and value-added resources it offers.

That said, like any online service, how you get the best benefit out of it really depends on your particular circumstances. For any serious Internet use, you should carefully consider the added benefits of the Internet Club pricing package offered to all CompuServe members.

> To find out the latest information regarding the Internet Club, type **internet** into the Go dialog box and then select Special Pricing - The Internet Club from the Internet Services main window.

CompuServe Forums

Unlike the Internet, which is made up of many varied services, CompuServe on the whole revolves around the concept of *forums*. In some ways this makes it difficult to compare Internet and CompuServe services directly. What you need to do is look at the various components that make up a CompuServe forum and contrast them with their correlating Internet services.

However, at the same time it is the very nature of CompuServe forums that highlights one of the many differences between the two services. Although there are many forums on CompuServe, the topics and categories they deal with are limited to those chosen by CompuServe's forum operators. The Internet, on the other hand, gives almost anyone with a computer the ability to provide services such as access to files via FTP or entire multimedia extravaganzas using the World Wide Web.

As a result, due to the anarchic nature of the Internet, it is easier for people to create their own "places" on the Internet than to obtain a forum on CompuServe. At the same time, though, there is still currently no direct equivalent to a CompuServe forum on the Internet, although the World Wide Web promises to equal this potential in the future. For the moment, the Internet is still a place of differing services that make up a whole, whereas CompuServe is still basically a single service.

Forums and Newsgroups

Where better to start the comparison than with Internet's main conversation facility, Usenet newsgroups, and CompuServe's forum message areas? Both services are basically discussion areas that allow people to publicly exchange messages and opinions on a wide variety of topics. At the same time, they both look after the distribution of these messages without any user intervention. Where they do tend to differ, however, is in their content and in the way they are moderated.

Firstly, let's look at the moderation issue. On CompuServe, each forum is administered by a *sysop*, who ensures that discussions are conducted in an orderly fashion and that, for the most part, decency and adherence to the forum's topic is maintained. Although forums aren't moderated in the strict mailing list sense of the word—where each message is approved by an administrator before being posted to the forum—most sysops do keep a fairly close watch on the discussions that take place and will intervene when necessary.

> A surefire way to attract the wrath of a sysop is to use foul or abusive language in a forum. This may also be the reason for the relatively small number of "flame wars," bouts of electronic insults and name-calling that occur on CompuServe forums.

Newsgroups, on the other hand, tend to be less controlled, although many do still have a person who acts as moderator. One of the main reasons for this is due to the way that Usenet operates. A new newsgroup message can come from any of the thousands of Usenet servers around the world. When such a message is posted, it is gradually distributed to all other Usenet sites and may not even be seen by some people, including the administrator, until days later. As a result, even if a message is unwelcome, in most cases it has already wound its way across the Internet before anyone can stop it. That said, as discussed in Chapter 8, most newsgroup members tend to conduct their own form of moderation and policing when unacceptable messages are received. This often takes the form of *spamming* or *mail dumps*, where sometimes thousands of messages are sent to a person's e-mail address telling him to behave.

This brings us to the second point—content. The diversity of Usenet newsgroups and the relative freedom of expression they allow—including the ability to easily create new newsgroups—mean that there are discussions taking place on Usenet that deal with just about every topic known to man. At last count there were over 12,000 newsgroups on the Usenet, compared to around 2,000 forums available on CompuServe. Of course, each CompuServe forum has up to 24 sections that often deal with different topics, so the total scope may be roughly comparable.

> Not all Usenet sites provide access to all of these newsgroups. Depending on your service provider, some of the less savory newsgroups in the `alt` section may be edited out. On CompuServe, the Internet Service administrators have chosen not to list many

of these newsgroups. However, if you do know a hidden newsgroup's name, you can still read it by entering the name directly using the Subscribe by Name option.

Based on the number of newsgroups and the variety of discussion topics, the Usenet would seem to be a better place to hang out. However, this is not always the case. Depending on what you are looking for, there are many reasons why you should consider using both services. For CompuServe's part, there are many discussions that take place in forums that have no corresponding newsgroups on Usenet. This is due to the way many software and hardware companies use CompuServe for online support and for beta testing programs. For these companies, Usenet is simply not an appropriate place to conduct discussions that require any level of privacy.

In addition, for many of these companies privacy is not the only issue that leads them to the use of CompuServe. Apart from the exchange of messages, the other major component of any beta or support service is the need for easy access to programs and support files. While it is possible to exchange files with Usenet, the simplicity of forum libraries far outweighs the complexities involved with binary encoding. (See Chapter 8 and Appendix D.)

FTP and CompuServe Libraries

This is not to say that forum libraries don't have an Internet equivalent. Of course, I am talking about the file transfer program (FTP) and anonymous FTP sites.

Both CompuServe and the Internet offer an extensive collection of public domain and shareware computer programs that can be downloaded to a person's local computer. As to how these two services compare, the answer lies not so much in how they operate but in the files they contain and how you locate them.

For general PC or Macintosh shareware and public domain software, there is relatively little difference between FTP and CompuServe. In most cases, if a program has been uploaded to CompuServe, it has also been uploaded to an FTP site. Where the two services tend to differ, however, is in the maintenance of more specialized files. Due to the UNIX-based nature of the Internet, you are more likely to find the UNIX file you are looking for on one of the many FTP sites than in the UNIX Forum archive. On the other hand, if you are looking for PC software support files or upgrades, CompuServe would be a better place to start your search.

> Unlike files found on CompuServe, there is no guarantee that files you download using FTP have been checked for viruses. To be sure, always scan any new files with a virus checker before using them on your system.

Tip

Apart from the different files each service contains, the other major difference springs from the way the two services organize their files. At CompuServe, all the files are held on the one system and stored in the forum libraries it operates. The Internet, on the other hand, consists of many unrelated FTP sites, each with its own organizational structure and unique naming conventions. For this reason, the way you locate and retrieve files using the two services tends to differ greatly.

Archie and CompuServe's File Finder

On CompuServe, you locate files using the CompuServe File Finder. (See Chapter 10, "File Transfer Protocol (FTP).") This tool allows you to search all of the forum libraries and identify files using keywords, descriptions, and a number of forum-related categories. As a result, you can very quickly narrow down your search and locate specific files.

Unfortunately, locating files stored at FTP sites can be a more difficult task. The most reliable way to search for files located on FTP sites involves the use of Archie. But unlike CompuServe's File Finder, you can only search for files by file name or directory name. This means that in most cases you need to know the name of the file before you begin your search. The other difficulty you face when using Archie is that not all FTP sites are currently indexed. This means that in some cases the file you are looking for may exist on an unindexed site, even though Archie reports that it does not exist.

To reduce this problem to some extent, a number of FTP sites also allow access to their files using Gopher. For these sites, you can locate files using Veronica, the Gopher search tool (see Chapter 13). This approach allows you to perform basic keyword searches using Gopher's file descriptions, which can greatly assist you by narrowing down the number of files located by a search request.

Tip

> If your time is important to you, the CompuServe File Finder offers the best approach. You'll be able to find files quickly and can be assured of a prompt downloading of virus-checked software.

Conferences and IRC

The last major component of many CompuServe forums is the Online Conferencing system and its Internet counterpart, IRC or *Internet Relay Chat*. Like IRC, CompuServe's online conferencing system allows users to conduct real-time discussions with other people. In addition, CompuServe also operates a forum devoted specifically to online conferencing called the CBFORUM.

The CBFORUM and the CB Simulator are designed to operate in much the same way as a CB radio, hence the name. Currently, CompuServe operates three 36-channel CB areas in the CB forum, in addition to the online conferences operated by individual forums. Listed in Table 15.1 are some of the more popular CB channels and a description of their discussion topics.

Table 15.1. Popular CompuServe CB channels.

GO	Channel	Description
CB-1	2	Newcomers
CB-1	3	Hospitality Suite
CB-1	4	Breakfast Club
CB-1	5	Cycle Shop
CB-1	7	The Holodeck
CB-1	9	Heart to Heart
CB-1	14	Sprechen Sie Deutsch
CB-1	23	Gone Fishin'
CB-1	27	Mac Mania
CB-1	35	Game Play 1
CB-2	1	Adult Band 1—Must be over 18 to Participate
CB-3	1	Adult Band 2—Must be over 18 to Participate

IRC, CB's Internet counterpart, offers similar features to CompuServe, although at this stage you will need to use NetLauncher and a dedicated IRC client (see Appendix C) to gain access to it. This is due to the fact that WinCIM does not currently support direct access to IRC.

Given this difficulty, using IRC is a relatively simple process. Like the CB Simulator, IRC consists of a number of channels where people meet and communicate in real time, but instead of using numbers to represent the channels, IRC uses names such as #chat, #amiga, or #IBM. Apart from this, the only real difference between the two services is that the participants on IRC are all connected by the Internet as opposed to CompuServe.

Other CompuServe Services

Although this book has spent a considerable amount of time discussing the use of CompuServe forums, there are a number of other services offered by CompuServe that also have complementary offerings on the Internet.

The following pages look at some of these services and discuss the different benefits each provides.

The World Wide Web and WinCIM

By far, the most difficult Internet service to compare with CompuServe is the World Wide Web. This is because in many ways it is not unlike WinCIM itself, when you consider the way it allows you to navigate around the Internet.

Like WinCIM, the World Wide Web lets you explore the electronic world without being concerned with all the complex technical issues such activities entail. As a result, the World Wide Web complements the services offered by CompuServe, and by WinCIM in particular. Moreover, the area in which the World Wide Web excels, Netsurfing, provides a major contrast between the two services that indicates why each service is so valuable in its own right. To paraphrase the comments of a number of CompuServe and Internet users, "When I want to find something, I go to CompuServe, and when I just feel like exploring, it's off to the World Wide Web."

With CompuServe's incorporation of a World Wide Web browser, its members have truly been given the best of both worlds. But more importantly, they can now pick and choose between the different services, allowing them to tailor their exploration of the information superhighway to suit their own particular needs.

The Electronic Mall and Internet Shopping

Since the inception of the CompuServe Information Service, CompuServe has been a leader in the world of electronic commerce and online shopping. Through the Electronic Mall, CompuServe offers its members a diverse range of products from many different sectors of the businesses community. Yet now it seems that the Internet is positioning itself to expand these services with its own brand of electronic commerce. So how do these two types of services shape up? And more importantly, which should you choose for your shopping explorations?

Probably the most significant difference between CompuServe's Electronic Mall and the online shopping services that are beginning to appear on the Internet is the location of these services. The Electronic Mall is located on CompuServe and can be entered by typing **MALL** into the Go… dialog box. This opens the mall's main window, as shown in Figure 15.1. From this menu, you can easily access all of the stores that operate storefronts in the mall.

Note

> As of September 1, 1995, even this distinction will be removed when the CompuServe Electronic Mall becomes accessible via the World Wide Web.

Finding stores on the Internet is a very different prospect. Following the near-global acceptance of the World Wide Web as the Internet navigator of choice, a number of inventive users realized that, due to its nature, it was an ideal platform for online commerce. In recent months, this has led to a deluge of new World Wide Web sites selling products and services online.

This has led to two problems. The first is, how do people find these stores on the World Wide Web? Because there is no starting point to the World Wide Web—no electronic front door—in order to find the WWW pages where stores are located, you need to put in some legwork. This is one of the big pluses for CompuServe's Electronic Mall—everything is in one place. However, if you use any of the World Wide Web search tools, this is not an insurmountable problem.

FIGURE 15.1.

The CompuServe Electronic Mall.

The CompuServe Internet Resources forum contains a regularly updated file called INMALL.TXT, which lists a wide variety of businesses that are accessible on the Internet. In addition, a number of lists are now beginning to appear on the Internet that contain similar information.

There is also another way that businesses are seeking to promote their wares on the Internet. A number of businesses have proposed the creation of shopping malls on the Internet similar to CompuServe's Electronic Mall. (See Figure 15.2.) By doing this, they increase their chances of being discovered and also benefit from the increased credibility such services provide.

FIGURE 15.2.

The Internet Shopping Network main directory.

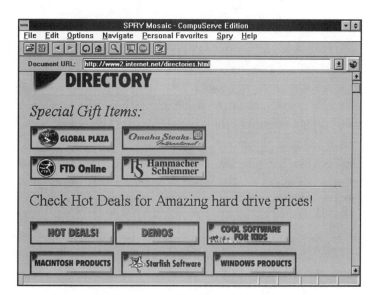

The second problem is a lot more difficult to deal with. Because of the lack of security on the Internet, there have always been concerns about the safety of personal financial details, particularly information such as credit card numbers. Until recently, this was a serious concern for anyone considering a purchase using the Internet. In the past, this was in fact the main argument for using CompuServe's Mall. It offered protection for your account details and the additional security of knowing that the store was approved by CompuServe.

To counter these concerns, a number of developments are currently taking place on the Internet in the search for secure World Wide Web servers. Amongst these developments are those being pursued by CompuServe in association with Terisa Systems. The two companies seek to develop S-HTTP and SSL technologies to make secure financial transactions a possibility on the Internet.

At this stage, however, there is no official standard. Netscape Communications, the developers of the Netscape WWW browser, have released their own secure transaction system, which only works if you are using their browsers. There is another system based on S-HTTP that some other WWW browsers already support, and possibly a third standard is in the pipeline. As a result, the whole secure transaction approach is still somewhat up in the air.

Note

> As with any shopping experience, consider the old saying "Let the buyer beware" whenever you venture out into the world of electronic commerce and online shopping.
>
> Firstly, always deal with respectable or well-known businesses where possible. Secondly, *do not* give out your credit card number or other financial details if you don't know who you are dealing with.

Electronic News Services

Following closely on the heels of electronic shopping in the popularity stakes is the ability to read the latest news of the day electronically.

For some time, CompuServe has offered access to direct newsfeeds from services such as the Associated Press and Reuters, giving its members the news of the day (or in most cases, of the minute) long before it could ever be delivered to their doorsteps.

To complement this almost instant coverage, the addition of direct access to electronic magazines and newsletters heralds the next wave of electronic news services. To the forefront of this new growth area comes the World Wide Web, which is ideally suited to the delivery of such services. (See the section on HotWired in Chapter 16 for a look at one of the more popular online magazines.)

Where this particular area of Internet development will end is very hard to say at this time. Already, a number of major newspapers are considering the possibility of offering online editions, while others are considering the merits of operating a newspaper purely in the electronic realm. What is certain is that, within a few years, you will just as likely read your newspaper online as buy a copy from the newsstand on the street corner.

Tip

Where better to find online newspapers than an electronic newsstand? Using the World Wide Web, go to the ENEWS home page at `http://www.enews.com/` to browse through the publications it offers.

IQUEST and WAIS

There is one CompuServe service that at the moment has no direct equal on the Internet, although that is not to say that in the future this will remain the case.

The service I am talking about is IQUEST, an extensive collection of databases that CompuServe members can search when conducting research on a wide variety of topics. To find an equivalent resource on the Internet, you need to look at the combined services offered by WAIS and those provided by the growing number of World Wide Web search tools that are rapidly attempting to index the Internet.

IQUEST highlights yet another example of the unique services that both CompuServe and the Internet offer. To the business world and as a research tool, IQUEST provides access to some of the largest commercial databases in the world. On the other hand, when you use search tools such as WAIS via the Internet, you have access to thousands of research papers, newsgroup discussions, and educational documents.

Again, each service offers you something different. This is the reality of both the Internet and CompuServe. Depending on what you are looking for, you need to choose the service that is right for the task.

Summary

Despite the fact that many of the services offered on the Internet are similar to those offered by CompuServe, each service brings with it a certain uniqueness of character.

With this uniqueness comes diversity and the ability to explore more widely the electronic world developing on the computer networks that now link the real world. Yet at the same time, the Internet services that CompuServe now offers don't so much reduce the need for its existing services as enhance and complement them. In doing this, they truly do combine the best of both worlds for CompuServe members.

With all this theory and comparison of services and resources, by now you are probably feeling a bit overloaded with computer terminology. So it's time to put your feet up for a while and simply explore some of what the Internet has to offer.

The next chapter takes you on a tour of the lighter side of the Internet, exploring family fun and, oh yes, we'd better look at education as well just to give the chapter some redeeming value.

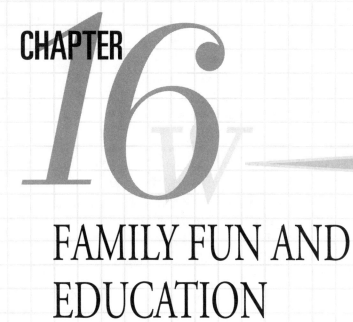

CHAPTER 16

FAMILY FUN AND EDUCATION

Although the ARPANET was originally designed as a tool for scientific research and distributed computing, it didn't take its users long to discover that it could also be used for many not-so-scientific endeavors.

Take, for example, one of the early mailing lists devoted to science fiction. Despite the wide variety of technical and scientific discussions available, this list rapidly became one of the most popular mailing lists ever. What was more interesting, however, was the fact that although the early administrators frowned on this non-scientific use of their new network, they were effectively forced to tolerate this non-standard usage due to the number of people choosing to use these mailing lists.

As ARPANET grew and was eventually replaced by NSFNET, this level of tolerance became the accepted norm for the emerging Internet. Despite many guidelines dealing with acceptable usage, the Internet has grown to become a veritable electronic playground. Ironically, it was this same level of freedom that eventually permitted the development of a number of Internet-based education- and community-based services.

It is these services and some of the more "fun" resources that will be covered in this chapter through the following topics:

◆ Games and other stuff

◆ Online news and magazines

◆ Education on the Internet

◆ Study and research

Games

"When you're tired of the Internet, you're tired of life," to plagiarize an overused quote. While saying such a thing may at first sound a bit trite, when you look at what the Internet has to offer, it isn't far from the truth. In the future, this same saying will probably become even more appropriate when the promised delivery of live television over the Net becomes a practical reality.

But enough of future dreams. What you want to know is what's available now!

Before looking at games you can play on the Internet, let's look at some of the games you can download from the Internet.

Without a doubt, the biggest software growth industry on the Internet—apart from writing WWW navigators—is the writing of shareware and public domain computer games. You would be very hard-pressed to locate an FTP site anywhere on the Internet that doesn't have at least one directory devoted to computer gaming.

Major Game-Related FTP Sites

To cater to this growing need, a number of FTP sites maintain archives containing a wide assortment of both DOS- and Windows-based computer games. These sites include these DOS game archives:

```
ftp.cdrom.com/pub/games
ftp.uml.edu/msdos/games
```

and these Windows game archives:

```
ftp.minash.edu.au/pub/win3/games
ftp.cica.indiana.edu/pub/pc/win3/games
```

In these archives you can find copies of public domain and shareware games, plus demonstration versions of many popular commercial games. Although these sites contain a large number of games, there are many other sites on the Internet that also contain various files—some dedicated to specific games and others holding more general archives.

To help you locate these sites, the best place to start is the World Wide Web, and more specifically, a WWW site called the Games Domain. (See Figure 16.1.) This WWW site has been designed to provide easy access to every Internet resource related to computer games. The links it provides include access to all of the major FTP sites, WWW servers for many commercial games, newsgroups, gaming FAQs, and one-click downloading of many shareware and public domain games. The home page for the Games Domain is `http://wcl-rc.bham.ac.uk/GamesDomain`.

FIGURE 16.1.

The Games Domain.

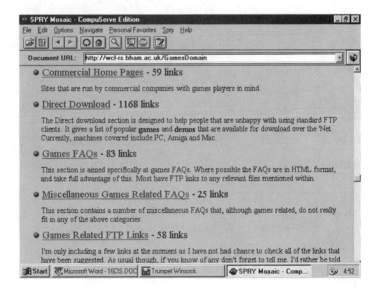

Doom

The distribution of computer games using the Internet has become so popular that one company in particular, id Software, has nearly turned the concept into an art form. In case you've been out to lunch, id Software, Inc., is the developer of Doom, Doom II, and Heretic. By offering fully playable versions of all their games on the Internet, this company created for itself an instant market when the final version (the commercial product), with all the bells and whistles, was released. In addition, they also encouraged the development of what can only be described as an aftermarket industry, which now sees new shareware support tools and many additional playing fields or *wads* being placed on the Internet each month.

There are a number of id Software game archives stored at various FTP sites, including mirrors of the host FTP archive at `ftp.cdrom.com` in the `/pub/idgames` directory. Alternatively, you can find a wealth of information about Doom, including pointers to many World Wide Web FTP sites. Figure 16.2 shows the home page for Doomgate, which is by far the most up-to-date Doom WWW site. Its http address is `http://doomgate.cs.buffalo.edu/`.

FIGURE 16.2.

*Doomgate—The gateway
to Doom.*

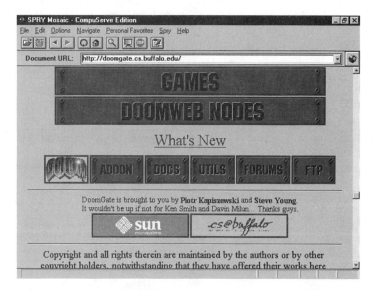

id Software has recently decided to set up a WWW server of their own at `http://www.idsoftware.com/`. However, at this stage, it is pretty much still under construction.

Apogee

If id Software is the writer of the most popular game, Apogee is the most prolific publisher of shareware games. With a software catalogue that includes Wolfenstein 3D, Commander Keen, and Duke Nukem, it is only natural that their software should also be available on the Internet.

For fans of Apogee software, the Games Domain has created a page providing direct access to all FTP sites containing Apogee shareware games. The http address for this page is `http://wcl-rc.bham.ac.uk/GamesDomain/Apogee`.

Newsgroups

Accompanying the many shareware games available using FTP, there are hundreds of newsgroups that discuss many of the more popular computer games.

alt.binaries

The `alt.binaries` area of USENET contains a few newsgroups that distribute the latest computer games as UUENCODED files stored in messages. Some of these are shown in Table 16.1. (See Chapter 8 for a discussion of UUENCODE and USENET.)

Table 16.1. `alt.binaries` **newsgroups.**

Newsgroup	Description
alt.binaries.descent	The latest Doom incarnation.
alt.binaries.doom	Doom I and II wads and editors.
alt.binaries.games.vga-planets	Not another Doom game—but a popular online computer game.
alt.binaries.heretic	Another Doom-like game from id Software.
alt.binaries.mac.games	Games for the Apple Macintosh.

alt.games

If fighting with UUENCODE isn't your style, some of the newsgroups in `alt.games` may be more to your liking. These newsgroups contain discussions ranging from hints and tips to game cheats. To get you started, Table 16.2 offers a list of some of the more popular newsgroups; however, just because a game isn't listed here doesn't mean that it isn't covered on the Internet.

Table 16.2. Popular `alt.games` **newsgroups.**

Newsgroup	Description
alt.games	Watch this newsgroup for announcements about new sections and computer gaming in general.
alt.games.apogee	A lively discussion of the many shareware games released by Apogee.

continues

Table 16.2. continued

Newsgroup	Description
alt.games.dark-forces	Having trouble winning at Dark Forces? Ask here for help.
alt.games.descent	Discussions and playing tips for Descent.
alt.games.doom	Enough said.
alt.games.doom.announce	This newsgroup is reserved for announcements about new wads, editors, and any other late-breaking Doom news.
alt.games.doom.ii	When you've tired of Doom, you're ready for Doom II.
alt.games.doom.newplayers	This is a good place to start if you're new to Doom. There are always people around who are willing to lend a helping hand.
alt.games.dune-ii.virgin-games	Dune, the computer game, not the book.
alt.games.heretic	Doom with a crossbow.
alt.games.playmaker-football	It's not a shoot-em-up, but for football fans it's just as much fun.
alt.games.tiddlywinks	Yes, there is even a newsgroup for this one.
alt.games.ultima.dragons	Adventure gaming at its best.
alt.games.x-wing	Star Wars for your PC.

To locate other game-related newsgroups, use the search options in CompuServe's Usenet dialog box. Type the word **game** into the Keyword: field and hit the **S**earch button, as shown in Figure 16.3. After a few seconds, WinCIM will open a results dialog box similar to the one shown in Figure 16.4, which lists the newsgroups it located. From this dialog box, you can **S**ubscribe to, or **P**review, any of the selected newsgroups.

FIGURE 16.3.

You can locate other computer game newsgroups by clicking the Search button.

FIGURE 16.4.

WinCIM reports that there are 131 game-related newsgroups.

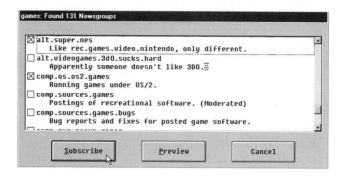

The *rec.games* Newsgroups

If you thought that the `alt` newsgroups covered the topic of computer games well, you're in for a big surprise. The `rec.games` area of Usenet is also crammed full of game-related newsgroups. To get you started, Table 16.3 lists some of the more active discussion areas.

Table 16.3. Popular `rec.games` **newsgroups.**

Newsgroup	Description
`rec.games.backgammon`	In this newsgroup you don't even need a computer. Backgammon anyone?
`rec.games.computer.doom.editing`	You guessed it, more Doom stuff.
`rec.games.corewar`	One of the more popular online games.
`rec.games.diplomacy`	Diplomacy buffs need look no further than this newsgroup.
`rec.games.rpg`	Role-playing games of all descriptions also receive good coverage on Usenet.
`rec.games.mud`	There are also a number of newsgroups that deal with multiuser dungeons.
`rec.games.pinball`	If you've ever played pinball, check out this newsgroup.
`rec.games.programmer`	This is a good place to talk with people about writing computer games.
`rec.games.xtank.play`	If you haven't heard about Xtank, have a look here.

Hardware-Related Newsgroups

To close out this topic, there are a number of other newsgroups dealing with computer games written for specific computer platforms. Some of these newsgroups are listed in Table 16.4.

Table 16.4. Hardware-specific games newsgroups.

Newsgroup	Description
alt.mac.games.binaries	Computer game files for the Apple Macintosh.
comp.os.os2.games	OS/2- and Warp-related computer gaming issues.
comp.sys.acorn.games	Devoted to computer games written for the Acorn Microcomputer system.
comp.sys.amiga.cd32	Commodore may be dead, but its computer games live on in the cd32 newsgroup.
comp.sys.amiga.games	For Amiga gaming discussion, this newsgroup is a good place to start.
comp.sys.ibm.pc.games.flight-sim	Flight simulators for those who love to fly.
rec.games.video.3do	The 3DO newsgroup.
rec.games.video.atari	Atari computer game machines also get a look in here.
rec.games.video.cd-i	CD-I, for those who have one.
rec.games.video.nintendo	Nintendo games machines are the topic of discussion here.
rec.games.video.sega	You can't mention Nintendo without someone saying Sega, so there is a newsgroup for it as well.

Online Games and the Internet

The Internet is not only a great source of computer game software, but it also offers a number of games and gaming environments that you can play while online.

These games tend to follow one of three main threads. The first relates to role-playing games (RPGs) not unlike the adventure games made popular by software houses like Sierra—the makers of Kings' Quest, Leisure Suit Larry, and Space Quest, just to mention a few. The second group falls into the category of interactive games, such as chess or checkers, which allow you to play with other people across the Internet. Finally, the last group is literally play-by-Internet games, where you play against the remote computer.

MUDs

Without a doubt, the most well-known role-playing game environment on the Internet is the MUD (*multiuser dungeon* or *multiuser domain*, depending on who you talk to).

MUDs are in many ways similar to text-based adventure games. When you enter a MUD, you are placed into an electronically generated world that you can explore by typing commands such as "north," "south," "up," and "down." As you enter commands, the MUD responds with descriptions describing your location, plus other important information. If you've ever played an adventure game, you will probably recognize the basic idea by now.

However, MUDs contain one vital element that separates them from your run-of-the-mill adventure game—the human element. When you join a MUD, you enter a world that is populated by other people—people like yourself who have entered the MUD and, like yourself, want to win. But win what? Fame, fortune, power, strength, magical abilities, or maybe the hand of a fair maiden or a prince. It really depends on which MUD you are playing. There are a number of different types, with varying rules and goals.

To participate in a MUD, you don't need any special program other than access to a Telnet client. Apart from this, all you need is the domain name of a MUD and away you go. Figure 16.5 shows the CompuServe Telnet Access a specific site dialog box. Using this dialog box, you can open a connection with a MUD called "The Final Challenge," whose domain name is `mud.primenet.com:4000`.

FIGURE 16.5.

You can use a CompuServe Telnet client to play a MUD.

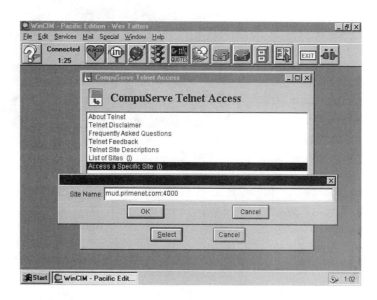

The `:4000` following the domain name refers to the port address of the MUD. You must include this number to ensure that your Telnet client connects to the MUD and not to a Telnet server associated with the same domain name. This address may be different for each MUD, so make sure you check out exactly which port you need to connect to.

When you hit the OK button, CompuServe opens a connection with the nominated MUD site and displays the MUD's logon screen. (See Figure 16.6.) If you are new to the MUD, you need to choose a name and a password. You will also be asked to enter configuration information depending on which MUD you are playing. You may be asked to nominate your sex and later your playing character for the game.

> **Tip**
> If you find that your Telnet connection displays symbols such as ^M when you hit the Enter key, you may need to use Ctrl+J instead of the Enter key.

FIGURE 16.6.

The Final Challenge MUD by Primenet.

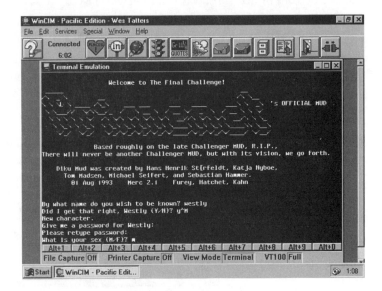

Once you enter the MUD itself, you are on your own. Part of the fun of playing a MUD is finding out how it works and learning its layout. There are often thousands of rooms to explore, objects to find, and people to meet (and sometimes do battle with). All MUDs are operated by gods and other minor deities who can be called upon for assistance, although some will expect adoration and worship in return. If you are really good, maybe one day you too can become a god—the highest level of achievement in any MUD game.

> **Tip**
> Playing a MUD does not need to be all guesswork. Most sites have a help facility that offers many useful tips and guidelines. To request the main help page, simply type the word **help.**

FIGURE 16.7.

*The Games Domain
MUD home pages listing.*

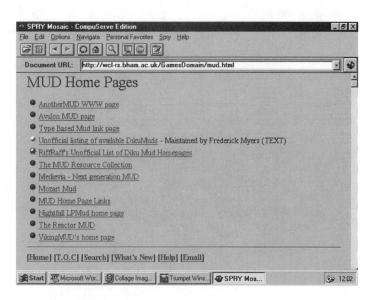

With over 450 MUDs of various types to be found on the Internet, listing them all here would be impractical. So instead, let's turn again to the World Wide Web and the Games Domain for a list of some popular MUDs and links to other MUD information pages. The http address for this page (Figure 16.7) is `http://wcl-rs.bham.ac.uk/GamesDomain/mud.html`.

MOOs, MUSHes, and MUSE

In addition to MUDs, there are a number of other multiuser environments on the Internet. Like MUDs, they allow people to interact in an online environment. However, where MUDs lean toward combat with the forces of evil, these other environments tend to be places for social interaction.

These environments fall into three main categories—MOOs, MUSHes, and MUSE. MOOs and MUSHes are different types of social MUDs, some of which feature worlds that often simulate places made popular by novels and movies, while others feature historical or futuristic worlds. Of the two, MUSHes tend to more closely adhere to the rules of dice-based role-playing games, with some closely replicating tabletop games of the same names. MUSE, on the other hand, are educational or tutorial worlds used by schools and colleges to teach human interaction and social sciences.

The best place to find information about MOOs, MUSHes, and MUDs in general is a WWW site called the MUD Resource Collection. (See Figure 16.8.) This site contains links to many games, plus related information including player guidelines, historical archives, and programming tutorials. The address for this site is `http://www.cis.upenn.edu/~lwl/mudinfo.html`.

However, for those of you who want to get started right away, Table 16.5 contains a short list of popular MUSHes and MOOs for you to explore.

FIGURE 16.8.

The MUD Resource Collection.

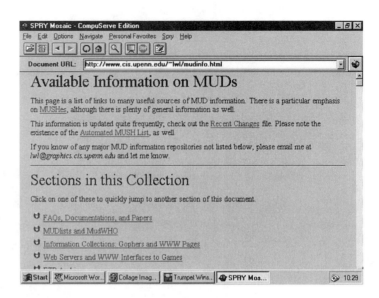

Table 16.5. Popular MOOs and MUSHes.

Site Address	Name	Description
sarcazm.resnet.cornell.edu:9000	AngrealMOO	This is a role-playing MOO based on Robert Jordan's novel *The Wheel of Time.*
omega.ru.ac.za:4201	Elenium MUSH	This game is set one hundred years after the events told in David Eddings' *Elenium Trilogy.*
colossus.acusd.edu:4444	ChromeMUSH	This is a cyberpunk MUSH set in Sacramento, California, in the year 2030.
omega.acusd.edu:9999	Danse Macabre	You guessed it, it's a "World of Darkness" game—well, at least loosely. This time, the setting is Paris in 1356.
dana.ucc.nau.edu:1892	Elendor MUSH	This MUSH is based loosely on J.R.R. Tolkien's *The Lord of the Rings.*

Site Address	Name	Description
`baymoo.sfsu.edu:8888`	BayMOO	This MOO is designed as a virtual reality world based around the San Francisco Bay Area.

Where to Find Other Games

As mentioned earlier, there are many other games on the Internet, some terminal-based and others built around the World Wide Web. To play any of these games, all you really need to know is the address of the site operating the game. Once you log on or open the appropriate WWW page, there are usually instructions provided to get you going.

There can be no doubt that the most concise list of online games ever compiled is Zarf's List of Interactive Games on the Web, a tiny section of which is shown in Figure 16.9. This site contains links to every known WWW-based game and a number of Telnet-based games as well. The http address for this site is `http://www.cs.cmu.edu/afs/andrew/org/kgb/www/zarf/games.html`.

FIGURE 16.9.

Zarf's List of Interactive Games on the Web.

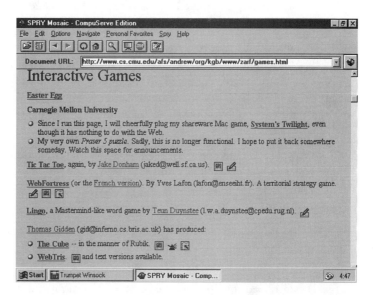

If your thirst for online games still isn't satisfied, you should also check out the other sites listed at the games domain. Many of these also contain links to online games.

Online News and Magazines

If playing games isn't your style, maybe browsing though online newspapers and electronic magazines is more your speed.

Ever since the first text editor was developed for computers, people have sought ways to publish their comments, criticisms, and views of the world. In the early days, many of these commentaries, or *e-zines* (electronic magazines), were disk-based. A number of articles would be collected on a disk with some pictures, and maybe a game or two or the source code of some program. The disks would then be distributed by the postal service or spread from hand to hand around university campuses and offices.

With the advent of widespread access to bulletin boards and modems, the popularity of disk-based magazines began to dwindle. In their place came electronically distributed versions. On the whole, the content did not change much, but now the publishers of these e-zines could reach a wider audience without the hassles and limitations of disk-based publication. Then came public access to the Internet, and again e-zine publishers adapted to meet the new technology.

Today, there are thousands of electronic magazines and newsletters published all over the world on a wide variety of topics, ranging from general interest to highly specific publications. Many of these e-zines are now distributed on the Internet. Some are delivered by e-mail using mailing lists, while others can be downloaded from various FTP and Gopher sites.

E-zines are not the only type of electronic publication available on the Internet. Since the arrival of the World Wide Web, a popular new concept has been sweeping the Internet—Web publishing. Of all the services offered on the Internet, none is more suited to the widespread delivery of electronic news and magazines than the World Wide Web. As a result, over the last two years hundreds of publications of all descriptions have begun to spring up all over the Web.

This section looks at some of the different types of e-zines, WWW publications, and even electronic newspapers that are now available on the Internet. In addition, it also looks at some of the best places to find new publications.

E-Zines

To get the ball rolling, first let's look at one of the oldest forms of electronic publishing, and still one of the most popular—electronic magazines, or e-zines.

The Internet is by far the most effective, and possibly the cheapest, method of electronic publication currently available. If you have access to a word processor and a modem, you can become an Internet publisher. While this may not be everyone's idea of a great way to spend the weekend, for many people it is just that—a hobby or, in many cases, a labor of love.

One of the more popular e-zine WWW pages currently lists over 350 well-known e-zines. These publications cover topics as diverse as cyberculture, independent filmmaking, time-wasting, and philosophical discussions at Phil and Bernie's Philosophical Steakhouse. In addition, there are literally thousands of other private publications devoted to just about every topic imaginable.

A large majority of these magazines are delivered by e-mail, although some of the more popular ones also operate World Wide Web pages that contain copies of not only the current edition, but also archives of back issues and, in many cases, subscription information as well. A small number are also available using FTP or Gopher, but most of these e-zines are being phased out in favor of the more popular World Wide Web distribution method.

To find one of the more popular e-zines, let's look first at the WWW site operated by a guy called John Labovitz. When John discovered that there was no concise listing of e-zines on the Internet, he set off on a personal journey to bring such a list to the world. The result was John Labovitz's E-Zine List (Figure 16.10), which can be found at `http://www.meer.net/~johnl/e-zine-list/index.html`.

FIGURE 16.10.

John Labovitz's E-Zine List.

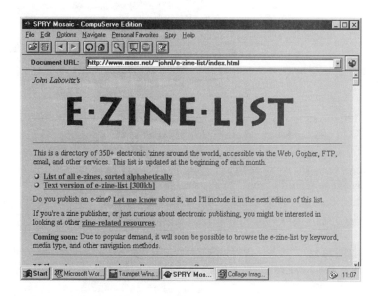

This site is regarded by many as the most up-to-date and accurate listing of currently available e-zines. At the moment, the list is available online in alphabetical order, or you can download a copy using FTP. However, by the time you read this book, a search tool should have been added to assist you with your e-zine exploration. There are currently over 350 e-zines listed on this site, which includes instructions on how to subscribe to each, as well as links to those e-zines whose publishers operate WWW, Gopher, or FTP sites.

One of the more impressive e-zines pointed to by this list is the Netsurfer Digest. This e-zine is published on a monthly basis and is available via e-mail or online using the World Wide Web. The link on John Labovitz's e-zine listing takes you straight to the Netsurfer WWW home page. (See Figure 16.11.) From here you can browse though the latest edition, look up articles from past editions, and subscribe to the e-mail version.

FIGURE 16.11.

The Netsurfer Digest home page.

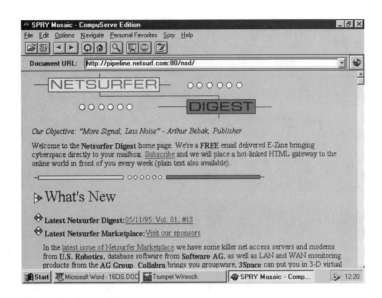

Subscribing to an e-mail version of any e-zine is the best way to read these publications, because you can look at them without being connected to the Internet. To encourage you to use this service, Netsurfer delivers each new edition to your CompuServe mailbox as an HTML page ready for you to load into your World Wide Web navigator. You can subscribe to Netsurfer by clicking on the word "Subscribe" in the first paragraph of the Netsurfer home page. Doing this opens a WWW form where you can enter your e-mail address and request a subscription. (See Figure 16.12.)

FIGURE 16.12.

Enter your CompuServe e-mail address to subscribe to Netsurfer.

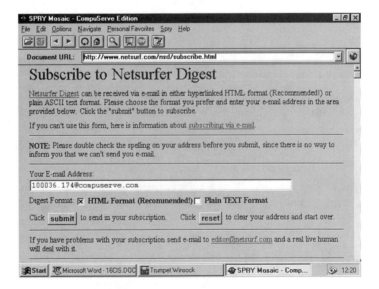

When entering your CompuServe e-mail address, remember to replace the comma in your ID with a dot, and use @compuserve.com as the domain name.

Note

Once you have subscribed to Netsurfer, you will begin to receive a monthly e-mail message containing the latest edition. To read Netsurfer, save this message as a file with an .htm extension and open your World Wide Web navigator. Using Spry Mosaic, open the **F**ile menu and select the Open **L**ocal File option. (See Figure 16.13.) This opens a file requester similar to the one shown in Figure 16.14. From here, select the file in which you saved a copy of the Netsurfer e-mail message and click on the OK button.

FIGURE 16.13.

Select the Open Local File option to load Netsurfer into Mosaic.

FIGURE 16.14.

Spry Mosaic's Open Local File requester.

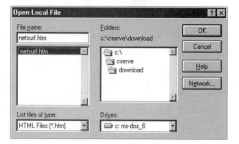

In this example, the e-mail message is saved as netsurf.htm and stored in the cserve\download directory. To keep track of past publications, you may wish to create a special directory to save all your Netsurfer zines and name each one with a date, but remember that to load them into Mosaic you must save them with a .htm extension.

After a few seconds, Mosaic loads Netsurfer and displays the text in your Mosaic window as though you had selected it while online. You can now read any of the articles in this edition using the hotlinks provided. In addition, many articles also contain links to other WWW sites that you can explore by simply clicking on the appropriate hypertext hotlinks. (See Figure 16.15.)

FIGURE 16.15.

Hot places on the Web this week.

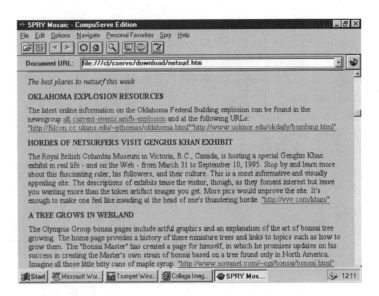

HotWired

Since the arrival of the World Wide Web, a new type of electronic magazine has begun to appear on the Internet—the interactive magazine. Unlike a traditional e-zine that you read and then put away, an interactive magazine invites you to become an active participant. After reading an article, you can add your own comments, criticisms, or even editorials.

At the leading edge of this type of publication technology, it isn't surprising to find one of the leading-edge magazines—*Wired*. In a bold move, *Wired* has created an alter ego on the Internet called HotWired. (See Figure 16.16.) To open HotWired, use `http://www.hotwired.com/`.

Note

> Before you can participate in HotWired, you must first become a subscriber. Although there are no costs involved in using HotWired, you must be a subscriber and have a valid user ID and password. To do this, follow the steps outlined on the HotWired home page.

This Web site is styled after *Wired* and offers the same level of insight into the emerging online world that people have come to expect. Where HotWired is different, however, is that it lets you become a part of the magazine by allowing you to make your own editorial comments, much like a global online letter to the editor. These commentaries are categorized into threads and grouped by subject, as shown in Figure 16.17. This level of interaction means that HotWired is always changing and growing as new members add their thoughts and ideas to the mix of cultures and ideologies.

FIGURE 16.16.

HotWired = Wired on the Web.

FIGURE 16.17.

HotWired's threads take you on a journey into the Wired world.

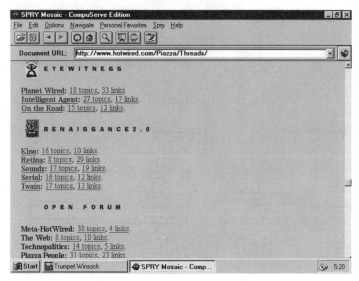

Not satisfied with offering a good service, but instead always wanting to offer the best, HotWired itself also grows and changes through the guidance and suggestions of the many people who use it. By the time you read this, HotWired 2.0 should be up and running, allowing a whole new level of interaction, with the added inducement of personal threads where people can create their own online editorials and possibly even electronic magazines in the future.

The Trib

Reading magazines may pass the time, but there are situations when what you really want is the latest news from around the world.

There's no better place to turn when you want the news than a newspaper or, in this case, the Internet newspaper shown in Figure 16.18. At `http://www.trib.com`, the news of the day is available online as it happens. Operated by the Casper *Star-Tribune* in Wyoming, this WWW site provides you with up-to-date national and global news, as well as links to many newsfeeds and newspapers operated by news organizations all around the world.

FIGURE 16.18.

The Trib online.

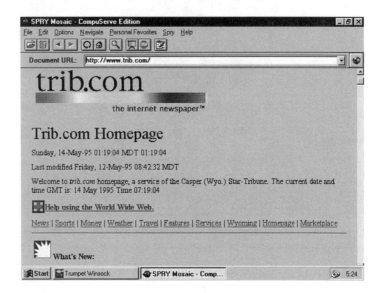

One of the main features of this service is its direct link to the Associated Press online news service—a first for the Internet—which allows you to read about the latest news as it happens. You can also search the Associated Press archives via this link and follow up on past news stories. The Trib also provides a link to CNN (Cable News Network), which offers the unique ability to download video clips of news stories. (See Figure 16.19.)

Warning

> Video clip files can be enormous, with even a short section of footage often requiring at least 1MB of storage space. As a result, downloading any of these files using a slow modem can sometimes take hours.

FIGURE 16.19.

Cable News Network on the Internet.

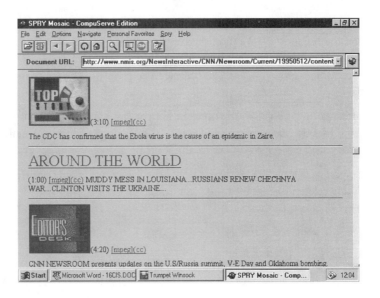

The Electronic Newsstand

Wherever there are magazines and newspapers, you can be sure that a newsstand isn't far behind, and the World Wide Web is no different.

So far you have looked at some of the magazines and journals published on the Internet, but what about the thousands of print magazines published each month? Many of these publications are also represented on the Internet at the Electronic Newsstand (Figure 16.20), whose address is `http://www.enews.com/`. It can also be reached by Telneting to `enews.com`.

FIGURE 16.20.

The Electronic Newsstand.

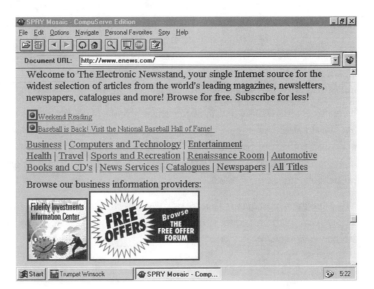

Every month, the magazines with a listing on The Electronic Newsstand upload copies of various articles and features published in the current print editions. Many also upload a copy of the table of contents to give you a better indication of what the magazine contains. Using The Electronic Newsstand, you can browse through any of the magazines and read the articles that have been uploaded.

After reading the articles, if you like what you have read, you can also use The Electronic Newsstand to subscribe to the printed edition. Due to a special arrangement with publishers, in most cases you can receive significant discounts or other benefits by subscribing online.

To give you some idea of the variety of magazines available online, here is a short list of randomly selected publications.

> *AV Video*
> *Best Friends Animal Magazine*
> *Guitar Player*
> *NBA Inside Stuff Magazine*
> *Technology Review!*
> *World Politics*

News Filtering

USENET is another good source of news and information, but for many people the sheer number of newsgroups available make it nothing short of impossible to keep track of all the various conversations. To help people keep track of what's happening on USENET, Stanford University has developed a news filtering service called Netnews as a part of its electronic library project.

Netnews lets you define search profiles for USENET. In these profiles you nominate keywords that you want Netnews to watch out for. Then, every day Netnews scans the thousands of messages that are posted to newsgroups all over USENET and captures any that contain the keyword you have defined. All of these captured messages are collated and sent to you on a regular basis via e-mail. By using Netnews, you can reduce the number of hours you spend wandering around USENET looking for interesting conversations.

Access to Netnews is available either through an e-mail list server-style service or a more flexible World Wide Web page. People interested in investigating the e-mail service should send mail to `netnews@db.stanford.edu` with the word HELP in the body of the message. On the other hand, if you prefer the World Wide Web, the Netnews World Wide Web home page can be found at `http://woodstock.stanford.edu:2000/`.

This page gives you access to a form for defining search profiles. (See Figure 16.21.) You can also use this form to update profiles you have already set up, as well as cancel profiles in which you are no longer interested.

FIGURE 16.21.

The Stanford Netnews profile form.

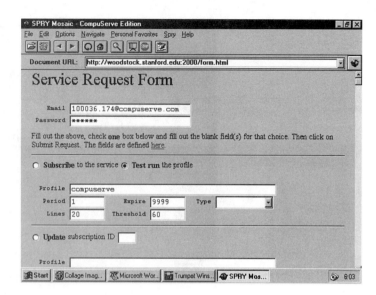

Before defining any profiles, it is a good idea to test them using the Test Run option. This option scans the current day's newsgroup discussions and generates a list of messages that meet your profile's requirements.

Tip

Education on the Internet

Although many people are often amazed by the fact that I like to talk about education and fun in the same breath, access to the Internet has changed the face of education forever. For the first time, even students are equating education with fun—especially when the Internet is involved.

One of the major strengths of the Internet is its capability to allow people to communicate with each other and share resources and information. This is an enormous boon to the educator. By providing access to resources that in the past have been simply unattainable or too expensive, the possibilities for expanding the educational experience are abundant.

In fact, the Internet has become so popular with educators that an entire service has been developed specifically for education purposes. Known collectively by the title K12, these services offer a number of benefits to educators and students alike.

AskERIC

The Educational Resources Information Center (ERIC), shown in Figure 16.22, is a federally funded information service that provides access to education-related resources using Gopher and the World Wide Web. To access this site, use the following http address: http://ericir.syr.edu/.

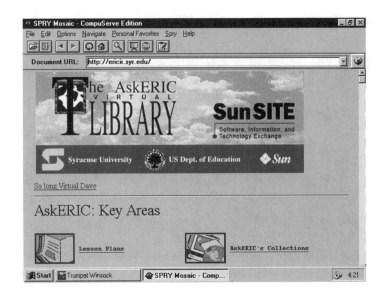

For educators at all levels, ERIC offers resources and teaching aids covering a wide range of subjects, including

◆ Lesson plans

◆ Digests and publications

◆ Reference tools

◆ Internet guides and directories

◆ Archives of education-related mailing lists

◆ Access to other education-related sites

To support these resources, the Educational Resource Information Center also operates AskERIC. This service is an e-mail feedback service that allows teachers, library media specialists, administrators, and other people involved in any field of education to send resource queries to the AskERIC staff. Because many educators are unfamiliar with the resources available on the Internet, AskERIC was created to help them locate the information they need. To quote from the information published about AskERIC:

> The hallmark of AskERIC is the human intermediary, who interacts with the information seeker and personally selects and delivers information resources within 48 working hours. The benefit of the human-mediated service is that it allows AskERIC staff to determine the precise information needs of the client and to present an array of relevant resources, both from the ERIC system and from the vast resources of the Internet.

To send an inquiry to AskERIC using e-mail, address your message to `askeric@ericir.syr.edu`.

Web66

Unlike ERIC, which is still strongly based on Gopher, the Web66 project shown in Figure 16.23 is built around the World Wide Web. To explore this site, open its home page: `http://web66.coled.umn.edu/`.

FIGURE 16.23.

Web66—The World Wide Web Education Project.

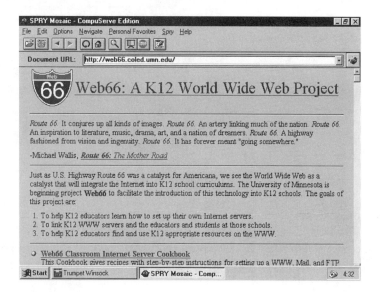

Begun by the University of Minnesota to facilitate the introduction of Internet and World Wide Web technology into K12 schools, this project aims to:

◆ Help educators set up their own Internet servers.

◆ Assist educators in linking these servers to the World Wide Web and other K12 schools connected to the Internet.

◆ Help educators locate K12-related resources on the Internet.

One of the main features of this page is the Web66 What's New page, which is updated daily. If you want to keep up-to-date with all the latest happenings in the online education world, this is the place to look. In addition, for Apple Mac users, there is a very good discussion of exactly what's involved in using a Mac as a WWW, Gopher, or FTP server.

GNN's Education Center

Another good source of educational information is the Education Center information (Figure 16.24) operated by GNN (Global Network Navigator), located at `http://www.gnn.com/hnn/meta/edu/index.html`.

FIGURE 16.24.

The GNN Education Center.

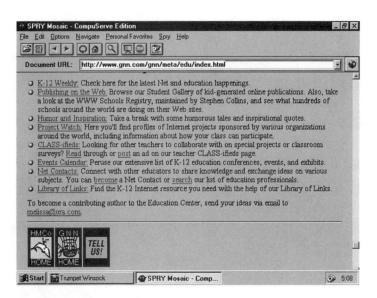

Although this site contains links to many of the same pages as Web66, it also maintains its own What's News catalog called K-12 Weekly. The Education Center also operates a classifieds service where teachers can advertise for collaborators when planning school projects and Internet-based classroom activities such as Travel Buddies. The Travel Buddies concept is an inter-classroom activity in which students from schools in distant locations—often on opposite sides of the world—exchange a small stuffed animal and report on the activities these Travel Buddies participate in while on holidays.

This page also features links to the GNN Library of Links, which is the ideal place to look for those hard-to-find K12 resources. There is also a link to a selection of notable quotes and humorous tales for those times when you really need to relax.

Tip

> Before you can take advantage of the services offered by GNN, you need to register yourself as a user. You can do this from either the Education Center index page or the GNN home page at `http://www.gnn.com/`.

Study and Research

As a research tool, the Internet offers capabilities unheard of in even the recent past. Many people wish that Internet access had been freely available during their time at school and college. With services such as the World Wide Web and WAIS now bringing the world to your desktop, finding information on many subjects is often just a few keystrokes away.

For example, assume that you are doing an assignment on the Hubble space telescope and want to find some information about what it does, and maybe locate a picture or two as well to show

Chapter 16 ◆ Family Fun and Education 343

what it looks like. There are a number of places you can begin a search, but by far the best approach is to again use the World Wide Web. From the World Wide Web, you can access two of the main Internet research tools: WWW search pages and WAIS.

The Web and Hubble

The weapon of choice for this Web search is Lycos, which was discussed in Chapter 12. To search for information on the Hubble space telescope using Lycos, follow these steps:

1. Call up the Lycos home page, shown in Figure 16.25, and select the "Search the big Lycos catalog" option.

   The home page for Lycos is `http://lycos.cs.cmu.edu/`.

FIGURE 16.25.

The Lycos home page.

2. Lycos displays a search form similar to the one shown in Figure 16.26.

   In the search field, enter the items you want to search for. For this example, enter **hubble picture.** This should find pages that are relevant to the Hubble space telescope.

   Once you have entered the parameters, click on the Search button to begin the search.

3. After a short wait, Lycos begins to display the results of your search on the screen, showing its name, http address, and a partial listing of its contents.

   After looking through the results of the search, find a site that looks right for your needs. Figure 16.27 shows part of the results list, which includes a site that seems to contain a number of press releases dealing with the Hubble telescope and possibly a number of pictures that may be useful for your assignment.

   To open this page, click on the highlighted http address shown at the beginning of the entry.

FIGURE 16.26.

Enter "hubble picture" in the search field.

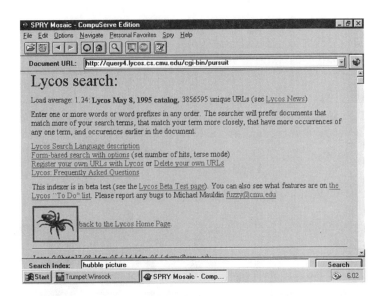

FIGURE 16.27.

Lycos lists the results on each search, including the http address of the site.

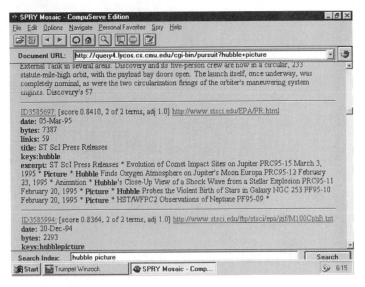

> **Tip**
>
> Using the simple search form, Lycos displays the first 10 entries it locates. To request additional entries, use one of the Search Form options on the Lycos home page.

4. When Mosaic finishes loading the selected page (Figure 16.28), it turns out that this is really the Hubble information mother lode. In fact, this site contains more information than you would ever need for your assignment, including a large collection of photos taken by the Hubble itself.

FIGURE 16.28.

The Hubble space telescope news and PR page.

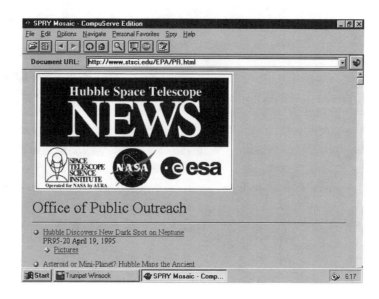

All things considered, these steps take no more than 10 minutes to complete, and in that time you can locate all the information you need as well as some suitable photographs.

WAIS and Hubble

Like Lycos, WAIS allows you to search for information stored on the Internet. But this time, instead of searching through WWW pages, you search the many databases linked by WAIS. To access WAIS, you can use either a dedicated WAIS client or a Web-based client like WAISgate. Both the dedicated client and the World Wide Web client achieve the same results, although each is somewhat different in its operation.

For this search you will use WAISgate, because you are already connected to the World Wide Web. (See Appendix C for information about obtaining dedicated WAIS clients.) To begin the search, you need to follow these steps:

1. To open WAISgate, call up the WAIS, Inc. home page shown in Figure 16.29, which is located at `http://www.wais.com/`.

2. Now click on the "Try a search yourself" link to open WAISgate. This will open a page similar to the one shown in Figure 16.30. From here you can select any of the options provided by WAISgate.

   In this case, you want to begin with the WAIS directory of directories, so click on the "Directory of Servers" hotlink. This allows you to search the topmost WAIS level. However, you could also select the "Other WAIS databases registered in the directory of servers" hotlink to move straight to a specific database.

FIGURE 16.29.

The WAIS, Inc. home page.

FIGURE 16.30.

WAISgate—The World Wide Web WAIS client.

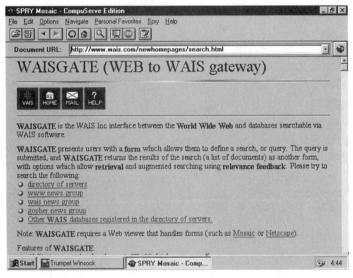

3. For this example, to find some up-to-date information on what the Hubble space telescope is doing, enter the word **hubble** into the search field as shown in Figure 16.31. Click on the Search button to get started.

4. When WAISgate completes the search, it generates a list of databases that match the search parameters. (See Figure 16.32.)

   Because you are trying to find out information about Hubble's status, the hst-status.src database seems like a good place to start. To open this database, click on its hotlink.

FIGURE 16.31.

The WAISgate directory of servers.

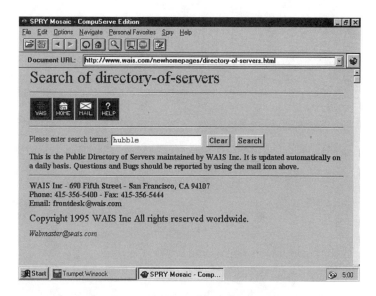

FIGURE 16.32.

WAISgate lists every database that matches search parameters.

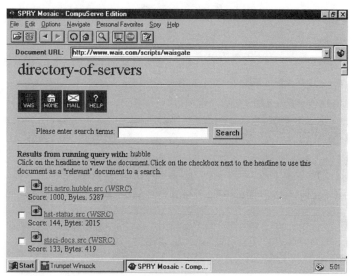

5. When you click on the `hst-status.src` item, WAISgate displays another search form similar to the directory of servers form. This time, however, it shows the name of the selected database. (See Figure 16.33.)

   You now want to search this database for any relevant entries. To do this, again type the word **hubble** into the Search field and then click on the Search button. You could also type any other word that would narrow down the files selected, because now you want to see every Hubble-related file.

FIGURE 16.33.

*To search the hst-status.src database, type the word **hubble** and click on the Search button.*

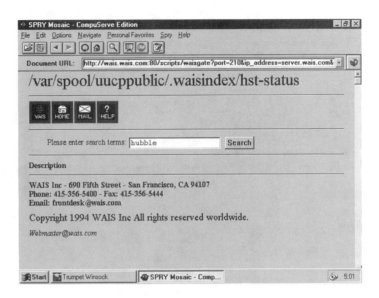

6. After WAISgate completes its search, it again creates a list showing all the files matching the search parameters. (See Figure 16.34.)

From here you can request copies of each of the files listed.

FIGURE 16.34.

The hst-status.src database contains a collection of text files.

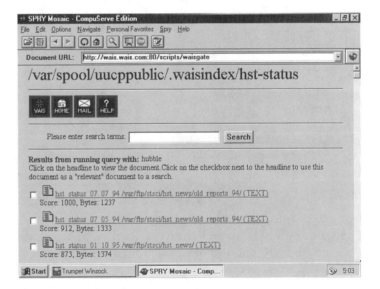

Like the World Wide Web search tools, WAISgate offers you another powerful research tool with hundreds of databases containing an extensive collection of text resources. The ways that each of these resources will suit your needs may differ greatly, but between the two of them you have access to a large percentage of the information available on the Internet.

Summary

The Internet contains resources suited to the different needs of all members of the community, be they games, magazines and newspapers, educational information, or study tools.

However, there is one aspect of the community that has not yet been discussed—the business community. To rectify this, "Business on the Internet" is the topic of discussion in the next chapter.

CHAPTER 17

BUSINESS ON THE NET

Until recently, many Internet users weren't open to the idea of companies doing business on the Net. For a long time there was strong resistance to any business activities on the Internet, with the operators of many network backbones actively participating in the lockout of business activities.

In fact, it was not until the formation of the *Commercial Internet Exchange* (CIX) that business activities began to be tolerated by much of the Internet. Gaining this acceptance came at a considerable cost, however, because CIX was effectively forced to set up its own communications backbone to bypass those areas of the Internet that insisted on locking it out. Thankfully, that period of conflict in the life of the Internet is behind us, and businesses, educators, and the public alike are now permitted to roam the Internet.

Since the resolution of this conflict, the commercial sector has consistently maintained its position as the fastest growth area on the Internet. As a result, the Internet Society reported that by the end of 1994, there were over 1.2 million commercial hosts connected to the Internet.

This chapter looks at why so many businesses are connecting to the Internet and explores some of the ways that even the smallest business can get a foothold. It looks at the following topics:

◆ The Internet Attraction

◆ CompuServe and the Net

◆ Business Services on the Internet

◆ Computer Companies on the Net

◆ WWW—The new Shopping Mall

The Internet Attraction

There are many reasons why companies of all sizes are now looking to the Internet. Some see the benefits of electronic mail, others see the potential of the World Wide Web, and some just want to use it because it's there. But regardless of the reason, it is a fair assumption that in the not-too-distant future, most businesses will be connected to the Internet in some way.

Commercial E-Mail

As the pace of daily life increases at near-breakneck speed, people have come to expect, and in many cases demand, instant feedback and around-the-clock support.

Unfortunately, the postal and courier services have reached a point where they simply cannot meet the turnaround requirements of 1990s business in the fast lane. To cope with these demands, the first innovation was the telex machine, an expensive device that required constant maintenance and trained operators—but at least they got the job done. Then came the fax machine, heralded as the business development of the century. No longer was there a need for telex operators, and even CEOs could be taught to use them.

From a resource perspective the fax machine is a wasteful tool, spewing out streams of paper when often all that is required is a simple one-line answer. It is also less useful within the office environment itself, although people have been known to send faxes from room to room just to make a point. Now, with the widespread acceptance of computer networking, electronic mail is rapidly replacing the fax in many business situations as the primary communications tool.

E-mail offers a new level of interaction to the business community. Using e-mail, messages can be sent and received almost instantly for considerably less cost than a corresponding letter or fax. This rapid transmission also leads to increased productivity because turnaround times for responses to messages can be reduced to a matter of hours or sometimes even minutes.

Global Presence

E-mail is a powerful tool, but the big attraction for many businesses is the potential for global exposure through services such as the World Wide Web.

To any business, the potential for greater public exposure, and hence the possibility of increased sales or greater market share, is a carrot that is hard to ignore. When this also means the possibility of international exposure, it becomes obvious why so many commercial sites are springing up all over the Internet.

Not since the advent of the telephone has a single communications service done more to bring about the advent of a global economic community. In real terms, it is now possible for even the smallest business to market its products and services on the global market for less than the cost of a good meal in an expensive restaurant. Businesses are not the only ones to benefit from the global reach offered by the Internet. For the first time, many consumers now have direct access to products and services that only a few years ago would not have been available to them.

Riding on the heels of this new consumer gold mine are the many credit card services, which also stand to benefit greatly from the upturn in online shopping. For their part, many of these services are very active in the area of secure transaction processing development, with both Visa and Mastercard now promoting these much-needed Internet security enhancements.

The Internet Industry

In addition to offering new opportunities to existing businesses, the growth in popularity of the Internet has fostered the development of an entirely new industry. This industry is devoted solely to the support and maintenance of the Internet and the services it provides.

To accompany the astounding growth of the Internet, new businesses are popping up all over the place that offer Internet connections, assistance with WWW development, FTP and HTML page storage, electronic shopping malls, and Internet-related software. If you want to get your business onto the Internet, these companies are the place to start. And where do you find these companies? On the Internet, of course.

Is it any wonder that so many people are talking about the Internet? While some regard it as a passing fad, others are calling it the overnight success story of the century. However, what it is now and what it has the potential to become suggest that the Internet is most definitely the place for business to be.

CompuServe and the Net

To cope with the level of interest being shown by the business community, CompuServe has instigated a number of new services designed specifically to help businesses get up and running on the Internet. Through CompuServe's Network Services division (Figure 17.1), businesses now have access to all of the tools and resources required to set up shop on the Internet.

FIGURE 17.1.

The CompuServe Network Services information page at http:// www.compuserve.com/.

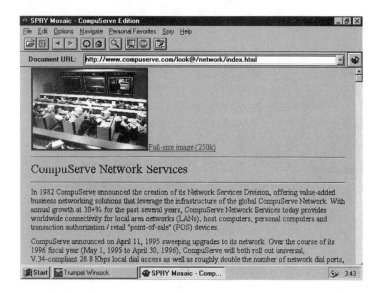

Internet Business Connections

In addition to dial-up PPP connections, CompuServe can also connect your business to the Internet on a more permanent basis. If you are interested in setting up your own FTP or WWW server, there is one important factor you need to consider. The main criterion you need to meet is being able to offer 24-hour-a-day access to your system. To do this, you will need to obtain a permanent TCP/IP link to the Internet.

Depending on your needs, CompuServe Network Services can provide you with a variety of connection options. These start with X.25 packet services at speeds up to 1.567 megabits per second (mbps) for U.S. users or up to 64 kilobits per second (kbps) throughout Europe. In addition, CompuServe can also connect high-usage businesses to their FRAME-Net® Frame relay service. Frame relays offer a flexible, high-bandwidth communications link between local area networks and the Internet. CompuServe currently offers FRAME-Net access to 15 countries around the world.

To work out what service is best for your needs, send an e-mail message to NETWORKINFO@cis.compuserve.com. In return, you will receive a message outlining all of the options currently available from CompuServe Network Services. Alternatively, you can always read about the latest services online at http://www.compuserve.com/look@/network/index.html.

> There are many ways to tailor a permanent Internet connection to meet a business's needs. One of the most important of these is finding the right Internet service provider. To find out more about locating other ISPs in your area, take a look at Appendix A.

World Wide Web Services

Once you've got your Internet connection organized, you need to consider the type of services you want to offer and how best to use them.

CompuServe has a number of services that can help you out in this area as well. These include online concept design, Web server installation and configuration, marketing consultancy, and even the design of your entire Web server including HTML page development and support. For the security conscious, CompuServe can also help to configure firewall security solutions that protect your company's resources.

Using the resources available at CompuServe Network Services, you can make your dreams for a World Wide Web storefront a reality. Depending on your level of ability, CompuServe can simply get you connected or manage the entire project for you.

Spry Mosaic Direct

Through CompuServe's new Internet Services Division, formed following the takeover of Spry Inc., you can also tailor the look of Spry Mosaic to suit your own business and corporate needs.

Spry Mosaic Direct is a companion product to NetLauncher that can be customized by adding personalized corporate hot lists and default links that automatically open your home page whenever Mosaic is running. This customized version of Spry Mosaic is then bundled on a single disk with a personalized installation program and all the connection tools needed to get your customers connected to the Internet.

By creating a customized version of Spry Mosaic for your customers, you can assist them greatly by helping them to get online with reduced hassles and none of the difficulties usually associated with the Internet. At the same time, you can promote your company's own Internet services to their best advantage.

To find our more about Spry Mosaic Direct (Figure 17.2), take a look at their World Wide Web site, located at http://www.spry.com/.

FIGURE 17.2.

The Spry Mosaic Direct information page at http://www.spry.com/.

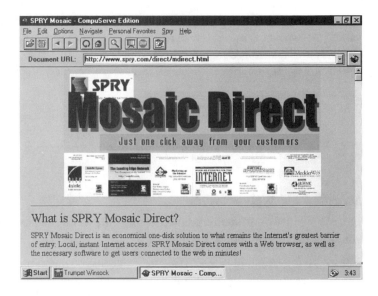

Online Service Providers

If setting up an Internet server is not within your budget, there is another option that may be more suited to your financial constraints. A number of companies have begun to set up servers on the Internet where you can rent space. Using one of these servers, you can set up your own FTP site or WWW home page without having to worry about operating your own permanent Internet connection or World Wide Web server.

The following pages look at two very different types of online service providers. The first service offers almost total access to its WWW server and allows you a high level of customization, but also requires a considerable amount of effort on your part. The second service offers you little or no access to its WWW server and requires very little work on your part. On the downside, this type of service usually does not provide a high level of flexibility and adaptability.

Web Communications

One of the most popular online Web servers is operated by a company called Web Communications—WebCom. (See Figure 17.3.) Using WebCom, you can create your own WWW pages and make them available to people on the Internet. The WebCom home page is located at http://www.webcom.com/.

Registration

The main feature of Web Communication's server is that the entire service can be managed using the World Wide Web. This includes the registration process and all contractual negotiations.

FIGURE 17.3.

At Web Communications you can set up your own private WWW home page or FTP server.

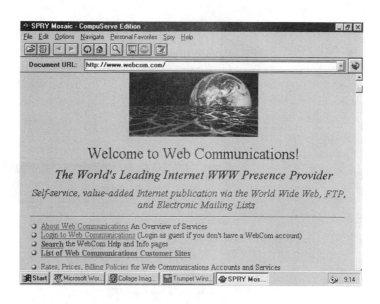

To open an account with WebCom, all you need to do is fill out an application form using your WWW Navigator and select a preferred payment method. If you choose to take advantage of the credit card payment facility, your WebCom account will be up and running about four hours after you make your request.

When you fill out your application, you will need to nominate the type of account you want to apply for. At WebCom, this is based on the way you intend to use the account and the size of your business. For private users, there is a personal account that can be used only for non-profit purposes. For companies with less than 15 employees, there is a special business rate. All other companies will need to select the corporate rate.

Regardless of which account you select, using a service like WebCom can save you thousands of dollars, not to mention the time and effort required to maintain an Internet server. To give you a better idea of the costs involved, Table 17.1 lists the current pricing structure for WebCom.

Table 17.1. WebCom pricing structure as of May, 1995.

Fee Description	Personal	Business	Corporate
One-time setup fee	$14.95	$44.95	$145.00
Monthly fee	$9.95	$29.95	$95.00
Mo. disk sp. allowance	5MB	5MB	10MB
Addtl. disk space/mo.	$1.95/MB	$2.95/MB	$4.95/MB
Net traffic allow./mo.	200MB	200MB	400MB
Optional addtl. traffic	$1.95/100MB	$3.95/100MB	$5.95/100MB

WebCom Services

Once you have created an account at WebCom, you can log onto your own private WWW server at any time. To maintain the WWW pages on this server, you use the online tools provided on the Web Communication - Customer Online Services page shown in Figure 17.4. From this page, you can access your private directories on the WebCom server, configure the various accounting and traffic reports available online, and keep track of your monthly account fees.

FIGURE 17.4.

Web Communications lets you maintain your WWW pages online.

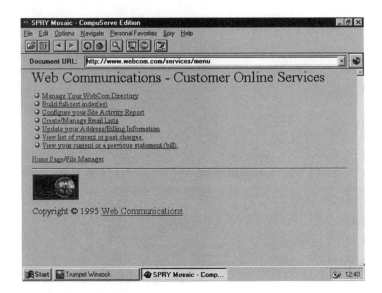

WWW Home Pages

For most people, the main reason for opening a WebCom account is the ability to create a personal WWW home page. The moment you open an account, a home page is automatically created for you using the account name you gave during the registration process.

The address for this home page is `http://www.webcom.com/~` plus your account name. When I opened an account at WebCom for Take Two, my film and television site, I gave it the account name `taketwo`. As a result, anyone who wants to access my home page uses the address `http://www.webcom.com/~taketwo`. (See Figure 17.5.)

If you are interested in film and television, why not drop in some time and say hi? I have links to every major film and TV page on the World Wide Web, and all the popular newsgroups as well. Oh, and if you like what you see, don't forget to nominate it for the Best of the Web. (So much for the shameless plug <G>.)

FIGURE 17.5.

Take Two, the film and television home page.

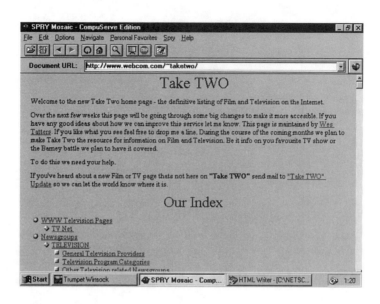

When it comes to online WWW maintenance, about the only thing that you can't easily do online is design your home page spectacular. WebCom does allow you to edit the HTML text of your WWW pages online, but for any serious work you need to consider using one of the many HTML editors now available. (See Chapter 13 for information about designing HTML pages.)

FTP Site

In addition to World Wide Web access, you can also use FTP to access your directory area at WebCom and selectively make directories available to the public as well.

Using the WinCIM FTP client, you can log onto WebCom using its FTP server. To access the WebCom FTP server, use this domain name: `ftp.webcom.com`.

Once connected, you will find that your files are stored in a subdirectory of `/pub/` with the same name as your account. In Figure 17.6, I located my TakeTwo files in the `/pub/taketwo` directory. The subdirectories of `/pub/taketwo` store any HTML pages you have created and can also be configured to hold files that other people can download just like a normal anonymous FTP server.

If you log onto `ftp.webcom.com` as an anonymous user, only those files and directories that have been marked as public on the WebCom WWW Directory Management page can be downloaded. To access protected files using FTP, log on using your WebCom account name and password.

Note

FIGURE 17.6.

Take Two via FTP.

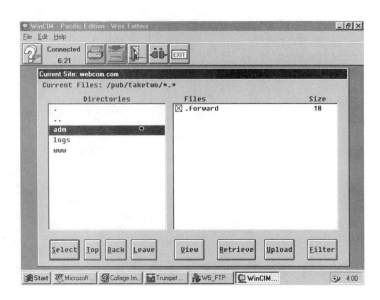

Mailing Lists

Probably the most unusual service offered by Web Communications is the ability to operate your own Majordomo mailing lists. (See Chapter 7 for a discussion of mailing lists and Majordomo.)

Using the instructions outlined on the Majordomo page and the Mailing List Management page shown in Figure 17.7, you can create any number of mailing lists. These mailing lists can contain any sort of information you wish to distribute and can be distributed as either digests or as regular mailing lists.

FIGURE 17.7.

The WebCom Mailing List Manager helps you maintain your mailing lists.

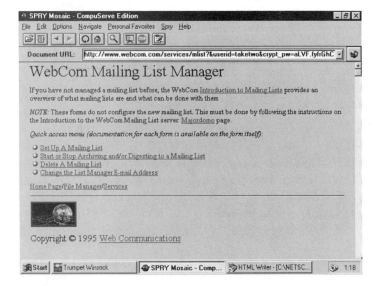

WebCom Support Services

To help you create your home pages, WebCom offers possibly the most comprehensive online guide to HTML ever produced. (See Figure 17.8.) There is information here for everyone who has ever considered using the World Wide Web, discussing topics as diverse as:

Tutorials on HTML
Forms management and WebCom
WWW marketing and advertising
A beginner's guide to the World Wide Web
Online help for all WebCom tools

FIGURE 17.8.

WebCom's Comprehensive Guide to the World Wide Web.

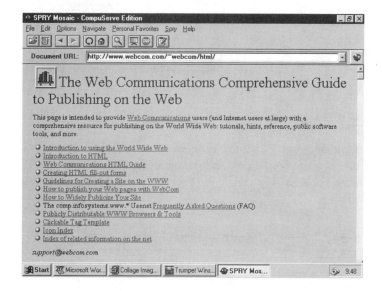

BizPro—Billboards on the Internet

For businesses that don't want to have to learn about HTML, there is another option. For a fee, some WWW operators will create the electronic equivalent of a billboard on their server where you can advertise your products and services.

One such server that specializes in this type of service is BizPro. When you purchase a billboard from BizPro, all you need to do is give them a copy of text you want to display on your billboard and any images, such as corporate logos or product graphics. BizPro then takes this information, creates your Web HTML pages for you, and places links to your billboard in their customer directory.

To find out more about the services offered by BizPro, take a look at their WWW server on `http://www.bizpro.com/bizpro/bilbord.html`. (See Figure 17.9.)

FIGURE 17.9.

Advertise your products on BizPro's Electronic Billboard.

Rates and Charges

Instead of charging a flat rate for space on their WWW server, BizPro charges you by the page, since they are actually doing all the maintenance work for you. To give you some idea of the costs involved in using this type of service, Table 17.2 lists the current charges for a listing on BizPro.

Table 17.2. BizPro billboard charges as of January, 1995.

	1/4 page	*1/2 page*	*Full page*
Page rental per year	$60.00	$120.00	$240.00
Each addtl. page per year	$30.00	$60.00	$120.00
Text updates	$10.00	$10.00	$10.00
Graphics updates	$20.00	$20.00	$20.00

Forms and Customization

If yours is a small business or one that does not plan to make many changes to its listing, this type of service can provide a quick way to get your business onto the Internet. However, if you plan to change your information on a regular basis or would like to use features like forms, services like BizPro should be considered only as a short-term option. At this stage, BizPro is strictly a billboard service and as such does not permit the use of data entry forms of any description.

If this is the case, you will probably be better off investing some time in learning about HTML and opting for a service like the one offered by WebCom.

Business Services on the Internet

With the rapid growth of interest in the Internet from the business community, it did not take long for some astute minds to realize that the Internet itself could be used to offer much-needed support.

As a result, several Internet business centers are now beginning to appear on the World Wide Web. These centers offer assistance to businesses interested in moving onto the Internet as well as support for existing services. This section looks at some of the businesses now available on the Internet.

CommerceNet

CommerceNet is a non-profit corporation formed in 1993 to facilitate the use of the Internet for electronic commerce. According to the CommerceNet charter, it aims to:

◆ Operate an Internet-based World Wide Web server with directories and information that facilitates an open electronic marketplace for business-to-business transactions

◆ Accelerate the mainstream application of electronic commerce on the Internet through fielding pilot programs in areas such as transaction security and electronic catalogues

◆ Enhance existing Internet services and applications and stimulate the development of new services

◆ Encourage broad participation from small, medium, and large companies and offer outreach programs to educate organizations about the resources and benefits available with CommerceNet

◆ Serve as a common information infrastructure for northern California and coordinate with national and international infrastructure projects

By doing this, CommerceNet hopes to stimulate the growth of a communications infrastructure that will be easy to use, oriented for commercial use, and ready to expand rapidly.

The first and most visible outcome of this project was the creation of the CommerceNet WWW server, shown in Figure 17.10. If you are interested in finding out more about what CommerceNet is doing or how you can take advantage of the services it offers, this is the best place to start. The HTTP address for this WWW site is `http://www.commerce.net/`.

FIGURE 17.10.

The CommerceNet home page at http://
www.commerce.net/.

The Internet Business Center

While CommerceNet offers you a considerable wealth of information about commerce on the Internet, there is another site that offers more general business-orientated information. The service I am referring to is the Internet Business Center (Figure 17.11), located at http://
www.tig.com/IBC/index.html.

FIGURE 17.11.

The Internet Business Center offers a wide variety of business information.

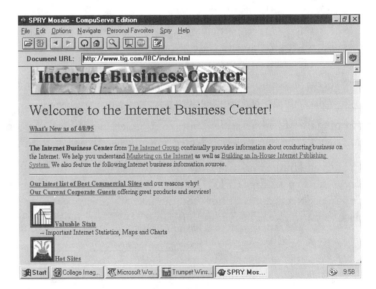

If you are planning to set up any sort of business venture on the Internet, spending a few hours browsing through the information stored at this site could save you many sleepless nights further down the line. Of all the information stored here, the section called "Building an In-House Internet Publishing System" should be considered required reading. In addition, there are some valuable insights into the art of marketing on the Internet, and a good collection of facts and figures that can help make your case for an Internet server to even the most wary board of directors.

This site also provides links to many other business-related sites, including financial and legal services and graduate business schools, through the Internet Business Center Hot Sites list (Figure 17.12), which can be found at `http://www.tig.com/IBC/Servers.html`.

FIGURE 17.12.

The Internet Business Center Hot Sites list.

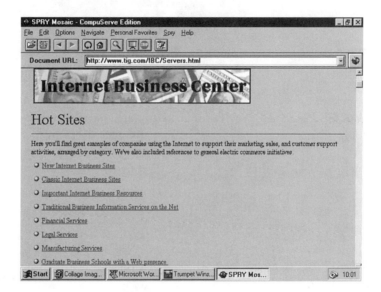

EINet Business and Commerce Directory

The most comprehensive directory of business- and commerce-related Internet sites is maintained by EINet Galaxy in its Business and Commerce directory. (See Figure 17.13.) This directory is maintained as a part of the EINet Galaxy directory service discussed in Chapter 12.

FIGURE 17.13.

The EINet Galaxy Business and Commerce directory.

You can access the directory from the EINet Galaxy home page or jump straight to it at `http://galaxy.einet.net/galaxy/Business-and-Commerce.html`.

Other Popular Listings

There are many other business-oriented lists on the World Wide Web that deal with a wide variety of business-related topics. To get you started, Table 17.3 lists some of the more popular business listings.

Table 17.3. Other popular business pages and listings.

Site Name	HTTP Address
Yahoo	`http://www.yahoo.com/Business/`
GNN	`http://www.gnn.com/gnn/bus/index.html`
Career Mosaic	`http://www.careermosaic.com/cm/`
Legal Information Institute	`http://www.law.cornell.edu/`
GE Corporate Toolkit	`http://ce-toolkit.crd.ge.com/`
Networth Info Page	`http://networth.galt.com/www/home/networth.htm`
Dow Jones Industrial Averages	`http://www.secapl.com/secapl/quoteserver/djia.html`
BizInfo	`http://www.dnai.com/~sharrow/bizinfo.html`

Computer Companies on the Net

As you would probably expect, many of the major computer manufacturers and software companies now present a variety of services on the Internet. Some companies offer online support to their customers, others provide software updates and patches, and a few even allow you to purchase software products online.

Software Manufacturers

To help you locate some of these companies, and since most of these companies now operate a server on the World Wide Web, Table 17.4 is a list of World Wide Web sites operated by software manufacturers.

Table 17.4. Computer software manufacturers on the World Wide Web.

WWW Home Page	Company Name
http://www.adobe.com	Adobe Systems, Inc.
http://www.microsoft.com	Microsoft Corporation
http://www.ncd.com	Network Computing Devices
http://www.novell.com	Novell, Inc.
http://www.sco.com	Santa Cruz Operations, Inc.
http://www.sgi.com	Silicon Graphics, Inc.
http://www.sun.com	Sun Microsystems, Inc.
http://www.synopsys.com	Synopsys

Hardware Manufacturers

Like software manufacturers, many hardware manufactures also operate WWW servers to support their various products and services. Table 17.5 lists the World Wide Web sites of some of the better known computer hardware manufacturers.

Table 17.5. Computer hardware manufacturers on the World Wide Web.

WWW Home Page	Company Name
http://www.amdahl.com	Amdahl Corporation
http://www.apple.com	Apple Computers, Inc.
http://www.cisco.com	Cisco Systems, Inc.
http://www.cray.com	Cray Research, Inc.
http://www.dell.com	Dell Computers

continues

Table 17.5. continued

WWW Home Page	Company Name
`continueshttp://www.digital.com`	Digital Equipment Corporation
`http://www.hp.com`	Hewlett Packard
`http://www.ibm.com`	IBM Corporation
`http://www.intel.com`	Intel Corporation
`http://www.qms.com`	QMS, Inc.
`http://www.racal.com`	Racal-Datacom
`http://www.rockwell.com`	Rockwell International
`http://www.tandem.com`	Tandem Computers

WWW—The New Shopping Mall

As discussed in Chapter 14, the Internet is rapidly becoming the shopping mall of the 1990s, offering goods and services to a global market that is just beginning to realize the potential of online shopping.

Discussing the diverse range of products and services now being offered is a job that begs for a book of its own. So instead, this section takes a look at some of the more popular electronic malls that offer access to these stores.

The Internet Mall

The Internet Mall is operated by Meckler Media, the publishing company that produces *Internet World* magazine, on its MecklerWeb site at `http://www.mecklerweb.com/`. (See Figure 17.14.)

Designed around the concept of a true shopping mall, the Internet Mall is divided into virtual floors (Figure 17.15) with different products and services available on each level. This site is by far the most comprehensive listing of commercial WWW sites currently available.

MecklerWeb also provides you with access to WWW pages dedicated to the various publications produced by Meckler Media: *Internet World, VR World, WebWeek,* and *Net.Day.* There are also links to information on Internet-related trade shows, the Career Web, and business activities on the World Wide Web.

FIGURE 17.14.

Meckler Media's World Wide Web site is the home of the Internet Mall.

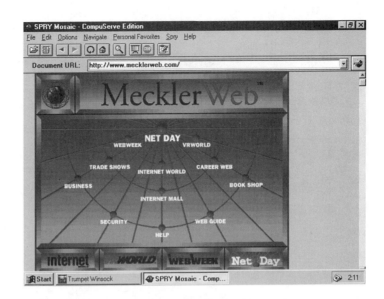

FIGURE 17.15.

The Internet Mall uses virtual floors to categorize the products and services available online.

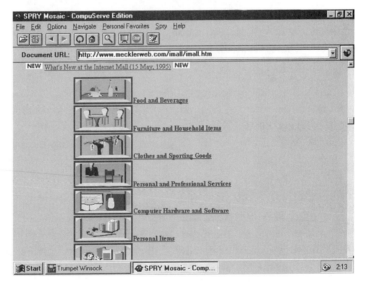

Netscape Galleria

Netscape, the developers of one of the most popular WWW navigators ever written, maintain their own listing of commercial WWW sites at the Netscape Galleria, `http://www.netscape.com/ escapes/galleria.html`. (See Figure 17.16.)

FIGURE 17.16.

Many of the WWW sites listed at the Galleria offer secure transaction processing.

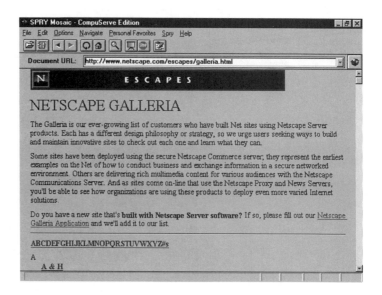

What is special about all of these sites is the fact that they all use a Netscape WWW server. In addition, many of them also support the use of secure transactions, which encode your purchase and credit information—protecting it from prying eyes.

> There are currently a number of different secure transaction specifications doing the rounds of the Internet. As a result, it will take some time before an official standard is agreed to and all WWW clients support each of the different protocols. Check with your WWW client provider to find out which protocols it supports.

The Open Market

Unlike other WWW servers, which provide services to other businesses by allowing them to create their own home pages, the Open Market Shopping Mall (Figure 17.17) looks after all the billing and accounting details for all of the stores it contains. To access the Open Market home page, use the following HTTP address: `http://www.openmarket.com/`.

For customers this means simpler online shopping, because all your billing details only need to be entered once. The first time you enter the Open Market, you will be asked to create a demonstration account by nominating a user name and password. Doing this allows you to explore some of what the Open Market offers. Then, if you decide to make a purchase, you register your billing details and your account is activated. After this, every time you purchase products and services from businesses in the Open Market, your accounting details are automatically updated and your credit card is billed as per your previous instructions.

FIGURE 17.17.

One-stop billing on the Open Market.

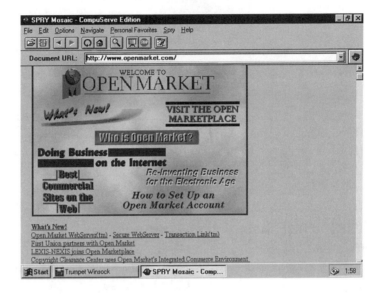

The Open Market supports secure transactions using the S-HTTP protocol. At this stage, however, only people using the latest version of NCSA Mosaic or Netscape 1.1 can take advantage of this capability. Check with your WWW client provider to find out if their latest version supports S-HTTP.

If you can't find the product you're looking for at Open Market, take a look at the WWW commerce directory that the Open Market maintains. (See Figure 17.18.) To explore the 5,000 commercial WWW sites listed in this directory, use the following HTTP address: `http://www.directory.com/`.

FIGURE 17.18.

The Open Market commerce directory.

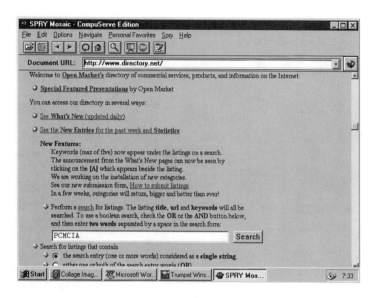

The Internet Shopping Network

If you enjoy the Home Shopping Network, you're bound to find something of interest on its new Internet service, the Internet Shopping Network, whose home page is located at `http://www2.internet.net/`. (See Figure 17.19.)

Like the Home Shopping Network, the Internet Shopping Network strives to offer you the best products at the cheapest prices, with overnight delivery of most products.

Before you can purchase any products on the Internet Shopping Network, you must become a member. To do this, select the Member option from the home page or any of the main product pages. When you fill out the membership application, you will be given your own private account number to use whenever you want to make a purchase.

More Malls and Internet Shopping Centers

In addition to these sites, there are a number of other WWW pages that provide lists of commerce-related Internet sites. Table 17.6 compiles a list of other popular sites that you may like to explore.

FIGURE 17.19.

Products offered at the Internet Shopping Network.

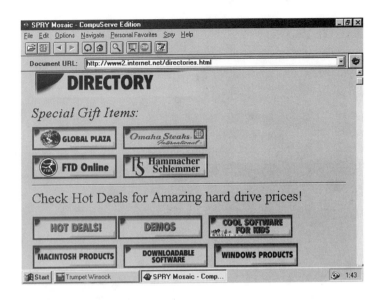

Table 17.6. Shopping malls on the World Wide Web.

Mall Name	HTTP Address
BizWeb	http://www.bizweb.com/
Canadian Business Pages	http://cban.worldgate.edmonton.ab.ca
Companies on the Net	http://www.primenet.com/links/companies.html
iMall	http://www.imall.com/
The Commerce Center	http://www.save.com/
Shopping 2000	http://shopping2000.com/
GNN Direct	http://www.gnn.com/gnn/gnndirect/index.html

Summary

Over the past two years, businesses all around the world have begun to realize the potential of the Internet, and in particular the World Wide Web.

As you have seen in this chapter, businesses of all descriptions are now using the Internet for communications, commerce, product support, and customer service. Where this growth will end is hard to say, but it would appear that if you want to remain in business in the very near future, you will need to be connected to the Internet. Eventually, consumers will come to expect this type of access in much the same way that people now simply assume that a business has a fax machine.

As this chapter comes to a close, you are nearing the end of your exploration of the Internet using CompuServe. So where do you go from here? The Internet offers many new avenues for research, education, business, fun, and entertainment. All you need to do is open the door and explore it.

The final chapter of this book takes a look at where you go from here and recaps some of the better departure points and places where you can find information about the Internet and its uses.

CHAPTER 18

THE NEXT STEP

Sadly, our time together is almost at an end. You now hold in your hands the final chapter, apart from the good stuff at the back—the appendices, the glossary, and the all-important index.

By now you are probably asking yourself, "What else is there to talk about?" You have already looked at:

◆ Sending messages using e-mail

◆ Mailing lists

◆ Usenet and newsgroups

◆ Remote connections via Telnet

◆ File transfers with FTP

◆ And of course, the World Wide Web

Well, the simple answer to "What else is there to talk about?" is "Nothing," and yet at the same time "Everything." If you have been following all of the examples and exploring the many sites discussed in this book, by now you should have a good understanding of the Internet and the many tools that CompuServe provides to give you access to it.

With all this knowledge under your belt, you should now be able to confidently explore the Internet. Yet at the same time, the Internet is so large that it continually offers up new sources of information, new means of accessing this information, and in some cases entirely new technology as well.

The Future of the Internet

If I had told you five years ago that there would be a computer network that spanned the globe by 1995, allowing people to communicate with each other for little more than the cost of a local phone call, you would probably have laughed in my face.

Today that story, which many would have considered a work of fiction, is a reality and the Internet is its name. But what if we take our crystal ball and try to look forward another five years? What sort of place will the Internet be, or will it even exist? Trying to answer such a question is at best a difficult proposition, but there are a number of pointers that can give you some indication of what the Internet may become.

Performance

For most people, the biggest single difficulty in using services like the World Wide Web and, to a certain extent, FTP is one of speed. Until modems capable of maintaining speeds in excess of 9,600bps became commercially available, even attempting to use the World Wide Web for any practical purpose was far from a viable proposition. When you consider the fact that many WWW pages are over 50KB in size, not including images and other graphics that can easily push the size of a complex page to close to 200 to 300KB, downloading such a page and displaying it on your computer can take a considerable amount of time.

With the introduction of 28,800bps modems, which can effectively achieve speeds of between 56,000bps and 110,000bps using on-the-fly data compression, the time it takes to load these pages can be considerably reduced. But at the same time, the complexity of WWW pages is also increasing to a point where even these high-speed serial modems are finding it difficult to keep up.

To keep pace with this increased need for improved performance, the next logical step seems to be ISDN. ISDN, which stands for Integrated Services Digital Network, is an emerging standard that provides both voice and data communications via a single cable. A number of major Internet service providers, including CompuServe, are currently either experimenting with the use of ISDN or are already offering ISDN as an alternative to slower dial-up modem options. Depending on the type of ISDN service you choose, it is possible to transfer data at rates of between 64KB and 128KB, providing much higher performance when you're using the World Wide Web.

However, even ISDN may only be a temporary step, and one that may already be doomed to fall by the wayside as the world's communications giants prepare to meet the Internet head on.

Cable TV and the Internet

One of the major disadvantages of ISDN in the past has been the high costs associated with maintaining the service and the expensive equipment that is required to connect your computer to it.

Yet in many households around the world, there is already another cable that may be able to provide direct access to the Internet in the very near future. This cable is the cable TV connection that sits on top of many television sets. Since late 1993, a number of cable TV providers and commercial telephone companies have been experimenting with the delivery of services such as the Internet using existing cable TV connections and through even higher-speed services such as fiber-optic cable. Although these systems are still in the late stages of development for the most part, the information that has begun to surface describing their potential is enough to make the mouth water.

The ambitious goal of much of this research is the delivery of video on demand, offering as many as 500 TV channels via a single cable. In addition, the same cable will be able to handle your telephone calls, including multiple lines, as well as provide you with a direct connection to the Internet at speeds approaching a megabyte of data per second.

If and when such services become available, you are likely to see full-motion video on your World Wide Web page, with IRC replaced by online video conferencing, and newspapers, magazines, and even virtual reality games all available from the comfort of your own home. The other change that you are also likely to see is a change in the appearance of your computer, which may eventually look more like a VCR sitting on top of your television. But what about the keyboard? Well, maybe voice recognition will become a practical reality as well.

Basically, who really knows? However, judging by the rapid growth in the popularity of the Internet and the imminent release of some exciting technology, chances are you won't have to wait another five years to find out for yourself.

The Future of CompuServe

With all these new developments taking place, what is the future of services like CompuServe? For CompuServe, at least, the answer is a bright future. However, that does not mean that you won't begin to see substantial changes in the way CompuServe looks and feels over the coming months and years.

What you will most likely see is a gradual integration of CompuServe services, such as its forums and news services, into the structure of the Internet. Having said that, all of the existing services will most likely remain, but in the future it is likely that they will be accessible using the World Wide Web or some future navigation tool based on WWW technology.

As an indication of their intention to move in this direction, CompuServe has already announced that as of September 1, 1995, all of the stores currently featured in its Electronic Mall will be accessible through the World Wide Web. Although they are yet to announce whether this new mall will be available to the general public or to CompuServe members only, such a move represents an enormous step forward in the integration of CompuServe and the Internet.

To accompany this release, it has also been rumored that a new version of WinCIM will be made available at the same time. It is expected that this version will remove the need for NetLauncher and Spry Mosaic by including a full WWW browser with secure transaction support as an integral part of WinCIM. Once this version is released, the integration on CompuServe and the Internet will be truly complete.

Where to Now?

But enough of this stargazing—what about now?

Where should you go next in your exploration of the Internet? The answer is really up to you. Depending on your interests, there are many directions that you can choose. However, there are a few possible steps that you should consider.

Winsock and Direct Internet Connections

One of your first ports of call at the end of this book should be Appendix C, "Internet Software." This appendix contains a brief introduction to the many Winsock-based Internet clients currently available. Although the capabilities offered by CompuServe via WinCIM and its various gateways are indeed very useful, to get the most out of the Internet, your computer really needs to be connected as a physical part of the network.

This is where programs such as NetLauncher and CompuServe's dial-up PPP connection come into their own, and in reality, it is where the future direction of services such as CompuServe lies. Already we are beginning to see the gradual transfer of CompuServe services such as the Electronic Mall to the Internet, and in the future, maybe you will even be able to access CompuServe forums using the World Wide Web or some other online navigation tool.

There is one important aspect of dial-up PPP connections and WinSock-based applications that makes them a valuable addition to your Internet resources. When you connect your computer to the Internet using a program such as NetLauncher, the computer itself becomes a physical part of the Internet network. This has been mentioned before, but what you probably didn't realize is that once you're connected in this way, you can take advantage of all of the capabilities offered by Windows when using Winsock-based applications that communicate with the Internet via the dialer program.

Of these capabilities, the most interesting is Windows' ability to run more than one program at the same time. This means that it is possible to have Spry Mosaic displaying a home page while a FTP client retrieves copies of files in the background, with a Usenet newsreader also running at the same time searching for the latest articles in your favorite newsgroups.

By taking advantage of these multitasking capabilities, you can greatly reduce the amount of time you spend online while at the same time getting more done.

Surfing the Net

It also goes without saying that the World Wide Web offers the best next-step option for most new Internet explorers. But in some ways its sheer size makes using it a daunting proposition.

The first concept you need to come to grips with when using the World Wide Web is the fact that as soon as someone creates something, there is someone else waiting in the wings, ready to step in and replace it with something better. In this sense, the World Wide Web is like a continually and rapidly evolving animal that continues to change, often while you are using it.

To keep ahead of this changing technology, you not only need to learn how to use the Web, but also how to surf it. In the past this meant spending hours logging onto new computers using Telnet and retrieving the latest copies of FAQs and Requests for Comment documents using FTP, but now this has all changed. With the introduction of the World Wide Web, the art of Netsurfing can now be learned by anyone with a little bit of time to spare and the desire to find out about the world around them.

Unlike environments such as CompuServe, which are designed primarily for interaction with a fixed set of resources, the World Wide Web is the ideal environment for exploration. Because there is technically no limitation to the number and diversity of pages that can be placed on the World Wide Web, it is an ever-changing world whose boundaries are limited only by your time and ability to explore them.

The art of Netsurfing, unlike ocean surfing, is relatively easy to pick up. Basically, you pick a point on the World Wide Web and then follow the pages and links like a surfer riding a wave. When you read a page on the World Wide Web, there will usually be at least one link to some other page of information, and if not, you can always skip back a few pages and follow another link to see where it leads. In addition, if you do manage to get yourself totally lost, a simple click on the home icon will take you quickly back to familiar ground.

But where do you start? This actually doesn't really matter, because you can start just about anywhere and still eventually wind up at a page that points you to many other sources of information. However, to recap some of the more popular World Wide Web directory listings mentioned in Chapter 12, "World Wide Web Productivity," here is a short list to get you started:

The Yahoo directory: `http://www.yahoo.com/`

CompuServe's home page: `http://www.compuserve.com/`

EINet Galaxy home page: `http://galaxy.einet.net/`

The Global Network Navigator: `http://gnn.com/gnn/gnn.html`

Mirsky's Worst of the Web: `http://turnpike.net/metro/mirsky/Worst.html`

Spry's HotLand Lists and Hotlinks: `http://www.spry.com/hotland/index.html`

Glenn Davis' Cool Site of the Day: `http://www.infi.net/cool.html`

Infinet's Explore the Net Page: `http://www.infi.net/explore/starting.html`

The Virtual Tourist: `http://wings.buffalo.edu/world/`

Matthew Gray's comprehensive list of Web sites: `http://www.netgen.com/cgi/comprehensive`

The OFFWORLD Metaplex: `http://tribble.com/index.html`

Online Help and FAQs

Other good sources of useful information are the online help screens provided by both WinCIM and Spry Mosaic. If you find yourself in a situation that does not make sense or are facing a dialog box whose contents you are not familiar with, clicking on the Help button will always bring up a screenload of information to help you better understand where you are.

You shouldn't be afraid to ask for help when using any Internet service, although you should always make sure that you have read any relevant Frequently Asked Questions (FAQ) documents to make sure that you are not asking a question that has been answered many times before. In fact, I cannot overemphasize the importance of reading every FAQ you come across. These documents have been created by people who want to help new users to better understand the Internet, but at the same time they may be very busy people who probably won't appreciate seeing messages asking questions they have collated into FAQs. Although there are many people who will be only too happy to assist a new user, the Internet also relies heavily on the concept of self-help. Basically, if you are willing to put in a little bit of effort to help yourself, others will be glad to guide you further.

What's New Announcements

With the number of changes CompuServe is currently implementing, the CompuServe What's New Page (GO NEW) should also be a top priority on your list of regular places to go.

To complement this list, CompuServe also features a regularly updated list of late-breaking Internet-related announcements on their World Wide Web server at `http://www.compuserve.com/`.

Similar services are also available at a number of World Wide Web sites, but instead of listing new happenings on CompuServe, these sites contain lists of new happenings on the World Wide Web.

One of the most popular of these services is operated by the NCSA in association with the Global Network Navigator. To access this site, use the following HTTP address: `http://www.ncsa.uiuc.edu/SDG/Software/Mosaic/Docs/whats-new.html`.

For a slightly different list, take a look at the What's New page operated by Netscape at `http://home.netscape.com/escapes/whats_new.html`.

Summary

In the immortal words of one of the world's great orators, "B'd, b'd, b'dee, that's all, folks!"

Well, not quite. In the pages that follow, you will find four appendices and a glossary of popularly used Internet terms. Appendix A explores some of the options available to those who are interested in exploring the use of other Internet service providers. Appendix B looks at how people with an alternative Internet service provider can take advantage of Telnet to log onto CompuServe using the Internet instead of the CompuServe dial-up network. Appendix C contains a list outlining the various Winsock-based applications that can be used in conjunction with NetLauncher and CompuServe's dial-up PPP connections. Appendix D examines some of the Windows-based encoding and encryption programs and discusses their use.

In closing, I hope this book has been of assistance to you as you begin your exploration of the Internet. For many people, the Internet is now a place where they can both work and play. It offers opportunities that were unimagined only a few short years ago, and allows you to communicate with people and exchange ideas, dreams, thoughts, and expectations. In addition, it offers people many opportunities for involvement, be it as a programmer, a World Wide Web publisher, or simply a lurker who enjoys what others have created. It is rapidly becoming a service that can be all things to all people.

However, at the same time it is a world that won't come to you. There is an entire world of information, entertainment, and interaction waiting for you on the Internet. All you need to do is reach out and grab it.

Good luck, and see you on the Net.

Wes Tatters (`wtatters@world.net`)

APPENDIX A

OTHER SERVICE PROVIDERS

What to Look for in a Service Provider

Where to Find Service Providers

Although CompuServe now offers access to the Internet in many parts of the world, its pricing structure may not be suited to the needs of every user. For people in countries like Australia, where network access fees are charged in addition to CompuServe's standard rates, there may be a local Internet service provider (ISP) who can offer more attractive pricing.

Note

> For information about your local CompuServe pricing, type **GO RATES**.

This appendix shows you what you should look for in an ISP and discusses ways to locate Internet connections in your part of the world.

What to Look for in a Service Provider

There are five important aspects that you need to consider when choosing an Internet service provider:

- ◆ Pricing
- ◆ Connection options
- ◆ Performance
- ◆ Customer support
- ◆ Value-added services
- ◆ Connectivity software

Pricing

If you thought trying to make sense of CompuServe's standard pricing plan was difficult, you'd better sit down. There are a multitude of options available in the Internet market.

Almost every ISP has come up with a different sort of pricing structure designed to give its members the best possible deal. The problem is, what may be the best possible deal for one sort of user is usually not the best deal for everyone else. As a result, when you are shopping around for an ISP, you need to pay careful attention to the fees it charges and exactly how and when they are calculated.

Flat Rate Services

The flat rate service, as its name implies, charges you a fixed rate for every hour you are online. Depending on the ISP and your location, the rates for these services can vary from as little as $0.50 an hour to as much as $10 or $15 an hour. But on average, you can probably expect to pay around $2.50 to $4 an hour for flat rate services.

If you plan to use the Internet only on an occasional basis, flat rate services allow the flexibility of pay for use. If you find yourself using the Internet on a more regular basis, you should probably consider taking advantage of one of the packaged services.

Flat Rate with After Hours

Another type of flat rate service that is becoming more popular is the after hours service. These services offer reduced connection rates for people who connect to the service outside of business hours. By taking advantage of these discount rates, you can often save up to 50% on your Internet usage bill. However, you do need to be careful when using such services because many of them charge much higher rates during business hours than a standard flat rate service.

If you don't mind the inconvenience of not being able to connect whenever you want and you're an infrequent Internet user, after hours rates offer good value for the money.

Packaged Services

Many ISPs now offer special prepaid connection packages. By taking advantage of these packages, you can often gain considerable savings over flat rate services.

There are two main types of packages on offer at the moment. The first allows you to purchase a fixed number of hours a month, which you can use whenever you choose. The second variety allows you to purchase a fixed number of hours each day for a month. Of these two packages, the first offers the best freedom and value for the money. With the second option, if you don't take advantage of the service every day, there is no way to recover the lost hours.

On the face of it, prepaid packages offer the best value for the money. But there is a nasty "gotcha" with most packaged services if you exceed your daily or monthly limit. Any additional hours are often charged at the highest rate the service charges, which can amount to $10 or $15 an hour.

Metered Usage

There is one other form of online charge used by some ISPs that needs to be used with some care, although it is being phased out by most sites.

This fee is calculated by metering the amount of data you send and receive while connected to the Internet. This includes file transfers, e-mail, WWW usage, and Telnet connections. Under this structure you are charged a fee for every 1,024 characters of data transmitted, at what appear to be very low rates of between half a cent and one cent.

Before the introduction of high-speed modems and services like the World Wide Web, using this sort of pricing structure was a very good way of keeping prices down. However, when you start to use 28,800bps modems to browse WWW pages that can cost up to 50 cents to load, things start to become very expensive.

In today's climate, metered usage is simply not practical for most users and should be avoided unless you fully understand how the charges will effect you. That said, for certain types of usage—Telnet in particular—metered charges can offer considerable savings over other pricing methods.

Connection Options

Price is not the only factor you need to consider when looking at Internet service providers. There are a number of different connection options available that can greatly effect the type of service you obtain, and in some case even the performance.

Connection Speeds

When you connect to the Internet, the speed of the connection is determined by the capabilities of your modem and that of the ISP. As a result, to get the best value out of your Internet connection, you should make sure that the ISP allows you to connect at 14,400bps or 28,800bps. On your end, you will also need to obtain as fast a modem as your budget allows.

If you plan to use the WWW with your Internet connection (and who doesn't?) you should make sure that the ISP selected offers 28,800bps connections, even if your current modem does not support it. You should also check to make sure that there are no additional fees and charges for higher connection speeds. When you connect at higher speeds, you get more done in your allotted time. As a result, some ISPs choose to add on additional charges to compensate them for the reduced time you spend online.

One of the ways they do this is by setting limits to the amount of data you can transfer to or from your computer. This includes screen displays and e-mail. When you connect at higher speeds, you are a lot more likely to exceed these limits and as a result attract additional charges.

Shell or Terminal Sessions

Some ISPs and even some bulletin boards offer shell- or terminal-based connections to the Internet.

To use these services, you use a communications program to dial into the service and from there connect to the Internet. In recent years, this type of service has began to lessen in popularity in favor of direct Internet connections, due to the fact that with a shell account it is difficult, if not impossible, to take advantage of tools such as graphical World Wide Web navigators and other Winsock client-based services.

On the plus side, a number of these sites offer access at rates far below those available from commercial service providers. To find out more about these sites, check out "Public Internet Service Providers Listing" in the following section.

SLIP and PPP Connections

By far the most popular method of connecting to the Internet is through the use of a TCP/IP connection. When you use TCP/IP, your computer actually becomes a physical part of the Internet instead of a fancy terminal emulator.

There are currently two ways of doing this using a dial-up connection: SLIP and PPP. SLIP is the older of the two methods, and should be avoided where possible due to the lack of error checking and compression. PPP, on the other hand, is rapidly becoming the standard protocol for dial-up TCP/IP connections. As a result, ISPs that offer PPP connections should as a rule be considered over those that offer only SLIP.

Occasionally you will also hear mention of a third dial-up protocol called CSLIP. This is an improved version of SLIP that offers more reliable connections and improved performance. Depending on who you talk to, this protocol is still not as good as PPP, but it should definitely be considered over services that only offer SLIP.

Performance

Even if you have the fastest modem ever made and your ISP has a matching one, it will be of little use if the ISP cannot feed it information fast enough.

Of all the criteria you should consider when selecting an ISP, the performance issue is by far the hardest to resolve. Obviously, every ISP is going to tell you that their service is the fastest and most reliable around. Your best bet in these situations is to talk with other people who are already using the service and see what they think of it. For starters, some astute queries in the Internet New Users Forum may give you some guidance, or maybe you can ask the ISP for some reference clients who you can talk to.

Most importantly, don't be baffled by the barrage of facts and figures that some ISPs will give you to explain just how great their service is. In all cases it comes down to usage. If you can, try to wrangle a look at a computer that is connected to the service before you make your final decision.

Customer Support

For CompuServe users who have come to expect a high level of customer support and simple-to-use navigation tools, getting connected to the Internet can be quite a culture shock.

It is important to check out the customer support offered by ISPs before you take the plunge. Because many of the cheaper services are often operated by only one or two people, getting help can sometimes be a difficult task. If you are fairly technically competent, you can probably afford to opt for reduced online charges over customer support. On the other hand, if you are not a hacker, you can expect to make at least one call to customer service while setting up your Internet connection. Good customer support should be considered a must.

Value-Added Services

When comparing some of the major ISPs, eventually the choice comes down to a comparison of the value-added products and services they offer.

Newsgroup Servers

In the past, people have often been caught out when subscribing to very cheap ISPs that seem to offer unbelievable prices. To achieve these prices, in many cases some things need to be left out.

For example, operating a Usenet connection requires a considerable investment of time and money, not to mention a large hard drive. To cut costs, some smaller ISPs simply don't operate a Usenet connection. As a result, even though they provide you with an Internet connection, you will not be able to use your account to read newsgroups.

Therefore, it is important to check what services are provided by the ISP, and in some cases what additional fees and charges are associated with using them.

Private Directories and FTP Access

Some ISPs allow you to store files on their host machine in your own private directory. Depending on the ISP, you may also be able to use this area as your own private FTP site and allow other people to access it via anonymous FTP.

If an ISP permits this type of activity, you should also check on any usage limitations and extra charges that might be incurred if you use more space than your designated allowance.

Home Page Links and the World Wide Web

With the growth in popularity of the World Wide Web, some ISPs are now beginning to allow their customers to create their own home pages and link them to the ISP's WWW server and customer pages.

Like sites that offer FTP access, most of these sites will set parameters that determine how much space you can use for your pages and images, while others also set limits to the level of access you have to things such as forms and other special WWW services. Given this, these sites offer their customers very affordable access to WWW publishing.

Connectivity Software

Some of the more organized ISPs are now offering special software packages like NetLauncher to help get you over the initial connection teething problems encountered by many people.

Depending on your skill level, services that offer one of these packages can take a lot of the heartache out of getting an Internet connection up and running. For this reason, when you're talking to ISPs it is a good idea to see if they offer one of these packages, and more importantly to try to find out if they are willing to bundle it with your connection fees.

Where to Find Service Providers

There are a number of sources that you can turn to for information about Internet service providers, but the best source of information is obviously the Internet itself.

In the past, this has then resulted in a crazy "chicken and the egg" scenario—to find out about connecting to the Internet, you needed to be connected to it already. Nowadays, with services like CompuServe providing you with the initial means of connecting to the Internet, this problem has pretty much disappeared.

The New Users Forum

CompuServe itself has a number of files in its Internet New Users Forum that contain information about Internet service providers. In the Accessing the Net library section shown in Figure A.1, there are a collection of files listing the services offered by Internet service providers in many parts of the world.

FIGURE A.1.

The Accessing the Net Forum section contains files that list the locations of Internet service providers.

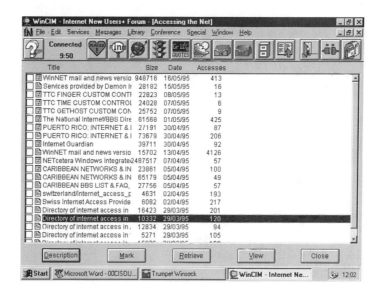

If this information still leaves you with questions, there are also many people in the Accessing the Net message area who will usually be only too happy to offer recommendations. Posting a message in this area with a subject line like "Help - Net connections in Peru ?" will usually be enough to invoke a flood of suggestions.

The Internet Society

As a service to the Internet, a gentleman named Barry Raveendran Greene, in association with the Internet Society, operates a collection of pages that contain a list of network service providers around the world. (See Figure A.2.) These pages are stored on the Internet Society WWW server at the following HTTP address: http://www.isoc.org/~bgreene/nsp-index.html.

To complement this listing, he has also compiled a do-it-yourself guide to finding an Internet service provider. If you are looking for an Internet service provider, you should definitely take a look at this page before you proceed any further.

FIGURE A.2.

*Network Service Providers
Around the World.*

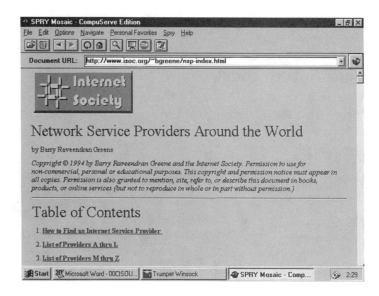

The Commercial Internet Exchange

If wading through lists of ISPs seems like a lot of hard work, maybe the novel approach offered by the Commercial Internet eXchange (CIX) will be more suited to your needs.

Instead of listing its member ISPs page by page, CIX has created a Map of the World page (Figure A.3) that allows you to simply click on the part of the world where you live. When you click on the map, CIX shows you a list of all the Internet service providers that offer Internet connections in that part of the world.

FIGURE A.3.

*CIX membership by
geographic location.*

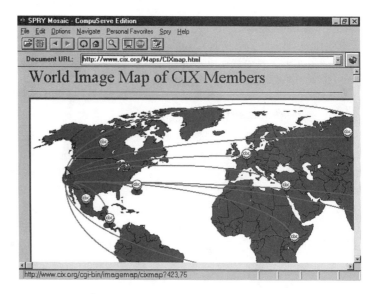

> Because all CIX members must agree to abide by the exchange's rules, using one of these service providers tends to ensure that your service will not disappear the day after you become a subscriber.
>
> This in itself is sufficient incentive for many people to consider only CIX-recognized commercial ISPs.

Public Internet Service Providers Listing

To cater to the growing number of public ISPs, Bux Technical Services maintains a listing of all known public sites.

You can obtain a copy of this listing by sending an e-mail message to mail-server@bts.com. In the body of the message, enter either **get PUB nixpub.long** or **get PUB nixpub.short**.

They also operate a mailing list for those people who want to keep up-to-date. To subscribe to this list, send an e-mail message to mail-server@bts.com with the following entry in the body of the message:

subscribe NIXPUB-LIST 'First Name' 'Second Name'.

Universities and Research Institutions

The last type of Internet service provider is one that not everyone has access to, but that at the same time offers a number of potential connection opportunities. If you haven't guessed already, these are educational service providers.

Every major university and research institution the world over has access to the Internet, and in many cases offers its students and employees access either through dial-up connections or in-house terminals. If you are a student, you should contact your campus computer center to find out about what types of Internet access they offer.

Non-profit organizations and grade schools should also consider these sites as a possible alternative, because many institutions offer special rates and sometimes even free connections for worthy causes.

CONNECTING TO COMPUSERVE FROM THE INTERNET

Shell Accounts and Terminal-Based Connections

Winsock TCP/IP Connections

For people who have access to the Internet through another service provider, CompuServe has set up a Telnet connection. This allows you to log on via the Internet using CompuServe's global network instead of the more common dial-up connection.

To open a Telnet connection with CompuServe, point your Telnet client to `compuserve.com`.

Even though for most people a dial-up connection is the simplest and most efficient method of connecting to CompuServe, for some users there are advantages to using a Telnet-based connection. There are a number or reasons why people choose to do this, but for many of them the main controlling factor is price.

If, like myself, you don't live in the U.S. or have access to a local CompuServe phone number, the additional costs associated with long distance telephone charges or network connection surcharges can easily make the cost of connecting to CompuServe prohibitive. To avoid this, I have reduced the hourly connection surcharges for CompuServe access in Australia from $15.00 to $1.40 by taking advantage of the $1.40-an-hour connection rates offered by my local Internet service provider.

For other users who have access to a permanent high-speed Internet connection, the attraction of a Telnet connection to CompuServe stems from the ability to take advantage of their existing Internet links to connect to CompuServe without the need for dedicated modems. For large corporate and educational institutions, this can lead to big savings by reducing the need for local phone calls and modem hardware.

Shell Accounts and Terminal-Based Connections

There are two ways that people can take advantage of a Telnet connection to CompuServe, and each depends on the type of service available from their Internet service provider.

If you have access to a shell- or terminal-based Internet account, you can configure programs such as WinCIM to dial the number for this service instead of dialing CompuServe directly. Then, using WinCIM's built-in scripting language, you can create a dialing script that will:

◆ Log you onto the Internet account

◆ Open a Telnet connection to compuserve.com

◆ Send "CISAGREE" to CompuServe

◆ Send "14400" to CompuServe

◆ Tell WinCIM to log you onto CompuServe

If you are interested in taking advantage of this type of connection, you should take a look at the Networks & Scripts library in the WinCIM Support Forum (GO WCIMSUPPORT). This library contains a file that documents the WinCIM scripting language and explains its use. There are also a number of example scripts that you can use for templates.

If you are still not sure about what you need to do, there is also a corresponding message area where you can discuss scripting issues. For specific Internet-related information, there is also a section on the Internet New Users Forum (GO INETFORUM) called Access: CompuServe.

> The support forums of the major CompuServe navigators each have an area devoted to logon or dialing scripts that often includes copies of scripts written by other users. If you need to create a script, it is not a bad idea to check out these files before you start, because it is possible that someone may have already done the job for you.

Note

Winsock TCP/IP Connections

With the increased popularity of TCP/IP connections using SLIP or PPP and the universal acceptance of the Winsock standard for Microsoft Windows, many CompuServe members—who had been using shell-based Internet accounts to connect with CompuServe—were presented with a problem when they converted these accounts to TCP/IP connections.

Due to the way that TCP/IP works, it was no longer possible to use WinCIM or any other Internet navigator to connect to CompuServe, because none of these programs were compatible with the Winsock environment. You could still connect using a Winsock-based Telnet client like Trumpet or EWAN, but this only allowed people to use the CompuServe ASCII interface (see Figure B.1) and not the more user-friendly graphical interface.

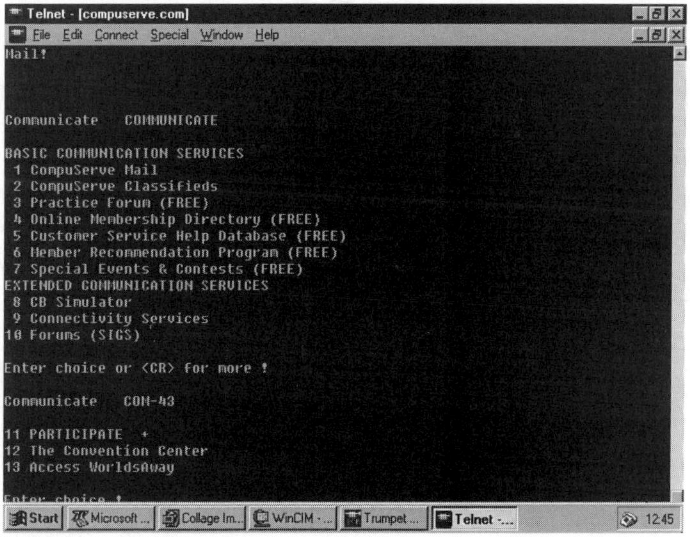

FIGURE B.1.
Trumpet Telnet connected to compuserve.com.

COMT

To get around this problem, a program called COMT was developed that allowed any of the popular CompuServe navigators, including WinCIM, to connect to CompuServe using Winsock. COMT achieved this by fooling these navigators into thinking that they were actually connected directly to a modem instead of to Winsock and the Internet.

To do this, COMT sets up a special software driver inside Windows that creates a fake COM port on your computer. Normally your computer will have two COM ports, called COM1 and COM2, which are connected to serial ports on the back of your computer. Unless you have an internal modem, you connect your modem to one of these ports and possibly a mouse to the other one.

When you install COMT on your system it creates a fake COM port, which will be called something like COM3 or COM4, depending on exactly how you configure COMT. Once this COM port is installed, you then tell your navigator to use this port instead of COM1 or COM2. Internally, your navigator will now think that it is talking to a modem connected to the new COM port, and Winsock will think it is talking to a normal Telnet client.

As a result, you can now use any Windows navigator to connect to CompuServe through the CompuServe Telnet port without needing to alter the way the program operates. Having said this, apart from installing COMT, there are a few changes that will need to be made to your navigator's settings before you can take full advantage of the capabilities offered by COMT.

In Figure B.2, OzWIN has been configured for use with COMT. You should note that in addition to changing the connector to COM3, the phone number entry has also been changed from a number to CompuServe's domain name, compuserve.com. Doing this tells COMT which site it needs to open a Telnet connection with.

FIGURE B.2.

OzWIN ready for use with COMT and a TCP/IP connection.

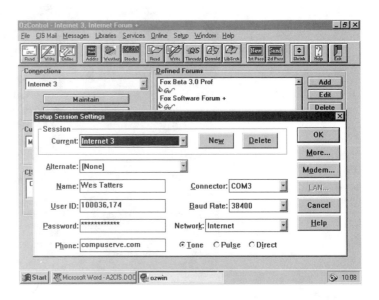

You will also need to change the dialing script to one that is suitable for use with COMT and the Internet. If you are using WinCIM or OzWIN, there is a script called "Internet" stored in the C:\CSERVE\SCRIPTS directory that is suitable. For other navigators, you will need to check with your supplier or create a dialing script yourself to negotiate the initial connection with CompuServe.

Because COMT is in effect pretending to be a modem when it talks to you navigator, you will also need to alter the modem settings for your navigator. (See Figure B.3.) To tell COMT how it should operate when connecting to CompuServe, set the modem initialization string to AT&F &C1 &D2 S1005=1 S1002=1 S1006=4^M.

FIGURE B.3.

For COMT to function properly, you need to add some special modem settings.

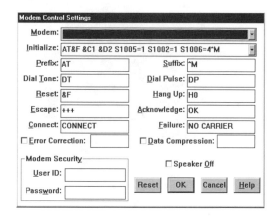

Although many people fail to read the instructions that come with software before installing it, this is one software package that demands that you read the manual first. To function, COMT makes some changes to your computer that in some circumstances can effect the way your machine operates.

You should also pay particular attention to the section dealing with setting up WinCIM for COMT, because it contains information that in most cases means the difference between COMT working and crashing.

To obtain a copy of COMT, you can either download it from the IBM Communications Forum (GO IBMCOM) on CompuServe under the name COMT.ZIP, or you can FTP a copy from ftp.std.com:/customers/software/rfdmail/.

WinCIM 1.4

Following the response to the release of COMT, CompuServe added an enhancement to version 1.4 of WinCIM that allows you to bypass the need for COMT and configured WinCIM so it communicates directly with Winsock. To set up WinCIM to take advantage of this new feature, open the **S**pecial menu and select the **S**ession Settings option, as shown in Figure B.4.

FIGURE B.4.

The Session Settings option lets you configure WinCIM's connection options.

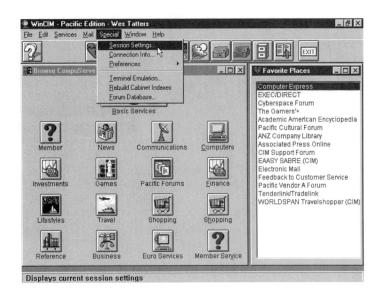

Doing this opens the Setup Session Settings dialog shown in Figure B.5. In this dialog box you can now select Winsock as a connection type using the Connector: field. This tells WinCIM that you have a TCP/IP Internet connection on your computer and instructs it to use this connection when logging onto CompuServe. If you choose to use this option, there is no need for COMT to be installed on your computer unless you plan to use other programs that don't have internal Winsock support.

FIGURE B.5.

Change the Connection: setting to Winsock to bypass the need for COMT.

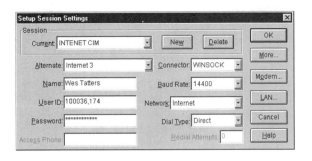

In addition to selecting the Winsock option, you will also need to change the network type to Internet and the dial type to direct. If you find that you are encountering problems, you many also need to select 14400 as the baud rate, although CompuServe does plan to permit faster connection rates over the Internet.

The **LAN** button on the right-hand side should also have become active when you selected Winsock as your connector. Click on this button to open the Winsock Settings dialog box shown on Figure B.6. In this dialog box you need to set compuserve.com as the host name, and depending on the performance offered by your Internet service provider, you may also need to set the connect timeout to 45 seconds or more. This is due to the fact that when you use the Internet, the time taken to open the initial connection with CompuServe can sometimes take longer than the normal WinCIM default.

FIGURE B.6.

Change the Connection setting to Winsock to bypass the need for COMT.

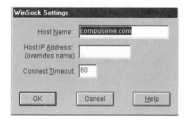

As the popularity of Telnet connections to CompuServe increase, it is likely that many of the other CompuServe navigators will eventually add the option of connecting to CompuServe via Winsock.

At the time of writing, CSNAV and WIGWAM have already added this capability, and OzWIN has indicated that its next release will support Winsock directly. For more information on the capabilities offered by these navigators, you should check with the various program developers.

APPENDIX C

INTERNET SOFTWARE

Telnet Clients

FTP Clients

E-Mail Clients

Usenet News Readers

WS_ARCHIE

WWW Tools

Gopher Clients

IRC Clients

WAIS Clients

When CompuServe released NetLauncher in April 1995, not only did it give every member access to the World Wide Web, but it also gave them access to Winsock and the many Winsock-based Internet client applications that continue to flood the Internet.

This appendix takes a look at some of the more popular Winsock-compatible programs to give you some idea of what's currently available. It's designed to give you a brief look at what's being offered, without any explanations or discussions of the way you use these programs. Such explanations are better left to the many books written specifically for that purpose.

Before looking at the various programs available, let's look at some of the places where you can obtain copies of them for yourself.

The best place to start, as a CompuServe member, is the Internet Resource forum (GO INETRESOURCE). In the PC Software area of this forum, you will find up-to-date copies of many of the programs mentioned in this appendix. For those that can be found on CompuServe, I have indicated the current file name, but you should always check the library for newer versions. To complement this library, you will also find a considerable number of discussions in both this forum and the Internet News Users forum (GO INETFORUM) dealing with the use of these programs.

Obviously, all of the programs are also available on the Internet from many anonymous FTP servers and software archives. To get started, you should take a look at the files available from the CICA archive, which is located at `ftp.cica.indiana.edu` in the `/pub/pc/winsock` directory.

If you prefer using the World Wide Web, E-Znet's Winsock Archive home page contains links to the most popular Winsock-based applications available on the Internet. The http address for this home page is `http://homepage.eznet.net/~rwilloug/ewa.html`.

This site is the home of the official FTP server for Forrest Stroud's Consummate Winsock Apps List. This list contains information about the latest release versions of each product, their status as freeware, shareware, or otherwise, and links to the host sites for each. To view the list directly, take a look at `http://homepage.eznet.net/~rwilloug/stroud/cwsapps.html`.

Telnet Clients

There are a number of different Telnet clients available on the Internet, each offering different capabilities. Of the programs available, the two most popular are the Trumpet Telnet program and EWAN, which is by far the most comprehensive, offering a totally configurable interface. In addition, for Windows 95 users there is a Telnet client supplied as a part of the TCP/IP package.

There is also another type of Telnet program designed specifically for connections to IBM computer systems requiring 3270 terminal emulation, instead of the more common VT100 emulation offered by most Telnet packages. This type of program is referred to as a TN3270 emulator.

Trumpet Telnet

CIS file name: `TTEL0_07.ZIP`

Status: Freeware

This Telnet program was developed by Peter Tattam—the man behind the Trumpet Winsock—in part to demonstrate the capabilities of his Winsock program. Although it's not the most configurable Telnet Client available, it performs reasonably well and does have the dubious honor of being the smallest Telnet program available.

When you download a copy, don't expect any fancy installation scripts or online help files. It's pretty much a what-you-see-is-what-you-get affair, but it will get you online if your Telnet needs are limited.

EWAN Telnet

CIS Filename: `EWAN10.ZIP`

Status: Freeware

EWAN is far and away the most powerful freeware Telnet application currently available. It offers VT100, VT52, and ANSI terminal emulation, which can be configured independently for each Telnet site stored in its configuration list. You can also define keyboard maps and input filters for each site and tailor the emulation in every way imaginable.

Support for the program is very good, with a comprehensive online help system built in and regular updates from the author. The current version of EWAN—version 1.052—or the most recent version is always available from the EWAN home page at `http://www.lysator.liu.se/~zander/ewan.html`.

IBM 3270 Terminal Emulation

CIS Filename: `QWS3270.ZIP`

Status: Freeware

Not all Telnet connections support the use of the standard VT100 terminal emulation. Principal amongst these sites are some of the older IBM-based services. To connect to any of these sites, you need to use an IBM3270 terminal emulator such as the Winsock 3270 emulation program. Like the Trumpet Telnet, this program seems to be unsupported these days, although the Readme file included with the program indicates that the developer still has further plans for it.

It is a what-you-see-is-what-you-get affair, with neither online help or anything approaching what could be called a user's manual. But then again, apart from selecting Connect and entering a domain name, what else would you expect a Telnet program to do?

FTP Clients

When it comes to FTP, there is only one option you need to consider as a Windows user. Windows 95 does bundle a terminal-based FTP client as a part of its TCP/IP package, but the only time you would even consider using it would be to download a copy of a real FTP client like WS_FTP.

WS_FTP

CIS Filename: `WS_FTP.ZIP`—16-bit

CIS Filename: `WS_FTP32.ZIP`—32-bit

Status: Freeware

WS_FTP is a Windows-based FTP client that allows you to log onto FTP sites using a graphical interface. Once connected, you can send and retrieve files by selecting them from the lists provided, in much the same way as you did when using the CompuServe FTP client.

There are two versions of WS_FTP currently available, one of which is designed for the older 16-bit Windows environment, the other for 32-bit platforms such as Windows 95 and Windows NT. If you own a copy of Windows 95 or Windows NT, you should consider using the 32-bit version, although the 16-bit version will work. This is because the newer 32-bit version has been designed so that it takes advantage of the improved multitasking features available in both Windows 95 and Windows NT.

E-Mail Clients

At this stage, CompuServe only partially supports the use of e-mail clients. You can use them to send e-mail messages, but currently you cannot retrieve messages from your CIS mailbox using them. In the future, this may change as CompuServe continues to enhance its Internet services.

To tell the e-mail client how to send e-mail via CompuServe, you will need to define the address of its SMTP mail server. This address is `mail.compuserve.com`.

Eudora

CIS Filename: `EUDORA.EXE`

Status: Freeware/Commercial

There are two versions of Eudora, a freeware and a more capable commercial version. Most users find that the freeware version is well suited to their needs, however, and for them there is no need to purchase the commercial version.

Eudora supports built-in MIME and BinHex encoding for file attachments and a nickname list for all your commonly used e-mail addresses. The only reason that many people would ever consider purchasing the commercial version would be to gain access to the intelligent mailbox features. They allow you to define parameters that tell Eudora how to sort your incoming mail. Because Eudora supports multiple mailboxes, it is possible to have mail from certain people, or mail containing certain words, automatically sorted into its own mailbox.

There is one downside to the freeware version of Eudora. It contains no help file and only limited usage instructions. That said, the layout and simple configuration options mean that Eudora is very easy to use.

Pegasus Mail for Windows

CIS Filename: `WINPM.ZIP`

Status: Freeware

Like Eudora, Pegasus offers users a wide variety of features that make it very much a personal preference issue when you're determining which one you prefer.

All the features available in Eudora—including many of the commercial-only features—can also be found in Pegasus, although I personally find the Pegasus layout is slightly less intuitive. There are some major advantages that give Pegasus the edge in some situations, however.

The first of these is the inclusion of a comprehensive built-in help system. There is also extensive support for the creation of mail distribution lists and a more powerful address book. In addition, the Incoming Mail filtering features that were available only in the commercial version of Eudora are all available in the freeware version of Pegasus.

Usenet News Readers

Instead of using the Usenet client provided by WinCIM, it is now possible to access the CompuServe Usenet server directly using any of the popular Winsock-based news readers.

CompuServe has made this possible by creating a Usenet NNTP port on its Internet server. To access this server, simply enter `news.compuserve.com` when asked to nominate a NNTP server. You will also need to nominate a SMTP mail server so that the newsgroup reader can send your messages. The address for this server is `mail.compuserve.com`.

Trumpet News Reader

CIS Filename: `WTWSK1.ZIP`

Status: Shareware

The Trumpet News Reader is yet another program from the stables of Peter Tattam. However, unlike the Trumpet Telnet application, this program comes compete with online help and detailed installation and configuration instructions. There does not appear to be much support in the way of ongoing development with this program, despite the fact that it is a shareware product. As a result, it is starting to show its age in the face of some stiff competition.

As a news reader, it allows you to subscribe to newsgroups and read the messages they contain. You can also reply to these messages either via e-mail or as a response to the original message. There is also built-in support for the decoding of UUENCODEd messages and the ability to attach files to messages you send. Trumpet can also double as a simple e-mail client through its built-in e-mail utilities.

WINVN

CIS Filename: `WINVN16.ZIP`—16-bit for Windows 3.*xx*

CIS Filename: `WINVN32.ZIP`—32-bit for Windows 95

Status: Freeware

WINVN is a highly Windows-integrated newsgroup reader that supports such features as multiple message areas, built-in encoding/decoding of MIME and UU/XX formats, extensive thread management, and full multitasking including background operations while download-ing messages. In addition, the developers of WINVN have put a lot of effort into its visual appearance, taking full advantage of all the capabilities offered by the Windows environment.

For Windows 95 users, the 32-bit version is not simply a recompile in 32-bit mode, but an extensive rebuild that adds support for the new Windows Explorer-style requesters and MAPI32 mail capabilities. About the only thing that it can't do is retrieve mail from your mailbox like an e-mail client.

This program is also well-supported by its developers, all of whom donate many hours of their free time to its maintenance and support. As a result, regular updates for both the 32-bit and 16-bit versions have been appearing regularly over the last 12 months. Although the version available on CompuServe will usually be fairly recent, to obtain a copy of the very latest version you need to use the official FTP site at `ftp://ftp.ksc.nasa.gov/pub/winvn/`.

News Xpress

CIS Filename: `NX10B2.ZIP`

Status: Beta Freeware

News Xpress is a relatively new entrant into the newsgroup reader fraternity. Its main claim to fame seems to be the fact that it is the first Windows MDI compliant program of this type. This allows it to multitask very well under Windows and handle more than one open newsgroup at a time.

It also supports thread-based access to newsgroup messages and background processing capa-bilities for message retrieval and thread sorting. For a program that is still in its early beta-testing stages, it is quite feature-packed and surprisingly stable.

Free Agent

CIS Filename: `AGENT055.ZIP`

Status: Beta Freeware

All of the newsgroup readers you have looked at so far have one thing in common. To use them effectively, you need to be online the entire time you are reading newsgroups and sending messages. Due to the fact that you are usually being charged for the time you are connected, it would appear that some sort of offline newsgroup reader would be a useful tool.

Until recently, no such tool was available for use with Usenet, which effectively forced people to waste a considerable amount of connection time. To remedy this inadequacy, a new program is currently being developed that can act both as an online and an offline newsgroup reader. To give people a sample of what's in store, the developers have released a beta version to the general public.

With Free Agent, you can nominate a group of newsgroups that you are interested in and then have Free Agent log onto your Usenet server and retrieve either a list of headings or all of the messages currently stored in each newsgroup. If you have retrieved a list of headings, you can scan through the headings while offline and select the ones you are interested in. Then when you are ready, reconnect to the server and have Free Agent retrieve a copy of all the messages associated with the headers you selected.

For those of you who are familiar with the use of offline readers on CompuServe, you will be right at home with Free Agent. However, you should be warned that some newsgroups can generate literally thousands of messages each day. As a result, you need to be somewhat selective about the number of newsgroups you choose to watch.

WS_ARCHIE

CIS Filename: `WSARCH.ZIP`

Status: Beta Freeware

WS_ARCHIE is currently the only Archie client available for Windows. It allows you to log onto any of the Archie servers around the world and request information about the location of files stored on FTP sites.

When you generate a request using WS_ARCHIE, it will attempt to retrieve a list of all the sites that contain files meeting your requirements. You can then select from the files listed and have WS_ARCHIE automatically open WS_FTP to retrieve a copy of the file for you.

WWW Tools

Apart from Spry Mosaic, there are a number of different World Wide Web navigators currently available, all of which offer different features and capabilities. To mention them all here, however, would be a waste of time, because it seems that as fast as one group brings out a new capability in their browser, someone else releases something different on theirs.

As a result, your best bet is to take a look at the latest list of WWW browsers in the Consummate Winsock Apps List. With this information in hand, download one or two and have a play with them. Choosing a WWW browser is a bit like buying a car—we all want one with at least four wheels, but apart from that, everyone has their eye on something different.

That said, the next sections mention two particular WWW browsers that, between them, offer the most features and are by far the most popular.

NCSA Mosaic

CIS Filename: `WMOSA9.ZIP`

Status: Beta Freeware

No discussion of World Wide Web navigators could ever be complete without mention of NCSA Mosaic, the WWW browser that all of the others are based upon.

In its latest incarnation, NCSA Mosaic is available only as a 32-bit application, but that does not mean that Windows 3.*xx* users cannot use it. Microsoft has released a special set of libraries called WIN32s that allow many 32-bit programs to operate on the older Windows operating system. To obtain a copy of this set of libraries, download a copy of `W320LE.ZIP`, located in the Internet Resource Forum, and install it according to the instructions included in the archive.

The latest version of Mosaic, version 2.0A9, includes a number of new features, including support for tables and embedded OLE integration. To find out what's happening on the leading edge of WWW technology, this browser is a good place to start.

Netscape

CIS Filename: N/A

Status: Freeware/Commercial

If NCSA Mosaic is the granddaddy of all Web browsers, Netscape is its upwardly mobile younger son. This is due, in no small part, to the fact that many of the developers who were originally responsible for the creation of Mosaic are now employed by Netscape. As far as features go, Netscape has them all—including many not provided by any other WWW browser. Like Mosaic, there is built-in support for tables and inline JPEG images, as well as background images and textures, dynamically updating pages, and even rudimentary animation capabilities.

For many people there is no other Web browser, and because its 16-bit version does not require the installation of the Microsoft WIN32s library, it is also the easiest program to set up. There is also a 32-bit version for Windows 95 and NT users.

To obtain a copy of Netscape, you should use the download page provided on the Netscape WWW server, which is located at `http://www.netscape.com/`.

Gopher Clients

With the rapid development of WWW browsers, the need for dedicated Gopher clients is currently on the downturn, because all of the features provided by even the most capable Gopher client are now included as a part of every WWW browser.

For those of you who would still like to take a look at a Gopher client, there is one available in the Internet Resource Forum called Gopher for Windows. Alternatively, the Consummate Winsock Apps List also contains links to BCGopher, HGopher, and WSGopher, each of which offers slightly different capabilities. In Chapter 13, "Gopher," there is a discussion of each of the major gopher clients.

IRC Clients

If you want to participate in IRC conversations using the Internet, you will need to obtain a copy of one of the IRC clients, because CompuServe does not currently support access to IRC through WinCIM.

WSIRC

CIS Filename: WSIRC.ZIP

Status: Freeware/Shareware/Registered

There are a number of different versions of WSIRC currently available, each of which offers slightly different capabilities. Both the freeware and shareware version offer a limited number of concurrent connections, reduced support for DCC chat, and no CTCP services. The help file for both of these versions is also limited to basic information and setup guidelines. The shareware version also includes a timed usage limitation that locks you out of the program after 30 days.

You can register the shareware version online via CompuServe, using the software registration service (GO SWREG) with 2442 as the program ID. The registered version allows you to open up to 255 concurrent public and private sessions, adds full DCC and CTCP support for file transfers and IRC games, and includes a detailed help file.

mIRC

CIS Filename: MIRC31.ZIP

Status: Freeware

According to its developers, this program has been released as unsupported software. It is not quite as full-featured as the registered version of WSIRC, but it compares favorably with both the freeware and shareware versions.

If you are looking for a good IRC client that does not overload you with millions of unnecessary options and that allows you to get up and running with a limited knowledge of IRC, this is the program for you.

WAIS Clients

Currently there are no WAIS clients available on CompuServe, possibly due to the size of their archives. As a result, the following sections list locations on the Internet where copies of the two main WAIS clients can be obtained.

Using a dedicated WAIS client has a number of advantages over the WWW-based gateways discussed in Chapter 12, "World Wide Web Productivity." Among these, the ability to store search queries and results for later use is without a doubt the most popular.

WAIS for Windows

CIS Filename: N/A

Status: Freeware

A number of the different WAIS clients currently available are based on the freely distributed source code for WAIS for Windows. This program has been though a number of different incarnations to arrive at the most recent version, known as `WWAIS24.EXE`. To obtain a copy of this version, which was released by Tim Gauslin of the U.S. Geological Survey, Information Systems Division, log onto their FTP server at `ridgisd.er.usgs.gov` and open the `/software/wais/` directory.

EINet winWAIS

Status: Shareware

The company that bought you the EINet Galaxy WWW directory also produces their own WAIS client called winWAIS. This version of WAIS is in many ways similar to WAIS for Windows, and demonstrates its obvious shared heritage both in its layout and usage. This version does add a number of new features, including better support for multimedia-based information and the ability to save existing queries.

It is not a freeware program, however, and as such you must register it if you choose to continue to use it after the 30-day trial period. To find out more information about EINet winWAIS, the best place to start is the EINet World Wide Web information page at `http://galaxy.einet.net/EINet/EINet.html`.

COMPRESSION AND ENCRYPTION SOFTWARE

WinZip

Wincode

WinPack

Internet Privacy

Throughout this book, a number of utilities have been mentioned that allow you to compress or encrypt files before they are transmitted across the Internet. To complement these tools, some others have been discussed that can unpack and decrypt such files.

By taking advantage of such programs, you can considerably reduce the amount of time required to send or retrieve large files. When you consider that many of the files available on the Internet are over a megabyte, reducing their size by up to 80% before transmission can add up to considerable savings in connection time. For the security-conscious, those tools that allow you to encrypt files provide the additional benefit of creating files that only the person they are intended for can read.

Some of these tools can also encode and decode files so that they can be transmitted via e-mail and Usenet. Because e-mail messages can consist only of ASCII text, files distributed this way need to be converted into a special format that is ASCII-text compatible.

This appendix looks at four programs that each perform one or more of these tasks and discusses places to obtain a copy of the latest version of each.

WinZip

Without a doubt, PKZIP is by far the best known file compression utility available today. Developed and distributed by a company called PKWare, during the past six years this program has become the standard compression system used by bulletin boards and commercial operations like CompuServe.

However, although PKZIP is an extremely popular compression tool, its command-line interface is not the most user-friendly. To get around this difficulty, a number of shell and graphical user interfaces (GUIs) have been developed that make using PKZIP a less complicated affair. For Windows users, the most popular of these is WinZip. (See Figure D.1.)

Instead of using a command line, with WinZip you can create compressed or "zipped" files using a simple point-and-click interface. It also allows you to decompress existing zip files using the same environment.

Decompressing a Zipped File

To decompress a zipped file that you have downloaded from the Internet or CompuServe, open WinZip and follow these steps:

1. Click on the Open button in the WinZip toolbar. This opens a file requester similar to the one shown in Figure D.2. (This is the Window 95 Requester. Under Windows 3.11 you may see a slightly different one.)

2. Using this requester, locate the file you wish to decompress and click on the Open Button. As a rule, files created with PKZIP or WinZip are given a `.zip` file extension to indicate that their contents have been compressed. The file selected in Figure D.2 was `df95.zip`.

FIGURE D.1.

WinZip is the first zip utility designed for Windows 95.

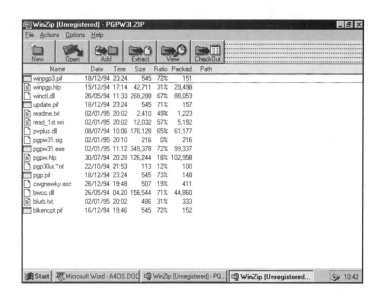

Depending on how you have configured WinZip, it can also decompress files created with a number of other compression utilities. These include ARJ, LZH, LHA and ARC. In addition, as of version 5.6a, you can also decompress files stored in many Internet specific formats that have file extensions such as TAR, GZ, Z, TAZ, and TGZ.

FIGURE D.2.

Under Windows 95, WinZip uses the standard File Open requester.

3. When you click on the Open button, WinZip scans the file you have selected and displays a list of all the files it contains. In Figure D.3, WinZip has displayed the contents of df95.zip.

Apart from being useful as a compression tool, using WinZip makes it easy to distribute many files at the same time. This is because it can store any number of files and even whole directories in a single file. This is why zip files are often referred to as *archives*.

FIGURE D.3.

*After you select a file,
WinZip displays its
contents.*

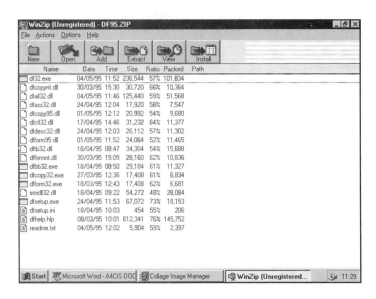

4. Once WinZip has opened the zip archive, you can perform a number of tasks that manipulate it. These include extracting the files it contains, viewing the contents on a single entry, or even installing it using the standard Windows SETUP.EXE program.

5. In this case, you want to simply extract the contents of df95.zip and place them on your hard drive. To do this, click on the Extract button located on the WinZip toolbar. You are presented with a requester similar to the one shown in Figure D.4. This is the Extract requester. Using it, select the location for WinZip to place the files you are extracting. You can instruct WinZip to store the files in any existing directory or create a new directory by clicking on the Create Dir… button.

6. Once you have located the directory where you want to store the extracted files, click on the Extract button to start the decompression. In Figure D.4 the \TEMP directory of the C: drive is selected.

FIGURE D.4.

*The Extract requester lets
you select the directory in
which the archive's contents
will be stored.*

Compressing a File with WinZip

Like decompressing a zip archive, compressing files and storing them in an archive using WinZip is a relatively straightforward process. Just follow these steps:

1. Click on the New Button in the WinZip toolbar to open a New Archive requester, like the one shown in Figure D.5.

FIGURE D.5.

Using the New Archive requester, select the location for your new zip file.

2. Select the directory in which to store your new zip archive.
3. Enter the name for the new zip archive in the File Name field.

You can also use WinZip to create compressed archives in ARJ and LZH format, provided that WinZip has been configured to use these programs. To use one of these programs, replace the .zip file extension with .arj or .lzh. However, you can't use WinZip to create ARC, TAR, or GZ files, even though you can use it to extract files stored in these archives.

4. Select the Add Dialog check box to tell WinZip that you want to open the Add Requester once the new archive is created.
5. Finally, click on the OK button to create your new archive. When you do this, WinZip opens the Add requester shown in Figure D.6.
6. This requester offers you a wide variety of options, allowing you to select the files you want to compress. If you want to compress all the files in a directory, all you need to do is click on the Add button.

To find out more about the various options provided by the Add requester, click on the Help button or hit the F1 key to bring up WinZip's online help system.

*The Add requester allows
you to select the files you
want to compress.*

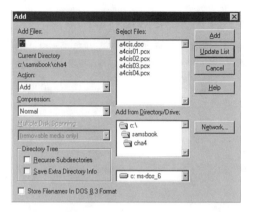

7. When WinZip finishes adding these files to the new archive, it returns you to the
   main WinZip window and displays the contents of your new archive. (See Figure
   D.7.) From here, you can click on the Add button again to include more files.

FIGURE D.7.

*WinZip instantly displays a
list of the files you have
added to your zip archive.*

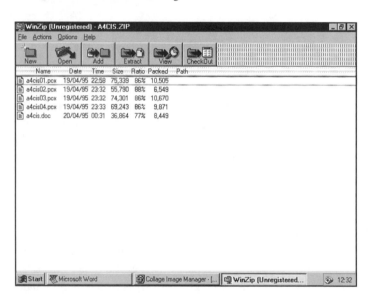

8. When you have finished working with your new archive, open the File menu and
   select the Close Archive option.

Downloading WinZip

To obtain a demonstration copy of the latest version of WinZip, you can either GO WINZIP
using CompuServe or go to the WinZip WWW home page at http://www.winzip.com/winzip.

WinZip is not a free program. If you continue to use WinZip after the 21-day trial period is over, you must pay a registration fee to Niko Mac Computing, WinZip's developer. At the time of this writing, this fee was $29 U.S.

Note

Wincode

To transmit a file using e-mail or Usenet, you must first convert it into an acceptable format. On the Internet, there are currently two main formats that achieve this goal: UUENCODE and MIME. Creating a file in one of these formats requires a special utility designed to perform this type of conversion. Under Windows, one of the more popular programs of this sort is called Wincode. (See Figure D.8.)

FIGURE D.8.

Wincode allows you to manipulate files in UUENCODE and MIME format.

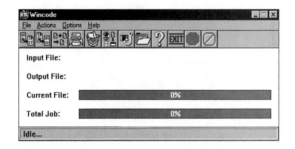

Wincode has developed a large following due to its ability to manipulate files stored in both UUENCODE and MIME format. For many people, this has made Wincode the only tool they need for e-mail file conversions.

Another reason for the popularity of this program is its status as a *freeware* program, although it should probably be called *work-it-out for-yourself-ware* for reasons that will become obvious. When you download a copy of Wincode from either CompuServe or the Internet, you receive a *free* full working version of Wincode—there are no registration requirements. However, what you do not receive is a copy of the manual or the online help file. As the program's author puts it:

> The HELP file is NOT required for Wincode to function properly. If you can figure out all of Wincode's features on your own, then by all means enjoy the FREE program. If you would like assistance and/or the HELP file to discover Wincode's FULL potential (i.e. network support, limited auto-line correction, etc.) then order the HELP and support…
>
> *George Silva—Snappy_Inc.*

Wincode Features

In deference to George Silva, how you use Wincode is not described here. Instead, some of its features and capabilities are discussed to give you some idea of what Wincode can do.

Supported Formats

Wincode can convert any 8-bit binary file into 7-bit UUENCODE format and convert it back. It fully supports both the UU and XX encoding specifications for UUENCODED files and allows you to create custom encoding specifications. For mail systems that set limits on the size of messages, Wincode can also automatically split large files into small UUENCODEd segments and recombine received messages containing split files.

> Once you convert a file into UUENCODE format, you can then transmit it using e-mail. For more information about sending e-mail messages, take a look at Chapter 6, "E-mail and CIS Mail."

Wincode also fully supports the MIME 1.0 standard that uses Base64 encoding. This format was designed for the distribution of multimedia files using e-mail. Wincode can also handle multipart MIME files and automatically launch image viewers, MPEG players, and audio players when decoding multimedia components.

When you are encoding files, Wincode can also be configured to compress the files with PKZIP before they are converted to reduce the size of the resulting ASCII encoded files.

> Currently, there are plans to add an additional format, known as BinHex, to Wincode. This format was made popular by the Apple Macintosh and has since been adopted by the developers of a number of e-mail packages as an alternate encoding format.

Menu Hooking

The most unique feature of Wincode is its ability to add itself to the menus of other programs. In Figure D.9, Wincode is hooked onto the WinCIM menu bar to simplify the handling of encoded messages using CIS Mail.

Using this feature, open the Wincode menu and select the **File -> Encode** option. This opens the Encode File requester, which lets you encode any files and store the results on the standard Windows Clipboard. Once the encoded information is stored on the Clipboard, you can then paste it onto the message you want to send. The reverse is also true for any encoded messages you receive. By copying the message to the Clipboard, you can easily decode the message by selecting the **File -> Decode** option from the Wincode menu.

FIGURE D.9.

With Wincode hooked onto the WinCIM menu, you can easily encode a file for transmission to the Internet.

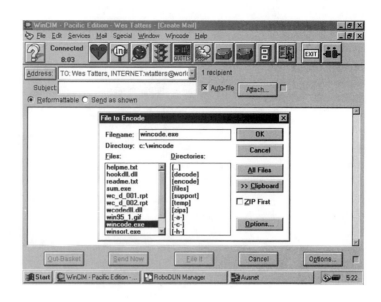

Downloading Wincode

A copy of Wincode can always be found on CompuServe in the Internet Resources forum (GO INETRESOURCE).

In addition, the author uploads a copy of each new version to ftp.cica.indiana.edu. However, he recommends Archie as the best method for finding copies of Wincode stored on the Internet.

WinPack

Another program has just arrived on the scene that promises to combine the best features of WinZip and Wincode into a single program, with some other added bells and whistles thrown in for good measure: WinPack. (See Figure D.10.) According to the WinPack press release, its developers aim to create a program that is easy to use and that can, at the same time, encode and decode every mainstream archive format currently available.

When this appendix was being written, WinPack was still in the early stages of beta testing. As such, the exact makeup of the final release version is still unknown. However, due to the nature of this program, its content is significant enough to include here—if only as a prelude for things to come.

Note

FIGURE D.10.

WinPack lets you create many different types of archives using one consistent interface.

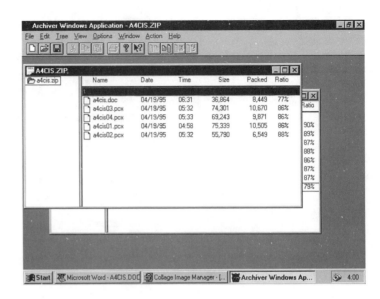

Pre-Release Information

In many ways, using WinPack is a lot like using WinZip, although WinPack lets you work with a wider variety of archive formats, including:

◆ Zip archives

◆ ARC archives

◆ Freeze archives

◆ GNU ZIP (UNIX) archives

◆ UNIX compressed archives

◆ UNIX Tar archives

◆ UUENCODE/UUDECODE

◆ BinHex encode/decode

◆ Stuffit archives

◆ Packit archives

◆ ARJ archives

◆ MIME encode/decode

Downloading WinPack

When WinPack is released in July, there will be two separate versions available: a shareware version that provides support for zip archives only, and WinPack Deluxe, a commercial version including all the archive modules.

Copies of the shareware version will be available on CompuServe and the Internet following the official release. The commercial version, on the other hand, will be available only from RetroSpect (WinPack's distributors) and should retail for around $20.00.

To find out more information about WinPack, please contact Randy Snow at RetroSpect—CompuServe: 71540,1240 or snow@retrospect.com.

Internet Privacy

The biggest problems facing the Internet today are privacy and security. Due to the unrestricted nature of the Internet, it is far from what anyone would call a secure system.

From the time a message leaves your computer to the time it arrives at its destination, it may pass through hundreds of different computer systems. At any stage during this journey, any unethical person with a little bit of knowledge and access to one of these systems could read your private message and even take a copy of it for their own use.

Although this may sound a bit like the story of the boy who cried wolf or someone's idea of Internet scare tactics, the unfortunate fact of life remains. In the past, and possibly still today, there are people who use systems like the Internet for activities that are not altogether legal. There are numerous stories that circulate on the Internet telling of credit card information and other private details being stolen from e-mail messages. For this reason, there is a silent rule on the Internet that says, "Thou shalt not use the Internet to send private or confidential information."

The problem is, the Internet is simply too convenient a method of communicating with people for such a rule to have any practical value. As a communications tool, many people want to use the Internet to send and receive confidential information. Yet at the same time, they also want their information to be secure.

Encryption

Because of the nature of the Internet, about the only reliable way of securing your information is to encrypt it before you send it. By encrypting your files, you are preventing prying eyes from viewing the contents of your private messages. Even though they may still have access to the contents of your transmissions, unless they have a suitable decoder, the information will be of little use to them.

There are two main types of encryption services you can use on the Internet, or anywhere for that matter: private key encryption and public key encryption.

Private Key Encryption

Private key encryption is a relatively straightforward process. You create a file that you want to send securely to another person. When you have created the file, a special program uses an encryption key to create an encrypted version of your original file. If you look at this new file, it will appear to be a jumble of letters and numbers that make no sense.

You can now send this file to its destination without any fear of a security breach. When the file arrives at its destination, the person who receives it must run the file through an encryption program identical to the one you used. They must also be able to tell the program exactly what encryption key you used when you created the file. Without knowledge of this key, it is impossible to decode the file.

As long as the contents of your encryption key remain a secret between yourself and the person you are communicating with, your security is guaranteed. This is the reason for the name "private key encryption"—you need to keep your key private to protect it.

Public Key Encryption

Although private key encryption may be suitable for communications with people you know, this reliability breaks down if you need to give the key out to many people. This type of key is also of little use for conducting activities such as online shopping, because it is not practical or viable for everyone you deal with to have a copy of your private encryption key.

This is where the concept of public key encryption comes into its own. Unlike private key encryption, which uses a single key to both encrypt and decrypt a file, public key encryption requires a pair of keys: one to encrypt the information, and a different one to decrypt it. The advantage of this approach is simple. Because the key used for the encryption process can't also be used to decrypt the file, you can freely give a copy of it to anyone who wants one. You can even publish it on the Usenet or in WWW pages. This key is called your *public* key. By using this key with an encryption program, anyone can create an encrypted file for you. Even the person who created the encrypted file for you using your public key cannot decode it. The file they created can be decoded only by you, because only you have the second part of the key—your secret key.

Like a private key, you need to keep this secret key's contents to yourself, but unlike a private key, no one else ever needs to know its contents. In this sense, public key encryption is actually a more secure method of encryption. There is no way for anyone to find out the contents of the key that decodes files encrypted by your public key—unless, of course, you leave it lying around.

Pretty Good Privacy

The most popular public key encryption system available today was developed by Philip R. Zimmerman in 1990. His aim was to create a public key encryption system that would provide a means of secure data transmission for all members of the Internet community. This program gives you *pretty good privacy* (PGP) and is distributed as freeware, provided that it isn't used for commercial purposes.

MIT also distributes a version of PGP. This version contains a different encryption module called the RSA public key cryptosystem. Although the program code for the encryption system in each version of PGP was written independently, both versions are sufficiently compatible to permit the exchange of encrypted files between the two systems.

PGP is also currently at the center of potential criminal proceedings between Philip Zimmerman and the U.S. Customs Department. This is because the government views the distribution of encryption software in much the same way as it views the sale of arms to foreign governments. Basically, the United States government contends that the distribution of encryption software by electronic means is a breach of ITAR restrictions (the restrictions controlling the export of munitions and cryptographic technology from the U.S. and Canada).

This is why there are currently two separate versions of PGP: one that can be used in the United States and Canada, and one that can be used only outside the United States. The version that can be used in the United States uses the RSA cryptosystem developed by MIT, while the international version is based on the algorithms designed independently by Philip Zimmerman. This second version, although based on an illegally exported version of PGP, can be used legally anywhere else in the world because it falls outside the restrictions of the RSA License and U.S. Customs limitations.

That said, the use of PGP may be illegal in different parts of the world, depending on local governments' views of encryption systems. For example, in the United Kingdom it is illegal to transmit encrypted data over the radio.

To confuse matters even further, there is also a commercial version of PGP that was licensed from Philip Zimmerman by ViaCrypt. This version cannot be used outside the United States for the reasons previously discussed, and because ViaCrypt also owns a license for the RSA cryptosystem.

Downloading a Copy of PGP

Depending on where you live, you need to obtain either the North American version of PGP or the international version.

North American Version

MIT operates a PGP home page containing the latest version of PGP (currently 2.6.2) for users in the United States and Canada. (See Figure D.11.) This home page also has a number of discussion pages on encryption technology and links to other PGP-related home pages.

To obtain a copy of PGP from this site, you are first required to fill out a declaration form. This form asks you to acknowledge that you agree to abide by the RSA and MIT licenses and certify that you are a resident of the United States or Canada.

To access this home page, use the following http address: http://web.mit.edu/network/pgp.html.

Copies of the latest U.S. version can also be found on CompuServe in the NCSA Forum (GO NCSAFORUM).

FIGURE D.11.

For users in the United States and Canada, the MIT PGP home page always contains a copy of the latest version.

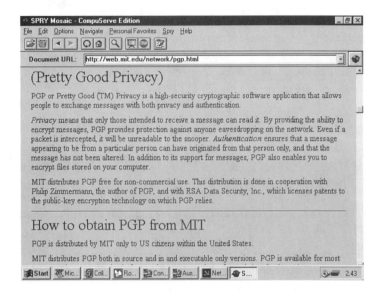

International Version

People outside the United States can obtain information about the latest international version from the International PGP Home Page (Figure D.12), located at `http://www.ifi.uio.no/~staalesc/PGP/home.html`.

FIGURE D.12.

The International PGP Home Page contains links to all the well known PGP sites.

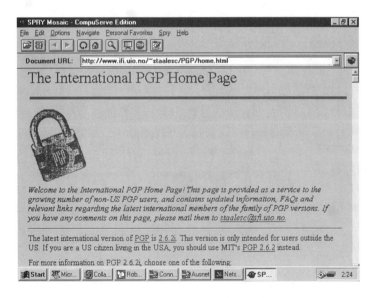

The current international version of PGP is 2.6.2i, although for legal reasons it is not an official version. In addition to housing a copy of the latest international version, this site also contains a wealth of information about the various versions of PGP and discussions of the technical and legal ramifications of PGP usage.

You may also be able to obtain a copy of the international version using CompuServe. The European forum (GO EUROFORUM) maintains a collection of PGP-related files and tools in its utility section. However, there is a legal question here that is still unanswered. Although the European forums are technically not U.S.-related, does downloading a copy of PGP from CompuServe, which is U.S.-owned, constitute a breach of the law? To be safe, international users are better off using the International PGP Home Page as their PGP source.

Warning

> People living in the U.S. and Canada should not use a copy of the international version, because it may also be illegal to do so. You should obtain either a copy of MIT's version or the commercial version distributed by ViaCrypt.

Using PGP

PGP, like PKZIP, is a DOS-based program that operates from the command line. To work with PGP, you type strings of switches and names at the DOS prompt.

For example, to create your own personal public and secret keys, enter the following command: **pgp.exe -kg**.

The PGP program then prompts you for some information, which it uses during the key creation process. You are first asked to give your name and possibly your e-mail address as a means of identifying your public key. I use Wes Tatters <wtatters@world.net> for my public key name, but it can be anything you choose.

The most important piece of information you are asked to provide is a *pass phrase*. This is the phrase you'll need to enter to unlock files encoded using your public key. It should be something you can easily remember but that can never be guessed by anyone else.

When PGP finishes creating your keys, you are returned to the DOS prompt. If you now look in the directory where you installed PGP, you'll find two new files: PUBRING.PGP and SECRING.PGP.

Stored in these two files, or *keyrings* as they are known, are your secret and public keys. PGP uses the keyring analogy for all its encryption information. This is also true for any public keys that you are given by other people. When you receive a public key, you need to place it on your public keyring before you can use it to encrypt files.

Signature Files

Apart from being an encryption system, PGP also provides you with an electronic method of signing documents to signify that their contents are yours.

For many people, this validation tool alone makes PGP a valuable addition to their software collection. Although a discussion of the actions required to use PGP as an electronic signature are beyond the scope of this book, it is important that you at least understand that the capability is there.

The best place to find out about using this capability and all the features included in PGP is the *PGP Users Guide,* written by Philip Zimmerman. Regardless of which version of PGP you obtain, a copy of the two files that constitute this guide are included. In most cases they are installed in a DOC subdirectory in the main PGP directory. The files you need to look for are PGPDOC1.TXT and PGPDOC2.TXT.

PGP WinFront

As you begin to work with PGP, it probably won't take very long before you become frustrated with the command line interface. To reduce the hassles associated with using PGP, a number of shells and front ends have been designed that allow you to replace the command line with a more user-friendly Windows interface.

> All the current PGP front ends and shells still require you to have a copy of PGP installed. You need to do this because each one actually uses PGP to perform encryption tasks. This avoids all the complex licensing and export restrictions discussed earlier.

One of the more popular contenders in the PGP shell stakes is WinFront, and in the spirit of PGP, WinFront is also freeware. (See Figure D.13.)

FIGURE D.13.

WinFront brings point-and-click simplicity to PGP.

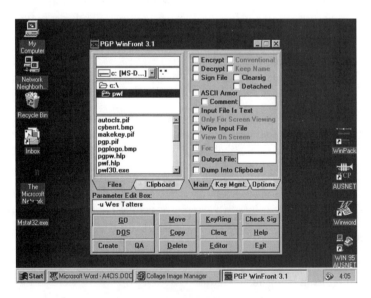

This shell provides you with point-and-click access to all of PGP's functions. You can encrypt and decrypt files using public and secret keys and manage the contents of your public keyring, including any public keys that you have been given.

Encrypting a File with WinFront

To encrypt a file using WinFront, follow these steps:

1. After opening WinFront, select the options shown in Figure D.14. Click on the check box next to the Encrypt option because you want to encrypt a file. In this case, the ASCII Armor option is selected so that you can send the file using e-mail. If you don't select this option, the encoded file is stored in binary format, not ASCII format.

FIGURE D.14.

Select the ASCII Armor option to encrypt a file for e-mail transmission.

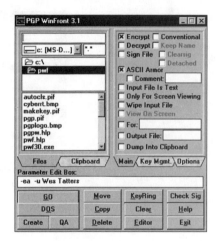

2. Click on the **K**eyRing button to select the people that can decode the file. This will open the Key Ring window, shown in Figure D.15. Using this window, you can select any of the people stored in your public keyring. In this example, Philip Zimmerman and Wes Tatters are the only people who will be able to decode the encrypted file. Once you have selected the recipients, click on the Hide Keyring button to return to the main WinFront window.

FIGURE D.15.

Select the people who can decode your message using the Key Ring window.

> In the next version of WinFront, the author plans to add the capability of automatically sending the encrypted file as an e-mail message to each of the people you select.

3. When you return to the main window, select the file you want to encrypt. Once you are happy with your selection, click on the **G**O button to begin the conversion.

FIGURE D.16.

Select the file you wish to encrypt and hit the GO button.

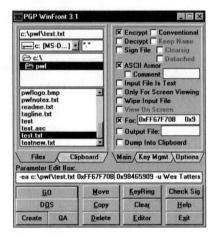

Note

> As you select from the various options available, WinFront displays the parameters it is going to send to PGP in the Parameter edit box. By studying these entries, you can learn a lot about the way PGP operates.

4. When you hit the **G**O button, WinFront launches PGP in a DOS window and performs the requested actions. (See Figure D.17.) As these occur, they are displayed one at a time down the screen.

5. When PGP completes the encryption process, it creates a new file with the same name as the original file. This new file has an .asc extension. You can now send this file to its intended recipients, confident that no one else can decode its contents.

Decrypting a File with WinFront

The process involved in decrypting a file is much the same as the encryption process. Naturally, you can only decode a file that has been encoded with your public key, but apart from that, the process is relatively straightforward.

FIGURE D.17.

WinFront launches PGP in a DOS window to perform the requested actions.

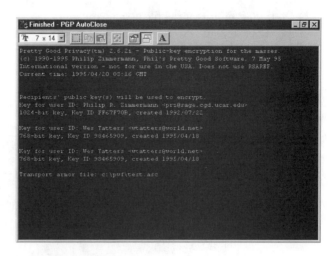

To decrypt a file using a WinFront, follow these steps:

1. After opening WinFront, select the Decrypt option, as shown in Figure D.18. Also select the Keep Name option to force PGP to store the decrypted file using the original file's name. If you don't select this option, PGP stores the decrypted file without a file extension.

FIGURE D.18.

If you don't select the Keep Name option, PGP saves the decrypted file without an extension.

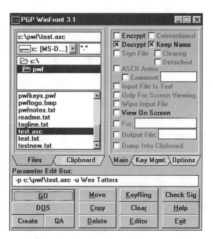

2. Select the file you want to decrypt. Files that are encrypted using PGP usually have either a .pgp or .asc extension. In this case, you want to decode the test.asc file you created earlier. Once you have selected the file, click on the **G**O button to launch PGP.

3. WinFront opens PGP in an MS-DOS window similar to the one shown in Figure D.19. If PGP finds that the file is valid and you have a secret key corresponding to one of the public keys used to encrypt the file, PGP asks you to enter the pass phrase for your secret key. Once you enter a valid pass phrase, PGP decrypts the file and saves it using the file's original name. In this case, PGP created a new file called `test.txt`.

FIGURE D.19.

Before PGP can decrypt a file, you must enter the pass phrase needed to unlock your secret key.

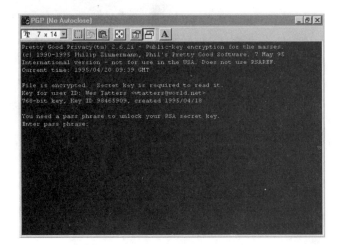

Downloading a Copy of WinFront

To obtain a copy of WinFront, open the NCSA forum on CompuServe (GO NCSAFORUM) and look in the Encryption library. The file name you are looking for should be something like `PWF31.ZIP`. Alternatively, you can use the IBM File Finder (GO IBMFF) to search for all PGP-related files by setting PGP as the keyword.

On the other hand, if you prefer to obtain a copy using FTP, there are a number of sites that currently maintain a copy of `PWF31.ZIP` as a part of the CICA archive. To obtain a copy of this file from the SUNET mirror, use the following FTP address and directory: `ftp.sunet.se/pub/pc/windows/mirror-cica/util`.

WinPGP™

If the up-front approach of WinFront seems a bit too complex for your needs, maybe WinPGP would be more to your liking. Instead of trying to give you everything at once, WinPGP uses the "big, friendly buttons" approach to guide you step by step through PGP's available options. (See Figure D.20.) This user-friendliness comes at a price, however. WinPGP is not a freeware program, but is instead released as shareware. If you continue to use WinPGP after the 30-day trial period, you must pay the author a licensing fee, either directly to the author or via CompuServe's software registration service (GO SWREG).

FIGURE D.20.

WinPGP uses big, friendly buttons.

Encrypting a File with WinPGP

To encrypt a file using WinPGP, you should follow these steps:

1. Open WinPGP and click on the Prefs button to open the PGP Preferences window, shown in Figure D.21. This window allows you to configure a number of default settings for PGP. For this example, select the ASCII Armor option to let PGP know that you want to create an e-mail-compatible file. Leave the Recover File Name on Decrypt option set to the default to force PGP to recover the original file name when decrypting files. After making these changes, click on the OK button to return to the main WinPGP window.

FIGURE D.21.

The Preferences window allows you to customize the way WinPGP operates.

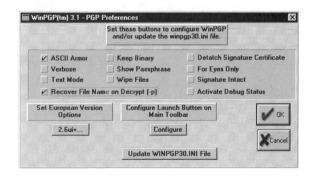

2. To encode a file, click on the Encrypt button (it looks like a combination padlock). Doing this opens a window similar to the one shown in Figure D.22. This window allows you to select from one of four different encryption types: signed encryption, unsigned encryption, idea encryption, and signing of a text file. For this example, let's

look at unsigned encryption, which is what you actually did in the WinFront. To do this, click on the Unsigned button.

FIGURE D.22.

PGP lets you choose from four different encryption options.

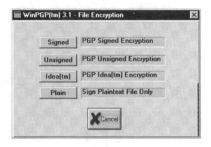

3. When you do this, WinPGP opens the Unsigned Encryption window, shown in Figure D.23. Into the first field, enter the name of the file you want to encrypt, or click on the Browse... button to open a file requester, which allows you to select the file you want. (See Figure D.24.) WinPGP requires you to enter an ID code from one of the public keys stored on your public keyring in the second field. To obtain the ID code that corresponds to the person you want to send the encoded file to, click on the ListNames button. This opens a Listing window, which lets you make your selection from any of the keys currently stored on your public keyring. (See Figure D.25.)

FIGURE D.23.

The WinPGP Unsigned Encryption window.

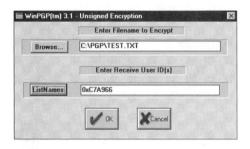

FIGURE D.24.

The Get File Name To Encrypt requester allows you to choose the file you want to encrypt.

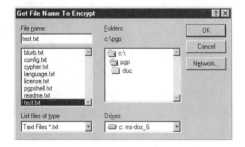

FIGURE D.25.

To locate a public key ID, use the View Key Names List.

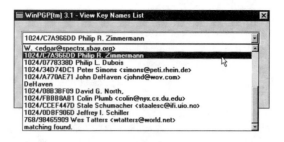

> The current version of WinPGP does not allow you select more than one recipient with the Listing window. However, if you know the ID codes of each person, you can enter them all into the ID Field one after the other, separated by spaces.

4. When you are satisfied that the correct information has been entered, click on the OK button to launch PGP. Like WinFront, WinPGP calls PGP with the appropriate codes and switches turned on. PGP then encrypts the file and stores the result in a file called `test.asc`.

Decrypting a File using WinPGP

To reverse the process and decrypt a file using WinPGP, follow these steps:

1. Click on the Decrypt button in the WinPGP main window to open the File Decryption window. (See Figure D.26.) The Decrypt button looks like an open combination padlock.

FIGURE D.26.

The File Decryption window is used to select the file you want to decrypt.

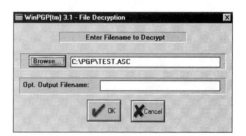

2. Either enter the name of the file you want to decrypt or click on the Browse… button to open a requester similar to the one mentioned during the encryption process. (See Figure D.24.) If you did not select the Recover File Name on Decrypt option, as shown in Figure D.21, you also need to enter the name that PGP is to use for the decrypted file. Otherwise, PGP creates a new file without an extension.

3. After you have nominated the file, click on the OK button to begin the decryption process. Like WinFront, once PGP starts, you are asked to enter the pass phrase for your secret key. (See Figure D.27.) When you enter this phrase, PGP decodes the file

and attempts to save a copy in the current directory. If a file with the same name already exists, as is the case in Figure D.27, you are given the opportunity to overwrite it or nominate a new name for the file.

FIGURE D.27.

If the file already exists, you are given the opportunity of either overwriting it or nominating a new name.

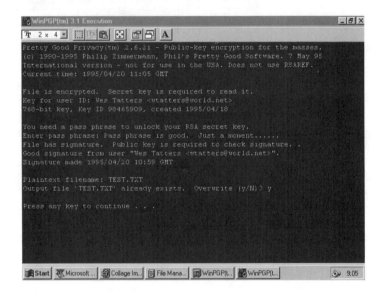

Downloading a Copy of WinPGP

Like WinFront, you can either obtain a copy of WinPGP from the NCSA Forum (GO NCSAFORUM) or you can use Archie to look for a copy on the Internet. Depending on the version, the file you are looking for will be called something like PGPW31.ZIP.

To get you started, all the SimTel mirror sites have a copy stored in the .../win3/security directory. This includes the UK Hensa FTP site, whose copy is stored at micros.hensa.ac.uk/mirrors/SimTel/win3/security.

You might also like to try the WWW server operated by the Electronic Frontier Foundation, which contains a considerable amount of information dealing with encryption and security issues in general. This server is located at http://www.eff.org/.

GLOSSARY

This glossary contains a short description of many of the words that you will find mentioned in Request for Comment documents, World Wide Web pages, Internet-related magazines, and trade and public newspapers and journals. Although this list is reasonably comprehensive, the Internet has a propensity for creating new words and jargon faster than any other area of interest.

As a result, if you come across a term or piece of Internet jargon not covered here, there are a number of resources on the World Wide Web that may be able to offer you further assistance. These include:

Collaborative Virtual HyperGlossary

`http://www.cryst.bbk.ac.uk/glossary/index.html`

WorldCom Network Services—Telecommunications Glossary

`http://www.wiltel.com/glossary/glossary.html`

The Glossary of Internet Terms

`http://www.matisse.net/files/glossary.html`

The Definitions and Acronyms Glossary

`http://www.itsi.disa.mil/cfs/glossary.html`

A Glossary of World Wide Web Terms and Acronyms

`http://www.ncsa.uiuc.edu/SDG/Software/Mosaic/Glossary/index.html`

You may also want to obtain a copy of the FYI 18—the Internet Users' Glossary from the InterNIC. This document is maintained by the User Glossary Working Group of the User Services Area of the Internet Engineering Task Force (IFTF), and is the basis upon which parts of the glossary that follows was based. Where a definition is based on this FYI or other sources, the reference will appear after the definition, such as [FYI18], which stands for "For Your Information" document 18.

A

acceptable use policy	Many transit networks have policies that restrict the use to which the network may be put. A well-known example is NSFNET's AUP, which does not allow commercial use. [FYI18]
address	There are many types of address to be found on the Internet: e-mail addresses, IP addresses, domain names, and URLs.
address resolution	When you type a domain name into an address field, it needs to be converted to an IP address before it can be

used by programs communicating via the Internet. This process is called address resolution. *See also* domain name system.

alias	Many e-mail clients allow you to define aliases or single words that represent much longer e-mail addresses. The Eudora e-mail client refers to these aliases as *nicknames*.
anonymous FTP	Using anonymous FTP, a person can retrieve files from an FTP server without the need for an account at the site that operates it.
ANSI	The American National Standard Institute is responsible for approving all U.S. standards for computer communications, software, and hardware.
application	Any computer program that can be run locally on a user's system or remotely using Telnet.
Archie	A client/server application that allows you to search FTP sites for specific files.
archive site	Any machine that permits access to its files by the use of anonymous FTP.
article	Any message sent to a Usenet newsgroup.
ARPANET	Advanced Research Projects Agency Network—A pioneering long-haul network funded by ARPA (now DARPA). It served as the basis for early networking research, as well as a central backbone during the development of the Internet. The ARPANET consisted of individual packet-switching computers interconnected by leased lines. [FYI4]
AUP	*See* acceptable use policy.

B

backbone	The highest level in the Internet network. NSFNET is an example of a backbone, as are AARNET and JANET.
bandwidth	Technically, the difference in Hertz (Hz) between the highest and lowest frequencies of a transmission channel. However, as typically used, the amount of data that can be sent through a given communications circuit. [FYI18]
BBS	*See* bulletin board system.
binary	The base 2 numbering system that is the foundation for all computer operations.

binary file	Any file that contains data stored in machine-readable format. *See* text file.
BITNET	The network responsible for the distribution of LISTSERV mailing lists, among other things. It is operated by academic institutions to allow for the exchange of information dealing with educational pursuits. *See* CREN.
bounce	When you send e-mail to an address that does not exist, the message is bounced back to you.
BTW	By the way.
bulletin board system	Any computer system operated for the purpose of the public exchange of electronic messages and files. BBS systems are as a rule not directly connected to the Internet, but instead use the FIDOnet network.

C

CCITT	Comite Consultatif International de Telegraphique et Telephonique—An organization that is a part of the United Nations International Telecommunication Union. It makes technical recommendations about telephone and data communications standards and acts as the regulatory body for the distribution of the standards it approves.
CIX	Commercial Internet Exchange—The organization responsible for the administration of the commercial Internet backbone.
client	A computer system or process that requests a service of another computer system or process. A workstation requesting the contents of a file from a file server is a client of the file server. [RFC18]
client/server	The term used to describe the process used by many Internet services. FTP, Usenet, and WWW are all example of client/server systems.
CREN	Corporation for Research and Education Networking— This organization is the result of the merger between CSNET and BITNET in 1989. Technically, it is now responsible for the operational oversight of BITNET.
CSNET	Computer and Science Network—When education institutions found that they were being denied access to ARPANET, they set up their own private network.

	CSNET no longer exists, following the creation of NSFNET and CREN.
cyberspace	A term coined by the novelist William Gibson to describe the electronic world he created for his series of cyberpunk novels—*Neuromancer, Count Zero*, and *Mona Lisa Overdrive*. The name has also become a popular method of describing the Internet to newbies.

D

decoding	*See* UUDECODE.
decryption	The process of converting an encrypted file back into a readable format. To do this, you need to know either the original key that the file was encrypted with or its secret key (if the file was encrypted using a public key system).
dial-up network	Any network that allows access using dial-up modems. To connect to the Internet using a dial-up network, you will usually need access to either a PPP or SLIP terminal server.
distributed database	A collection of several different data repositories that looks like a single database to the user. A prime example in the Internet is the domain name system. [FYI18]
domain name system	This system provides the mechanism that allows domain names to be converted into IP addresses.

E

EEF	The Electronic Frontier Foundation was formed to address the many legal issues people face when dealing with electronic communications using computers.
e-mail	Electronic mail—The term used to describe the exchange of messages electronically via computers and typically across the Internet.
e-mail address	The address used to describe the location of the intended recipient of an e-mail message. This address takes the form `userid@domain.name`.
encoding	*See* UUENCODE.
encryption	The process that converts a file into a seemingly scrambled format to ensure its secure transmission across the Internet. The file must then be decrypted before it can be read by anyone at the receiving end.

F

FAQ

Frequently Asked Questions—Documents published on many sites and servers that contain a list of questions and answers relating to the service on which they are contained.

finger

A small program used to display information about a person logged onto the Internet.

flame

A strongly worded message sent in response to an article posted on an Usenet newsgroup or in a mailing list.

flame war

What happens when a flame triggers a stream of responses and counter-flames.

fragmentation

The IP process in which a packet is broken into smaller pieces to fit the requirements of a physical network over which the packet must pass. [FYI18]

FTP

File Transfer Protocol or File Transfer Program. A program that allows files to be transferred from one computer to another via the Internet.

FWIW

For what it's worth.

FYI

For Your Information—Documents maintained by the InterNIC that contain useful information about the Internet and its operation.

G

<G>

A grin emoticon. Also <g>, <grin>, and <bg>.

gateway

A communications tool used to exchange information between different networks. CompuServe uses a gateway to exchange information between itself and the Internet.

GD&RFC

Grinning, ducking, and running for cover.

Gopher

A text-based predecessor to the World Wide Web that is still in use on many systems.

H

hacker

Any person who has a detailed understanding of computer systems and networks. In recent years this term has also come to refer to people who attempt to break into computer systems, although the term "cracker" more correctly applies to such people.

hardware	Any physical components of a computer system, including CPUs, keyboards, hard drives, monitors, and printers.
hierarchical routing	The complex problem of routing on large networks can be simplified by reducing the size of the networks. This is accomplished by breaking a network into a hierarchy of networks, where each level is responsible for its own routing. The Internet has, basically three levels: the backbones, the mid-levels, and the stub networks. The backbones know how to route between the mid-levels, the mid-levels know how to route between the sites, and each site (being an autonomous system) knows how to route internally. [FYI18]
host	A term used to refer to any computer that allows people to connect to the Internet. The CompuServe dial-up PPP service is a form of host computer system.
host name	The domain name of a host computer system. CompuServe's host name is `compuserve.com`.
HTML	Hypertext markup language—The language used to define pages that can be displayed by World Wide Web navigators.
http://	The URL protocol entry that defines a document as a WWW page.

I

IAB	The Internet Architecture Board oversees the Internet Engineering Task Force and the Internet Research Task Force.
IETF	The Internet Engineering Task Force is the technical body formed by the IAB to develop protocols and design strategies for the Internet.
IMHO	In my humble opinion.
Internet protocol	The Internet Protocol is defined in RFC 791 as the network layer for the TCP/IP protocol suite.
Internet registry	The registry operated by InterNIC that is responsible for the allocation of IP addresses and the registration of domain names.
IP address	The individual address assigned to every computer connected to the Internet that distinguishes it from

every other machine. This address is usually represented as a dotted quad—four numbers separated by dots, as in 192.190.215.5, which represents the IP address of my Internet host at world.net.

IRC

Internet Relay Chat—The CB radio of the Internet world.

IRTF

The Internet Research Task Force is charted by the IAB to examine the future of the Internet and discuss the long-term implications of services such as Internet radio and the possibility of video on demand.

ISDN

Integrated Services Digital Network—An emerging technology that is beginning to be offered by the telephone carriers of the world. ISDN combines voice and digital network services in a single medium, making it possible to offer customers digital data services as well as voice connections through a single "wire." The standards that define ISDN are specified by CCITT. [RFC1208]

ISOC

The Internet Society is a non-profit, professional membership organization that facilitates and supports the technical evolution of the Internet; stimulates interest in and educates the scientific and academic communities, industry, and the public about the technology, uses, and applications of the Internet; and promotes the development of new applications for the system. The Society provides a forum for discussion and collaboration in the operation and use of the global Internet infrastructure. The Internet Society publishes a quarterly newsletter, the *Internet Society News*, and holds an annual conference, INET. The development of Internet technical standards takes place under the auspices of the Internet Society with substantial support from the Corporation for National Research Initiatives under a cooperative agreement with the U.S. Federal Government. [FYI18—V. Cerf]

K

Kermit

An early file transfer protocol that is still in use on some systems. Unlike FTP, Kermit is not a network transfer protocol but is instead a computer-to-computer protocol.

L

LAN
Local Area Network—A popular method of connecting computers in a network that are situated in the same physical location.

LISTSERV
The mailing list management software supported by BITNET.

layer
Communication networks for computers may be organized as a set of more or less independent protocols, each in a different layer (also called a *level*). The lowest layer governs direct host-to-host communication between the hardware at different hosts; the highest consists of user applications. Each layer builds on the layer beneath it. For each layer, programs at different hosts use protocols appropriate to the layer to communicate with each other. TCP/IP has five layers of protocols; OSI has seven. The advantages of different layers of protocols is that the methods of passing information from one layer to another are specified clearly as part of the protocol suite, and changes within a protocol layer are prevented from affecting the other layers. This greatly simplifies the task of designing and maintaining communication programs. [FYI18]

lurkers
Any person who reads messages posted to newsgroups, mailing lists, or CompuServe forums but does not post any responses. As a rule, newbies are encouraged to lurk for a while before participating to get the feel of the style of messages and the nature of the conversations.

M

mail gateway
A gateway that permits two separate networks to exchange electronic mail. CompuServe uses such a gateway to exchange messages with the Internet.

mailing list
A form of distributed messaging system that forwards a copy of every message it receives to all participants in the mailing lists. The two most common mailing list managers are LISTSERV and Majordomo.

mail server
A Internet site that acts as a post office for a number of users by collecting and distributing their electronic mail.

Majordomo	The mailing list manager designed for UNIX-based computer systems, which is based on the popular PERL scripting language.
Martin packets	A humorous term applied to packets that turn up unexpectedly on the wrong network because of bogus routing entries. Also used as a name for a packet that has an altogether bogus (non-registered or ill-formed) Internet address. [RFC1208]
MIME	Multipurpose Internet Mail Extension is regarded by many as the replacement for the tiring UUENCODE format, which sometimes cannot properly encode files that relate to multimedia-based activities like compressed video and audio.
moderator	The term used to refer to the person who moderates or determines which messages are distributed to all the recipients of a mailing list or newsgroup.
MOO	*See* MUD.
MUD	Multi-User Dungeon—Interactive, text-based role playing games that can be played across the Internet.

N

Netiquette	A pun on "etiquette," referring to proper behavior on a network [FYI18].
network	Any collection of computers connected for the purpose of real-time data transfers. The Internet is considered to be a network of networks.
newbie	A term used to describe new Internet users.
newsfeed	In the Internet world, this refers to sites that provide access to Usenet traffic, while in the commercial world it refers to services that provide access to news from organizations like Associated Press and CNN.
newsreader	A client program that can access articles stored in newsgroups on a Usenet server.
NIC	A Network Information Center—The most well known of which is the InterNIC site at ds.internic.net.
NNTP	Network News Transfer Protocol—This protocol allows Usenet servers to exchange newsgroup articles using the Internet instead of the older UUCP process.

NSF

National Science Foundation—The government agencies that administer the NSFNET, which for a long time was regarded as the primary backbone of the Internet.

O

OCLC

Online Computer Library Catalog—A nonprofit membership organization offering computer-based services to libraries, educational organizations, and their users. The OCLC library information network connects more than 10,000 libraries worldwide. Libraries use the OCLC system for cataloging, interlibrary loan, collection development, bibliographic verification, and reference searching. [OCLC]

P

packet

The unit of data sent across a network. A generic term used to describe a unit of data at all levels of the protocol stack, but it is most correctly used to describe application data units. [FYI18]

ping

A small program used to test your Internet host's ability to reach another point on the Internet. Usually, it also reports the amount of time taken for a message to transverse the Internet as well.

point of presence

CompuServe currently has over 450 points of presence around the world where you can dial up the CompuServe network.

POP3

The standard e-mail post office protocol that allows users to retrieve messages from their mailbox on a Internet mail server.

PPP

Point-to-Point Protocol—The common method of connecting a computer to the Internet via a dial-up connection using a serial line.

R

reassembly

The IP process in which a previously fragmented packet is reassembled before being passed to the transport layer. [FYI18]

remote login	The process of logging onto a computer using the Internet. *See* Telnet.
RFC	Request for Comment documents are an integral part of life on the Internet. Now numbering in the thousands, these documents describe all of the protocols used by the Internet and discuss all nature of Internet usage. The informational RFCs are also known as FYIs, and those that contain published standards are STDs.
ROTFL	Rolling on the floor laughing.
route	The path that a packet of information takes as it travels from one host to another.
RTFM	Read the [censored] manual. (I'll let you work out what the F stands for. Some people say it could be "fabulous," but I doubt it <G>.)

S

server	Any computer that provides services to the Internet community. FTP sites, WWW hosts, and Usenet providers are all examples of servers. To access the information contained on a server, you need to have a complementary client program running on your local system.
signature	The tag line that is appended to the end of messages by e-mail clients and Usenet newsreaders. These lines often contain quotes and information about the message's sender.
SLIP	The original serial line IP process, which allows a computer to become a part of the Internet via a dial-up connection. On most hosts, SLIP is being phased out in favor of the more reliable PPP method.
smileys	:-) and all his friends.
SMTP	Simple Mail Transfer Protocol—A protocol, defined in STD 10, RFC 821, used to transfer electronic mail between computers. It is a server-to-server protocol, so other protocols are used to access the messages. [FYI18]
snail mail	A derogative term used for mail sent through the Postal Service that reflects the amount of time taken for the mail to be delivered.

sneaker mail	The process of delivering mail by hand. Computer programs distributed this way are often said to have used sneakernet.
SNMP	Simple Network Management Protocol—The Internet standard protocol, defined in STD 15, RFC 1157, developed to manage nodes on an IP network. It is currently possible to manage wiring hubs, toasters, jukeboxes, etc. [FYI18]
STD	The Request for Comments documents that contain official Internet standards.

T

T1	A high-speed digital connection that can transmit data at speeds up to 1.544 megabits per second.
T3	A high-speed digital connection that can transmit data at speeds up to 44.746 megabits per second.
TCP	Transmission Control Protocol—An Internet standard transport layer protocol defined in STD 7, RFC 793. It is connection-oriented and stream-oriented, as opposed to UDP. [FYI18]
TCP/IP	The suite of protocols that allow computers to communicate with each other using the Internet.
Telnet	The standard communications protocol used for remote terminal logins across the Internet.
terminal emulator	Any computer program that emulates a terminal.
text file	A file that contains only the characters that can be read by text editor. They are often referred to as ASCII text files.
TN3270	Another version of the Telnet program that lets you log onto IBM mainframe computers by making the mainframe think that it is connected to a 3270 terminal.
TTFN	Ta ta for now. A common way to sign off services such as IRC.

U

UDP	User Datagram Protocol—An Internet standard transport layer protocol defined in STD 6, RFC 768. It is a connectionless protocol that adds a level of reliability and multiplexing to IP. [FYI18]
UNIX	The operating system developed by AT&T Bell Labs. Most Internet servers are UNIX-based. One of the main features of the UNIX operating system is its ability to handle many tasks at once. This is called multitasking.
URL	Uniform Resource Locator—This is the common method used by the World Wide Web to describe the location of a document by defining its type, site, and directory path, along with its name.
Usenet	A collection of thousands of topically named newsgroups, the computers that run the protocols, and the people who read and submit Usenet news. Not all Internet hosts subscribe to Usenet, and not all Usenet hosts are on the Internet. [FYI18]
UUCP	UNIX to UNIX Copy—This program was originally the primary method of distributing articles published in Usenet newsgroups. It has now been replaced for the most part by NNTP.
UUDECODE	The UNIX program used to convert binary files encoded as ASCII text files back to binary files.
UUENCODE	The UNIX program that converts binary files into ASCII text files. Once a file is encoded into this format, you can send it using e-mail.

V

virus	A small program that is capable of replicating itself on computer after computer in much the same ways as a virus infects humans. Some computer viruses are harmless, but others are more malicious and have been known to destroy hard drives and wipe files.
virtual reality	VR is the latest catch phrase of the computer industry. It refers to computer programs that create virtual worlds where people can interact in a variety of ways. MUDs, and their counterparts, MOOs, are often referred to as text-based virtual reality environments.

W

W3	*See* World Wide Web.
WAIS	Wide Area Information Servers let you search thousands of documents stored on computers all over the Internet.
Web	A common method of referring to the World Wide Web.
worm	A lot like a computer virus. The main difference is that worms are designed primarily to work in network environments like the Internet. Not all worms are malicious—some often perform useful tasks such as roaming the World Wide Web looking for new home pages to add to indexes.
WWW	*See* World Wide Web.
World Wide Web	The Internet equivalent of WinCIM that allows you to navigate the Internet using a graphical point-and-click interface based on the popular hypertext system.

X

X Window	A UNIX-based graphical user interface popular with users of Sun workstations that fully supports the TCP/IP protocol as an integral part of its working environment.
X.500	A directory standard that one day may result in the creation of the ultimate white pages for the Internet.

INDEX

X-Y-Z

Add to Your Sams Library Today with the Best Books for Programming, Operating Systems, and New Technologies

The easiest way to order is to pick up the phone and call

1-800-428-5331

between 9:00 a.m. and 5:00 p.m. EST.

For faster service please have your credit card available.

ISBN	Quantity	Description of Item	Unit Cost	Total Cost
0-672-30617-4		World Wide Web Unleashed	$35.00	
0-672-30667-0		Teach Yourself HTML Web Publishing in a Week	$25.00	
0-672-30466-x		Internet Unleashed (Book/Disk)	$44.95	
0-672-30705-7		Navigating the Internet, Third Edition	$25.00	
0-672-30764-2		Teach Yourself Web Publishing with Microsoft Word in a Week	$29.99	
0-672-30599-2		Tricks of the Internet Gurus	$35.00	
0-672-30595-x		Education on the Internet	$25.00	
0-672-30627-1		Plug-n-Play Mosaic	$29.99	
0-672-30594-1		Programming WinSock	$35.00	
0-672-30627-1		Plug-n-Play Internet	$35.00	
0-672-30638-7		CD-ROM Madness (Book/CD-ROM)	$39.99	
❏ 3 ½" Disk		Shipping and Handling: See information below.		
❏ 5 ¼" Disk		TOTAL		

Shipping and Handling: $4.00 for the first book, and $1.75 for each additional book. Floppy disk: add $1.75 for shipping and handling. If you need to have it NOW, we can ship product to you in 24 hours for an additional charge of approximately $18.00, and you will receive your item overnight or in two days. Overseas shipping and handling adds $2.00 per book and $8.00 for up to three disks. Prices subject to change. Call for availability and pricing information on latest editions.

201 W. 103rd Street, Indianapolis, Indiana 46290

1-800-428-5331 — Orders   1-800-835-3202 — FAX   1-800-858-7674 — Customer Service

Book ISBN 0-672-30761-8

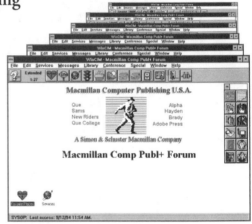
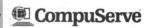